S0-AHL-110

DISCARD

Aggression and Violence

An Introductory Text

Edited by

Vincent B. Van Hasselt
Nova Southeastern University

Michel Hersen
Pacific University

Allyn and Bacon

Boston ■ London ■ Toronto ■ Sydney ■ Tokyo ■ Singapore

616.8582
Ag38

Executive editor: *Carolyn Merrill*
Series editorial assistant: *Susan Hutchinson*
Marketing manager: *Joyce Nilsen*

Copyright © 2000 by Allyn & Bacon
A Pearson Education Company
Needham Heights, MA 02494

Internet: www.abacon.com

All rights reserved. No part of the material protected by this copyright notice may be reproduced or utilized in any form or by any means, electronic or mechanical, including photocopying, recording, or by any information storage and retrieval system, without written permission from the copyright owner.

Library of Congress Cataloging-in-Publication Data

Aggression and violence : an introductory text / edited by Vincent B.
    Van Hasselt and Michel Hersen.
        p.   cm.
    Includes bibliographical references and indexes.
    ISBN 0-205-26721-1
    1. Aggressiveness (Psychology)   2. Violence.   I. Van Hasselt,
Vincent B.   II. Hersen, Michel.
    RC569.5.A34A366   1999
    616.85'82--dc21   99-30549
                                                                              CIP

Printed in the United States of America

10 9 8 7 6 5 4 3 2 1   03 02 01 00 99

CONTENTS

PREFACE

It is almost axiomatic that on a daily basis the media will detail some form of human aggression, whether it be on its grandest scale in the form of war, serial murder, random bombings and shootings in the streets, torture in a prison camp, murder by gangs, wife abuse resulting in the murder of the husband, or the physical abuse of children, sometimes resulting in their death. However, despite the upsurge of professional, lay, and media attention directed to this area, the academic aggression books that have appeared to date have exclusively targeted graduate level or professional audiences. Further, most previous efforts have emphasized theoretical aspects of aggression and violence with little or no attention directed to actual problem areas. By contrast, this textbook is specifically geared toward the upper undergraduate level and lower graduate level, and therefore is directed to filling in that gap in the literature. Moreover, the focus of our book is on the major forms of aggression and violence that are currently of greatest societal concern. It is anticipated that the audience for this should traverse disciplinary lines, including psychology, criminology, rehabilitation counseling, and social work.

Aggression and Violence: An Introductory Text is divided into three parts. In Part One, we provide an overview, the major theoretical perspectives on aggression and violence, and a chapter on neuropsychological factors. Following an Introduction by Wilcox, Van Hasselt, and Hersen, Felson articulates A Social Psychological Approach to Interpersonal Aggression; Eron outlines A Psychological Perspective; and Golden, Jackson, Peterson-Rhone, and Gontkovsky examine the Neuropsychological Factors in Violence and Aggression.

Part Two deals with the specific forms of aggression and violence, including Child Abuse, Child Sexual Molestation, Incest, Partner Abuse, Elder Abuse, Sexual Assault, Paraphilias, Homicide, and Serial Murder and Sexual Homicide. In order to ensure comparability across chapters in Part Two, a similar format was followed when possible: Description of the Disorder, Epidemiology, Characteristics of the Offender, Assessment, Intervention with Case Illustration, and Summary.

Finally, Part Three deals with special topics that we feel are most timely in light of the significant and growing social concern for these areas. This interest is largely attributable to recent and highly publicized crimes and court cases that have focused on Alcohol, Drugs, and Violence and Prediction of Violence.

Many people have been involved in the development and production of this textbook. First and foremost, we thank our experts who took time out to write the chapters in order to share their expertise with us. Second, we thank our friends at Allyn and Bacon for their encouragement. And third, but hardly least of all, we appreciate the technical assistance of Carole Londerée, Benjamin Toll, Eleanor Gil, and Erika Qualls.

ABOUT THE EDITORS

Vincent B. Van Hasselt, Ph.D., is Professor of Psychology and Director of the Family Violence Program at Nova Southeastern University, Fort Lauderdale, Florida. Dr. Van Hasselt received his M.S. and Ph.D. from the University of Pittsburgh and completed an internship in clinical psychology at Western Psychiatric Institute and Clinic of the University of Pittsburgh School of Medicine. He is editor of the *Journal of Family Violence, Aggression and Violent Behavior: A Review Journal, Journal of Child and Adolescent Substance Abuse, Handbook of Family Violence, Sourcebook of Psychological Treatment Manuals for Adult Disorders,* and *Handbook of Psychological Approaches with Violent Offenders: Contemporary Strategies and Issues.* Dr. Van Hasselt has been the recipient of grants from Buhl Foundation, March of Dimes Birth Defects Foundation, National Institute of Disabilities and Rehabilitation Research, National Institute of Mental Health, U.S. Department of Education, and the National Institute of Justice. He has published over 150 journal articles, books, and book chapters including several on the assessment and treatment of family violence, substance abuse, and police issues. Dr. Van Hasselt is also a certified police officer and a lecturer at the Broward County, Florida Police Academy and the FBI National Academy on the topics of police stress and mental health, domestic violence, and suicide prevention. His clinical and research interests are in the areas of police psychology, crisis negotiations, and behavioral criminology.

Michel Hersen (Ph.D., ABPP State University of New York at Buffalo, 1966) is Professor and Dean, School of Professional Psychology, Pacific University, Forest Grove, Oregon. He is past president of the Association for Advancement of Behavior Therapy. He has coauthored and coedited 112 books, including the *Handbook of Prescriptive Treatments for Adults* and *Single Case Experimental Designs.* He has also published more than 220 scientific journal articles and is coeditor of several psychological journals, including *Behavior Modification, Clinical Psychology Review, Journal of Anxiety Disorders, Journal of Family Violence, Journal of Developmental and Physical Disabilities, Journal of Clinical Geropsychology,* and *Aggression and Violent Behavior: A Review Journal.* With Alan S. Bellack, he is coeditor of the recently published 11-volume work entitled: *Comprehensive Clinical Psychology.* Dr. Hersen has been the recipient of numerous grants from the National Institute of Mental Health, the Department of Education, the National Institute of Disabilities and Rehabilitation Research, and the March of Dimes Birth Defects Foundation. He is a Diplomate of the American Board of Professional Psychology, Distinguished Practitioner and Member of the National Academy of Practice in Psychology, and recipient of the Distinguished Career Achievement Award in 1996 from the American Board of Medical Psychotherapists and Psychodiagnosticians.

ABOUT THE CONTRIBUTORS

Howard E. Barbaree, Ph.D., is the clinical director of the Forensic Program at the Centre for Addiction and Mental Health in Toronto, Canada, and is a professor in Psychiatry at the University of Toronto. He has published extensively in the areas of sexual aggression, paraphilias, and sex offender treatment.

Allen G. Burgess, D.B.A., has a background in the computer industry of over twenty-five years and has been a lecturer for several colleges for over ten years. During his industrial career he worked for Honeywell, Raytheon, and Nixdorf Computers before founding Data Integrity in 1984. Data Integrity is a software consulting firm primarily providing services to solve the Year 2000 problem. His publications are in the areas of crime classification, violent offender characteristics, interpersonal stalking, and infant abductors.

Ann W. Burgess, R.N., D.N.Sc., is van Ameringen Professor of Psychiatric Mental Health Nursing at the University of Pennsylvania School of Nursing. She, with Lynda Lytle Holmstrom, cofounded one of the first hospital-based crisis intervention programs for rape victims at Boston City Hospital in 1972. She served on numerous governmental councils and was elected to the National Academy of Sciences Institute of Medicine in October 1994. Her research and publication areas include victimology, the use of children in pornography; sexual homicide and patterns of crime scenes; infant kidnapping; stalking and domestic violence; workplace violence; and threat communication.

Dr. Martha Coulter, Ph.D., is an associate professor of Public Health and Social Work at the University of South Florida. She is the director of the James and Jennifer Harrell Center for the Study of Domestic Violence. Her experience, research, and publications are focused in the areas of family violence and public health.

John E. Douglas, Ed.D., has a doctorate in education and served with the Federal Bureau of Investigation from 1970 until his retirement in 1995. As unit chief at the FBI Academy in Quantico, Virginia, Dr. Douglas supervised the Bureau's Criminal Investigative Analysis Program. He has provided consultation and guidance in over 5,000 cases involving both violent crime and white-collar crime investigations. He is coauthor of books and articles in the areas of criminal investigation, offender motivation, crime scene analysis, and offender profiling.

Leonard D. Eron, Ph.D., is past president of the International Society for Research on Aggression, and former editor of the *Journal of Abnormal Psychology*. He has received the APA award for Distinguished Professional Contributions to Knowledge (1980) and the Gold Medal for Life Contributions to Psychology in the Public Interest (1995).

Shari Feldbau-Kohn, M.A., is a doctoral candidate in clinical psychology at the State University of New York at Stony Brook. She was a graduate research fellow on a NIMH training grant in the area of partner aggression. She has written and contributed to papers studying the causes and effects of marital distress and partner aggression, and issues associated with the treatment of partner aggression. She is currently designing and teaching a course related to issues of violence.

Richard B. Felson, Ph.D., is a professor of Sociology at Pennsylvania State University. His research is concerned with situational factors in interpersonal violence. He is the author of numerous articles and is the coauthor (with James Tedeschi) of *Violence Aggression and Coercive Actions* (APA Books, 1994).

Michael P. Gamache, Ph.D., is a clinical assistant professor of Psychology in the Department of Neurology at the University of South Florida. His research and publications have been in the areas of psychological and neuropsychological assessment and the criminal profiling of serial sex offenders. He also maintains a private practice specializing in forensic psychological assessment.

Charles J. Golden, Ph.D., is a Diplomate in Clinical Psychology and Clinical Neuropsychology. He received his Ph.D. from the University of Hawaii in 1975. He is currently a full professor at Nova Southeastern University in Fort Lauderdale, Florida. Dr. Golden is a fellow of the APA and a past-president of the National Academy of Neuropsychologists.

Samuel T. Gontkovsky is currently a clinical psychology intern at the Department of Veterans Affairs Medical Center in Little Rock, Arkansas. He has presented numerous outcome studies at national and state conventions on topics including psychophysiology, EEG entrainment, and sexual aggression, and has published in the areas of neuropsychology, psychometric testing, aggression, and behavioral medicine.

Michele L. Jackson, Ph.D., is a graduate of Nova Southeastern University in Fort Lauderdale, Florida. She has worked as a mitigation specialist/forensic social worker for the Capital Crimes Unit of the Public Defender's office in Dade County, Florida. She is also a certified forensic examiner in the state of Florida.

Dr. Kathryn Kuehnle, Ph.D., is an adjunct assistant professor at the Department of Mental Health Law and Policy, Louis de la Parte Florida Mental Health Institute, University of South Florida. Her research and publications are focused on topics of child abuse. She also maintains a private practice, specializing in child abuse cases.

Kenneth E. Leonard, Ph.D., is a senior research scientist at the Research Institute on Addictions and director of the Division of Psychology in Psychiatry at the University at Buffalo Medical School. A fellow in Division 50 of the American Psychological Association, his research has focused on alcohol and marital/family violence.

John R. Lutzker, Ph.D. (University of Kansas), is the Florence and Louis Ross Professor and Chair of the Department of Psychology and director of Graduate Training at the University of Judaism in Bel-Air, California. Also, he is an adjunct professor of Human Development at the University of Kansas and president of Behavior Change Associates, a psychological corporation that provides services to regional centers in California serving people with developmental disabilities, and provides consultation to school districts. Dr. Lutzker has published over 100 professional articles and chapters: he has presented nearly 300 professional papers. He is a fellow of the American Psychological Association, the American Psychological Society, and The American Association of Applied and Preventive Psychology.

Barry M. Maletzky, M.D., is professor of clinical psychiatry at Oregon Health Sciences University, Portland, Oregon. He is also director of The Sexual Abuse Clinic, an organization devoted to treating the sexual offender. Dr. Maletzky is editor-in-chief of the international journal *Sexual Abuse: A Journal of Research and Treatment.* Although specializing in treatment of the sexual abuser, Dr. Maletzky has published 3 books and more than 60 articles and has delivered numerous presentations in the United States and abroad on a variety of topics. His areas of specialty and publication include treatment of refractory affective disorders and forensic and management aspects of crimes of violence. He serves on the Editorial Board of *Aggression and Violent Behavior: A Review Journal.* Dr. Maletzky is a founding member of the Association for the Treatment of Sexual Abusers.

Liam E. Marshall is assessment manager at the Bath Institution Sexual Offenders Program in Canada. He is involved in research projects evaluating the range of sexual behaviors and attachments in child molesters.

William L. Marshall, Ph.D., is professor of Psychology and Psychiatry at Queen's University in Canada. He has been doing research and clinical work into sexual offenders for 29 years, and has over 200 publications. He is currently president-elect of the Association for the Treatment of Sexual Offenders.

Daniel K. O'Leary, Ph.D., is distinguished professor of Psychology at the University of New York at Stony Brook. He was president of the American Association for Advancement of Behavior Therapy and received Distinguished Scientist Award from the Clinical Division of the American Psychological Association.

Brian M. Quigley, Ph.D., received his doctorate in Social Psychology from State University of New York, Albany and is currently a Research Associate at the Research Institute on Addictions. His research focuses on the interpersonal and social cognitive aspects of anger and aggression.

Marc Riedel is associate professor for the Center of Crime, Delinquency, and Corrections at Southern Illinois University. He does research on prescribed and proscribed forms of violence. Articles on the death penalty and homicide have appeared in the *Annals of the American Academy of Political and Social Science, Journal* *of Criminal Law and Criminology,* and *Temple Law Quarterly.* His ninth book, *Research Strategies for Secondary Data: A Perspective for Criminology and Criminal Justice* will be published by Sage Publications in 2000. Riedel has served on the Executive Council and as Vice-President of the American Society of Criminology. In 1985, Riedel received the Herbert A. Bloch award from the American Society of Criminology for outstanding service to the society and the profession.

Phillip J. Resnick, M.D., is a professor of Psychiatry and director, Division of Forensic Psychiatry at Case Western Reserve University (CWRU) School of Medicine. He is also a lecturer at CWRU School of Law. He has served as president of the American Academy of Psychiatry and the Law.

Angela Peterson-Rohne is a recent graduate of the clinical psychology program at Nova Southeastern University. She is currently in clinical practice involved with a wide range of client populations.

Charles L. Scott, M.D., is an assistant professor and director of Child Psychiatry and the Law at Tulane University School of Medicine. Dr. Scott is board certified in general, child and adolescent, and forensic psychiatry. He oversees a maximum security unit for those with mental illness and violent behavior.

Julie Schumacher, M.A., is a doctoral candidate in clinical psychology at the State University of New York at Stony Brook. She was a graduate research fellow on a NIMH training grant in the area of partner aggression. She has conducted numerous interviews with college students on the causes and consequences of dating aggression, and has written and contributed to works on the topic. She is currently designing and teaching a course related to issues of violence.

Michael C. Seto, Ph.D., is a psychologist in the Forensic Program at the Centre for Addiction and Mental Health in Toronto, Canada. He is also an assistant professor in Psychiatry and Criminology at the University of Toronto. He has published extensively in the areas of sexual offending and paraphilias.

Alisa B. Wilcox is a current psychology intern and lieutenant in the United States Navy, stationed at the National Naval Medical Center in Bethesda, Maryland. She is both a Ph.D. and Psy.D. candidate in psychology at Nova Southeastern University's Center for Psychological Studies in Fort Lauderdale, Florida. Some of her work experiences include Miami-Dade Police Department, the FBI's Behavioral Sciences Unit, South Florida prisons, a juvenile offenders program, and the Broward County Public Defender's Office.

Rosalie S. Wolf, Ph.D., is executive director, Institute on Aging, at UMass Memorial Health Care, Worcester. She is president of the National Committee for the Prevention of Elder Abuse, chair of the International Network for the Prevention of Elder Abuse, and editor of the international *Journal of Elder Abuse & Neglect.*

1 Introduction

ALISA B. WILCOX
Nova Southeastern University

MICHEL HERSEN
Pacific University

VINCENT B. VAN HASSELT
Nova Southeastern University

A crime is committed every 2 seconds; a violent crime every 19 seconds. This entails one aggravated assault every 31 seconds, one robbery every 59 seconds, one forcible rape every 6 minutes, and one murder every 27 minutes (Federal Bureau of Investigation, 1997). Based on these figures, it is not surprising that the United States is the most violent country in the industrialized world, with aggression and violence having reached epidemic proportions as we approach the new millennium. According to Palermo (1997), "a sense of insecurity and disenchantment with life has swept across much of society, often leading to feelings of anger, hostility, and frustration" (p. 1). Such feelings are believed to be major contributors to the current level of violence. However, even with these alarming statistics, this country has witnessed a recent trend emerge in the late 1990s regarding violent crime. Specifically, in 1996, an estimated 1.7 million violent crimes were reported to law enforcement officials throughout the country. This represents a decrease of 6 percent from 1995 estimates. Moreover, it marks the lowest total for violent crime nationally recorded in the 1990s (Federal Bureau of Investigation). Accuracy of such findings, however, has been the focus of controversy in light of recent media reports suggesting a tendency for some law-enforcement agencies to either underreport or reclassify more violent crimes as lesser offenses.

This introductory chapter briefly defines and discusses general trends of violence and aggression with an additional emphasis on violent crime in the United States. The main information source for violent crime figures used for this chapter is the *Uniform Crime Reports,* a publication by the Federal Bureau of Investigation. The Uniform Crime Reporting Program is a cooperative nationwide statistical collaboration, involving over 16,000 city, county, and state law-enforcement agencies. These law-enforcement organizations gather and submit data on crimes that have been reported to them or that have been committed in their areas. Over the years, the Uniform Crime Reporting Program has come to be one of the country's most influential and highly regarded social indices of crime. The Uniform Crime Reports document has been used not only in this country as a barometer of criminal activity, but also by various professionals (e.g., criminologists, sociologists, psychologists, and legislators) for research directions and policy decisions.

Regionally, the southern portion of the nation accounted for the greatest occurrence of violent crime, totaling 39 percent in 1996. Following the South was the West with 24 percent, the Midwest with 20 percent, and the Northeast with 17 percent. A decline was observed in all four regions from 1995 to 1996. The Northeast and the West recorded 9 percent drops, and the Midwest and the South recorded 8 percent and 3 percent declines, respectively. Further, the highest incidence of violent crime was in the months of July and August; the lowest month was February (Federal Bureau of Investigation, 1997).

Aggression and Violence in the Family

Several statistics from the 1980s demonstrate how many incidents of aggression and violence are not limited to strangers. For example, approximately 3 to 4 million American and 500,000 Canadian families experience familial abuse every year (Stark et al., 1981). A study conducted by Richters and Martinez (1993) using Washington, DC, schoolchildren, revealed that 13 percent of the violent incidents reported by fifth- and sixth-graders were committed by family members; family members also comprised 13 percent of the victim population. The same investigation obtained a positive correlation between number of domestic violence incidents and geographic regions with a high crime rate.

In addition, approximately one-third of marriages in the United States are characterized by physical violence between spouses (Straus, Gelles, & Steinmetz, 1980). Further, one in eight adults can recall at least one occasion during their adolescence where one or both parents hit the other (Straus, 1992). A woman is beaten every 12 seconds (Waits, 1985) and killed by her husband or boyfriend every 6 hours (Schneider, 1990). Every year, 4 percent of elderly Americans are abused by a family member (Pagelow, 1984). Three to five thousand children die each year in the United States due to parental abuse (Pagelow, 1984). According to Taylor and colleagues (1994), as violence in communities and schools continues to rise, a majority of children will witness or be victims of aggressive and/or violent behavior during their developmental years. Relatedly, the study by Richters and Martinez (1993) with Washington, DC, schoolchildren found that over one-third indicated that they had observed a shooting. Eleven percent of fifth- and sixth-graders reported having been a victim of a shooting; within this group, 22 percent said they had been the victim of a mugging, 47 percent had experienced physical threats, and 37 percent had been chased by a gang. Sixteen percent of children report inflicting physical harm on their siblings (Wiehe, 1997). And when examining incidents of familial violence, in conjunction with the increase of juvenile violence, it is no surprise that research findings have suggested that children who are directly or indirectly exposed to violence are at risk for employing aggressive and violent tactics themselves (Helfer & Kempe, 1976), usually as a means to solve interpersonal conflicts and cope with stress (Garrett, 1997).

Violent Crime

A violent crime usually involves one of four offenses: murder and nonnegligent manslaughter, forcible rape, aggravated assault, and robbery. All violent crimes involve some type of force or threat of force. According to Palermo (1997), violent behavior, particularly homicide, suicide, and mass murder, "is an expression of the inability to control negative emotions" (p. 6). Each one of the aforementioned offense categories will be briefly covered. In addition, hate crime, another aggressive and violent act that is too often overlooked, will be discussed.

Murder and Nonnegligent Manslaughter

Murder and nonnegligent manslaughter is the willful and intentional killing of one person by another. Another form of homicide, mass murder, is an offense in which multiple victims are killed in a single incident, typically by one individual and in a certain given social context (Palermo, 1997). According to 1997 statistics homicide is now the second leading cause of death in 15- to 24-year-olds, and is the third leading cause of death among elementary school children, ages 5 to 14 years (Osofsky, 1997). However, despite the increase in homicide incidents in the past decade, a recent trend has developed in the 1990s: While adult violence has actually decreased, juvenile violence has dramatically increased. Homicide by offenders aged 14 to 17 years climbed from 16.2 per 100,000 juveniles in 1990 to 19.1 per 100,000 in 1994 (Herbert, 1996). Additionally, the number of juveniles under age 15 years arrested for murder increased by 50 percent from 1984 to 1992 (Greenwood, 1995).

One explanation may be that access to lethal weapons is easier than ever before. Assaults among adolescents frequently result from an argument that escalates into either a physical alteration or use of a weapon (Hawkins, 1986). Indeed, in 1996, firearms were the weapons used for 29 percent of all homicides, robberies, and aggravated assaults; a knife or cutting instrument was used in 15 percent; while 26 percent consisted of other dangerous weapons. Personal weapons (e.g., hands, fists, or feet) were used in 30 percent of the incidents. Despite the increased accessibility of guns, however, the proportion of violent crimes committed with firearms in the general adult population, overall, has remained relatively constant in the late 1990s (Federal Bureau of Investigation, 1997). Appelbone (1996) documented a poll targeting juveniles (including suburban and rural areas) in their demographics. Of the 2,000 juveniles from around the country who responded, one in eight youths, and almost two in five from violent neighborhoods, replied that they carried a weapon for protection. One in nine youths, and more than one in three from neighborhoods considered violent, said they had been truant from school because of fear of crime (Appelbone, 1996).

The estimated number of murder victims in the United States in 1996 was 19,645. Despite the dramatic increase in juvenile homicide, the 1996 figure for homicide dropped 9 percent since 1995, and 17 percent since 1992. A comparison of years 1995 and 1996 also shows that the murder rate dropped 10 percent throughout the nation's cities, and 6 percent in rural areas. It should be noted that cities with populations exceeding 1,000,000, and cities with populations ranging from 250,000 to 499,999, registered the largest decrease (13%) (Federal Bureau of Investigation, 1997).

It is encouraging that all four regions in the United States recorded decreases in their homicide rates, with the South and Midwest decreasing by 7 percent, and the Northeast and West dropping 13 percent. In 1996, the South accounted for 43 percent of the murders, the West, 23 percent, the Midwest, 20 percent, and the Northeastern States, 14 percent. Figures show that most murders in 1996 occurred in August, while the fewest were committed in March and April (Federal Bureau of Investigation, 1997). Of 18,108 homicide offenders in 1996, 90 percent were males, 86 percent were 18 years or older, 69 percent were ages 17 through 34 years, 52 percent were African American, and 45 percent were Caucasian.

An interesting trend in the 1990s is that incidents involving one victim and one offender were typically intraracial in nature. Ninety-three percent of African American homicide victims were killed by another African American. Christoffel (1990) documented that assaults and murders of a majority of African American adolescents over the age of 12 were typically committed by a peer who was at minimum, acquainted with their victim. Eighty-five percent of Caucasian victims were murdered by another Caucasian. Similarly, males were usually killed by other males (89%); however, figures also show that 9 out of 10 female homicide victims were killed by males (Federal Bureau of Investigation, 1997).

Forcible Rape

In 1996, the United States witnessed the lowest incidence of forcible rapes reported to law-enforcement agencies since 1989, with a total 95,769. This figure is 2 percent lower than 1995 and 12 percent lower than 1992. Thirty-nine percent of forcible rapes occurred in the southern region, while 25 percent occurred in the midwestern region, 23 percent in the western states, and 13 percent in the northeastern states. The number of reported forcible rapes dropped 5 percent in the Midwest and 3 percent in the West since 1995. Figures for the Northeast and the South, however, remained essentially unchanged for that period. The fewest number of incidents occurred in December, while the greatest number occurred during the month of July (Federal Bureau of Investigation, 1997).

Aggravated Assault

According to *Uniform Crime Reports* (1997), aggravated assault is "an unlawful attack by one person upon another for the purpose of inflicting severe or aggravated bodily injury" (p. 31). This act of aggression and violence is typically committed with a weapon that is likely to cause death or serious bodily harm. Rate of aggravated assaults decreased 6.3 percent from 1995 to 1996. This marks the third consecutive year of decline.

By region, southern states accounted for 41 percent of the aggravated assault incidents in the United States in 1996, while western states accounted for 24 percent, the midwestern region 20 percent, and the northeastern region, 15 percent. All four regions experienced a decline in reported incidents since 1995. The most incidents of aggravated assault were recorded in July, while the lowest occurred during the months of February and November.

With regard to the nature of aggravated assault incidents, in 1996, most were committed using a blunt object or other dangerous weapon (34%); personal weapons (i.e., hands, fists, or feet) were used in 26 percent; firearms in 22 percent; and knives or other cutting instruments in 18 percent.

A closer examination of weapon usage reveals that use of all four types of weapons (blunt object, personal, firearm, and knife or cutting instrument) declined since 1995. Use of firearms saw a 10 percent decline, while use of personal weapons (e.g., hands, fists, or feet) had a 9 percent decrease; knives or other cutting instruments a 7 percent decrease; and blunt objects or other dangerous weapons a 3 percent decrease (Federal Bureau of Investigation, 1997).

Robbery

Robbery is the unlawful taking or attempting to take anything of value from the care, custody, or control of an individual or individuals by force or threat of force or violence, and/or by putting the victim in fear. The estimated number of incidents of robbery totalled 537,050 nationally in 1996. This is the lowest number of reported incidents since 1987. From 1995 figures alone, a 7 percent total decline was registered, with an 8 percent decrease registered for the nation's cities.

On closer examination, 35 percent of all reported robberies took place in the southern states; 24 percent in the western states; 22 percent in the northeastern states; and 19 percent in the midwestern states. In the past two years, the Northeast and the Midwest recorded an 11 percent decrease, while the West and the South registered an 8 percent and 3 percent decline in reported robbery incidents, respectively (Federal Bureau of Investigation, 1997).

Approximately $500 million in losses was attributed to robberies in 1996. While the main objective in a robbery is to obtain some sort of monetary or property gain, use of force or threat of force is always employed, and many individuals suffer serious personal injuries as a result.

Fifty-one percent of robberies in 1996 occurred on streets and highways, an 11 percent decrease since 1995. Commercial and financial establishments accounted for 24 percent of robbery incidents, and residences accounted for 11 percent. Miscellaneous types of robbery accounted for the remaining percentages. All types of robberies saw a decline since 1995, with the exception of bank robbery, which saw a 14 percent increase (Federal Bureau of Investigation, 1997).

According to *Uniform Crime Reports* (1997) figures, in 1996, 41 percent of all robberies involved use of a firearm; 39 percent involved "strong-arm tactics"; knives or other cutting instruments were used in 9 percent of robberies; and other dangerous weapons in the remaining cases. Since 1995, use of a knife or other cutting instrument decreased 9 percent; strong-arm tactics dropped 8 percent; firearm use dropped 7 percent; and use of other dangerous weapons dropped 6 percent.

Hate Crime

A hate crime is a criminal offense committed against a person, property, or society, which is primarily motivated by the perpetrator's bias against a race, religion, ethnic/national origin group, or sexual orientation. Not all hate crime involves person-to-person contact; however, when it does, the contact, or threat of contact, is often of an aggressive and violent nature.

In 1996, of 10,702 offenses reported, 69 percent involved a hate crime against a person. Of the crimes committed against another person, intimidation accounted for 56 percent, while simple and aggravated assault accounted for 24 percent and 20 percent, respectively. A closer examination of bias motivation showed that 63 percent of reported hate crimes were due to race, 14 percent to religion, 12 percent to sexual orientation, and 11 percent to ethnicity. Eighty-six percent of all reported hate crimes involved destruction, damage, or vandalism (Federal Bureau of Investigation, 1997).

Violence and Gender

When considering aggressive and violent behavior, one of the more controversial issues is that of gender differences (Bograd, 1990; McNeely & Mann, 1990). Research has commonly reported that acts of aggression and violence are more common in males than females (Eagly & Steffen, 1986; Richardson, Vandenberg, & Humphries, 1986; Steinmetz & Lucca, 1988). This has especially been the case with more serious acts of violence (Bograd, 1990), such as sexual abuse (Burke, Stets, & Pirog-Good, 1988) and homicide (Daly & Wilson, 1990; Mercy & Saltzman, 1989). However, studies in which females were found to be the primary aggressors have been documented (McNeely & Mann, 1990; Riggs, O'Leary, & Breslin, 1990; Sugarman & Hotaling, 1989). Most research in this area has involved female victims of spouse or date abuse.

Purpose of This Book

Given the wide range and magnitude of problems encompassed by aggression and violence, combined with the increased professional, public, and legislative attention they have received, we believe that the ever-burgeoning information warrants being under one cover. An introductory text on aggression and violence is, in our opinion, long overdue. In the present volume, we review the major developments in light of the theoretical perspectives, specific forms of aggression and violence, and special topics relevant to the field.

REFERENCES

Appelbone, P. (1996, January, 12). Crime fear is seen forcing changes in youth behavior. *New York Times*, p. A6.

Bograd, M. (1990). Why we need gender to understand human violence. *Journal of Interpersonal Violence, 5*, 132–135.

Burke, P. J., Stets, J. E., & Pirog-Good, M. A. (1988). Gender identity, self-esteem, and physical and sexual abuse in dating relationships. *Social Psychology Quarterly, 51*, 282–285.

Christoffel, K. K. (1990). Violent death and injury in U.S. children and adolescents. *American Journal of Diseases of Childhood, 144*, 697–706.

Daly, M. & Wilson, M. (1990). Is parent-offspring conflict sex-linked? Freudian and Darwinian models. *Journal of Personality, 58*, 163–189.

Eagly, A. H. & Steffen, V. J. (1986). Gender and aggressive behavior: A meta-analytic review of the social psychological literature. *Psychological Bulletin, 100*, 309–330.

Federal Bureau of Investigation. (1997). *Uniform Crime Report, 1996*. Washington, DC: U.S. Department of Justice.

Garrett, D. (1997). Conflict resolution in the African American. *Aggression and Violent Behavior, 2*, 25–31.

Greenwood, P. (1995). Juvenile crime and juvenile justice. In J. Q. Wilson & J. Petersilia (Eds.), *Crime* (pp. 91–117). San Francisco: ICS Press.

Hawkins, D. (1986). Longitudinal-situational approaches to understand Black-on-Black homicide. In *Report of the Secretary's Task Force on Black and Minority Health, 5*, 97–116. Washington, DC: U.S. Department of Health and Human Services.

Helfer, R. E. & Kempe, C. H. (1976). *Child Abuse and Neglect, the Family and the Community*. Cambridge, MA: Ballinger.

Herbert, B. (1996, March 4). In trouble after school. *New York Times*, p. A15.

McNeely, R. L. & Mann, C. R. (1990). Domestic violence is a human issue. *Journal of Interpersonal Violence, 5*, 129–131.

Mercy, J. A. & Saltzman, L. E. (1989). Fatal violence among spouses in the United States, 1976–1985. *American Journal of Public Health, 79*, 595–599.

Osofsky, J. D. (1997). *Children in a Violent Society*. New York: Guilford.

Pagelow, M. D. (1984). *Family Violence*. New York: Praeger.

Palermo, G. B. (1997). The bérserk syndrome: A review of mass murder. *Aggression and Violent Behavior, 2*, 1–8.

Richardson, D. R., Vandenberg, R. J., & Humphries, S. A. (1986). Effect of power to harm on retaliative aggression among males and females. *Journal of Research in Personality, 20*, 402–419.

Richters, J. E. & Martinez, P. (1993). The NIMH Community Violence Project: I. Children as victims of and witnesses to violence. *Psychiatry, 56*, 7–21.

Riggs, D. S., O'Leary, K. D., & Breslin, F. C. (1990). Multiple correlates of physical aggression in dating couples. *Journal of Interpersonal Violence, 5*, 61–73.

Schneider, E. M. (1990, July). *Legal Reform Efforts to Assist Battered Women: Past, Present, and Future*. Unpublished manuscript.

Stark, E., Flitzcraft, A., Zuckerman, D., Grey, A. J., & Frazier, W. (1981). Wife abuse in the medical setting: An introduction for health personnel. *Domestic Violence, 1*, 1–54.

Steinmetz, S. & Lucca, J. S. (1988). Husband battering. In V. B. Van Hasselt, R. L. Morrison, A. S. Bellack, & M. Hersen (Eds.), *Handbook of Family Violence*. New York: Plenum.

Straus, M. (1992). Children as witnesses to marital violence: A risk factor for life-long problems among a nationally representative sample of American men and women. *Children and Violence: A Report of the Twenty-Third Ross Roundtable on Initial Approaches to Common Pediatric Problems*, 98–109.

Straus, M. A., Gelles, R. J., & Steinmetz, S. K. (1980). *Behind Closed Doors: Violence in the American Family*. New York: Doubleday.

Sugarman, D. B. & Hotaling, G. T. (1989). Dating violence: Prevalence, context, and risk markers. In M. A. Pirog-Good & J. E. Stets (Eds.), *Violence in Dating Relationships*. New York: Plenum.

Taylor, Zuckerman, Harik, & Groves. (1994). Witnessing violence by young children and their mothers. *Developmental Behavioral Pediatrics, 15,* 120–123.

Waits M. (1985). The criminal justice system's response to battering: Understanding the problem, forging the solutions. *Washington Law Review, 60,* 267.

Wiehe, V. R. (1997). *Sibling Abuse: Hidden Physical, Emotional, and Sexual Trauma.* Thousand Oaks, CA: Sage.

A Social Psychological Approach to Interpersonal Aggression

RICHARD B. FELSON
Pennsylvania State University

A social psychological approach focuses on the situational factors that lead to aggression. Situational factors involve present circumstances rather than an actor's past history. Present circumstances include characteristics of the immediate environment, such as the setting and the other people present. They also include the current thinking or subjective point of view of the actor. For example, a homicide offender's perception that the victim insulted or wronged him is likely to have influenced his behavior (whether the victim actually wronged him or not). Also included are the motives that lead actors to use aggression and the beliefs that inhibit them from doing so. These motives and inhibitions are likely to have a strong social component.

From a social psychological perspective, it is also important to consider the role of the target of aggression. Aggressive encounters often stem from interpersonal conflicts and grievances. The target may provoke an attack by engaging in some offensive behavior. In addition, verbal aggression can escalate into physical violence when the target retaliates. It is important to examine the give-and-take that occurs during aggressive social interactions.

Finally, third parties often have an impact. They may instigate or mediate the conflict, or they may serve as an audience or ally. They may alter the balance of power in favor of one party or the other. For example, when parents intervene on behalf of younger siblings, such siblings fight more frequently. As a result of parental protection, a younger sibling is more willing to fight with an older, and usually stronger child. The balance of power has been altered in the little one's favor.

Defining Aggression

People use the terms *aggression* and *violence* loosely in everyday life. In science, we need to be more careful or we will talk past each other. We recognize that there are no true definitions—dictionary meanings are based on common usage, not scientific truths. We must settle for a definition that is useful.

A definition should classify together behaviors that have common motives and exclude behaviors that have different motives. We do not want to classify the behavior of the aggressive salesmen with the behavior of the serial killer if we think their motivations are different. We do want to classify together the behavior of both the punishing parent and the serial killer if we think that their motivations are similar (in spite of many differences between them).

Interpersonal aggression is usually defined as any behavior involving an intent to harm another person. The definition includes the components of harm and intention. Harm is relatively straightforward. If I do something to you that you would prefer to avoid, I have harmed you.

People can harm each other in a variety of ways. They can use verbal methods, such as insults and threats, or physical methods, such as punches and kicks. They can harm bodies, self-images, and property. The term *violence* usually refers to actions that either involve physical means or produce physical harm.

For an action to be identified as aggression, the person must have intended to produce harm. Whether the attack was successful or not does not matter. For example, the sniper who shoots and misses is engaged in an act of aggression even if he harms no one. If harm has been done, it must have been done on purpose for the act to be aggression; it cannot be accidental. For example, the drunk driver who kills someone has engaged in an act of recklessness, not aggression, because he did not have the intent to harm.

Does an intent to harm mean that the aggressor wanted the victim to suffer? Not necessarily. For example, robbers may be indifferent about harming the victim. The typical robber desires the victim's compliance (which will bring him a profit), not harm. He uses a threat to force the victim to give him money. The robber is willing to harm the victim, but it has no positive value for him.

Do we want to label all behaviors that deliberately produce harm *aggression?* If we did, we would include competitive activities, since winners gain (deliberately) at the expense of losers. For example, if you get the job that I wanted, I was harmed partly as a result of nonaccidental behavior on your part. How is the competitor different from the robber? Both are willing to harm someone, but neither typically attaches a positive value to that harm. The difference is that the robber uses coercion, while the competitor does not. The robber imposes a harm on an unwilling participant. This consideration leads to an amendment of the original definition of aggression. I define *aggression* as *coercive* behavior in which an actor intends to harm another person. People who use aggression expect the target will be harmed (whether they value it or not), and they impose harm on the target.[1]

We should not confuse anger with aggression. When people are upset, they may curse or pound their fist, but that is not aggression because they have no intent to harm. Anger is the emotional reaction people have to other people when they believe they have been treated unfairly—when they have a grievance. Sometimes anger leads to aggression, but more often it does not. In addition, people are not necessarily angry when they engage in aggression. However, we may consider a *display* of anger an act of aggression if a person uses it to threaten others.

We sometimes use the word *aggressive* as an adjective to describe intense effort or activity. However, the aggressive salesman who annoys us on the telephone is not engaged in aggression because he has no intent to harm and is not using coercion. Pete Rose was an aggressive base runner, but his intent (I believe) was to reach the next base, not to injure the opposing player. If he did attempt to injure an opponent in a particular instance, as some claimed, then he was engaged in an act of aggression.

It is important not to allow our value judgments to influence our definitions. Thus, we must avoid defining aggression as a harmful act that we believe is antisocial or wrong. A moral approach leads to endless debate over whether a particular harmful act was justified or not; we will often disagree. It is more useful to say that people harm other people for good reasons and bad, or more precisely, that we approve of some acts of aggression and disapprove of others. We may approve of violence used in self-defense, for example, but it is still useful to describe it as an act of aggression, because it involves coercion and an intent to do harm. In addition, it is important not to label some behavior as aggression just because we disapprove of it (e.g., drinking and driving)—not all antisocial behavior or harm-producing behavior is aggression.

Punishment is aggression given a positive face. When teachers, judges, and parents punish, they intentionally harm an offender in order to deter unwanted behavior and to encourage future compliance. Calling the aggression punishment legitimizes it because it implies that the target deserved to be harmed. However, there is still an intent to do harm, at least in the short term. (Over the long term, a harm may help, by rehabilitating the target, for example.) If the target does not experience the punishment as a harm, it is not effective punishment. As we shall see, some criminal violence involves an attempt by an offender to punish someone for an alleged wrong.

Frustration-Aggression Hypothesis

One popular conception of aggression is that it is an irrational, involuntary outburst. In the scientific literature, this point of view is expressed in the frustration-aggression hypothesis (Berkowitz, 1989; Dollard et al., 1939). The basic idea is simple: People become aggressive when their goals are blocked or when bad things happen to them. Psychological stress, depression, anxiety, failure, physical pain, sadness, embarrassment, and guilt should all lead to aggression. For example, analysts attribute the violent return of the disgruntled postal worker to years of frustration. He must have just "snapped."

According to the frustration-aggression hypothesis, aggression satisfies an innate desire to harm other people when one is feeling bad or frustrated. People prefer to attack the source of their suffering, but if that is too costly, they *displace* their aggression onto someone else. Engaging in aggression reduces their aggressive drive and they experience a *catharsis*. After catharsis, they are less likely to engage in aggression.

This type of behavior is called angry or reactive aggression. It is compelled by an aggressive drive—a biological force inside the person. If the person engages in a harmful act, the drive is reduced. The aggressive drive is like the sexual drive, in that it arises from outside stimulation, seeks release, and then returns the body to its original state.

The frustration-aggression hypothesis (and revisions of it) have received much criticism. One criticism centers on the concepts of catharsis and aggressive drive. People do not become less aggressive after they have been aggressive, according to experimental evidence (see Tedeschi & Felson, 1994, for a review). Expressing angry emotions—letting it all out—does not calm us down and make us peaceful. Sometimes it makes us more aggressive.

Another problem with this approach is that people who feel bad or frustrated do not generally engage in aggression. For example, we feel bad when we blame *ourselves* for a problem; but blaming others, not self-blame, leads to aggression. The death of a loved one is one of our most negative experiences. Yet, aggression rarely occurs at funerals or other situations involving mourning.

The type of negative situation that leads to aggression is more specific. People tend to become aggressive when they believe that someone has attacked or wronged them in some way. In the laboratory, the best way to get subjects to be aggressive is to attack them, not frustrate them. An insult has much more impact than losing a contest, for example. Some studies do show small frustration effects, if the subject is also attacked, but frustration has no effect by itself (see Tedeschi & Felson, 1994 for a review).

People respond to frustrations and negative events in other ways. They become upset, they get drunk, they engage in problem solving, or they give up and try something else. It is primarily *unjustifiable* frustrations that lead people to want to engage in aggression, according to laboratory evidence. In other words, blaming someone else is critical in determining whether a negative experience leads to aggression.

In fact, in a laboratory study subjects retaliated for intended shocks even when they did not actually receive the shock (Epstein & Taylor, 1967). *Bad intentions*, not bad experiences, lead to aggression, because they imply blame. Other laboratory studies show that subjects are more likely to retaliate when a person shocks them than when a machine shocks them (e.g., Sermat, 1967). The pain is the same, but the meaning differs. When someone zaps them, and subjects think that person has mistreated or humiliated them, they want to retaliate.

The frustration-aggression theorists do not claim that all aggression is due to feeling bad. They recognize that some aggression is instrumental to a goal—a means to an end. They recognize that sometimes individuals harm others because it brings them some benefit or reward. For example, they claim that robbery is usually instrumental aggression, while assault is usually angry aggression. The robber usually wants the victim to comply and hand over the money. His goal is not to harm.

From the perspective described here, *all* aggression is instrumental. People use aggression to get what they want. Maybe they want justice, maybe they want to save face, maybe they want to influence someone's behavior. Whatever their goal, the victim's suffering has no intrinsic value for them—it is a means to some other end. It is not compelled by a mysterious inner force. We don't need a special mechanism to account for aggression. Aggression is similar to other human behavior in that it is oriented toward rewards and costs.

Decisions—Impulsive and Otherwise

People use aggression when they think it will achieve something they value. They are likely to avoid using aggression if they think it will be too costly, or if they think it is morally wrong. However, violent encounters often involve quick decisions, strong emotions, and alcohol. These factors may lead to a failure to consider costs, morals, or alternative approaches.

Aggression can also be like a "bad habit." People may strike out habitually in certain circumstances. For example, a mother habitually screams at her disobedient child. Like people who smoke, or overeat, aggressors may feel compelled or out of control, but they can break the habit if they want to badly enough.

People often inhibit habitual aggression when they think the costs are too high. For example, the angry mother may refrain from screaming at her child in the grocery store, and wait until they are alone. On the other hand, if she is impulsive, she may lash out in front of others without giving it much thought. However, the aggression is a learned habit, not an explosion produced by an internal aggressive drive.

We must keep in mind that an act of aggression, no matter how impulsive or spontaneous it appears, involves a string of decisions. Consider the baseball batter who charges the pitcher after being hit with a pitch. He is clearly angry, and to some, he may appear out of control. But he remembers, on the way to the mound, to drop his bat. He knows that going after the pitcher with a bat would mean the end of his career. As he approaches the pitcher he has more decisions to make: Should he throw a punch? Should he grab or push the pitcher? Should he make verbal threats from a distance? When players, coaches, and umpires intercede, he allows himself to be contained, screaming all the while.

Even when people use violence in a rage, they are still engaged in decision making. They must decide whether to attack or bide their time, how to attack, and how to respond to their adversary's counterattack. While they may behave impulsively, in the sense that they fail to consider long-range consequences, they are still making decisions. The fact that decisions are sometimes impulsive does not mean that decisions are not being made. Of course, there is variation in the amount of thought given to decisions about whether to use aggression; sometimes people are calculating and sometimes they are not. Frustration can facilitate aggression if it interferes with the ability to make careful decisions, but it does not have an innate link to aggression.

What about violent offenders who kill someone when they know they will be caught and sent to prison? Perhaps they are so angry at the victim that they are willing to pay the price. More likely they do not even consider the cost. They are acting in the heat of the moment, overwhelmed by their desire for revenge, or fooling themselves about the likely consequences. Perhaps frustration or emotional arousal interferes with careful thought. Perhaps things happen too quickly for reflection. Perhaps they are lost in a cloud of drunkenness. Alcohol inhibits one's ability to make thoughtful decisions.

You may still find some violent behavior incomprehensible and want to attribute it to an inner compulsion. Maybe that is because your moral inhibitions prevent you from understanding why someone would choose to commit heinous acts of violence. Maybe you have difficulty understanding this behavior because you have high self-control—you give more thought to your behavior than people who commit these acts. You have enough self-control to sit down and read this book. This characteristic may prevent you from a full understanding of the impulsive person who engages in criminal violence. You are having trouble getting into the criminal mind.

Motives for Aggression

If aggression is not due to an inner compulsion, then what is its motivation? Why do we sometimes impose harms on others? People engage in aggression for primarily three reasons: (1) in order to control the behavior of the target; (2) for retribution or justice; and (3) to promote or defend their self-image.[2]

Control

People often desire to influence or control the behavior of others: Parents want their children to behave; spouses want to change each other's behavior when they find it offensive; robbers and rapists want their victims to comply; and judges want to deter criminals. Aggression is a social influence tactic, sometimes used as a last resort, sometimes as a first resort. It is used to compel a target to do something they would otherwise not do, or to deter a target from what they are doing.

For example, how does a mother get a resistant child to go to bed? She could try persuasion: "You'll be tired tomorrow." This might be her first method, but children often disobey. They respond to commands with counterarguments and negotiation. The mother could promise a reward: "I'll read you a story if you'll go to bed afterward." This might work, but it will take some time, and she will miss the television show she is watching.

So she turns to a tried-and-true technique. Her voice becomes stern or angry to convey her threat. It is like the dog's growl. If the child continues to resist, she makes her threat explicit: "Go straight to bed, or no television tomorrow." The child understands this *contingent threat* and complies. Aggression is quick, easy, and effective as an influence technique.[3]

Some children are more difficult and disobedient, and some parents are ineffective as agents of social control, and lack self-control. Put these factors together and there is the possibility of child abuse. Child abuse usually develops out of discipline situations in which aggression escalates.

Contingent threats are a common method for controlling others through force. Threats can be communicated verbally or through the display of a weapon. The robber threatens to harm the victim ("Your money or your life") unless the victim complies. The rapist uses the threat of harm to force a woman to engage in sexual relations. The blackmailer threatens to reveal incriminating information to the police unless the target makes a payoff.

Interpersonal conflict is a ubiquitous aspect of social life. When two people want the same object and are unwilling to share it, they sometimes use aggression to get their way. Scarcity leads to conflict, which can lead to aggression and violence. For example, aggression is common between siblings. Siblings fight over the use and distribution of property in the home (e.g., over what television show to watch). When the rules regarding property are unclear, as they are in many homes, conflict and aggression are more likely.

Retribution

We punish offenders to achieve justice or retribution (as well as deterrence). When people do wrong—particularly when they wrong us—we believe they deserve to be punished.[4] The more serious the offense the more severe the punishment: "An eye for an eye, a tooth for a tooth." Historically, this rule of retribution was used as an argument against punishment that was viewed as too severe. As society has become less punitive, it has come to stand for greater severity of punishment.

Sometimes people rely on the criminal justice system to handle their grievances, sometimes they take the law in their own hands. Much criminal violence is a form of vigilantism or self-help, where someone with a grievance seeks retribution. Self-help violence is more likely when the criminal justice system is unavailable or ineffective in addressing a grievance (Black, 1983). For example, violence frequently occurs in conflicts over illicit drug sales, because the police are not sought out to handle grievances over illegal actions.

It is ironic that people who use violence often feel self-righteous. From their point of view they are doing a good deed, and their behavior is an act of justice. From their point of view, nonaggression is immoral when someone deserves to be punished. To fail to punish the misdeeds of others would be wrong.

Assigning blame is therefore a key factor producing aggression and violence. We punish people when we blame them for negative outcomes. We assign blame when we think that they have misbehaved intentionally or recklessly. We wish to harm people when we think they have wronged us, not when they have harmed us through no fault of their own.

However, some people are "blame-mongers." That is, they tend to assign blame even when it is undeserved. They may ignore exonerating circumstances or fail to understand the perspective of the person they accuse of wrong. Sometimes they blame others to avoid self-blame. For example, students can avoid their own responsibility for a failing grade by blaming their teachers. Sometimes blaming others can help explain traumatic events that are otherwise difficult to understand. For example, we may assign blame for a terrible accident, even when it was unavoidable.

Grievances are common in social life because people frequently break rules and offend each other. When people are dependent on each other and living together, conflict is inevitable, and there are many opportunities for grievances to develop. These conflicts can lead to domestic violence. Discussions of violence between husbands and wives must recognize the important role of conflict and grievances.

People often do not express their grievances to the offending party. They are silent because they want to avoid an embarrassing scene, or they want to avoid damaging their relationship. Politeness helps regulate interpersonal relations by preventing aggression (although sometimes it prevents conflicts from being resolved).

The tendency to express grievances openly varies across cultures. For example, Americans are more confrontational than the Japanese (Ohbuchi, 1991), but less likely to say what is on their mind than Israelis. Some Americans feel the need to express their grievances more often. They might purchase books and attend assertiveness training seminars that exhort them to do so.

Some people are more likely than others to generate grievances because they engage in offensive behavior. Obnoxious people are probably more likely to become involved in violent interactions because they get people angry at them. Politeness is expected in social life, and the failure to follow ritualized forms of respect is sure to offend others (Felson, 1992). Men probably generate more grievances than women, because they engage in more deviant behavior. This probably leads to more violence against men than would otherwise be the case.

People under stress are also more likely to generate grievances. Stress interferes with competent performance, and angers the people affected. Because of their mood, people under stress are less likely to be polite and friendly. For example, when a husband comes home after a difficult day at work, and does not greet his wife warmly, she is likely to feel aggrieved. She may admonish him and he may then retaliate.

Self-Image

People use aggression to enhance or protect their self-images. For example, by using violence, a young man demonstrates that he is powerful, tough, and courageous. By showing skill with his fists, he can increase his status among his friends. If winning is impossible, standing up to the antagonist maintains some level of honor and provides a measure of satisfaction.

When someone insults us, we may believe that we have been "put-down," or made to appear weak. By putting our adversary down we can nullify that image, and make ourselves appear powerful. Retaliation is a way of *saving face* or maintaining one's honor when one has been attacked. However, the counterattack is a put-down for the other person who may then retaliate, creating a *conflict spiral*. Adversaries try to win this face-saving contest rather than limit the punishments to fit the offense. Sometimes small disputes escalate into physical violence. This is particularly likely to occur when an audience is watching, because the threat to image is greater. Thus, verbal conflicts between men are more likely to escalate to physical violence if an audience is present (Felson, 1982). On the other hand, the presence of an audience prevents escalation in conflicts between men and women.

Sometimes the audience encourages the adversaries, making it difficult for them to back down. Sometimes the audience pulls the parties apart. Third-party mediation allows both sides to back down without losing face. The response of third parties is a key factor in the escalation of aggressive interactions.

School-aged bullies are motivated by concerns for self-image. They prey on vulnerable targets in order to show how tough they are. For the bully, dominating the victim is an accomplishment, a way of demonstrating power to himself and others. When bullies pick on other children, they usually do so in front of their friends.

Multiple Motives

A particular violent incident may involve all of these motives. For example, consider why a person might retaliate when attacked. First, by retaliating, targets deter their tormentors and others from future attacks. Second, the target is likely to perceive an attack as wrongdoing, and therefore deserving of punishment. Finally, by retaliating, targets save face by making adversaries look weak, not themselves.

In some instances, talk about justice is a justification not a motivation. The person retaliates in order to save face, and is able to legitimate the counterattack by claiming that the target deserved it. One might describe this as a case of "justice in the service of revenge."

Most violent disputes begin with criticism and other attempts at social control. Offended parties want justice and redress of their grievances. Concerns for justice and deterrence are central in this initial stage of the encounter. People who have been accused often see things differently. They interpret the criticism as an attack, and they retaliate in response. Verbal attacks are reciprocated, as the incident escalates into a battle to save face. Finally, one of the adversaries, perhaps thinking that they are losing the verbal battle, engages in a physical attack.

Concerns for justice and self-image do not always have the same effects. Aggrieved individuals are interested in seeing that the wrongdoer receives a punishment that is proportional to the offense, while individuals concerned with face-saving want to win the battle and make a good show of themselves. They prefer to dominate antagonists, which means delivering greater harm than they have received.

Explaining Displacement

The motive for aggression almost always has something to do with the victim. Either the actor and target have a dispute, or the target has something the actor wants (Felson & Steadman, 1983). Random attacks on victims by serial killers, for example, are rare. Even serial killers may have some imagined grievance with the strangers they victimize. Delusional thinking can play a role in aggression.

Displaced aggression, however, is an exception that requires explanation. Why, after some provocation, does someone attack an innocent third party? The frustration-aggression hypothesis has an explanation: Displaced aggression provides a catharsis, relieving the aggressive drive produced by frustration when the frustrating agent is too costly to attack. However, evidence suggests that catharsis does not occur when people engage in aggression (see Tedeschi & Felson, 1994). How, then, can we account for displacement?

First, the misperception of aggression leads to an exaggeration of the frequency of displacement. When people are in a bad mood, they tend to be irritable and impolite, which often does not involve an intent to do harm. People are expected to be warm and friendly to each other. When they fail to show proper etiquette, their behavior can be misperceived as displaced aggression.

Second, displacement may reflect a concern for self-image after a failure or loss of face (Melburg & Tedeschi, 1989). A successful attack against a third party may help the person restore, at least to some extent, a favorable image as tough or competent. By putting another person down, people can bring themselves up in comparison. By changing competitors, the actor shifts to a contest that is winnable: "If you can't beat 'em, beat someone else."

Third, displaced aggression may also be due to guilt by association when the offending party and an innocent third party are members of the same group. The aggressor may assign collective guilt to all members of the group. Blood feuds, bias crimes, and perhaps some rapes, are examples of aggression carried out against members of a group.

Is Violence Involving Women Special?

Men are much more likely to engage in violence, and they also are much more likely to be the target of violence. As a result, the typical violent encounter involves two or more men. When women are involved in violence, their adversaries are usually men.

The fact that men are usually bigger and stronger has an important impact on conflicts between the sexes. Size and strength give men a tremendous advantage over women in a physical altercation. Gender differences in fighting skills, and the willingness to use violence are also factors to consider.

Women might use heavy objects to counter the physical advantages of men, or they may sometimes use more lethal weapons. They may seek assistance from third parties, including the criminal justice system. In primitive societies, a woman's kin may intervene on her behalf when her husband assaults her. The farther a woman lives from her kin, the more likely she is to suffer abuse from her husband. This fact affects the attitudes of the villagers, for example, Yanamomo women abhor being married to men in distant villages, because they know their fathers and brothers cannot protect them (Chagnon, 1977).

The norm of chivalry discourages violence against women. In other words, we believe that hitting a woman is worse than hitting a man (and women get first crack at the lifeboats when ships are sinking). Because of the norm, men are the target of violence more frequently than women (in spite of the fact that it is less dangerous to attack women). In addition, we punish those who harm women more severely (Bureau of Justice Statistics, 1992).

If violence against women is considered so bad, why is it sometimes tolerated? The privacy of family life may be the answer. Most violence against women is within the family, and family violence tends to occur behind closed doors, hidden from outsiders. In addition, outsiders are reluctant to intervene in disputes between family members. Historically, privacy concerns have increased the vulnerability of women to their husband's violence.

Special Motives

To a large extent, men and women have similar motives when they use aggression. Both have grievances and a desire to punish the "guilty" party. Both have an interest in controlling the behavior of others for their own purposes. Both are likely to retaliate when attacked in order to avoid losing face. The difference between men and women is primarily in the methods, not their motives. Men use physical violence much more often than women; women engage in verbal attack as often as men do, and indirect forms of aggression more often (Eagly & Steffen 1986; Björkqvist, Lagerspetz, & Kaukiainen, 1992).

There *are* some differences in motivation in violence involving women. Face-saving is more likely to motivate the aggression of men than women. Men care more about not looking weak or cowardly. They are more likely to retaliate when attacked than are women, particularly if there is an audience watching. Face-saving is also more important when men fight men than when men fight women; conflicts between men are more likely to become contests over image. These contests help explain why in homicides involving love triangles men usually kill their male rivals, while women usually kill their cheating husbands (Felson, 1998).

It is widely believed that men who assault their wives have a control motive. There is some evidence that the control motive is more *likely* to be involved when husbands assault their wives than when men assault other men, or when they assault women who are not their wives (Felson & Messner, unpublished). However, men who assault their wives probably have a variety of motives.

In addition, both husbands and wives want to control each other at times. Because men are stronger and have a greater proclivity to use violence, they are more likely to use violent means. When a woman wants to control her husband, she may use other methods. She may express anger at him, refuse sexual relations, or threaten to leave him. A study of disputes involving couples shows that women are more likely to engage in control behavior than men (Stets & Burke, 1996). Women complained about and criticized their spouses more often than the men did; however, women probably have more to complain about, since men misbehave more often than women.

There is also evidence that when women commit homicide, it is more likely to involve self-defense than when men commit homicide (Felson & Messner, 1998). However, self-defense is not a very common motive for either gender.[5]

Sexual Coercion

A common form of male violence against women involves sexual coercion. Almost all rape offenders are male and most victims (about 92%, according to one estimate) are female.

Some scholars believe that men who use sexual coercion are attempting to demonstrate their power. This is a plausible idea, but there is no scientific evidence as yet to support it. And there are reasons to be skeptical. Males are more likely to demonstrate power by attacking males than by attacking females. Attacking females implies weakness, which is why some people call a man who is violent toward a woman a coward. In addition, males often publicly display their violence against other males (recall the schoolyard bully), while they usually hide violence toward females.

There is some evidence that sexual motivation plays an important role in rape and other forms of sexual coercion. Sex differences in sexuality provide the context. Males are much more likely than females to be indiscriminate and casual in their attitudes toward sexual relations. Females, on the other hand, are more likely to interpret sexual activity as romance rather than recreation.

These differences in sexuality lead to conflict between the sexes. Men often attempt to influence women to have sex using a variety of techniques, some men use coercion. Rape allows a man without moral qualms or fear of consequences to have sex with anyone he wants.

Most date rapes occur during consensual sexual activity when the man is sexually aroused. He wants intercourse, but she does not want to go that far. Men who engage in date rape tend to use it as a last resort after persuasion and other techniques have failed. In addition, sexually coercive men tend to be young men with high sexual aspirations. They masturbate frequently and spend a lot of time searching for sexual partners. Rapists express a preference for attractive victims, and they overwhelmingly choose young women (Felson & Krohn, 1990).

Most rapists use the force necessary to complete the crime, but no more. Their violence is usually tactical, not gratuitous. However, men who rape their ex-wives and ex-girlfriends are more likely to beat up the victim during the rape. The motive of these rapists is probably retribution and revenge, not sexual compliance.

Most rapists and wife beaters commit other crimes as well. They are likely to be versatile criminals, not sexists who specialize in violence toward women (Alder, 1984). Low self-control and a lack of moral inhibitions allow them to victimize both men and women.

Summary

There are reasons to be skeptical that aggression is produced by an innate drive triggered by frustration. The evidence casts doubt on the idea that there is a special mechanism to explain aggression. Instead, I have suggested that aggression is instrumental action like other human behavior. Harming others is a means to various ends, not an end in of itself. Sometimes aggressive behavior reflects careful calculation of reward and costs, and sometimes it is impulsive or habitual. In either case, it is readily understood using well-established social psychological principles.

NOTES

1. In our work, we often prefer the term *coercion* over aggression (e.g., Tedeschi & Felson, 1994). Coercion involves verbal impositions (e.g., insults) as well as physical impositions.
2. A fourth motive is the desire for excitement. Some people use violence for entertainment.
3. It can be less effective and more costly in the long run, however. Evidence suggests that reasoning with a child is also important.
4. Jealousy can also produce aggression. When people think that someone has received an unfair share of some reward, they may attempt to restore equity by harming the person, even when that person is not held responsible for the injustice.
5. Even if a woman kills her husband after continual abuse, she may do so for retribution or revenge rather than self-defense.

REFERENCES

Alder, C. (1984). The convicted rapist. A sexual or a violent offender? *Criminal Justice and Behavior, 11,* 157–177.

Björkqvist, K., Lagerspetz, K. M. J., & Kaukiainen, A. (1992). Do girls manipulate and boys fight? Developmental trends in regard to direct and indirect aggression. *Aggressive Behavior, 18,* 117–127.

Berkowitz, L. (1989). The frustration-aggression hypothesis: An examination and reformulation. *Psychological Bulletin, 106,* 59–73.

Black, D. J. (1983). Crime as social control. *American Sociological Review, 48,* 34–45.

Bureau of Justice Statistics. (1992). Criminal victimization in the United States—1990. U.S. Department of Justice. Bureau of Justice Statistics. Washington, DC: USGPO.

Chagnon, N. A. (1977). *Yanomamo, the Fierce People.* New York: Holt, Rinehart and Winston.

Dollard, J., Doob, N., Miller, N. E., Mowrer, O. H., & Sears, R. R. (1939). *Frustration and Aggression.* New Haven: Yale University Press.

Eagly, A. H. & Steffen, V. J. (1986). Gender and aggressive behavior: A meta-analytic review of the social psychological literature. *Psychological Bulletin, 100,* 309–330.

Epstein, S. & Taylor, S. P. (1967). Instigation to aggression as a function of degree of defeat and perceived aggressive intent of the opponent. *Journal of Personality, 35,* 265–289.

Felson, R. B. (1982). Impression management and the escalation of aggression and violence. *Social Psychology Quarterly, 45,* 245–254.

Felson, R. B. (1992). Kick 'em when they're down: Explanations of the relationship between stress and interpersonal aggression and violence. *Sociological Quarterly, 33,* 1–16.

Felson, R. B. (1996). Big people hit little people: Sex differences in physical power and interpersonal violence. *Criminology, 34,* 433–452.

Felson, R. B. (1997). Anger, aggression and violence in love triangles. *Violence and Victims, 12,* 345–362.

Felson, R. B. & Krohn, M. (1990). Motives for rape. *Journal of Research in Crime and Delinquency, 27,* 222–242.

Felson, R. B. & Messner, S. F. (1998). Disentangling the effects of gender and intimacy on victim-precipitation in homicide. *Criminology, 36,* 405–424.

Felson, R. B. & Steadman, H. J. (1983). Situational factors in disputes leading to criminal violence. *Criminology, 21,* 59–74.

Melburg, V. & Tedeschi, J. T. (1989). Displaced aggression: Frustration or impression manage-ment? *European Journal of Social Psychology, 19,* 139–145.

Ohbuchi, K. (1991). Interpersonal conflicts among Japanese and Americans. Unpublished paper, Tohoku University, Sendai, Japan.

Sermat, V. (1967). The possibility of influencing the other's behavior and cooperation: Chicken vs. prisoner's dilemma. *Canadian Journal of Psychology, 21,* 204–219.

Stets, J. E. & Burke, P. J. (1996). Gender, control and interaction. *Social Psychology Quarterly, 59,* 193–220.

Tedeschi, J. T. & Felson, R. B. (Eds.). (1994). *Violence, Aggression, and Coercive Actions.* Washington, DC: APA Books.

3 A Psychological Perspective

LEONARD D. ERON
University of Michigan

It is apparent from the varied chapters in this volume that aggression and violence are not caused by any one factor or circumstance, whether biological, sociological, or psychological. However, whatever the underlying causes, ultimately these behaviors are learned, and are usually learned very early in the development of a young child. This is the conclusion reached by the Commission on Violence and Youth of the American Psychological Association which issued its final report, *Reason to Hope* (Eron, Gentry, & Schlegel, 1994) a few years ago. The title for this report was selected because members of the commission believed, on the basis of their extensive review of the findings by psychologists and others over the past 50 years, that violence in our society is not an intractable problem. If aggression is learned, then it can be unlearned; and it should be possible to implement prevention and treatment programs based on sound, theoretically driven, psychological principles. Such programs should have an impact on the prevention and amelioration of aggression and violence in our society.

In this chapter the terms *aggression* and *violence* will be used interchangeably. Much of the research on violence to date has dealt with physical violence, probably because psychological harm is more difficult to observe and measure. The definition of aggression used in this chapter is "a behavior that is intended to injure another person," which includes both physical and psychological injury. This commonly accepted definition includes both behavior motivated primarily by a desire for tangible awards and behavior motivated primarily by hostility. However, it does not include many commonplace meanings of *aggression,* including assertive behaviors (e.g., an aggressive salesperson). There are numerous gray areas in which the classification of behaviors as aggressive or nonaggressive is problematic. For some of these areas (e.g., contact sports and war), the key distinction may be whether the behavior is restricted to the game, played under specific rules and sanctioned by society. In war, for example, one might argue that most individual acts of killing derive from prosocial rather than antisocial motives.

Many psychiatrists and psychologists who work with people who engage in aggresive behavior, consider aggression to be the result of some kind of psychopathology. And, when working with children and adolescents who present with aggressive behavior, they place them in a category labeled conduct disorder. However, it is an error to apply a categorical disease model to a phenomenon, aggressive behavior, that is essentially noncategorical and is not an illness.

Aggressive behavior in children and adults falls on a continuum, not into discrete categories. Children do not suddenly "come down" with aggression or "catch aggression." Aggression is not something you either have or do not have. Everyone's behavior can be evaluated on its aggressiveness. Such evaluations inevitably produce a continuum on which everyone can be placed. This continuum is most often, if not always, positively skewed, with a few persons scoring zero, many persons scoring toward the low end, some scoring toward the high end, and a few persons scoring very high. This distribution of scores is obtained, regardless of the measure used. This continuum, of course, can be divided into categories which may fit the conceptual framework that medical practitioners and epidemiologists are accustomed to using. But it is a distortion. Defining people as pathological who are in the upper 5 percent, or over some other arbitrary score, gives a meaning to the results that they do not deserve. It is possible, of course, to define categories and create consensus across research groups by adopting similar definitions, but unless the underlying phenomena are categorical, the result is a distortion of the truth.

Causes of Aggression

As stated previously, violent human behavior is not caused by any one factor. It is multiply determined. The factors involved range from genetics, neuroanatomy, endocrinology, and physiology, through exogenous substances and firearms, to peer, gang, family, and community influences. There has been a plethora of research on each of these factors. However, none of these factors by itself can explain much of the variance in the extent and/or intensity of violent behavior in the population, much less predict who will engage in such behavior. It is only when there is a convergence of a number of variables that aggressive or violent behavior occurs (Eron, 1982).

However, aggressive or violent behavior does not routinely occur even when these factors do converge. And all children are not similarly affected by these physical, social, and economic factors. Not every African American, late-adolescent male, living in a single-parent family in the inner city in the midst of a high-crime neighborhood, the victim of poverty and lack of opportunity to advance economically or socially, becomes violent; only a minority of them do. The individual most likely to behave aggressively and violently is one who has been programmed to respond in this way through previous experience and learning (Eron, 1982). Individuals with given genetic, neurological, and physical endowment, living under circumstances that put them at risk for violence still vary in their likelihood of behaving violently. Aggressive behavior must somehow have been learned in the past and incorporated into the individual's repertoire of responses before it can be elicited by some external situation and/or stimulation from within the individual. In addition, alternative prosocial behaviors must not have been learned, or at least, were not learned as well as aggressive behavior.

Violence is not a behavior that springs forth spontaneously when a child reaches adolescence. The groundwork has been prepared long before this. Somewhere in the youngster's background, bombarded by all the genetic, physiological, social, and economic conditions mentioned previously, he or she must have learned to solve interpersonal problems with the use of violence, to relieve frustration that way, and similarly to acquire material possessions by the use of violence. As a *youngster*, the violent adolescent *must* have seen this type of behavior at home, in the neighborhood, in school, or on the TV screen. He or she must also have seen it rewarded and approved, might subsequently have fantasized about it, and perhaps engaged in it and been rewarded for it. Although aggression is caused by many factors, ultimately it is a learned behavior. This is the one hopeful note in the depressing concatenation of causal factors. If aggression is learned, as I said before, then it can be unlearned, or conditions can be arranged so it is not learned in the first place.

Learning Aggression

How is aggression learned? Several different learning theories of aggression were proposed in the 1960s and 1970s by Bandura (1973), Berkowitz (1962), Buss (1961), Eron, Walder, and Lefkowitz (1971), Patterson (1986), and others. More recently, researchers have introduced learning models based on current thinking in cognitive psychology (Berkowitz, 1990; Dodge, 1980; Huesmann, 1988). The various learning theories have differed in terms of exactly what is learned—whether they be specific behaviors, cue-behavior connections, response biases, beliefs, or scripts. In all cases, though, learning is hypothesized to occur both as a result of one's own behaviors and as a result of viewing how others behave.

The specific conditions that have been shown empirically to be most conducive to the learning and maintenance of aggression are those in which the child is rewarded for his or her own aggression (e.g., Patterson, 1986); is provided many opportunities to observe aggression (e.g., Bandura, 1973; Eron, Huesmann, Lefkowitz, & Walder, 1972); is given few opportunities to develop positive affective social bonds with others (e.g., Hawkins & Weis, 1985); and is the target of aggression (e.g., Dodge, Bates, & Pettit, 1990). While these conditions can exist in all social classes, they are more likely in the inner-city environment with its extreme economic and social deprivation (McLoyd, 1990). Thus, this environment increases the general level of risk for all children growing up there.

Early Predictors of Adult Aggression

One of the clearest findings concerning adolescent and adult aggression and antisocial behavior is that such behavior is predictable statistically from early antisocial, aggressive, and hyperactive behavior. The more aggressive child is likely to become both the more aggressive adult and the more antisocial and criminal adult. No other factor measured in childhood, whether physiological, cognitive, environmental, or familial, has been shown to predict more of the variation in adult antisocial behavior than does early aggression. For example, in a study in which data were collected on over 800 youngsters, it was found that peer-nominations of a child's aggression measured at age 8 years predicted a whole variety of aggressive and antisocial behaviors displayed 22 years later at age 30 years, including officially tallied criminal convictions (Huesmann, Eron, Lefkowitz, & Walder, 1984).

Does that mean, as has been suggested, that all criminal behavior is aggressive behavior? No, of course not. What it does suggest, however, is that the developmental, psychological processes underlying aggressive behavior also underlie other forms of antisocial and criminal behavior. Furthermore, aggression is a behavior that occurs frequently among even very young children, and therefore is amenable to study as part of a developmental process.

Individual differences in social behavior related to aggression (e.g., early temperament) have been detected before age 2 years (Kagan, 1988), and it has been shown that at least by age 6 years, a number of children have adopted aggressive patterns of behavior in their interactions with others (Parke & Slaby, 1983). The extent of aggressive behavior in children tends to increase into adolescence. However, by age 8 years, children are characteristically more or less aggressive over a variety of situations; and aggression becomes a stable characteristic of the individual youngster (Huesmann et al., 1984; Olweus, 1979).

Implications of such stability and the relation between adult criminality and child aggression are relevant to planned interventions that are aimed at preventing criminal behavior. Because aggression is already apparent with wide individual differences by age six years, and becomes a stable characteristic of the individual by age eight years, that leaves only a brief period of developmental years during which preventive action must begin by parents, teachers, and other socializing agents. How these persons respond to the first indications of aggression will probably be more important in determining subsequent development or inhibition of such behaviors than any organized efforts of the criminal justice establishment at later ages. By the time a youngster is an adolescent, aggressive behavior has been so well learned as a response to angry feelings or as an instrumental act, that it is difficult to change. Despite occasional or even frequent attempts to discourage or control aggression, the individual rewards, social approval, and media portrayals that support this behavior are so abundant that it persists. Although it is never too late to make changes in one's violent behavior patterns, by late adolescence it is extremely difficult because distinctive ways of behaving aggressively and, furthermore, of justifying this behavior, have become so firmly established that they are resistant to change. Therefore, interventions are most likely to succeed when they start in early childhood and continue throughout adolescence.

Theoretical Issues

Not only must preventive programs start early, they must also be based on sound knowledge of the causal mechanisms that contribute to the development of violence and aggression. The first major attempt by psychologists to account for the development of aggression on the basis of learning principles and observable behavior appeared in the monograph, *Frustration and Aggression* by Dollard, Doob, Miller, Mowrer, and Sears (1939). It was the authors' premise that when individuals become frustrated, they respond with aggression. What was *unusual* about their position was the assumption of the inevitability and inexorability of the relation. Frustration always leads to some form of aggression, and when aggression occurs it can be presumed that frustration was an antecedent event. Early on, this position was seen by researchers as too extreme. In fact, one of the authors, Neal Miller, just two years later (1941) denied the inevitability of the relation stating, "Frustration produces instigation to a number of different types of responses, one of which is an instigation to some form of aggression" (p. 338). The frustration-aggression premise was further called into question by a number of researchers (Berkowitz, 1989; Buss, 1961; Cohen, 1955; Pastore, 1952), and the theory itself lost its explanatory power, but not before stimulating many other researchers to investigate the validity of the factors that had been specified by its authors as the factors that lead to aggression and determine how and when it can be expressed. Thus, the frustration-aggression hypothesis has probably stimulated more research than any other proposition in psychology over the last 50 years.

Operant Psychology

From the perspective of operant psychology, the concept of frustration as an instigator of aggression is irrelevant. What is important to operant psychology is the reaction of the environment to any specific aggressive response elicited from the individual. Aggressive responses that are rewarded over time are repeated; those which are punished tend to extinguish. It should be remembered, however, that very important to operant behaviorists is the availability of an alternative unpunished response, preferably one that could be rewarded to replace the punished response (Azrin & Holz, 1966).

Such operant principles have been employed successfully by Gerald Patterson and his colleagues, who have proposed a theory of the development of antisocial behavior based almost exclusively on operant principles. Their coercion theory places the genesis of aggressive behavior in the parent-child relationship and the disciplinary practices used by the parent—that is, inept or inconsistent discipline and poor monitoring lead to antisocial behavior in the child. Their correlational data gathered in the observation of parent-child interactions have been supported by manipulative experiments (Patterson, Dishion, & Chamberlain, 1993).

Patterson and his colleagues invoke the concept of mutual reinforcement, both negative and positive, between parent and child to explain the development and amelioration of aggressive behavior. They do recognize that other processes such as modeling, social attribution, and affective expression can also influence the development of aggressive behavior. However, Patterson believes that neither cognitive nor social skills training is "necessary or sufficient for the treatment of antisocial children" (Patterson, Dishion, & Chamberlain, 1993) and that behavioral training of both parent and child is an essential component of any "treatment package."

Social Learning Theory

The point of view described previously, however, is *not* shared by other psychologists who believe that, in order to understand the development and reduction of aggressive behavior, it is necessary to consider the learned cognitions that are associated with aggressive behavior, either as antecedents or consequent. For example, Bandura (1986) has expanded his social learning theory of aggression, which earlier had emphasized observation of such behavior and its subsequent reinforcement as the essential ingredients. He has found it necessary to include internal, cognitive factors to account for aggressive behavior and its stability in children. According to Bandura, it is the cognitive evaluation of events taking place in the child's environment and how competent he or she feels in responding in different ways, which is important in determining the child's behavior at that time and in the future. This is what has been termed self-efficacy. Berkowitz (1988), on the other hand, emphasizes the importance of enduring associations. Aggression is a behavior which is stimulated by aversive events that produce negative affect. In most people, this negative affect is associated with "expressive-motor reactions, feelings, thoughts and memories that are associated with both fight and flight tendencies" (p. 8). The strength of these tendencies is affected by a number of factors (e.g., genetic, situational, and learned). The stronger tendency is the one acted on, and if fight is stronger than flight, the emotional experience is interpreted as anger. The generation of the behavior and the associated anger are relatively automatic although attributions about the behavior may occur later as a controlled cognitive process.

Cognitive-Behavioral Approaches

Dodge (1980) emphasizes the importance of attributional biases. Aggressive children are viewed as possessing defective cognitive processes for interpreting behavior of others and in the selection of their own behavior from a previously learned repertoire. Huesmann (1988) views the child as a processor of information who develops programs or scripts to guide social behavior. The aggressive child is one who has developed many aggressive scripts and few prosocial ones. A script suggests what events are to happen in the environment, how the person should behave in response to these events, and what the likely outcome of that behavior would be. Scripts may be used to guide behavior in a controlled manner, producing seemingly reflective behavior, or, after they are well learned, in an automatic manner generating seemingly impulsive behavior (Schneider & Shiffrin, 1977).

According to Huesmann (1988), individuals differ markedly in terms of both the range of different types of scripts they have available, as well as the specific content of their most utilized scripts. For example, aggressive children who are less skilled at processing social information probably have fewer, but more aggressive scripts available, and they rely on these aggressive scripts more frequently than children who are more skilled in processing social information. Therefore, during the course of social interaction, aggressive children are more likely to rely on these aggressive scripts. Furthermore, to the extent that a child's environment is characterized by randomness, disorder, and emotional distress, he or she is also more likely to rely on very well-learned scripts in order to keep the information-processing load within his or her capabilities during this chaos. This is because automatic cognitive processing dominates controlled processing under conditions of high stress (Huesmann, 1988).

Effect of Contextual Factors

These recent theoretical approaches have the common theme that the child's cognitions play a key role in maintaining the stability or in changing the developmental trajectory of aggressive behavior over time and across situations. However, the cognitions the child forms are not unaffected by what goes on around her or him. Contextual variables both within the family (socioeconomic status, parent child-rearing practices, stressful life events, parental substance abuse) and those outside the family (neighborhood violence and poverty level, association with deviant peers, exposure to violent media) all help mold the cognitions which then exert a more direct influence on aggressive behavior. Although cognitive schemata are critical to understanding social behavior, they do not operate in a vacuum. Environmental conditions continuously interact with previously learned attributions, scripts, and beliefs to exert a strong influence on aggressive behavior.

A large number of macro and micro contextual factors ranging from poverty to a violent environment, from community efficacy to social control, and from peer rejection to parental restrictiveness have the potential to serve as frustrators and instigators to aggression and to provide models of violent behavior. But it is the way the children process information about such stimuli and react cognitively to them that determines if they will become instigators. For example, a punishment for aggression may inhibit aggression or stimulate further aggression depending on the child's cognitions about it (Eron, 1987; Eron, Walder, & Lefkowitz, 1971). If a child encodes the event as an instance of his or her own misbehavior being followed by an appropriate parental response, then the punishment may have the desired effect. Thus, punishment often works with children who identify with their parents. On the other hand, with a different cognitive interpretation, the child may encode the event as an instance of another person's successful problem solving with aggression. In this case a different effect is produced.

More generally, it has been demonstrated that social behavior is controlled to a great extent by attributional biases, world schemas, scripts, and normative beliefs about behavior that are established during a person's early development (Huesmann, 1988). Attributional biases (Dodge, 1980) direct the individual's interpretation of social cues to help determine the intent of others. These attributions are influenced by the kind of "world schema" that an individual has acquired (for example, "the world is mean"). These attributions influence emotions and the type of script that an individual will retrieve to deal with the social situation. Scripts (Abelson, 1981) can be viewed as cognitive programs that are stored in a person's memory and are used as guides for behavior and social problem solving. Not all scripts that occur to the child will be employed. Before acting out the script, the child reevaluates the appropriateness of that script in light of existing internalized social norms—called normative beliefs (Huesmann & Guerra, 1997)—and examines the likely consequences. There may be great individual differences in the extent of this evaluation. Some children may not have the cognitive capacity to engage in a thorough evaluation. Even among children with similar capacities, differing reinforcement histories and differing perceptions of social norms may lead to quite different evaluations.

According to Huesmann (1988; Huesmann & Eron, 1991), the primary process through which scripts and other cognitions are acquired is a learning process involving both observational learning, and conditioning. Additionally, these cognitions are modified by information processes such as rehearsal, abstraction, and reactance. It is presumed that while these cognitions are first being established, they influence the child's behavior through *controlled* mental processes (Schneider & Shiffrin, 1977), but that these processes become *automatic* as the child matures. Correspondingly, cognitions that persist in a child's repertoire as they are rehearsed, enacted, and generate consequences, become increasingly more resistant to modification and change.

Thus, there are four distinct cognitive structures and processes particularly relevant to the control of aggressive behavior. First, the attributional biases of the child interact with his or her emotional reactivity and situational influences to affect anger. Second, the specific repertoire of scripts for social behavior that the child has observed, rehearsed, and encoded will affect the likelihood of aggressive behavior. Third, the more the child rehearses or ruminates (fantasizes) about aggressive scripts, the more these scripts will become accessible. Fourth, the child's internalized normative beliefs about the appropriateness of aggression can inhibit the emission of aggressive behavior, or, on the other hand, buffer the use of aggressive scripts.

A number of recent studies conducted by a variety of researchers have produced results consistent with these conceptions (e.g., Dodge & Crick, 1990; Huesmann & Guerra, 1997; Huesmann, Guerra, Miller, & Zelli, 1992; Winter & Uleman, 1984; Zelli, Huesmann, & Cervone, 1995). However, it is important to stress that this cognitive/information-processing view of aggression does not ignore macro-contextual or microcontextual influences in the development of aggressive behavior. To the contrary, the model asserts that to understand the development of aggressive behavior, the joint effects of contextual and cognitive factors must be examined. Thus, for example, in order to understand the cross-generational transmission of aggressive behavior, it is necessary to examine not only how parents' aggression-related cognitions and behaviors are related to their children's aggression-related cognitions and behaviors, but how changes in macrocontextual and microcontextual factors (e.g., community efficacy, socioeconomic status, parental psychopathology, and substance use) might affect the trajectory of aggression-related cognitions and behaviors across generations.

Continuity across Generations

While the processes involved are not well understood, there is substantial evidence that aggressive and antisocial parents are more likely to have aggressive and antisocial children (Bouchard, 1984; Cloninger & Gottesman, 1984; Huesmann, Eron, Lefkowitz, & Walder, 1984; Mednick, Gabrielli, & Hutchings, 1984; Osborne & West, 1979; Widom, 1989). A variety of adoption studies, for example, have revealed relations between children's aggressiveness or antisocial behavior and the aggressive or antisocial behavior of both their natural and adoptive parents. These studies, along with twin studies, suggest that there may be certain genetic factors that predispose some children to be more at risk for developing aggressive or antisocial behavior. However, it seems clear that these predisposing factors interact with social and personal factors to determine what is the actual risk (Raine et al., 1994). Furthermore, the fact that there are relations of children's aggression to the behavior of their adoptive parents suggests that the processes involved are more complex than simple genetic transmission.

Parents, of course, play key roles in a variety of developmental processes that will affect later social behavior ranging from how they respond to early temperament (Kagan, 1992), to their role in attachment (Bowlby, 1969), to socializing the child (Bandura, 1986; Dodge & Crick, 1990; Eron, Walder, & Lefkowitz, 1971; Huesmann, 1988; Patterson et al., 1992). It is easy to see how more-aggressive parents could be deficient in any of these areas; so the risk for antisocial and aggressive behavior in a child should be affected by how more-aggressive parents behave in each of these domains. However, it is hypothesized that the risk for a young child developing aggression depends not only on any genetic predispositions, the parents' overt behaviors in these domains, and the current family and contextual environment, but also on the cognitions that the parents have developed and how these interact with the contextual environment in which childrearing is occurring. It is hypothesized that these cognitions may be reflected by similar cognitions in the developing child, and that such cognitions are important mediators in maintaining the trajectory of aggression within families from parent to offspring.

Similarities of Cognitions and Behaviors across Generations

Over ten years ago, it was pointed out that in order to understand the effects of parenting, it is necessary to study the relation between the ideas held by parents and those held by their children, a circumstance which has been termed *mutual cognitions* by Maccoby and Masters (1983). The dyadic nature of the parent-child relation has been described by Holden (1995), who pointed out that many characteristics of children have a direct influence on the childrearing behavior of parents. According to Bugental (1992), different cognitions about a child's aggressive behavior are evoked, depending on whether the parent considers the child a problem. Mothers of aggressive children hold beliefs about social development that may vary from mothers of nonaggressive children, and they use different strategies to deal with their children's aggressive behavior (Rubin et al., 1995). Miller (1990) found that maternal cognitions were more closely related to the child's behavior than to either any maternal behavior itself or any cognitions of the child, leading to the conclusion that maternal cognitions about a child's behavior are often reactions to the child's actual behavior.

It has been pointed out by Rubin and colleagues (1995) that not only parental behavior but parental cognitions and affect vary with the characteristics of the child, and change with the child's age and whether the behavior is viewed as intentional. As the child gets older, the affective reactions of parents of aggressive children become increasingly negative (Dix & Reinfield, 1991). Mills and Rubin (1990) reported that by the time the children in their study were 4 years old, parents expressed concern about the aggressive behavior of their children, and had various thoughts about the strategies for dealing with this. By middle childhood, parents are even more concerned about aggression (Bacon & Ashmore, 1988). As children grow older, the parents' beliefs about aggression and its causes change, and attitudes toward the behavior also change (McNally, Eisenberg, & Harris, 1991).

There has been considerable research on how parental behaviors affect the development of aggression in children and predict the adult aggressive behavior of these children (Rubin, Stewart, & Chen, 1995). However, there has been little research on how the behavior of the offspring, whether as children, adolescents, or adults, affects the behavior of the parents. What has been the effect of children's aggressive behavior on the parents' cognitions, affect, and behavior? Lytton (1990) cites evidence that the type of control responses used by parents of children with conduct disorder are instigated by the child's acting-out behavior. Mills and Rubin (1990) found, according to parents' reports, that aggressive behavior in their young children causes anger and disappointment, which then leads to the use of high-power, assertive disciplinary strategies. Sanson and Rothbart (1995) have reviewed the extensive literature on the effect of temperamental differences in young children on parenting behavior, and have concluded there is indeed such child-to-parent effect, but the quality and extent of the effect depends on the "particular combinations of parent behavior and child temperament." Thus, in the case of young children, there is some evidence of the effects of young children's behavior on the behavior of parents. However, although it is a reasonable supposition, there is no evidence that the aggressive behavior of adolescent children affects the behavior of the parents to such an extent that it interferes with their own adjustment and marital interaction (see, for example, chapter on marital interaction and parenting by Wilson and Gottman (1995), which cites no study detailing the effect of aggression in adolescent children on the marital relations of the parents).

These cognitions cannot be treated in isolation, however. Rather, they must be understood as interacting with the environmental context in which the child is raised—a context which in turn may promote continuity of aggression in time and across generations through its own continuity.

The intergenerational transmission of aggression has recently been noted in the child development literature (Constantino, 1996; MacEwen, 1994; Muller et al., 1995). All of these studies were based on self-report, retrospective questionnaire data and only one (Muller et al., 1995) obtained such data from two generations. Response bias problems cloud the interpretation of such findings. In an earlier review of the literature, Widom (1989) concluded that while there are considerable data indicating that "violence begets violence," and that many professionals subscribe to this thesis, the long-term consequences of abusive home environments are not all that clear because of the lack of convincing empirical evidence. What prospective studies there are have attrition rates unaccounted for (e.g., whether due to early death, hospitalization, imprisonment), and do not consider factors which might alter the relation, that is, protective factors (Garmezy, 1981). A well-designed study should thus obtain a variety of measures independently from at least three generations. Then it would be possible to compare data, both self-report and reports by others, as well as archival data across generations. Such data can minimize response bias and provide information as to protective factors that might account for any discontinuities and reasons for attrition of subjects.

Discontinuities in the Trajectory of Aggression: Protective Effects and Competence

While there is substantial continuity of aggression over time and across generations, reports of extensive intervention efforts suggest that aggressive behavior can be modified (see the Special Section of the *Journal of Consulting and Clinical Psychology*, 1995, Vol. 63). For example, a recent report on a large-scale preventive intervention for high-risk, urban children would indicate that aggression is not intractable (Guerra, Eron, Huesmann, Tolan, & VanAcker, 1997).

The critical issue is to identify those variables that play a role in deflecting the trajectory of aggression over time and across generations. How does an aggressive child develop into a socially competent adult? What factors account for how an individual who was highly aggressive during childhood and adolescence is now the parent of a competent child? To investigate these questions, it is necessary to define *competence*. Although there has been some debate over the definition of competence (see Coatsworth & Sandler, 1992), the definition of Masten and colleagues (1995) focuses on the "performance of salient developmental tasks (across) broad dimensions of effective behavior" (p. 1636). Through structural equation modeling, these researchers have identified three dimensions of competence (academic, social, and behavioral conduct) during childhood (ages 8–12 years) and two additional dimensions (romantic, vocational) during late adolescence/early adulthood (ages 17–23 years). Several researchers in the field of resilience (Cowen & Work, 1988; Garmezy & Rutter, 1983; Luthar & Zigler, 1991) have identified a triad of protective factors that are hypothesized to operate in youth who exhibit competent outcomes despite exposure to significant risk conditions:

1. Dispositional/temperamental attributes of the child (e.g., easy temperament, intellectual ability)
2. Warm and secure family relationships
3. Availability of extra-family support (e.g., teachers, peers)

Contextual variables, such as family and peer support, and individual variables such as intellectual ability, self-esteem, and cognitive social problem-solving skills have been found to protect diverse samples of children from the potentially deleterious effects of risk factors (e.g., Cowen, Wyman, Work, & Parker, 1990; Dubow & Tisak, 1989; Rutter, 1990; Werner & Smith, 1992). To this list of potential protective factors there are added macroenvironmental variables such as neighborhood factors (e.g., collective efficacy, neighborhood violence), changes in which might also buffer the effects of risk on the development of aggression (Kupersmidt et al., 1995).

Gender

For many years there has been concern with the gender differences in aggressive behavior and how they can be accounted for in terms of differential socialization of boys and girls (Eron, 1979; Eron, Walder, & Lefkowitz, 1971; Lefkowitz, Eron, Walder, & Huesmann, 1977). It has also been noted that there has recently been a lessening of this difference. This has been ascribed to changes that have been developing over the years in the way that females are being socialized (Eron, 1987; 1992). A 1997 issue (Vol. 3, no. 2) of the *Journal of Social Issues* is devoted to gender "differences." The point is made by many authors that the assumption of gender difference is misleading and overdrawn. Over time, the observed differences have been diminishing: "As men's and women's lives become more similar, there are fewer and fewer psychological differences" (Barnett, 1997, p. 357). Indeed, recent findings on the effects of viewing television violence between the ages of 6 and 8 years indicate little difference in the effects of TV violence on males and females 13 years later (Moise et al., 1997). This is in marked contrast to earlier findings (Eron, 1992) of no TV violence effect over 11 years for girls who were the same age as these girls just 17 years earlier. Recent research also suggests that females simply are aggressive in different ways than males. For example, Björkqvist, Lagerspetz, and Kavkiainen (1992) and Lagerspetz and Björkqvist (1994) have reported that females tend to aggress more indirectly (e.g., "shun another," "spread lies about another") than do males. Crick and colleagues (Crick, 1996; Crick & Grotpeter, 1995) have reported similar results although they call indirect aggression *relational* aggression to emphasize its damage to social goals. The importance of assessing indirect aggression, as well as the more typically assessed overt aggression, is further indicated by findings suggesting that aggression during childhood may be manifested in different ways in later developmental periods (Eron et al., 1987), and this degree of *heterotypic* expression (Kagan & Moss, 1984) of aggression might be gender dependent. For example, it has been found that childhood aggression in females is linked to later forms of psychopathology that are nonaggressive in nature (Eron, Lefkowitz, Walder, & Huesmann, 1974).

Summary

A psychological perspective on the nature of violent and aggressive behavior would emphasize that, although this behavior is always the product of a number of interacting factors—genetic, physiological, social, and economic—ultimately it is learned. Thus, in order to understand the development of aggression and violent behavior, it is essential to understand how such behavior is learned in the presence of these interacting factors. Current thinking about the learning of aggression stresses the importance of cognition in the learning process. Attention is paid to the attributions the developing youngster makes about the motives and behavior of others, feelings about self-efficacy, attitudes, and normative beliefs about the extent and appropriateness of aggressive behavior in the population. Also important are the scripts for behavior, which the child learns by observing the behavior of others and by the rewards and punishments obtained for specific behaviors.

Contextual influences, such as socioeconomic status, community efficacy, parental behaviors, and stressful life events continually interact with these processes and must also be evaluated. Many protective factors that can deflect the developmental trajectory of aggressive behavior have been observed. These are such variables as good intelligence and competence in life tasks, as well as support from family and peers, The intergenerational transmission of aggression is also of interest. One of the vehicles for this transmission is similarity in cognitions between parent and child. Finally, the child's gender must be considered as an important variable affecting the development of aggression.

REFERENCES

Abelson, R. P. (1981). The psychological status of the script concept. *American Psychologist, 36,* 715–729.

Azrin, N. H. & Holz, W. C. (1966). Punishment. In W. K. Honig (Ed.), *Operant Behavior: Areas of Research and Application* (pp. 380–447). New York: Appleton-Century and Crafts.

Bacon, M. K. & Ashmore, R. D. (1988). How mothers and fathers categorize descriptions of social behavior attributed to daughters and sons. *Social Cognition, 3,* 193–217.

Bandura, A. (1973). *Aggression: A Social Learning Analysis.* Englewood Cliffs, NJ: Prentice Hall.

Bandura, A. (1986). *Social Foundations of Thought and Action: A Social Cognitive Theory.* Englewood Cliffs, NJ: Prentice Hall.

Bandura, A. (1991). Social cognitive theory of moral thought and action. In W. M. Kurtines & J. L. Gewirtz (Eds.), *Moral Behavior and Development: Advances in Theory, Research, and Applications* (Vol. 1, pp. 45–103). Hillsdale, NJ: Erlbaum.

Barnett, R. C. (1997). How paradigms shape the stories we tell: Paradigm shifts in gender and health. *Journal of Social Issues, 53,* 351–368.

Berkowitz, L. (1962). *Aggression: A Social Psychological Analysis.* New York: McGraw Hill.

Berkowitz, L. (1988). Frustrations, appraisals, and aversively stimulated aggression. *Aggressive Behavior, 14,* 3–12.

Berkowitz, L. (1989). The frustration-aggression hypothesis: An examination and reformulation. *Psychological Bulletin, 106,* 59–73.

Berkowitz, L. (1990). On the formation and regulation of anger and aggression: A cognitive-neoassociationistic analysis. *American Psychologist, 45,* 494–503.

Björqvist, K., Lagerspetz, K. M. J., & Kavkiainen, A. (1992). Do girls manipulate and boys fight? *Aggressive Behavior, 18,* 117–127.

Bouchard, T. J. (1984). Twins reared together and apart: What they tell us about human diversity. In S. W. Fox (Ed.), *Individuality and Determinism: Chemical and Biological Basis* (pp. 147–184). New York: Plenum.

Bowlby, J. H. (1969). *Attachment and Loss.* New York: Basic Books.

Bugental, D. (1992). Affective and cognitive processes within threat-oriented family systems. In I. E. Sigel, A. V. McGillicuddy-De Lisi, & J. J. Goodnow (Eds.), *Parental Belief Systems: The Psychological Consequences for Children* (pp. 219–248). Hillsdale, NJ: Erlbaum.

Buss, A. H. (1961). *The Psychology of Aggression.* New York: Wiley.

Cloninger, C. R. & Gottesman, A. (1987). Genetic and environmental factors in antisocial behavior disorders. In Mednick, S. A., Moffitt, T. E., & Stack, S. A. (Eds.), *The Causes of Crime: New Biological Approaches* (pp. 92–109). New York: Cambridge University Press.

Coatsworth, J. D. & Sandler, L. (1992). Defining and measuring children's competence: Issues for community psychology. *The Community Psychologist, 26,* 16–17.

Cohen, A. R. (1955). Social norms, arbitrariness of frustration and status of the agent of frustration in the frustration-aggression hypothesis. *Journal of Abnormal and Social Psychology, 51,* 222–226.

Constantino, J. N. (1996). Intergenerational aspects of development of aggression. *Journal of Developmental and Behavioral Pediatrics, 17,* 176–182.

Cowen, E. L. & Work, W. C. (1988). Resilient children, psychological wellness, and primary prevention. *American Journal of Community Psychology, 16,* 591–607.

Cowen, E. L., Wyman, P. A., Work, W., & Parker, G. M. (1990). The Rochester child resilience study: Overview and summary of first year findings. *Development and Psychopathology, 2,* 193–212.

Crick, N. R. (1996). The role of overt aggression, relational aggression, and prosocial behavior in the prediction of children's future social adjustment. *Child Development, 67,* 2317–2327.

Crick, N. R. & Grotpeter, J. K. (1995). Relational aggression, gender, and social-psychological adjustment. *Child Development, 66,* 710–722.

Dix, T. J. & Reinfield, D. P. (1991). Chronic and temporary influences on mothers' attributions for children's disobedience. *Merrill Palmer Quarterly, 37,* 251–271.

Dodge, K. A. (1980). Social cognition and children's aggressive behavior. *Child Development, 53,* 620–635.

Dodge, K. A., Bates, J. E., & Pettit, G. S. (1990). Mechanisms in the cycle of violence. *Science, 250,* 1678–1682.

Dodge, K. A. & Crick, N. R. (1990). Social information processing basis of aggression in children. *Personality and Social Psychology Bulletin, 16,* 8–22.

Dollard, J., Doob, L. W., Miller, N. E., Mowrer, O. H., & Sears, R. R. (1939). *Frustration and aggression*. New Haven: Yale University Press.

Dubow, E. F. & Tisak, J. T. (1989). The relation between stressful life events and adjustment in elementary school children: The role of social support and social problem-solving skills. *Child Development, 60,* 1412–1423.

Eron, L. D. (1979). Differential effects of television violence viewing on aggressive behavior of boys and girls. In A. Solnit (Ed.), *Proceedings of International Year of Child Conference, Child Advocacy* (pp. 215–235). New Haven: Yale University Child Study Center.

Eron, L. D. (1982). Parent-child interaction, television violence and aggression of children. *American Psychologist, 37,* 71–77.

Eron, L. D. (1987). The development of aggressive behavior from the perspective of a developing behaviorist. *American Psychologist, 42,* 435–442.

Eron, L. D. (1992). Gender differences in violence: Biology and/or socialization. In K. Björkqvist (Ed.), *Of Mice and Women.* New York: Academic.

Eron, L. D., Gentry, J., & Schlegel, P. (1994). *Reason to Hope.* Washington, DC: American Psychological Association.

Eron, L. D., Huesmann, L. R., Dubow, E., Romanoff, R., & Yarmel, P. (1987). Aggression and its correlates over 22 years. In D. Crowell, I. Evans, and C. O'Donnell (Eds.), *Childhood Aggression and Violence* (pp. 249–262). New York: Plenum.

Eron, L. D., Huesmann, L. R., Lefkowitz, M. M., & Walder, L. O. (1972). How learning conditions in early childhood—including mass media—relate to aggression in late adolescence. *American Journal of Orthopsychiatry, 44,* 412–413.

Eron, L. D., Lefkowitz, M. M., Walder, L. O., & Huesmann, L. R. (1974). Relation of learning in childhood to psychopathology and aggression in young adulthood. In A. Davids (Ed.), *Child Personality and Psychopathology* (pp. 53–88). New York: Wiley.

Eron, L. D., Walder, L. O., & Lefkowitz, M. M. (1971). *The Learning of Aggression in Children.* Boston: Little Brown.

Garmezy, N. (1981). Children under stress: Correlates of vulnerability and resistance to psychopathology. In A. I. Rabin, J. Aronoff, A. M. Barclay, & R. A. Zucker (Eds.), *Further Explorations in Personality* (pp. 196–269). New York: Wiley.

Garmezy, N. & Rutter, M. (Eds.). (1983). *Stress, Coping, and Development in Children.* New York: McGraw Hill.

Guerra, N. G., Eron, L. D., Huesmann, L. R., Tolan, P., & VanAcker, R. (1997). A cognitive/ecological approach to the prevention and mitigation of violence and aggression in inner city youth. In D. Fry & K. Björkqvist (Eds.), *Cultural Variation in Conflict Resolution: Alternatives to Violence* (pp. 199–214). Mahwah, NJ: Erlbaum.

Hawkins, D. & Weis, Y. (1985). The social development model: An integrated approach to delinquency prevention. *Journal of Primary Pediatrics, 6,* 73–97.

Holden, G. W. (1995). Parental attitudes towards childrearing. In M. H. Bornstein (Ed.), *Handbook of Parenting, Vol. 3: Status and Social Conditions of Parenting.* Mahwah, NJ: Erlbaum.

Huesmann, L. R. (1988). An information processing model for the development of aggression. *Aggressive Behavior, 14,* 13–24.

Huesmann, L. R. & Eron, L. D. (1991). Modeles structurels du development de l'agressivite. [Structural models for the development of aggression.] In R. E. Tremblay (Ed.), *Les Comportements Agressifs* (pp. 181–214). Montreal: University of Montreal Press.

Huesmann, L. R., Eron, L. D., Lefkowitz, M. M., & Walder, L. O. (1984). Stability of aggression over time and generations. *Developmental Psychology, 20,* 1120–1134.

Huesmann, L. R. & Guerra, N. G. (1997). Children's normative beliefs about aggression and aggressive behavior. *Journal of Personality and Social Psychology, 72,* 408–419.

Huesmann, L. R., Guerra, N. G., Miller, L., & Zelli, A. (1992). The role of social norms in the development of aggression. In H. Zumckly & A. Fraczek (Eds.), *Socialization and Aggression.* New York: Springer-Verlag.

Kagan, J. (1988). Temperamental contributions to social behavior. *American Psychologist, 44,* 668–674.

Kagan, J. (1992). *Early Temperament and Environmental Interactions.* Presentation at American Psychological Association Meetings, Washington, DC.

Kagan, J. & Moss, H. A. (1984). *Birth to Maturity: A Study in Psychological Development.* New York: Wiley.

Kupersmidt, J. B., Griesler, P. G., DeRosier, M. E., Patterson, C. J., & Davis, P. W. (1995). Childhood aggression and peer relations in the context of family and neighborhood factors. *Child Development, 66,* 360–375.

Lagerspetz, K. M. J. & Björkqvist, K. (1994). Indirect aggression in boys and girls. In L. R. Huesmann (Ed.), *Aggressive Behavior: Current Perspectives* (pp. 131–150). New York: Plenum.

Lefkowitz, M. M., Eron, L. D., Walder, L. O., & Huesmann, L. R. (1977). *Growing Up to Be Violent: A Longitudinal Study of the Development of Aggression.* New York: Pergamon.

Luthar, S. S. & Zigler, E. (1991). Vulnerability and competence: A review of research on resilience in childhood. *American Journal of Orthopsychiatry, 61,* 6–22.

Lytton, H. (1990). Child and parent in boys' conduct disorder: A reinterpretation. *Developmental Psychology, 26,* 683–697.

Maccoby, E. (1992). The role of parents in the socialization of children: An historical overview. *Developmental Psychology, 28,* 1006–1017.

MacEwen, K. E. (1994). Refining the intergenerational transmission hypothesis. *Journal of Interpersonal Violence, 9,* 350–365.

Masten, A. S., Coatsworth, J. D., Neeman, J., Gest, S. D., Tellegan, A., & Garmezy, N. (1995). The structure and coherence of competence from childhood through adolescence. *Child Development, 66,* 1635–1659.

McLoyd, V. C. (1990). The impact of economic hardship on black families and children: Psychological distress, parenting and socioemotional development. *Child Development, 61,* 311–346.

McNally, S., Eisenberg, N., & Harris, J. P. (1991). Consistency and change in maternal child-rearing practices: A longitudinal study. *Child Development, 62,* 190–198.

Mednick, S. A., Gabrielli, W. F., & Hutchings, B. (1984). Genetic influences in criminal convictions: Evidence from an adoption cohort. *Science, 224,* 891–894.

Miller, L. S. (1990). *Relations among Cognitions and Behaviors of Aggressive Children and Their Mothers.* Unpublished doctoral dissertation. University of Illinois at Chicago.

Miller, N. E. (1941). The frustration-aggression hypothesis. *Psychological Review, 48,* 337–342.

Mills, R. S. & Rubin, K. H. (1990). Parental beliefs about problematic social behavior in early childhood. *Child Development, 61,* 138–151.

Moise, J. F. & Huesmann, L. R. (1996). Television violence viewing and aggression in females.

Annals New York Academy of Sciences, 194, 380–383.

Muller, R. T., Hunter, J. E., & Stollak, G. (1995). The intergenerational transmission of corporal punishment. *Child Abuse and Neglect, 19,* 1323–1335.

Olweus, D. (1979). The stability of aggressive reaction patterns in males: A review. *Psychological Bulletin, 85,* 852–875.

Osborne, S. G. & West, D. G. (1979). Conviction records of fathers and sons compared. *British Journal of Criminology, 19,* 120–133.

Parke, R. D. & Slaby, R. G. (1983). The development of aggression. In P. Mussen (Ed.), *Handbook of Child Psychology* (pp. 547–642). New York: Wiley.

Pastore, N. (1952). Role of arbitrariness in the frustration-aggression hypothesis. *Journal of Abnormal and Social Psychology, 47,* 728–731.

Patterson, G. R. (1986). Performance models for antisocial boys. *American Psychologist, 41,* 432–444.

Patterson, G. R., Dishion, T. J., & Chamberlain, P. (1993). Outcomes and methodological issues relating to treatment of antisocial children. In T. R. Giles (Ed.), *Handbook of Effective Psychotherapy* (pp. 43–88). New York: Plenum.

Patterson, G. R., Reid, J. B., & Dishion, T. J. (1992). *Antisocial Boys: A Social Interactional Approach* (Vol. 4). Eugene, OR: Castalia.

Raine, A., Brennan, P., & Mednick, S. (1994). Birth complications combined with early maternal rejection at age 1-year predispose to violent crime at age 18-years. *Archives of General Psychiatry, 51,* 984–988.

Rubin, K. H., Stewart, S. L., & Chen, X. (1995). Parents of aggressive and withdrawn children. In M. H. Bornstein (Ed.), *Handbook of Parenting* (Vol. 1, pp. 255–284). Hillsdale, NJ: Erlbaum.

Rutter, M. (1990). Psychosocial resilience and protective mechanisms. In J. Rolf, A. S. Masten, D. Cicchetti, K. H. Nuechterlein, & S. Weintraub (Eds.), *Risk and Protective Factors in the Development of Psychopathology* (pp. 181–214). New York: Cambridge University Press.

Sanson, A. V. & Rothbart, M. K. (1995). Child temperment and parenting. In M. H. Bornstein (Ed.), *Handbook of Parenting: Vol. 14, Applied and Practical Parenting.* Mahwah, NJ: Erlbaum.

Schneider, W. & Shiffrin, R. M. (1977). Controlled and automatic human information processing: I. Detection, search, and attention. *Psychological Review, 84,* 1–66.

Werner, E. E. & Smith, R. S. (1992). *Overcoming the Odds: High-Risk Children from Birth to Adulthood*. Ithaca, NY: Cornell University Press.

Widom, C. S. (1989). Does violence beget violence? A critical examination of the literature. *Psychological Bulletin, 106,* 3–28.

Wilson, B. J. & Gottman, J. M. (1995). Marital interaction and parenting. In M. Bornstein (Ed.), *Handbook of Parenting, Vol. 1. Applied and Practical Parenting* (pp. 33–56). Hillsdale, NJ: Erlbaum.

Winter, L. & Uleman, J. S. (1984). When are social judgements made? Evidence for the spontaneousness of trait inference. *Journal of Personality and Social Psychology, 47,* 237–252.

Zelli, A., Huesmann, L. R., & Cervone, D. P. (1995). Social inferences and individual differences in aggression: Evidence for spontaneous judgements of hostility. *Aggressive Behavior, 21,* 405–418.

4 Neuropsychological Factors in Violence and Aggression

CHARLES J. GOLDEN
Nova Southeastern University

ANGELA PETERSON-ROHNE
Nova Southeastern University

MICHELE L. JACKSON
Nova Southeastern University

SAMUEL T. GONTKOVSKY
Nova Southeastern University

We have chosen to view aggression in humans as a result of free will or under the control of the environment. However, it has become increasingly clear that if we truly wish to understand aggressive behavior, we must understand how it arises from neural structures and, more importantly, how dysfunction of those structures can lead to aggression. While there is no evidence to suggest that aggression is solely the result of neurobiology, its role is likely much larger than is generally acknowledged. Studies have increasingly recognized the importance of these factors, especially in individuals with histories of recurrent aggressive episodes.

Neuropsychology is the study of how brain processes influence and change behavior. Neuropsychological studies use a wide variety of measures to evaluate cognitive and personality changes that accompany injuries or changes in the brain. Neuropsychologists evaluate basic functions, such as motor and sensory skills, as well as more developed skills, such as intelligence, reading, writing, memory, speech, psychosis, depression, insight, awareness, flexibility, and problem-solving abilities.

The social implications of increasing violence necessitate a thorough understanding of the neuropsychological indicators that may lead to new ways to control or predict aggressive behavior. Neuropsychological factors appear to predispose certain people toward violence. This predisposition interacts with the client's environmental and social milieu. A violence-prone person raised in a hostile atmosphere will be much more likely to engage in violence. A violence-prone individual raised in a setting that appropriately acts to control violent acts may show less violent behavior.

In some cases, where the neuropsychological tendency toward violence and acting out is extremely high, the environment may play a negligible role. In cases where there is no unusual tendency toward violence, the environment may play the only role in determining the occurrence of violent and aggressive behavior.

Neuropsychological Theories of Aggression

In order to fully understand how neuropsychological factors may predispose people toward violence and aggression, we need to identify those mechanisms which influence such behavior. There are multiple neuropsychological mechanisms involved in this process. Jones (1992) has identified four ways in which brain function can lead to aggression: (1) increased arousal interfering with the ability to think; (2) decreased ability to inhibit impulses; (3) impairment of attention, concentration, memory, and higher mental processes; and (4) misinterpretation of external stimuli and events.

These mechanisms point to impairment of specific areas of the brain. Most approaches emphasize one or more of the following areas: (1) damage to the very front of the brain, which is called the prefrontal cortex; (2) damage to the temporal areas of the brain (located around the sides of the brain), which include the emotional centers called the limbic structures; and (3) more extensive impairment to the brain arising from generalized damage to the brain as a whole, resulting in dementia or delirium. Although the problems in any individual may involve complex relationships between these areas, we will treat them as independent disorders for this chapter.

Frontal Lobe Functions

Luria (1980) characterized the frontal lobes as the seat of higher abstraction, judgment, planning, sustained motivation, and self-regulation. The frontal lobes are the last areas of the brain to fully develop. Substantial changes take place in these areas during adolescence and into one's early twenties (Golden, Zillmer, & Spiers, 1992). While intellectual and cognitive skills are relatively well established by age 12 years, these frontal lobe skills are responsible for the changes that enable individuals to move from being children to being responsible adults.

The general functions of the frontal lobes include: (1) deciding what is worth attending to and what is worth doing; (2) providing continuity and consistency of behavior across time, central to planning and predictability of behavioral responses; (3) controlling emotional and interpersonal behavior so that drives are satisfied within the constraints of reality; and (4) monitoring, evaluating, and adjusting behavior (Hart & Jacobs, 1993).

It should be emphasized that prefrontal development, like the development of most higher levels of the cortex, is not dependent on neurological development alone. While biology provides the neural foundation for developing the skills mediated by the prefrontal areas, learning and experience must also take place so that the proper final structures are developed. Thus, unlike most organs of the body, development is dependent not only on the physical environment and DNA, but also on psychological and cognitive influences.

In an overview of neuroanatomy and neuropathology, Stuss and Benson (1984) described six specific manifestations of prefrontal damage. The first is an inability to use knowledge to regulate behavior. This means that although we may be aware that a behavior is wrong or inappropriate, we are unable to stop ourselves from doing the behavior. In such cases, what one thinks and says may be at odds with what one does. The prefrontal areas are important for turning what we want to do into our actual behavior, especially when what we want to do is at odds with our impulses (e.g., when we are angry at someone).

The second symptom is an impaired ability to handle sequential behavior. Specifically, people with prefrontal injuries are unable to follow a series of instructions. Thus, if they are taught a series of steps for anger management or what to do when threatened by someone else, they can follow the first or second step, but not the remainder of the sequence of behaviors. As a result, their ability to use socially approved methods to handle anger, challenge, or distress can be substantially damaged.

The third symptom is a tendency toward inflexibility. Inflexibility interferes with the client's ability to change their mind and to approach problems in different ways. This can influence aggression in two ways. In the first, the client uses problem-solving methods that are ineffective. This leads to increased frustration and emotional behavior. When someone tries to help, the client is unable to learn and becomes more hostile and aggressive. The second mechanism occurs when the client develops negative or paranoid ideas. These ideas usually involve the belief that someone is against or out to hurt him or her. Even when the client is shown that this isn't true, however, the client is unable to give up his or her belief. They continue to interpret anything the person does as supporting this belief. As anger escalates in response to this belief, violence becomes more likely.

Prefrontal injuries can also cause the opposite problem: the inability to maintain a mental set. Thus, the person may be erratic in mood and behavior. These frequent changes in mood or behavior can irritate others, leading to confrontations that may escalate into violence.

Individuals with prefrontal injuries may also be impaired in their ability to monitor their own behavior. Monitoring skills are important because they allow us to see whether our behavior is happening as we intend it to happen, as well as allow us to evaluate the impact of our behavior on others. In such cases, playful aggression may turn into violence as the person fails to see how his or her behavior is escalating.

In other cases, unintended insults and other irritating behaviors go unnoticed by the client, but set off confrontational behavior in others. The prefrontal client is unable to deal effectively with the confrontational behavior, leading again to possible aggressive behavior which the client sees as being solely instigated by the other person or persons involved. Individuals without monitoring skills are generally seen as having poor awareness and poor insight.

A final defect seen in prefrontal clients is apathy. These clients, however, are very unlikely to be aggressive or violent. They generally ignore even provocative situations, and, in extreme cases, may be content to sit in one place for hours at a time. The clients generally fail to recognize that there is any problem with these symptoms.

These cognitive deficits may occur in an individual with normal intellectual abilities (Mattson & Levin, 1990). Thus, the person may superficially appear to be normal. The most typical form of expression of violent behavior arises from an intermittent period of irritability that escalates into an emotional response, the magnitude of which is quite disproportionate to the eliciting event (Wood, 1987). Such behaviors generally have a clear cause, although the cause does not justify the severity of the response.

Afterward, while clients may express sorrow for their behavior, they generally have little insight and see others as provoking the aggressive act. In many cases, they will be unaware of the severity or the impact of their response. Such individuals are generally highly egocentric and unable to appreciate damage or pain to anyone but themselves. They are unable to show a long-term understanding of the impact of their behavior or its implications for future behavior. Consequently, behaviors are likely to be repeated.

However, frontal lobe impairment does not always lead to violence or aggression. Indeed, the literature makes it quite clear that frontal lobe clients vary considerably from one another (Hart & Jacobs, 1993). The expression of a frontal lobe disorder appears to be substantially affected by the timing of the injury, the severity of the injury, the cause of the injury, and the nature of the person's premorbid personality.

In the case of many individuals, premorbid tendencies toward aggression or irritability become expanded as frontal lobe controls are lost. In general, individuals who are older when injured and have well developed internal control systems show less of an impact than those with poorly developed internal controls. Not surprisingly, younger people, who have had no chance to develop controls, and older individuals, who have weak controls, are the most likely to show these symptoms.

Because prefrontal patients may be intellectually intact, they can be well aware that violence is inappropriate behavior. However, they are unable to use such abstract ideas in modulating or changing their own actions. When made aware that they have violated commonly accepted rules, their tendency is to place blame on others, due to their inability to see their own responsibility.

Temporal Lobe Dysfunction

Temporal lobe impairment is often demonstrated by episodes of unprovoked or exaggerated anger, memory and intellectual impairment, auditory or visual hallucinations, delusions, and receptive language impairment. Episodic dyscontrol is most commonly associated with damage to the deeper portions of the temporal lobes, which contain limbic system structures important for regulating emotion and behavior (Miller, 1990).

Episodic dyscontrol was first described by Kaplan in 1899, when he demonstrated that it sometimes follows head injury. Meninger and Mayman (1956), who originated the label of episodic dyscontrol, noted that individuals who had a history of illness or injury involving the central nervous system were often subject to recurrent acts of rage in response to minor provocation.

Episodic dyscontrol, however, is not a specific disorder, and can be found in a variety of diagnostic categories, including psychoses, neuroses, borderline personality disorders, conduct disorders, psychopathy, organic brain syndromes, epilepsy, mental retardation, metabolic diseases, and in developmental syndromes including attention deficit hyperactivity disorder (ADHD) and specific learning disorders (Elliott, 1992). In each of these cases, the etiology can be emotional or due to neurologic impairment.

The clinical presentation of episodic dyscontrol varies in severity and form. In more severe cases, the aggressive behavior can appear as sudden, unprovoked outbursts that are primitive and poorly organized in nature and directed at the nearest available object or person. Outbursts in less severe cases, however, may appear less out of control, more organized, and more clearly directed against the source of the irritation.

In general, the aggression following temporal lobe damage involves a loss of behavioral control, is unpatterned, is not confined to particular situations, times, and individuals, and occurs with minimal provocation and no premeditation (Miller, 1990). It does not have the clear antecedents or goals that frontal lobe aggression appears to demonstrate. In many cases, frontal lobe or temporal lobe dysfunction are mistaken for one another because of a failure to note these important differences.

Episodic dyscontrol has been associated with some forms of epilepsy, a disorder characterized by sudden surges of disorganized electrical impulses in the brain. This will not usually be accompanied by gross motor problems or sudden absences, which the general public usually associates with seizures. Epilepsy is the most common chronic neuropsychological disease affecting the general population. The disorder can be associated with a clear etiology (e.g., a tumor or head trauma) or may have no discernible cause (idiopathic epilepsy.) The ictal event of a seizure is the actual seizure itself. There are additional nonictal periods representing the time before the seizure (preictal), after the seizure (postictal), and between seizures (interictal).

Episodic violence associated with epilepsy can appear during any one or more of these phases. The preictal phase is a period of minutes, hours, or even days prior to the onset of a seizure. Aggression seems to be a relatively rare occurrence during this stage. More common are nonspecific psychological changes, such as irritability, anxiety, depression, or changes in behavior (Fenwick, 1989).

Second, although extremely rare, are ictal furies (Elliott, 1987; 1988; 1992). Aggression during the ictal phase is characterized by acts that may be highly coordinated, but that occur in a confused mental state and are inappropriate to the situation (Fenwick, 1989). According to Jones (1992), the majority of ictal violence is resistive in nature rather than goal directed or purposeful. Such violent behavior may be the first clinical manifestation of the seizure, or it may develop as the seizure progresses.

Aggression may occur as acts that reflect *postictal automatisms* and those that are part of a postictal confusional state (Fenwick, 1989). Epileptic automatisms are regarded as a subgroup of complex partial seizures. They are often preceded by hearing things that are not there. They are generally brief and most are nonviolent (Hindler, 1989).

Violent acts occurring during a postictal confusional state are generally the result of the patient being crowded and/or physically restrained during or following a seizure (Perrine & Congett, 1994). While regaining consciousness, a patient may make clumsy movements, appear disoriented, and be very irritable (as some people are when woken from a deep sleep). If interfered with, he or she may become resentful and, while still confused, strike out (Fenwick, 1989).

Finally, a proposed link between epilepsy and violence has been hypothesized as resulting from permanent changes in personality functioning produced by seizure activity itself. This, however, has not been supported by the research to date, which indicates that such individuals are no more likely to be violent than other groups (Elliott, 1992; Jones, 1992; Mendez, Doss, & Taylor, 1993).

Jones (1992) discusses another postulated path of epileptic violence through subictal foci or by electrical irritation from foci in deep subcortical structures. By electrical dysfunction, epilepsy produces violent or aggressive behavior of a partial complex type, but without producing the more frequently observed stereotyped behaviors identified with seizure activity. Individuals in this category are typically amnestic for the event.

While there exists a general consensus that the parts of the brain that compose the limbic system (in the deep areas of the temporal lobe) are involved in intense emotional states, debate continues regarding whether seizures predominantly involving limbic structures can be associated with directed aggression. The belief that patients with epilepsy are prone to directed violent acts during seizures has been perpetuated by the myths and the stigma surrounding the condition, as well as by the attempt of attorneys to use epilepsy as a defense in criminal cases (Perrine & Congett, 1994). However, research indicates that individuals rarely exhibit organized, directed violence due to ictal phenomena (Kaplan, Sadock, & Grebb, 1994; Lewis & Pincus, 1989; Perrine & Congett, 1994). Violence exhibited by such individuals is generally random and unconnected to specific events. However, it must be noted that seizures themselves can be set off by physical and/or psychological stress, so that the seizures are more likely in threatening and stressful situations.

Delirium and Dementia

Delirium represents a generalized state of brain impairment that arises suddenly and most often for limited periods of time. Numerous organic causes for delirium exist, including the ingestion of substances, such as PCP, LSD, cocaine, heroin, alcohol, and similar substances, the use of legal medications in improper doses or as the result of improper prescriptions, meningitis, encephalitis, head trauma, hypoxia, diseases of major organ systems, metabolic imbalances, and poison (Jones, 1992).

Delirium results in a confusional state that impairs the individual's judgment and perception of reality. There may be frank hallucinations and delusions, or in less-severe versions, misperceptions and misinterpretations. The individual generally shows many symptoms of a frontal lobe disorder as well: disinhibition, inability to plan or anticipate consequences, irritability, inability to integrate information, and a heightened state of emotional arousal (Jones, 1992). Delirium does not necessarily affect the person's ability to move and strike out (although coordination may be affected) or to speak or to execute plans (although these plans may not achieve their goals because of poor anticipation of consequences).

Delirious individuals may engage in aggression for a wide variety of reasons. They may believe that they are defending themselves from external threats; they may react to heightened internal emotions without any inhibitory abilities; or they may overreact to real events because of heightened irritability. Disinhibition may also allow them to perform acts that they want to perform, but would not as long as frontal inhibitory mechanisms are functional. Unlike frontal lobe injuries, delirious individuals are generally easy to identify because of a wide range of physical and psychological symptoms that are more pronounced than focal prefrontal injuries. In addition, the violence is limited to the acute times they are affected by the cause.

However, individuals with existing prefrontal problems may show symptoms of delirium more quickly than normal individuals. They appear to be much more sensitive to the effects of drugs (illegal or legal) and various medical disorders. It appears that the preexisting injuries leave them with little reserve to cope with the normal effects of a substance or condition. Thus, they are more likely to overreact to a normal illness or prescribed medication (such as some cough syrups), causing a variety of inappropriate behavior ranging from irritability to violence.

Dementia represents a loss of previous neuropsychological skills that is chronic and generally permanent. Many causes of dementia result in symptoms that develop slowly over time, although rapid onset of symptoms is possible as well. The most commonly recognized form of dementia is Alzheimer's Disease. Although there are widespread individual differences, neuropsychological problems commonly associated with Alzheimer's dementia include memory problems, visual spatial disorders, complex language, planning, inhibition, confusion, disorientation, delusions, and hallucinations (Kolb & Whishaw, 1990). Other dementing processes have similar symptoms, although the pattern and extent of deficits may vary widely with the specific cause.

Aggression in dementia arises out of several mechanisms, similar to what is seen in delirium. First, individuals may misperceive their environment and believe they are protecting themselves. Memory disorders may make people believe others are stealing from them, or cause disorientation and confusion about where they are. This can result in *flashbacks,* where individuals conclude they are in a place they were in earlier in life. If this is a negative or dangerous situation, then aggression may occur against caretakers.

Patients may react against doctors or nurses performing medical procedures, interpreting them as attacks. Other aggression may occur only when caretakers attempt to stop them from leaving or carrying out behaviors the patients believe to be important. Some aggression may be the result of delusions, misperceptions, or hallucinations.

Many clients with dementia show symptoms that vary during the day. They generally will do better when well rested, showing a tendency to deteriorate as the day progresses. Symptoms may also increase as the result of medical illness or medication. In a descriptive survey of 14 elderly patients who attempted or committed homicide, Ticehurst, Ryan, and Hughes (1992) found that the patients showed a high level of neuropsychiatric disturbance, with dementia diagnosed in over half of the cases.

Brain Injury in Specific Aggressive Populations

A major focus in the field has been exploring the presence of neuropsychological deficits in specific populations. This section will include reviews of the literature on marital violence, juvenile delinquency, adult criminal behavior, sex offenders, and antisocial behavior, which represent the major areas within this literature.

Marital Violence

In an initial study investigating the prevalence of head injury in maritally violent men, Rosenbaum and Hoge (1989) found that 19 of 31 male batterers had a history of severe head injury. Results indicated that the rate of head injury in their sample, 61.3 percent, far exceeded that found in the population at large, estimated at 5.9 percent. Rosenbaum, Hoge, Adelman, Warnken, Fletcher, and Kane (1994) found a history of head injury in 53 percent of the batterers, compared with 25 percent of a group of nonviolent, maritally discordant men, and 16 percent of a group of nonviolent, satisfactorily married men. Based on examination of the temporal order of the head injury and violence, the authors found that in 93.1 percent of the head-injured batterers, the head injury preceded the first instance of marital aggression.

Warnken, Rosenbaum, Fletcher, Hoge, and Adelman (1994) conducted a historical review of 982 male patients who had sustained either an orthopedic or head injury between 1985 and 1990. They found increased aggression and hostility in marital relationships after the head trauma compared to orthopedic injury. The female partners of the head-injured men reported significantly higher increases in verbally abusive behavior and dependency in their male partners following the injury, as well as significant decreases in communication skills and positive feelings about themselves when compared to the reports of partners of the orthopedically injured men. Changes in temperament and mood were also significant between groups, with the head-injured men and their partners reporting more depression and anger than the orthopedically injured men and partners.

Juvenile Delinquents

Much of the literature examining neuropsychological correlates of violence and aggression have focused on juvenile males who exhibit violent behaviors. Individuals who sustain frontal lobe damage early, before developing adequate patterns of self control, are thought to be more likely to show aggressive patterns. These individuals are of concern because we would predict that individuals who are violent as a result of chronic brain injury would be more likely to continue to be violent as they grow up, and more susceptible to the effects of street drugs and alcohol, further adding to the likelihood of criminal behavior. Research has shown that juvenile delinquents with violent propensities are more likely to continue to offend as adults when compared to conduct-disordered adolescents who do not manifest violent, impulsive behavior (Detre, Kupfer, & Taub, 1975).

Researchers have looked at many possible causes for juvenile delinquency. While sociological theories contend that the violent behavior is an adaptive, learned response to adverse environmental situations, other theories suggest a neurobiological cause arising from genetic abnormalities or acquired medical problems.

Lewis and colleagues (Lewis & Shanok, 1979; Lewis, Pincus, & Feldman, 1986; Lewis, Pincus, Bard, Richardson, Prichep, Feldman, & Yeager, 1988) found that trauma to the central nervous system (CNS) was commonly seen in violent juveniles and adults. These CNS trauma included prenatal distress, interpersonal violence, and serious accidents involving head injury.

Spellacy (1977) compared violent and nonviolent delinquent adolescent males on a comprehensive set of neuropsychological tests. Spellacy found the violent group to be impaired on 12 of 31 variables. These results indicated that the violent group, characterized by poor impulse control and consistently aggressive behavior, had more group members who manifest neuropsychological impairment than the nonviolent group. Their impaired performance was readily apparent in cognitive, perceptual, and psychomotor abilities. Interestingly, none of the organically impaired violent delinquents had been diagnosed as brain injured prior to or during their institutionalization.

Adult Criminal Populations

The literature examining the connection between violent and aggressive behavior and neurological impairment in adult criminal offenders reaches similar conclusions to the studies using juvenile delinquent samples—violent offenders tend to have several neuropsychological indicators of brain damage, as well as decreased intellectual functioning.

Studies examining the relationship between aggression and intellectual functioning have found lower IQ scores (Syverson & Romney, 1985; Valliant, Asu, Cooper, & Mammola, 1984). The first major study to utilize a comprehensive neuropsychological battery in the assessment of violent behavior and the relationship to neuropsychological impairments was conducted by Bryant, Scott, Golden, and Tori (1984). Violent subjects were those who had committed assaultive crimes against persons. The control group of nonviolent inmates were convicted of property crimes.

The violent offenders were found to be significantly more impaired on all measures. When the profiles were classified for the presence or absence of brain injury, it was found that only 28 percent of the non-brain-damaged group had committed violent crimes, while 73 percent of the brain-damaged group had committed violent crimes. The violent group in this study demonstrated impaired performance on complex tasks that required integration of sensory information from the auditory, visual, and somesthetic processing systems. The violent group also lacked the ability to create, plan, organize, and execute goal-directed behavior. Sustained concentration and attention were also impaired in the violent offenders.

Langevin, Ben-Aron, Wortzman, Dickey, and Handy (1987) examined neuropsychological functioning for comparative discrimination of homicidal, violent, and nonviolent male offenders. On one neuropsychological test battery, they found that 33 percent of the murderers and 17 percent of the assaulters were significantly impaired according to Reitan's scoring criteria. None of the nonviolent sample was significantly impaired. On a second neuropsychological test battery, none of the nonviolent controls were impaired, but 21 percent of the murderers and 19 percent of the assaulters were classified as brain injured.

Sexual Assault

Evidence of brain dysfunction is frequently found in individuals who exhibit a variety of sexual aberrations (see Cummings, 1985). Of interest here are those criminal sexual behaviors which are recognized to be the result of aggressive rather than sexual feelings.

The temporal lobes of the brain, in particular, are considered important to the expression and possible development of sexual anomalies. Kluver-Bucy Syndrome, resulting from bilateral lesions of the anterior temporal lobes, produces bizarre hypersexuality and inappropriate sexual behavior. Oppenheimer (1971) suggests that this behavior occurs when inhibitory controls are removed, similar to the dyscontrol of psychomotor seizures.

Inappropriate sexual behavior is also evident in individuals suffering from central nervous system degeneration caused by disorders such as Alzheimer's disease and Huntington's chorea. One study of Huntington's patients found inappropriate sexual behaviors in 30 of 48 patients providing sexual histories (Dewhurst, Oliver, & McNight, 1970). Disinhibition can also be a major factor in such crimes.

The poor impulse control present in sexual offenders implicates impairment in the executive functions of the frontal lobes. Sexual assaulters often describe their own behavior as impulsive and unplanned, occurring during the commission of an unrelated criminal activity, such as robbery. Research suggests that this failure to control behavior may be related to limbic system dysfunction, specifically as a failure of the cortical structures to inhibit impulses (Eysenck, 1964; Mark & Ervin, 1970). This lack of sexual impulse control may be part of the syndrome of *episodic dyscontrol* which is also marked by hyperagressivity and pathological intoxication (Mark & Ervin, 1970).

Graber, Hartmann, Coffman, Huey, and Golden (1982) presented a series of six case histories of mentally disordered sex offenders. Three of the six subjects were found to be impaired on neuropsychological measures. These subjects tended to engage in more primitive sexual behavior and tended to lack impulse control regarding their sexual behavior. The brain damage noted was primarily localized in the temporal and frontal lobes. Decreased blood flow to the brain and decreased brain density was found in these three subjects.

Scott, Cole, McKay, Golden, and Liggett (1984) studied 36 men arrested for sexual assault. The sexual assaulters performed worse than the control group on nearly all neuropsychological measures utilized. When the sexual assaulters were separated into groups of rapists and pedophiles, the results indicated that 55 percent of the rapists and 36 percent of the pedophiles were brain damaged.

Antisocial Personality

The psychopathic or antisocial personality can be described as being impulsive, self-centered, and aggressively opportunistic. Such individuals seem to enjoy taking unnecessary chances, appear easily bored, cannot delay prospects for immediate gratification, and evidence a low tolerance for frustration (Miller, 1987). Compared with other male criminals, individuals with antisocial personality disorder commit disproportionate numbers of crimes that are more violent and aggressive than those of other criminals (Elliott, 1992).

Yeudall (1977) presents the results of a series of studies in which individuals with forensic disorders were assessed for neuropsychological impairment. His overall findings indicate that more than 91 percent of the criminal psychopaths studied at Alberta Hospital were characterized as having dysfunction of the anterior regions of the brain.

According to Miller (1987), more impulsive and violently aggressive psychopaths tend to be less intelligent, although a causal relationship between low IQ and aggressive behavior remains to be proved. Those factors that seem to be associated with the presence of both low intelligence and aggressiveness include unsocialized personality characteristics, poor cognitive control, poor impulse control, and less anxiety and sensitivity. Subjects classified as delinquent or psychopathic who also have histories of violent or aggressive criminal acts against persons test out as less intelligent and do worse on many neuropsychological measures than do nonviolent subjects drawn from equivalent populations. In addition, there seems to be an association between frontal-lobe-like neuropsychological and behavioral manifestations and the results of similar measures obtained with adult male psychopaths.

It is necessary to recognize that what is called an antisocial personality may represent two or more subgroups. From the perspective of brain dysfunction, the first group represents individuals with prefrontal dysfunction (with or without other brain damage) who are impulsive, childish, unable to support themselves through normal means, and drawn into criminal behavior by their own lack of control, as well as the inducements of others. When faced with stress, they overreact and get into frequent confrontations.

The second group are criminals with intact brains, who show good planning and organizational skills. Such individuals engage in aggression for gain and as a result of planning, rather than the more impulsive aggression of the first group. These individuals are amoral, not because of brain injury, but because of environment and upbringing. These individuals may recruit others from the first group to commit crimes and aggressive acts under their direction. It is likely that this group is underrepresented in prisons compared to the first group.

Complicating Conditions

The issue of aggression in brain-injured clients is complicated by conditions that may raise the likelihood of aggression (as well as other undesirable behaviors) in this population. One of the most important areas is the interaction between brain injury, substance abuse, and aggression (Bond, 1984; Langevin et al., 1987; Rosenbaum & Hoge, 1989; Ticehurst et al., 1992). Alcohol, a depressant, is the most commonly used and abused drug (Elliott, 1992). The main effect of alcohol intoxication is the depression of inhibitors, which predisposes even normal individuals toward aggressive behavior. Some authors note that alcohol abuse and brain damage may have a synergistic effect on the disinhibition of behavior, together predisposing, to a greater extent, individuals with developmental or acquired brain defects toward aggression (Miller, 1990; Elliott, 1992). However, separating the impact of the substance abuse from the brain injury itself is difficult.

Alcohol abuse may trigger explosive rage characterized by episodic dyscontrol (Elliott, 1992); however, the literature has found discrepant results regarding the incidence of alcohol abuse and consumption at the time of violent crime. Ticehurst and colleagues (1992) found that almost half of their elderly subjects who had attempted or committed homicide had been previous abusers of alcohol, although none reported being intoxicated at the time of the offense. Langevin and colleagues (1987) found that killers and assaulters were more often considered alcoholic, and were found to abuse alcohol with a higher frequency than nonviolent criminals. These effects may occur in individuals without brain damage, but appear more severe when the client has a preexisting brain injury.

Similar but less dramatic effects may be seen with any condition that increases the clients fatigue or ability to concentrate. These conditions may include routine illnesses like the flu or colds, but can also include more severe medical disorders such as kidney or liver failure. Excessive fatigue due to lack of sleep or high activity levels may also increase the likelihood of aggressive responses, as can any kind of significant stressor (which in turn may be real or imagined). Clients may appear to be normal when healthy and unstressed, only to show violent behavior when stressed or fatigued.

Summary

This review points to a strong role for neuropsychological factors in aggression and violence. As new techniques develop in neuropsychology and related areas, such as neuroradiology (e.g., Raine, Buchsbaum, & LaCasse, 1997), it is becoming increasingly evident that violent individuals—especially those who perpetuate the worst crimes and those who are repeat offenders—show substantial neuropsychological and neurological problems that must be understood and addressed if we are to deal effectively with violence in our society. An understanding of the neurobiological factors can lead to an analysis of how social and environmental policies on guns, the role of stress in modern societies, changes in medical treatments, attitudes toward violence, and childrearing practices may interact to produce violence and aggression. While our overall knowledge must be considered rudimentary in these areas, we have made substantial strides in the past two decades and are likely to see equal growth in the near future.

REFERENCES

Bond, M. R. (1984). The psychiatry of closed head injury. In D. N. Brooks (Ed.), *Closed Head Injury: Psychological, Social, and Family Consequences.* New York: Oxford University Press.

Bryant, E., Scott, M., Golden, C., & Tori, C. D. (1984). Neuropsychological deficits, learning disability, and violent behavior. *Journal of Consulting and Clinical Psychology, 52,* 323–324.

Cummings, J. L. (1985). *Clinical Neuropsychiatry.* New York: Grune & Stratton.

Detre, T., Kupfer, D. J., & Taub, S. (1975). The nosology of violence. In W. S. Fields & W. H. Sweet (Eds.), *Neural Bases of Violence and Aggression.* St. Louis: Warren Green.

Dewhurst, A., Oliver, J. E., & McNight, A. L. (1970). Sociopsychiatric consequences of Huntington's Disease. *British Journal of Psychiatry, 116,* 255–258.

Elliott, F. A. (1987). Neuroanatomy and neurology of aggression. *Psychiatric Annals, 17,* 385–388.

Elliott, F. (1988). Neurological Factors. In V. B. Van Hasselt, R. L. Morrison, A. S. Bellack, & M. Hersen (Eds.), *Handbook of Family Violence* (pp. 359–382). New York: Plenum.

Elliott, F. A. (1992). Violence: The neurologic contribution: An overview. *Archives of Neurology, 49,* 595–603.

Eysenck, H. (1964). *Crime and Personality.* Boston: Houghton Mifflin.

Fenwick, P. (1989). The nature and management of aggression in epilepsy. *Neuropsychiatric Practice and Opinion, 1,* 418–425.

Golden, C. J., Zillmer, E., & Spiers, M. (1992). *Neuropsychological Assessment and Rehabilitation.* Springfield, Illinois: Charles C. Thomas.

Graber, B., Hartmann, K., Coffman, J. A., Huey, C. J., & Golden, C. J. (1982). Brain damage among mentally disordered sex offenders. *Journal of Forensic Sciences, 27,* 125–134.

Hart, T. & Jacobs, H. (1993). Rehabilitation and management of behavioral disturbances following frontal lobe injury. *Journal of Head Trauma and Rehabilitation, 8,* 1–12.

Hindler, C. G. (1989). Epilepsy and violence. *British Journal of Psychiatry, 155,* 246–249.

Jones, H. (1992). Neuropsychology of violence. *Forensic Reports, 5,* 221–233.

Kaplan, H. I., Sadock, B. J., & Grebb, J. A. (1994). *Synopsis of Psychiatry* (7th ed.). Baltimore: Williams and Wilkins.

Kaplan, J. (1899). Kopftrauma und Psychosen. *Allgemeiner Zeitschrift Fur Psychiatrie, 56,* 292–297.

Kolb, B. & Whishaw, I. (1990). *Human Neuropsychology* (3rd ed.). New York: Freeman.

Langevin, R., Ben-Aron, M., Wortzman, G., Dickey, R., & Handy, L. (1987). Brain damage, diagnosis, and substance abuse among violent offenders. *Behavioral Sciences and the Law, 5,* 77–94.

Lewis, D. O. & Pincus, J. H. (1989). Epilepsy and violence: Evidence for a neuropsychotic-aggressive syndrome. *Journal of Neuropsychiatry, 1,* 413–418.

Lewis, D. O., Pincus, J. H., Bard, B., Richardson, E., Prichep, L., Feldman, M., & Yeager, C. (1988). Neuropsychiatric, psychoeducational and family characteristics of 14 juveniles condemned to death in the United States. *American Journal of Psychiatry, 145*, 584–589.

Lewis, D. O., Pincus, J. H., & Feldman, M. (1986). Psychiatric, neurological and psychoeducational characteristics of 15 death row inmates in the United States. *American Journal of Psychiatry, 143*, 838–845.

Lewis, D. O. & Shanok, S. (1979). Perinatal difficulties, head, and face trauma and child abuse in the medical histories of seriously delinquent children. *American Journal of Psychiatry, 136*, 419–423.

Luria, A. R. (1980). *Higher Cortical Functions in Man* (2nd ed.). New York: Basic Books.

Mark, V. H. & Ervin, F. R. (1970). *Violence and the Brain*. New York: Harper & Row.

Mattson, A. & Levin, H. (1990). Frontal lobe dysfunction following closed head injury: A review of the literature. *The Journal of Nervous and Mental Disease, 178*, 282–291.

Mendez, M. F., Doss, R. C., & Taylor, J. L. (1993). Interictal violence in epilepsy: Relationship to behavior and seizure variables. *The Journal of Nervous and Mental Disease, 181*, 566–569.

Meninger, K. & Mayman, M. (1956). Episodic dyscontrol: A third order of stress adaptation. *Bulletin of the Meninger Clinic, 20*, 153–160.

Miller, L. (1987). Neuropsychology of the aggressive psychopath: An integrative review. *Aggressive Behavior, 13*, 119–140.

Miller, L. (1990). Major syndromes of aggressive behavior following head injury: An introduction to evaluation and treatment. *Cognitive Rehabilitation, 14*, 14–19.

Nestor, P. (1992). Neuropsychological and clinical correlates of murder and other forms of extreme violence in a forensic psychiatric population. *Journal of Nervous and Mental Disease, 180*, 418–423.

Oppenheimer, H. (1971). *Clinical Psychiatry: Issues and Challenges*. New York: Harper & Row.

Perrine, K. & Congett, S. (1994). Neurobehavioral problems in epilepsy. *Neurologic Clinics, 12* 129–152.

Raine, A., Buchsbaum, M., & LaCasse, L. (1997). Brain abnormalities in murdererd indicated by positron emission tomography. *Biological Psychiatry, 42*, 495–508.

Rosenbaum, A. & Hoge S. (1989). Head injury and marital aggression. *American Journal of Psychiatry, 146*, 1048–1051.

Rosenbaum, A., Hoge, S., Adelman, S., Warnken, W., Fletcher, K., & Kane, R. (1994). Head injury in partner-abusive men. *Neuroscience and Biobehavioral Reviews, 18*, 487–495.

Scott, M. L., Cole, J. K., McKay, S. E., Golden, C. J., & Liggett, K. R. (1984). Neuropsychological performance of sexual assaulters and pedophiles. *Journal of Forensic Sciences, 29*, 1114–1118.

Spellacy, F. (1977). Neuropsychological differences between violent and nonviolent adolescents. *Journal of Clinical Psychology, 33*, 966–969.

Stuss, D. & Benson, F. (1984). Neuropsychological studies of the frontal lobes. *Psychological Bulletin, 95*, 3–28.

Syverson, K. L. & Romney, D. M. (1985). A further attempt to differentiate violent from nonviolent offenders by means of a battery of psychological tests. *Canadian Journal of Behavioral Science, 17*, 87–92.

Ticehurst, S. B., Ryan, M. G., & Hughes, F. (1992) Homicidal behaviour in elderly patients admitted to a psychiatric hospital. *Dementia, 3*, 86–90.

Valliant, P. M., Asu, M. E., Cooper, D., & Mammola, D. (1984). Profile of dangerous and non-dangerous offenders referred for pretrial psychiatric assessment. *Psychological Reports, 54*, 411–418.

Warnken, W., Rosenbaum, A., Fletcher, K., Hoge, S., & Adelman, S. (1994). Head-injured males: A population at risk for relationship aggression? *Violence and Victims, 9*, 153–166.

Wood, R. L. (1987). *Brain Injury Rehabilitation: A Neurobehavioral Approach*. Rockville: Aspen.

Yeudall, L. T. (1977). Neuropsychological assessment of forensic disorders. *Canadian Mental Health, 25*, 7–18.

5 Child Abuse

JOHN R. LUTZKER
University of Judaism

Description of the Disorder

Child abuse was first recognized professionally in 1962 when Kempe, Silverman, Steele, Drogemueller, and Silver published their seminal paper in the *Journal of the American Medical Association*, "The battered child syndrome." It is a problem of huge proportion in the United States. In 1994, there were over 1 million substantiated incidents of child abuse and neglect in 48 United States (U.S. Department of Health and Human Services, 1994). This represented a 27 percent increase over 1990. This chapter will address physical child abuse. Simply defined, this involves adult intentional infliction of pain on a child in a severe enough manner to leave marks, bruises, or other trauma, and can often result in the death of the child.

After the Kempe and colleagues (1962) article, theories were proposed to account for why parents would intentionally inflict injury on a child. The early theories were psychodynamic in nature, largely exploring intrapersonal parental factors. Later came sociological theories examining the role of poverty, low education, and similar sociological variables. Recently, the problem has come to be seen as a developmental/ecological/transactional disorder (National Research Council, 1993). That is, there are social/ecological factors, such as parent and child variables, economic/employment variables, and sociological and psychological factors that appear to contribute to child abuse.

Epidemiology

That there were over one million incidents of child maltreatment in the United States in 1994 means that there were over two million reports concerning almost three million children. Twenty-six percent of those reports were for physical child abuse, 14 percent for sexual abuse, and 5 percent for emotional abuse. It is estimated that these figures underestimate the actual prevalence of child maltreatment. Indeed, these figures are thought to be underestimates by as much as one-third (Warner & Hansen, 1994).

The short- and long-term consequences to children of child maltreatment and abuse, in particular, are many. They include poor perceptual-motor deficits, poor academic performance, lower scores on intelligence and achievement tests, and negative social behaviors (Lutzker, Bigelow, Swenson, Doctor, & Kessler, 1999). The long-term effects appear to affect many adults in a number of ways, such as substance abuse, interpersonal problems, suicidal behavior, and emotional problems (Lutzker et al., in press).

Intergenerational abuse is difficult to assess because of the reliance on retrospective self-report. Thus, the estimates of its occurrence range from 7 percent to 70 percent (Malinosky-Rummell & Hansen, 1993). Children who were victims of child maltreatment display significantly more conduct disorders than comparison children (Ammerman, Cassisi, Hersen, & Van Hasselt, 1986).

Characteristics of the Offender

Perpetrators of child maltreatment have been characterized as having numerous disorders such as substance abuse, emotional lability, impulse control problems, antisocial personality, and difficulty with relationships (Lutzker et al., 1999). Although biological variables such as predisposition to violence have been examined, no clear evidence suggest that biological variables play a role in child maltreatment.

The research on perpetrator characteristics is largely correlational and remains tentative. Among the problems of accruing accurate information on perpetrators is that of ever being sure of who is the perpetrator or an given instance of child maltreatment. For example, it is not uncommon for a mother to "take the rap" for an abuse report that may have been perpetrated by a boyfriend. In any case, there are some reliable data to suggest some characteristics of a parent at risk for child maltreatment.

Low warmth and authoritarian parenting styles have been associated with child maltreatment and appear to be possible risk factors. A cycle of aversive parent-child interactions has been suggested by Lorber, Felton, and Reid (1984) as a potentiator for abuse. On the other hand, Dumas and Wahler (1985) have suggested that indiscriminate parenting is a risk factor. That is, their research has suggested that it might not necessarily be the temporally proximate interactions of parent and child (as seen by Lorber and colleagues, 1984) that triggers an incident of abuse. Rather, it might be a more temporally distant setting event, such as a boyfriend or spouse physically abusing the mother the night before she abuses the child.

Azar, Povilaitis, Lauretti, and Pouquette (1998) also suggest that faulty parental attributions and expectations may be responsible for child maltreatment. They have shown that some parents may attribute inborn tendencies to their child's aversive behavior and thus feel that severe punishment may be the only way to control the child. Similarly, some parents actually believe that the devil may be in a child and, thus, sever beatings are the only way to exorcise the devil. Knowledge deficits about normal child development may be a risk factor.

In addition to offender characteristics, it should be noted that there are some child characteristics that have been associated with child maltreatment. Research on child risk factors has examined prematurity, temperament, age, and gender. There are, in fact, some data to suggest that low birth weight is a risk factor for children. Further, there is some evidence that infants who are irritable are at risk (National Research Council, 1993). Additionally, boys, especially those with troublesome behavior, are at more risk for maltreatment (National Research Council, 1993).

Assessment

There are a host of direct and indirect assessment tools for child maltreatment. By direct assessment, it is meant that trained observers record actual parent and/or child behavior directly in the presence of the person or persons being observed. Indirect assessment involves "paper and pencil" self-report data or ratings scales from other observers of the parent or child.

Risk Assessment

Risk assessments are aimed at trying to identify parent behaviors or self-reports that suggest that the parent has the propensity to place the child at risk of maltreatment. Some risk assessments have been used without adequate verification of the psychometric properties (Lutzker, Bigelow, Swenson, Doctor, & Kessler, 1999). Others have received considerable validation.

One of the most frequently used, validated risk assessments is the Child Abuse Prevention Inventory, also known as the CAP-Inventory (Milner, 1986). The CAP-Inventory is a measure of potential risk for physical child abuse. It yields one abuse potential score and six additional scales: Rigidity, Unhappiness, Distress, Problems with Child and Self, Problems with Family, and Problems with Others. Further, the CAP-Inventory has three distortion indices: Faking Good, Faking Bad, and Random responding. These are derived from combinations of scores from three validity scales: Lie, Random Responding, and Inconsistency.

The CAP-Inventory has a readability for third grade. It also has a Spanish version that has been subject to some questionable predictive validity (Lutzker et al., in press). The CAP was originally designed as a tool that might aid child protective service workers.

The Childhood Levels of Living Scale (Hally, Polansky, & Polansky, 1980) is a measure of essential elements of child care and neglect. It is designed to be administered to parents whose children are between 4 and 7 years. It has nine factors, four that are descriptive of emotional/cognitive aspects of child care, and five that measure physical care.

Some researchers have used the MMPI-2 (Butcher, Dahlstrom, Graham, Tellegen, & Kaemer, 1989) with parents involved in maltreatment. There is no specific scale for risk of child maltreatment. However, when combined with more relevant assessment tools, the MMPI-2 might be useful in identifying psychopathology that may correlate with maltreatment.

The Home Simulation Assessment (MacMillan, Olson, & Hansen, 1991) can be used to assess parent behavior in simulated child behavior management situations. This is truly a simulation in that an adult actor supervised by the researcher plays the role of the child in a variety of scenarios aimed at predicting risk by the manner in which the parent responds to the simulations. This assessment device can be useful when it is not possible to directly assess parent-child interactions in the home.

An adaptation of the Home Simulation Assessment is the High Deviance Home Simulation Assessment. In this version, the actor escalates the amount of simulated child deviant behavior. This tool helps researchers or clinicians determine if they might derive benefit from stress reduction or anger management training related to the parent's child behavior management practices.

The Parent Behavior Checklist (Fox, 1994) is a coding system relevant to children ages 1 to 4 years. It measures three aspects of parent behavior: expectations, discipline, and nurturing.

There are also some measures of parent-infant interactions. A direct assessment was developed by Lutzker, Lutzker, Braunling-McMorrow, and Eddleman (1987) to assess the quantity and quality of parent-infant interactions. It examines smiling, affectionate words, guided play, assuming the physical level of the child, affectionate touch, and eye contact. These measures were validated by experts in parent-infant interactions.

The Dyadic Interaction Coding System (Eyberg & Robinson, 1981) asses positive and negative parent and child behaviors, such as parent commands, descriptive and reflective statements, questions, labeled praise, and critical comments. The child behaviors assessed are whine, cry, yell, compliance, noncompliance, and destructive behaviors. A very similar coding system is the Behavioral Coding System (Forehand & McMahon, 1981).

The Parenting Stress Index has been used in several studies evaluating stress among parents involved in child maltreatment (Lloyd & Abidin, 1985). It was designed to screen and assess the magnitude of family stress among three domains: parent characteristics, child characteristics, and other parent/child situations. There are long and short forms.

Parental anger can be assessed using the Novaco Anger Control Scale (Novaco, 1975). This is a self-report measure designed to evaluate anger and arousal control problems. The Parent Anger Inventory is a self-report measure aimed at evaluating anger and arousal control problems. Another anger measure is the Parental Anger Inventory (DeRoma & Hansen, 1994). Parents are asked to rate 50 child-related situations. Internal consistency and content validity have been demonstrated by these measures.

Parent expectations have been assessed by the Parent Opinion Questionnaire (Azar, Robinson, Hekimian, & Twentyman, 1984). This is a 80-item questionnaire that assesses parents' unrealistic or realistic expectations about child behaviors and development. It has shown that parents involved in child maltreatment have unrealistic expectations about their children's behavior compared to parents who are not involved in maltreatment.

A similar measure is the Family Beliefs Inventory (Roehling & Robin, 1986). It also measures unreasonable beliefs of parents; however, it is their beliefs toward adolescents.

Problem Solving

Problem Solving is another domain that is useful to assess when looking for risk factors in child maltreatment. The Parent Problem-Solving Instrument (Wasik & Bryant, 1989) presents to parents 10 scenarios from stories in assessing parent responses. Maltreating parents elaborate less on solutions, use fewer content categories in their solutions, and generate fewer solutions overall in their descriptions than comparison parents.

Hansen, Palotta, Tishelman, Conaway, and McMillan (1989) developed the Parental Problem Solving Measure. It evaluates problem-solving abilities in child and nonchild situations. Problematic situations are read to the parent, who is then asked to imagine being in the scenario and describe what they would do in that scenario.

Coping styles have been assessed using the Ways of Coping Checklist-Revised (Lazarus & Folkman, 1984). It has eight scales aimed at determining parents' abilities to cope with life's stressors. The Community Interaction Checklist was developed by Wahler, Leske, and Rogers (1979) to assess the frequency and quality of community interactions that a mother has, and to determine if she is what Wahler (1980) has called "insular." Many mothers reported for child maltreatment are, in fact, insular, thus making it difficult to provide services to them.

Child Measures

In addition to assessing parental behaviors that suggest a child's risk for being a maltreating parent, there are a number of tools that have been used to help determine if the child has characteristics that have been associated with children at risk for maltreatment.

The Child Behavior Checklist (Achenbach & Edelbrook, 1983) is a long valued standard in assessing a number of child characteristics. Similarly, the Eyberg Child Behavior Inventory (Eyberg & Ross, 1978) is useful for assessing children between ages 2 and 16 years.

Environmental Risk

Assessing the conditions of the home is another way of looking at risk to children. The Home Accident Prevention Inventory (HAPI) (Tertinger, Greene, & Lutzker, 1984) and the Home Accident Prevention Inventory-Revised (HAPI-R) (Mandel, Bigelow, & Lutzker, 1998) are direct assessment tools that involve observing and recording the number of hazards in homes that are accessible to children. The HAPI and HAPI-R are content validated, and are reliable tools for assessing home hazards—a problem that often causes parents to be referred for child maltreatment. It has been tested exclusively in homes of families reported for child maltreatment.

The HAPI and HAPI-R are very conservative measures of accessible hazards in homes. They represent direct observation methodology rather than ratings of home conditions. These tools examine fire and electrical hazards; suffocation by ingested items and mechanical objects; and accidents involving firearms, solid and liquid poisons, balconies, and water hazards (drowning).

The Checklist for Living Environments to Assess Neglect (CLEAN) is used to assess the presence of nonorganic or organic decaying matter in the home; clothes and linens in inappropriate places within the home; and other objects not belonging in the home (Watson-Perczel, Lutzker, Greene, & McGimpsey, 1988). In other words, it measures filth and clutter in homes. The CLEAN has also been content validated, has good reliability, and represents a direct assessment tool.

Intervention

The earliest behavioral strategies reported in treating families reported for child abuse appeared in the 1970s. Gilbert (1976) described simple behavior management strategies in working with parents involved in child abuse.

A more comprehensive parent training approach was reported by Wolfe and Sandler (1981). For parents reported for child abuse, they provided reading assignments; modeled behavior management skills; required the parents to role-play; and provided feedback based on direct observation of the parents.

Wolfe, Edwards, Manion, and Koverola (1988) reported considerable improvement in parents who received parent training and stress reduction procedures. Azar and colleagues (1984) used a combination of stress reduction, communication training, and cognitive restructuring to produce dramatic improvements over an insight-oriented treatment group and a control group of parents.

As a social ecological perspective took hold in the 1980s, Project 12-ways was created to try to address the multiple factors that appear responsible for child abuse (Lutzker, 1984). Thus, instead of providing only parent training or stress reduction, Project 12-Ways attempted to address many factors related to child abuse. In addition to teaching effective parenting skills (Dachman, Halasz, Bickett, & Lutzker, 1984) and stress reduction (Campbell, O'Brien, Bickett, & Lutzker, 1983), parents were provided with self-management skills (Lutzker, 1984), marital counseling (Campbell et al., 1983), job finding, money management, nutrition training (Sarber, Halasz, Messmer, Bickett, & Lutzker, 1983), home safety (Barone, Greene, & Lutzker, 1986), home cleanliness training (Watson-Perczel, Lutzker, Greene, & McGimpsey, 1988), infant stimulation training (Lutzker, Lutzker, Braunling McMorrow, & Eddleman, 1987), and infant health care skills (Delgado & Lutzker, 1988).

A systematic replication of Project 12-Ways, Project SafeCare (Lutzker, Bigelow, Doctor, Gershater, & Greene, 1998) has taught bonding skills (Bigelow & Lutzker, in 1998), home safety (Mandel et al., 1998), and health care skills (Cordon, Lutzker, Bigelow, & Doctor, in press). Project 12-Ways demonstrated the ecobehavioral approach (based on a social/ecological perspective) in rural southern Illinois. Project SafeCare demonstrated this ecobehavioral model in urban Los Angeles with a predominately Latina sample.

The ecobehavioral model focuses on direct assessment and the training of skills to parents in their homes and other in situ settings.

Fantuzzo, Delgaudio Weiss, and Coyle Coolahan (1998) have described a community-based partnership in providing social skills to children who have been abused in urban inner-city Philadelphia. They had the community help develop the assessments so that they were not offensive to families. This was done because families had previously reported that traditional assessments were, in fact, offensive because of their perceived focus on deficits rather than skills.

These researchers also used community members to recruit participants and involved them in the skills training programs. Children with exemplary social skills were used to help teach social skills to isolated children suffering from child abuse to help them achieve socially in preschool.

A wrap-around treatment approach very similar to the ecobehavioral model, which integrates the community, has been described by Striefel, Robinson, and Truhn (1998). In rural Utah, at-risk families have been provided with 10 services. These are: early childhood education, early intervention for at-risk children with developmental delays, nutritional services, child care, child health services, mental health services, substance abuse education, substance abuse treatment, parent education and training, and vocational training.

Youth violence, which often later leads to child abuse, has been addressed by Yung and Hammond (1998). Their program, Positive Adolescent Choices Training (PACT), teaches a number of violence-prevention strategies and communication skills to adolescent African Americans. Cognitive strategies are also employed. Youth who participate in the PACT program have higher observer ratings from videotaped role-plays; higher ratings by teachers and parents; and better self-ratings. Additionally, from school records, these youth display less physical aggression, verbal intimidations, and other misbehavior than youth who do not participate in the program. Further, they have fewer violence-related police and court offenses, as well as fewer criminal acts and status offenses.

Also attempting to prevent violence, Pittman, Wolfe, and Wekerle (1998) have taught Canadian adolescents communication skills through the Youth Relationships Project (YRP). Data from the YRP show that participants display less coercion and emotional abuse and display considerably more positive communication as compared to their own baseline measures.

Preventing child abuse is especially difficult with parents who have intellectual deficits. Feldman (1998) has used modeling, role-playing, and picture cues to teach such parents a variety of child care skills, such as feeding, washing, sleep safety, bottle cleaning, nutrition, crib safety, diapering, bathing, and treating diaper rash. Contingent on successful progress throughout training the parents are given coupons which are redeemed for tangible items. Similar strategies have been utilized by Tymchuk (1998).

Treatment adherence has been an especially difficult issue for researchers and service providers working in child abuse. Lundquist and Hansen (1998) have noted that failure to adhere to treatment regimens among families involved in child maltreatment can be as high as 70 percent. They point out that many complex social/ecological variables may be responsible for this problem. Among the solutions that they propose are to keep treatment as simple as possible; to not be confrontive with parents; to be sensitive with assessments; to use written protocols when possible; to use behavioral strategies such as shaping, feedback, and reinforcers; and to make use of social validation information. Finally, they suggest using behavioral generalization principles such as training diversely and incorporating functional mediators.

Case Illustration

Rather than use one case illustration from Project SafeCare, presented here is a composite family. That is, described here are several families as if they were one. This composite family will be called the Lopez family. The mother was referred for child abuse after a report that she had burned her 6-year-old son's (Raul) lip with a cigarette because he had failed to comply to her commands. The mother, Eugenia, was a 26-year-old immigrant from Mexico who also had a 3-year-old daughter (Gloria). She lived with her two children in a one-bedroom apartment in the San Fernando Valley area of Los Angeles, California. Eugenia worked part time as a housekeeper for several families. She reported that when she worked, a cousin took care of the children.

Project SafeCare was asked to provide bonding training, safety training, and health care training. As with all families served by Project SafeCare, several indirect and direct assessments and a lengthy interview/questionnaire were applied with the family during a four-week assessment period. The questionnaire yielded considerable data, the most interesting of which was that Eugenia had been physically abused by her mother as a child and that as a young adolescent she had been sexually abused by an uncle.

The Parenting Stress Index yielded a baseline score of 160; the Child Abuse Potential Inventory (Spanish version) yielded a score of 210, and the Beck Depression Inventory yielded a score of 24. Thus, from these indirect data it can be seen that Eugenia showed clinical levels of stress about being a single parent, she was moderately depressed, and she had clear potential for more child abuse.

The direct observation data indicated that she displayed poor parenting skills. That is, she gave poor commands and showed little affect when interacting with her children. Further, she engaged in nearly no activities with them, and rarely made any positive comments to her children. Her verbalizations toward her children consisted mostly of commands and criticisms.

As with many of the homes served by Project SafeCare, there was not much filth or clutter as measured by the CLEAN, but there were numerous safety hazards accessible to her children. For example, under the kitchen sink there were many toxic cleaning agents, and the cabinet doors under the sink were not latched. There were three electric sockets in the apartment without covers, and there were many small items on the floor and coffee table, which the children could swallow, and from which they could suffocate.

Eugenia scored very poorly on the task analyses/scenarios required to show adequate health care skills. She did not know how to take a temperature; she could not describe how to treat several childhood illnesses, and she could not identify most child health problems.

The first training component offered to her was Planned Activities Training (PAT). She was taught in five sessions how to schedule and plan activities for her children. She was provided laminated activity cards from which to choose activities. PAT also involves teaching the parent to use incidental teaching skills (Lutzker, Huynen, & Bigelow, 1998). This requires the parent to require language from the child and to include teaching in all activities.

PAT also involves teaching the parent to ignore minor challenging behaviors and to use simple positive consequences for successful activities. The parent is taught affective skills, such as proper voice intonation, positioning at the child's level, clear instructions, and positive touch.

After PAT was taught, the Home Safety Program was implemented. The parent is provided with latches for the cabinets, and instructions on how to make each room safe and how to keep hazards away from the children. In Eugenia's apartment, the first target room was the kitchen. When that room was safe, the bathroom was made safe, followed by the living room (where she slept), and then the children's bedroom.

Finally, Eugenia was taught to identify and report her children's illnesses. She was given a thermometer and some other medical supplies (e.g., cotton swabs). Using role-playing, modeling, feedback, and positive practice, she was taught how to take a temperature. These behavioral procedures, in conjunction with flow charts and a manual, were also used to teach her how to identify and report health problems, and what to do in an emergency. This took six sessions.

The entire treatment program lasted 16 sessions. Direct observation data showed that Eugenia learned the PAT skills to a 90 percent criterion. Of particular note was that during baseline, the children followed instructions less than 30 percent of the time. After PAT for Eugenia, Raul followed instructions 83 percent of the time and Gloria 82 percent. Eugenia said that the skills that she learned through PAT were allowing her to take the children to community settings much more frequently, and to visit relatives with greater ease.

Home safety hazards were reduced dramatically. The average baseline data of over 120 hazards accessible to her children was reduced to an average of 9 hazards after the home safety program was administered.

Eugenia met the criteria for identifying and reporting child illnesses and demonstrated how to treat them properly. Four weeks after health training was completed, she correctly identified a medical problem and took Gloria to a clinic in a timely manner.

A six-month follow-up showed that treatment gains were maintained for all three programs Eugenia had received. Of considerable interest were the reduced scores on the Beck, the Parent Stress Index, and the Child Potential Inventory. Her Beck score had been reduced to 11, which showed her moving to the mild depression range. Her PSI was 22, showing considerably less, and not clinically significant, stress related to parenting, and the Child Abuse Potential Inventory scores were lowered to the normal range (100).

Summary

Treatment and research in child abuse began in the 1960s. Early theories on its etiology focused on parents; however, the contemporary view is social/ecological. Several assessments are available (indirect and direct) that examine many variables correlated with child abuse. None are completely adequate; however, when used in the proper combination, these tools can be useful in determining risk, and assessing need and progress in treatment.

There are some predictable characteristics of parents who are at risk of abusing their children, and there are also predictive child characteristics. These characteristics reflect only correlations and should therefore be considered cautiously.

Early interventions in child abuse attempted to treat parents by providing parent training or stress reduction techniques. More recent treatment has been more multifaceted, involving parent training that is more comprehensive, and including self-management strategies, attempts to make changes in the families' social ecologies, and other community efforts.

Child abuse appears to be an increasing problem. There is a need for all levels of prevention and intervention. In addition to comprehensive treatment programs for families already involved, there is a need for secondary and primary prevention efforts. One suggestion is a human development curriculum offered from preschool through high school (Lutzker, 1998; Wurtele, 1998). All programs must be culturally sensitive and community driven.

REFERENCES

Achenback, T. M. & Edelbrock, C. S. (1983). *Manual for the Child Behavior Checklist and Revised Child Behavior Profile*. Burlington, VT: Thomas M. Achenbach.

Ammerman, R. T., Cassisi, J. E., Hersen, M., & Van Hasselt, V. B. (1986). Consequences of physical abuse and neglect in children. *Clinical Psychology Review, 6*, 291–310.

Azar, S. T., Povilaitus, T. Y., Lauretti, A. F., & Poquette, C. L. (1998). The current status of etiological theories of intrafamilial child maltreatment. In J. R. Lutzker (Ed.), *Handbook of Child Abuse Research and Treatment* (pp. 3–30). New York: Plenum.

Azar, S. T., Robinson, D. R., Hekimian, E., & Twentyman, C. T. (1984). Unrealistic expectations and problem-solving ability in maltreating and comparison mothers. *Journal of Consulting and Clinical Psychology, 52*, 687–691.

Barone, V. J., Greene, B. F., & Lutzker, J. R. (1986). Home safety with families being treated for child abuse and neglect. *Behavior Modification, 10*, 94–114.

Bigelow, K. M. & Lutzker, J. R. (1998). Using video to teach planned activities to parents reported for child abuse. *Child and Family Behavior Therapy, 20* 1–14.

Butcher, J. N., Dahlstrom, W. G., Graham, J. R., Tellegen, A., & Kaemer, B. (1989). *Minnesota Multiphasic Personality Inventory-2 (MMPI-2): Manual for Administration and Scoring*. Minneapolis: University of Minnesota Press.

Campbell, R. V., O'Brien, S., Bickett, A., & Lutzker, J. R. (1983). In-home parent-training, treatment of migraine headaches, and marital counseling as an ecobehavioral approach to prevent child abuse. *Journal of Behavior Therapy and Experimental Psychiatry, 14*, 147–154. (Indexed in the *Inventory of Marriage and Family Literature*, Vol. X, Family Resource Center, 1984.)

Cordon, I. M., Lutzker, J. R., Bigelow, K. M., & Doctor, R. M. (1998). Evaluating Spanish protocols for teaching bonding, home safety, and health care skills. *Journal of Behavior Therapy and Experimental Psychiatry, 29*, 41–54.

Dachman, R. S., Halasz, M. M., Bickett, A. D., & Lutzker, J. R. (1984). A home-based ecobehavioral parent-training and generalization package with a neglectful mother. *Education and Treatment of Children, 7*, 183–202.

Delgado, L. E. & Lutzker, J. R. (1988). Training young parents to identify and report their children's illnesses. *Journal of Applied Behavior Analysis, 21*, 311–319.

DeRoma, V. M. & Hansen, D. J. (1994, November). *Development of the Parental Anger Inventory*. Poster presented at the Association for the Advancement of Behavior Therapy Convention, San Diego, CA.

Dumas, J. E. & Wahler, R. S. (1985). Indiscriminate mothering as a contextual factor in aggressive-oppositional child behavior: "Damned if you do and damned if you don't." *Journal of Abnormal Child Psychology, 13*, 1–17.

Eyberg, S. M. & Robinson, E. A. (1981). *Dyadic Parent-Child Interaction Coding System: A Manual*. Unpublished manuscript, Oregon Health Sciences University.

Eyberg, S. M. & Ross, A. W. (1978). Assessment of child behavior problems: The validation of a new inventory. *Journal of Clinical Child Psychology, 7*, 113–116.

Fantuzzo, J., Delgaudio Weiss, A., & Coyle Coolahan, K. (1998). Community-based partnership-directed research: Actualizing community strengths to treat child victims of physical abuse and neglect. In J. R. Lutzker (Ed.), *Handbook of Child Abuse Research and Treatment* (pp. 213–237). New York: Plenum.

Feldman, M. A. (1998). Parents with intellectual disabilities: Implications and interventions. In J. R. Lutzker (Ed.), *Handbook of Child Abuse Research and Treatment* (pp. 401–420). New York: Plenum.

Forehand, R. & McMahon, R. (1981). *Helping the Noncompliant Child: A Clinician's Guide to Parent Training*. New York: Guilford.

Fox, R. A. (1994). *Parent Behavior Checklist*. Brandon, VT: Clinical Psychology Publishing.

Gilbert, T. (1976). Behavioral approach to the treatment of child abuse. *Nursing Times, 72*, 104–143.

Hally, C., Polansky, N. F., & Polansky, N. A. (1980). *Child Neglect: Mobilizing services* (DHHS Publication No. OHDS 80-30257). Washington, DC: U.S. Government Printing Office.

Hansen, D. J., Palotta, G. M., Tishelman, A. C., Conaway, L. P., & MacMillan, V. M. (1989). Parental problem-solving skills and child behavior problems: A comparison for physically abu-

sive, neglectful, clinic, and community families. *Journal of Family Violence, 4,* 353–368.

Kempe, C. H., Silverman, F. N., Steele, B. F., Drogemueller, W., & Silver, H. K. (1962). The battered child syndrome. *Journal of Medical
Association, 181,* 105–112.

Lazarus, R. S. & Folkman, S. (1984). *Stress, Appraisal,
and Coping.* New York: Springer.

Lorber, R., Felton, D. S., & Reid, J. (1984). A social
learning approach to the reduction of coercive
processes in child abusive families: A molecu-
lar analysis. *Advances in Behavior Research and
Therapy, 6,* 29–45.

Lloyd, B. H. & Abidin, R. R. (1985). Revision of the
Parenting Stress Index. *Journal of Pediatric Psychology, 10,* 169–177.

Lundquist, L. M. & Hansen, D. J. (1998). Enhancing
treatment adherence, social validity, and generalization of parent-training interventions
with physically abusive and neglectful families. In J. R. Lutzker (Ed.), *Handbook of Child
Abuse Research and Treatment* (pp. 449–471).
New York: Plenum.

Lutzker, J. R. (1984). Project 12-Ways: Treating child
abuse and neglect from an ecobehavioral perspective. In R. F. Dangel & R. A. Poslter (Eds.),
*Parent training: Foundations of Research and
Practice* (pp. 260–291). New York: Guilford.

Lutzker, J. R. (1998). Child abuse and neglect: Weav-
ing theory, research, and treatment into the
twenty-first century. In J. R. Lutzker (Ed.),
Handbook of Child Abuse Research and Treatment
(pp. 563–570). New York: Plenum.

Lutzker, J. R., Bigelow, K. M., Doctor, R. M.,
Gershater, R. M., & Greene, B. F. (1998). An
ecobehavioral model for the prevention and
treatment of child abuse and neglect: History
and applications. In J. R. Lutzker (Ed.), *Handbook of Child Abuse Research and Treatment* (pp.
239–266). New York: Plenum.

Lutzker, J. R., Bigelow, K. M., Swenson, C. C., Doctor, R. M., & Kessler, M. L. (1999). Problems
related to child abuse and neglect. In S. Neth-
erton, C. E. Walker, & D. Holmes (Eds.), *Comprehensive Handbook of Child and Adolescent
Disorders,* (pp. 520–548). Oxford: Oxford University Press.

Lutzker, J. R., Huynen, K. B., & Bigelow, K. M.
(1998). Parent training. In V. B. Van Hasselt &
M. Hersen (Eds.), *Handbook of Psychological
Treatment Protocols for Children and Adolescents,*
(pp. 467–500). Mahwah, NJ: Erlbaum.

Lutzker, S. Z., Lutzker, J. R., Braunling-McMorrow,
D., & Eddleman, J. (1987). Prompting to
increase mother-baby stimulation with single
mothers. *Journal of Child and Adolescent Psychotherapy, 4,* 3–12.

MacMillan, V. M., Olson, R. L., & Hansen, D. J. (1991,
November). *The Development of an Anger
Inventory for Use with Maltreating Parents.*
Paper presented at the Association for the
Advancement of Behavior Therapy Conven-
tion, New York.

Malinosky-Rummell, R. & Hansen, D. J. (1993).
Long-term consequences of childhood physical abuse. *Psychological Bulletin, 114,* 68–79.

Mandel, U., Bigelow, K. M., & Lutzker, J. R. (1998).
Using video to reduce home safety hazards
with parents reported for child abuse or
neglect. *Journal of Family Violence, 13,* 147–162.

Milner, J. S. (1986). *The Child Abuse Potential Inventory: Manual* (2nd ed.). Webster, NC: Psytec,
Inc.

National Research Council. (1993). *Understanding
Child Abuse and Neglect.* Washington, DC:
National Academy.

Novaco, R. W. (1975). *Anger control: The Development
and Evaluation of an Experimental Treatment.*
Lexington, MA: Lexington Books.

Pittman, A. L., Wolfe, D. A., & Wekerle, C. (1998).
Prevention during adolescence: The Youth
Relationship Project. In J. R. Lutzker (Ed.),
Handbook of Child Abuse Research and Treatment
(pp. 341–356). New York: Plenum.

Roehling, P. V. & Robin, A. L. (1986). Development
and validation of the Family Beliefs Inventory: A measure of unrealistic beliefs among
parents and adolescents. *Journal of Consulting
and Clinical Psychology, 54,* 693–697.

Sarber, R. E., Halasz, M. M., Messmer, M. C., Bickett,
A. D., & Lutzker, J. R. (1983). Teaching menu
planning and grocery shopping skills to a
mentally retarded mother. *Mental Retardation,
21,* 101–106.

Striefel, S., Robinson, M. A., & Truhn, P. (1998).
Dealing with child abuse and neglect within a
comprehensive family support program. In J.
R. Lutzker (Ed.), *Handbook of Child Abuse
Research and Treatment* (pp. 267–289). New
York: Plenum.

Tertinger, D. S., Greene, B. F., & Lutzker, J. R. (1984).
Home safety: Development and validation of
one component of an ecobehavioral treatment
program for abused and neglected children.
Journal of Applied Behavior Analysis, 17, 159–174.

Tymchuk, A. J. (1998). The importance of matching
educational interventions to parent needs in
child maltreatment: Issues, methods, and rec-

ommendations. In J. R. Lutzker (Ed.), *Handbook of Child Abuse Research and Treatment* (pp. 421–448). New York: Plenum.

U.S. Department of Health and Human Services, National Center on Child Abuse and Neglect. (1995). *Child Maltreatment 1993: Reports from the States to the National Center on Child Abuse and Neglect.* Washington, DC: U.S. Government Printing Office.

Wahler, R. G. (1980). The insular mother: Her problem in parent-child treatment. *Journal of Applied Behavior Analysis, 13,* 207–219.

Wahler, R. G., Leske, G., & Rogers, E. S. (1979). The insular family: A deviance support system of oppositional children. In L. A. Hamerlynck (Ed.), *Behavioral Systems for the Developmentally Disabled: I. School and Family Environments.* New York: Brunner-Mazel.

Warner, J. E. & Hansen, D. J. (1994). The identification and reporting of physical abuse by physicians: A review and implications for research. *Child Abuse and Neglect, 18,* 11–25.

Wasik, B. H. & Bryant, D. (1989). Parent means-end problem solving instrument (abstract). In J. Touliatos (Ed.), *Handbook on Family Measurement Techniques.* Newbury Park, CA: Sage.

Watson-Perczel, M., Lutzker, J. R., Greene, B. F., & McGimpsey, B. J. (1988). Assessment and modification of home cleanliness among families adjudicated for child neglect. *Behavior Modification, 12,* 57–81.

Wolfe, D. A., Edwards, B., Manion, I., & Koverola, C. (1988). Early intervention for parents at risk of child abuse and neglect: A preliminary investigation. *Journal of Consulting and Clinical Psychology, 56,* 40–47.

Wolfe, D. A. & Sandler, J. (1981). Training abusive parents in effective child management. *Behavior Modification, 5,* 320–335.

Wurtele, S. K. (1998). School-based sexual abuse prevention programs: Questions, answers, and more questions. In J. R. Lutzker (Ed.), *Handbook of Child Abuse Research and Treatment* (pp. 501–516). New York: Plenum.

Yung, B. R. & Hammond, R. (1998). Breaking the cycle: A culturally sensitive violence prevention program for African American children and adolescents. In J. R. Lutzker (Ed.), *Handbook of Child Abuse Research and Treatment* (pp. 319–340). New York: Plenum.

6 Child Sexual Molestation

W. L. MARSHALL

Queen's University

LIAM E. MARSHALL

Bath Institution Sex Offender's Program

The sexual molestation of children constitutes a serious problem for our societies. This is a very extensive problem involving the sexual abuse of many children, and resulting, all too often, in severe and long-lasting impairment to their functioning. Damage of this kind to so many innocent children ought to be reason enough to take preventive and remedial action, but the resultant reduced productivity and ineffective social functioning of the victims should give impetus to an all-out attack on this social malady. Unfortunately, societies have not taken the necessary steps to deal with this issue. Increasingly punitive measures have been enacted against the perpetrators of child sexual molestation with little regard to how effective these procedures are in addressing the problem. Punitive responses are an appropriate part of a response to child sexual molestation, and severe punishment of the offenders on its own may satisfy the public's understandable need for retribution; however, this simply gives the *impression* of doing something, rather than actually achieving the sensible goal of protecting children.

Treatment of the perpetrator is one way in which a reasonable society, truly committed to protecting children and maximizing the utility of all its members, might attempt to reduce this scourge. While the evidence to date on the value of treating sexual offenders is not conclusively positive, such an approach can only improve if practitioners are given the wherewithal to continue to develop treatment methods. Of course, treating the offender is only one aspect of a truly serious social effort. Providing assistance and counseling to the victims and their families is an essential, but largely neglected, component of a comprehensive response to the sexual abuse of children, as is the development of preventive procedures.

As we have noted, there are several fronts on which society could make efforts that might help to reduce this problem. This chapter, however, is limited to addressing the issues of the offender. We will do this by first describing the problem and its frequency of occurrence, in the hope that this will make clear the need to deal with child sexual abuse. We will then focus on identifying the nature of the offenders, their heterogeneity, and the ways in which we can identify, and meet, their treatment needs.

Description of the Problem

The current *Diagnostic and Statistical Manual (DSM-IV)* (American Psychiatric Association, 1994) supposedly identifies all problems of psychological functioning that need some sort of psychiatric treatment or management. Unfortunately, its definition of the problem of child sexual molestation is restricted to identifying only a specific subgroup of offenders (i.e., those who meet the criteria for pedophilia), and to classifying the victims, if, and only if, they meet one or another of the set of independently identified disorders. Victims of child sexual abuse, for example, may be found to have post-traumatic stress disorder or dissociative identify disorder. Many, however, may have serious problems that nevertheless do not meet the criteria for a *DSM-IV* disorder. Among the offenders, some may meet the criteria for pedophilia (a paraphilic disorder), but far too many do not. Refer to Marshall (1997) for a more complete discussion of the problems arising from the discrepancies between *DSM-IV* criteria for pedophilia and current clinical practice in dealing with child molesters.

The sexual molestation of children also cannot be adequately described in legal terms since, across jurisdictions, the laws are remarkably different. All too often, legal descriptors do not clearly indicate the age of the victim or of the offender, and yet these features are critical to defining abuse as child molestation. While guidelines on the issue of victim and perpetrator age have not been agreed upon, clinicians typically use some age discrepancy criterion, although clinicians working with juveniles often ignore the age of the offender.

Whatever the future resolution of these problems may be, the behavioral criteria for child sexual molestation is relatively simple. Any sexual act perpetrated on a child by someone sufficiently older to exercise, by nature of that age discrepancy, power over the child, or who exercises power by more direct coercion, constitutes child sexual abuse. The range of sexual acts perpetrated on children includes what has been called *hands off* as well as *hands on* actions. The former refers to exhibitionism, invitations to sexual acts, voyeurism, obscene phone-calling, and similar behaviors that do not involve direct physical contact. *Hands on* sexual acts with children involve direct physical contact. Offenders may simply touch children's breasts, genitals, or buttocks either over or under their clothing. They may kiss the child in a sexual way, they may engage in oral-genital, oral-breast, or oral-anal activities; they may digitally penetrate the child or penetrate the child's orifices with some object, or they may simulate intercourse or have actual intercourse (oral, genital, or anal) or have the child penetrate their anus.

In earlier days, based primarily on the reports of offenders, researchers often took the view that child molestation was primarily restricted to fondling, it being assumed that penile penetration of a child's body by an adult penis would be all but impossible (e.g., Mohr, Turner, & Jerry, 1964). This view was clearly mistaken. Both Finkelhor (1979) and Haugaard (1987) report a low but significant rate of intercourse by child abusers, whereas Russell (1984) reports a far higher rate. Russell's respondents indicated that when the abuser was extrafamilial, the rate of intercourse was 23 percent, whereas 53 percent of incest offenders had intercourse with their victims. However, the source of the data has a significant influence on the relative rates of different sexual acts with children. Table 6.1 illustrates this point with the data collected by the Committee on Sexual Offenses against Children and Youths (1984) of Canada. Rates of both intercourse and the use of force clearly varied considerably across the different agencies surveyed. However, it is also clear that the rates for both intercourse and coercion are very high and obviously reflect the intrusive and abusive nature of child molestation.

In an examination of the child molesters attending our prison and community clinics, we found that over a third had intercourse with their victims, and almost one quarter used excessive force (Marshall & Christie, 1981). It should be apparent from these data that the sexual molestation of children involves quite distressing behaviors. Adding to this unfortunate scenario is the fact that these offenses are quite widespread.

TABLE 6.1 Canadian Data on the Types of Sexual Molestation of Children

Type of Behavior	Population Surveys of Victimization		Victims Identified by Police		Victims Presented at Hospitals		Victims Reported to Child Protection Agencies	
	Males	*Females*	*Males*	*Females*	*Males*	*Females*	*Males*	*Females*
Fondling	15.8	47.4	71.1	91.6	35.2	44.8	40.8	68.6
Kissing	0.3	3.0	9.9	14.8	5.4	4.0	7.5	13.5
Oral sex	3.1	2.1	32.2	7.5	27.0	14.0	10.8	7.5
Digital/object penetration	0.5	5.5	3.3	7.8	8.2	16.8	3.3	10.7
Vaginal intercourse	0.0	9.7	0.0	24.1	0.0	48.9	0.0	22.5
Anal intercourse	1.6	1.6	12.6	1.9	39.2	6.2	20.9	2.6

Source: Adapted from the Report of the *Committee on Sexual Offenses Against Children and Youths* (1984).

Note: Figures are percentages of total samples.

Epidemiology

The previous section showed that the source of data determined the identified frequency of particular sexual behaviors enacted by child molesters; the same is true for the data on the incidence and prevalence of the sexual abuse of children. For example, in surveys of adults where they were asked to recall child abuse, Haugaard (1987) found that different participation rates affected the reported incidence of victimization. When Haugaard secured full participation, the reported rates of child sexual abuse were higher than when the response rate was 78 percent. This, however, is somewhat reassuring since the majority of the most commonly cited surveys (e.g., Finkelhor, 1979; Russell, 1984; Wyatt, 1985) report participation rates somewhere between 50 to 80 percent, suggesting that the data obtained from such studies should represent an underestimate of the actual prevalence of child molestation.

Considering contact abuse only (i.e., hands on abuse), the rates for female children range from 10 percent (Haugaard & Emery, 1989) to 36 percent (Wyatt, 1985). The rates for male children range from 0 percent (Reed & Kenning, 1987) to 7 percent (Risin & Koss, 1987). Surveys have consistently indicated far higher rates of sexual abuse of girls than boys. It has been variously estimated that the ratio of boy-to-girl victims is somewhere between 1:6 and 1:12 (Knopp, 1986). Refuting the possible argument that these rather high prevalence figures are the result of recent attention to the issue that has artificially inflated the rates, or as a result of a recent increase in all abusive crimes, Salter (1992) describes data collected over the period 1929 to 1965. These data reveal prevalence rates that are, if anything, even higher than the more recent estimates (24 to 39% for girls and 27 to 30% for boys). Evidently, child sexual molestation has been a feature of our societies throughout the twentieth century.

Characteristics of the Offender

The most obvious characteristic of child molesters is that most are males. In fact, until recently, it was thought that almost all offenders were male. Somewhat contrary to this notion, Harrison (1993) reports that, of the 8,663 callers to a children's helpline who were sexually abused, 9 percent (i.e., 780 children) said their abuser was female. Finkelhor and Russell (1984) analyzed data collected by the American Humane Association and determined that 14 percent of the male victims and 6 percent of the female victims of child sexual abuse were molested by females. Whatever the true figures are, it is clear that female child molesters do not represent a trivial problem.

Similarly, it has only recently been recognized that a substantial proportion of child molesters are either adolescents or children themselves (Barbaree, Marshall, & Hudson, 1993). Related to this is the fact that many juveniles who molest children go on to become adult offenders (Abel, Osborn, & Twigg, 1993), indicating that the sexual activities of these young people cannot be dismissed, as they were in the past (Roberts, Abrams, & Finch, 1973), as youthful experimentation. It has been estimated, for example, that as many as 30 to 50 percent of cases of child sexual molestation are committed by juveniles (Davis & Leitenberg, 1987).

Over the past 20 years, in particular, researchers in the field have learned a considerable amount about other characteristics of child molesters. What emerges from this literature, however, is that while group differences have been observed between child molesters and various comparison groups, there is considerable overlap no matter what feature is being examined. This is perhaps not so surprising as it first seems. Finkelhor and Lewis (1988), for example, found that 17 percent of adult males admitted in an anonymous survey that they had sexually molested a child at some time during their adulthood but had not been reported. In our studies of child molesters, we have the nonoffender volunteers fill out a form asking questions about their sexual fantasies and behaviors. The subjects complete these forms in private and place them in a coded envelope (so that we cannot identify their name) that they then seal before giving it to our experimenter. Counting as deviant those subjects who indicate persistent sexual fantasies of children, or who say they have engaged in sex with a child since they were adults, we have persistently identified as deviant over 30 percent of all our volunteers. Obviously, there are many supposedly "normal" males who have deviant attractions to children, and yet most studies reported in the literature do not indicate the use of any screening procedure. We will describe those group differences that have been found, but we caution the reader not to assume that these are clearly distinguishing features.

Cognitive Processes

Depending on the particular author's view, cognitive distortions can include the offender's misperception of the victim's behavior, his refusal to accept responsibility, and his belief that children desire sex with adults. Cognitive distortions can also include a failure to recognize harm, various distorted attitudes about children, or a process (cognitive deconstruction) that excludes consideration of anything but the offender's immediate needs or sexual goals (Langton & Marshall, 1997; Ward, Hudson, & Marshall, 1995). Bumby, Langton, and Marshall (1997) have considered issues of guilt and shame to be part of the cognitive processes that allow child molesters to continue to offend. In addition, Howells (1978) and Horley (1988; Horley & Quinsey, 1995) demonstrated that child molesters perceive children as less threatening and as more attractive than adults. Thus, children make child molesters feel more comfortable and are, therefore, more attractive to them. With these sorts of perceptions, it is no wonder that these offenders seek out children for sex or take advantage of opportunities when they arise.

Abel, Becker, and Cunningham-Rathner (1984) were the first to describe what they called *cognitive distortions*. These distortions include faulty beliefs about children's sexuality, inaccurate perceptions of the behavior of potential victims, the idea that having sex with a child will not hurt them, and that sex with a child is a way of showing love. While Abel and colleagues (1984; 1989) found that these features distinguished child molesters, other researchers report no differences (Langevin, 1991), and this has been attributed to the ease with which offenders can dissimulate on these tests (Hanson, Gizzarelli, & Scott, 1994).

Social Competence

Although it has frequently been declared that child molesters suffer deficits in social competence (Barnard, Fuller, Robbins, & Shaw, 1989; Cohen, Seghorn, & Calmus, 1969; Crawford & Allen, 1979), in fact, the evidence in support of such deficits is weak (McFall, 1990; Stermac, Segal, & Gillis, 1990). There is reasonable support for the notion that child molesters are unassertive (Marshall, Barbaree, & Fernandez, 1995; Segal & Marshall, 1985); however, their unassertiveness may not be entirely due to a skill deficit. Marshall and colleagues (1995) found that child molesters, unlike other subjects, believed that obsequious acquiescence was the most appropriate response to an unreasonable request from an assertive acquaintance.

It has also been assumed that child molesters have a deficit in their capacity for empathy (Hildebran & Pithers, 1989) that is in need of treatment (Knopp, Freeman-Longo, & Stevenson, 1992; Wormith & Hanson, 1992). Reviews of the literature, however, have not revealed convincing evidence of such a generalized deficit among child molesters (Hanson, 1997; Marshall, Hudson, Jones, & Fernandez, 1995). What has been found (Fernandez, Marshall, Lightbody, & O'Sullivan, 1997) is that child molesters show significant deficits in empathy for their own victims, somewhat greater empathy, but still deficient, toward the child victims of other offenders, and no deficits at all to children in general.

In contrast to the limited support for the ideas that child molesters are unassertive and lack empathy, there is far clearer evidence indicating that these offenders have problems in forming effective relationships with adults. Marshall (1989) proposed that an inability to develop intimacy with adults might compel some men to attempt to meet their sexual and intimacy needs with children. Subsequently, studies have revealed deficits in intimacy and elevated levels of loneliness among child molesters (Garlick, Marshall, & Thornton, 1996; Seidman, Marshall, Hudson, & Robertson, 1994).

It has also been proposed that child molesters lack confidence, particularly in social contexts (Marshall & Barbaree, 1990; Williams & Finkelhor, 1990). A review of the literature indicates that low self-esteem does, indeed, characterize child molesters (Marshall, Anderson, & Champagne, 1996). However, whether this is an etiological or maintaining feature, or whether it is simply the product of being identified as an offender, is not clear at the present time.

Deviant Sexual Arousal

It was assumed by early behavior therapists that sexually deviant behavior, including child molestation, was driven by a preference for particular acts or partners (Abel & Blanchard, 1974; McGuire, Carlisle, & Young, 1965). The measurement of sexual arousal has not, however, fully supported these claims.

As a group, men who persistently molest nonfamilial children (i.e., offenders who have more than one victim), and who admit to having done so, display, relative to nonoffenders, greater sexual arousal to children and usually, but not always, less arousal to adults (Freund, 1981; Lang, Black, Frenzel, & Checkley, 1988; McConaghy, 1993; Quinsey & Chaplin, 1988). Men who molest their own children, however, have not been consistently found to display deviant sexual arousal to children (Frenzel & Lang, 1989; Freund, Watson, & Dickey, 1991; Marshall, Barbaree, & Christophe, 1986; Quinsey, Chaplin, & Carrigan, 1979).

Barbaree and Marshall (1989) examined in greater detail the sexual responses of a group of child molesters and found they were a quite heterogeneous group. Among the nonfamilial offenders against girls, 22 percent were not aroused by either adults or children, 30 percent displayed a relatively normal profile, 21 percent did not discriminate for age (i.e., they were equally aroused by adults, teenagers, and children), while 27 percent were more aroused by children than by adults. Apparently, not all child molesters sexually prefer children; only those who admit to victimizing several children clearly have such preferences.

Other Features

The personality of child molesters has been thoroughly investigated, both projectively and by the use of more objective measures; unfortunately, however, inconsistency in findings across studies has been the rule (Levin & Stava, 1987; Marshall & Hall, 1995). In a detailed examination of those studies employing the Minnesota Multiphasic Personality Inventory (MMPI), Marshall and Hall (1995) found little support for the contention that this instrument could identify child molesters, despite the confident conclusions of many authors that these offenders display a specific personality profile (i.e., elevations on scales 4 and 8, or elevations on deviant indices derived from the MMPI).

In recent years, researchers have concentrated on one particular aspect of offenders' personality; namely, their tendency to display psychopathy. Quinsey and colleagues (Quinsey, Harris, & Rice, 1995; Quinsey, Lalumière, Rice, & Harris, 1995) report that more than 30 percent of child molesters are psychopathic, and Prentky and Knight (1986) found much the same. However, both of these sets of studies examined child molesters held in psychiatric institutions where we might expect a disproportionate number to be psychopaths. When Serin and colleagues (1994) evaluated child molesters housed in prisons, only 7.5 percent were determined to be psychopathic.

Many child molesters either abuse alcohol or some other intoxicant, or are intoxicated at the time of their offense. For example, Pithers and colleagues (1989) reported that 30 percent of sexual offenders against children used intoxicants immediately prior to offending. Langevin and Lang (1990) found that 55.8 percent of 123 child molesters scored above the cutoff for alcoholism, and 17.8 percent were identified as having a drug abuse problem.

Finally, child molesters appear to have unusually high rates of being sexually victimized themselves as children. A review by Hanson and Slater (1988) revealed that between 0 to 67 percent of child molesters said they were victims of childhood sexual abuse, with an average of 28 percent overall reporting such victimization. Employing both questionnaires and extensive follow-up interviews, Dhawan and Marshall (1996) found that 50 percent of child molesters interviewed reported hands on sexual abuse as children, whereas only 20 percent of nonsexual offenders reported such abuse.

Assessment

The justifiable reasons for assessing sexual offenders are (1) to evaluate risk to reoffend; (2) to determine the specific areas to address in treatment; and (3) to evaluate treatment efficacy. While some clinicians are apparently willing to conduct assessments in order to assist in the determination of guilt or innocence, there are, in fact, no grounds to support such an evaluation. Neither phallometric testing (Barbaree & Peacock, 1995) nor a more comprehensive assessment (Marshall, 1996a) have been shown to reliably identify the innocent from the guilty among men accused of a sexual offense.

We will not attempt to describe all the methods that have been employed in the assessment of sexual offenders, as there are far too many. Almost all treatment programs choose some unique testing procedures. However, there are reasonably common assessment targets across programs, which we will describe, along with some typical measures. First, let us set aside from consideration both polygraphy and projective testing as their empirical status as useful procedures with sexual offenders is in some doubt (Lalumière & Quinsey, 1991; Levin & Stava, 1987).

The clinical interview represents perhaps the most important source of information. All other forms of assessment are to be done in concert with a thorough interview. Interviews should be conducted in a supportive, respectful, and non-confrontational, although challenging, fashion (Miller & Rollnick, 1991), both to facilitate the acquisition of accurate information and to create an appropriate relationship for subsequent treatment. It is also necessary to gather information from other sources, such as court documents, police records, victim accounts, institutional history, and any other relevant sources. This will aid in the assessment and treatment process.

The targets for assessment and the corresponding measures are listed in Table 6.2. These targets should each be addressed in the interviews with additional input from the test procedures. Indeed, the test procedures can be seen as ways of evaluating hypotheses generated from the interview information, although many programs simply have a standardized battery with which they evaluate all clients.

Sexual Interests, Behavior, and History

Information from interviews to determine appropriate and deviant sexual history, and current masturbatory fantasies, is compared with phallometric results and self-report measures. When there are discrepancies between any of these reports, or between the test results and the information provided at interview, a reinterview or possibly repeated testing, may be necessary.

Self-report questionnaires that we have found useful in assessing sexual functioning are listed in Table 6.2, although other measures are also available. Phallometry, for example, has been a widely used method of assessing sexual offenders since the early 1970s. As noted earlier, there are limits to the value of phallometry. However, there does seem to be some utility in assessing nonfamilial child molesters. A recent study by Hanson and Bussière (1997) found that phallometric responses to children (but not responses to rape) combined with sexual offending history were the best predictors of recidivism for all types of sexual

TABLE 6.2   Assessment Target Methods

Target	Method
1. Sexual interests, behavior and history	Phallometric testing (Murphy & Barbaree, 1994) Sexual Interest Card Sort (Abel & Becker, 1985) Clarke Sexual History Questionnaire (Langevin, 1983) Multiphasic Sex Inventory (Nichols & Molinder, 1984) Sone Sexual History Form (Maletzky, 1991)
2. Social functioning	Anxiety (Watson & Friend, 1969) Assertiveness (Rathnus, 1973) State-Trait Anger Expression Inventory (Speilberger, 1988) Child Molester Empathy Measure (Fernandez, Marshall, Lightbody, & O'Sullivan, 1997) Social self-esteem (Lawson, Marshall, & McGrath, 1979) Social intimacy (Miller & Lefcourt, 1982) UCLA Revised Loneliness Scale (Russell, Peplau, & Cutrona, 1980)
3. Life history	Hassles Scale (Kanner, Coyne, Shafer, & Lazarus, 1981) Social Network Scale & Social Buffers Scale (Flannery & Wieman, 1989) Multiple Screen Sexual Abuse Questionnaire (Dhawan & Marshall, 1996) Family Environment Scale (Moos & Moos, 1986)
4. Cognitive processes	Abel's Cognitive Distortions Measure (Abel et al., 1989) Bumby's Child Molester and Rapist Cognitive Distortion Scales (1996) Hostility Toward Women Scale (Check, 1984)
5. Personality	Hare's Psychopathy Checklist-Revised (Hare, 1991) Minnesota Multiphasic Personality Inventory 2 (Graham, 1993)
6. Substance abuse	Michigan Alcoholism Screening Test (Selzer, 1971) Drug Abuse Screening Test (Skinner, 1982)
7. Physical problems	Hormonal assays and brain dysfunction testing (see text)
8. Relapse-related issues	Situational Competency Test (Miner, Day, & Nafpaktitis, 1989)

offenders, including child molesters. Therefore, phallometric tests may usefully be combined with interviews and self-report measures, and a clinical decision should be based on information derived from all these sources.

Social Functioning

The targets of this area of assessment cover all domains of social functioning, including interpersonal and relationship skills. Interpersonal functioning examines conversational skills, assertiveness, anxiety, anger, empathy, and self-esteem. Examining relationship history and social functioning to determine intimacy, attachment styles, and loneliness tells us about the offender's general social skills and his ability to form meaningful relationships. These areas of assessment are particularly relevant to decisions regarding treatment targets. Measures of interpersonal functioning that we have found to be useful are listed in Table 6.2, but again, other procedures are also available.

Life History

The developmental history of the sexual offender is the target in this component of the assessment process. The offender's relationship with his parents and his history, if any, of physical, emotional, and sexual abuse are important. Also, his ability to handle stress, his educational attainment, employment history, current support system, and his physical and emotional health are all factors relevant to treatment and predicting recidivism.

Interviews are an excellent source for this information as are autobiographies provided by the offender. However, we also use the measures listed in Table 6.2.

Cognitive Processes

Assessment of cognitive processes focuses on the offender's inappropriate attitudes toward women and children, his distorted perceptions of his own behavior, and the reactions of his victim(s), as well as the extent of his denial and minimization of his offenses. We also assess the degree of his understanding of the impact on his victim and his more general procriminal attitudes. The interview is, again, a useful tool. However, as noted earlier, it is necessary to have police records and court transcripts available to challenge the offender's self-serving perspective, because when presented with contradictory evidence, at least some offenders give more accurate details.

Although the measures listed in Table 6.2 can provide useful information on problematic aspects of cognitive processes, offenders typically have a vested interest in presenting themselves in a positive light. Often later in therapy, or at interview, they reveal far more inappropriate or distorted perceptions than is evident at assessment.

Personality

The offender's personal style and whether or not he has a personality disorder are the assessment targets in this area. The two most commonly used measures of personality are the Minnesota Multiphasic Personality Inventory 2 (MMPI-2) and Hare's Psychopathy Checklist-Revised. The results concerning a distinctive personality type associated with sexual offending have, as we noted, been inconsistent (Marshall & Hall, 1995). However, the MMPI can be useful for determining whether the offender displays any other sign of psychopathology. Hare's PCL-R is particularly useful in determining recidivism (Quinsey, Lalumière, Rice, & Harris, 1995) and may also assist in assigning clients to various levels of intensity of treatment.

Substance Abuse

As we have seen, substance abuse and dependence (alcohol and drug) is common among sexual offenders. If an offender meets the criteria for dependence or abuse, then it is almost certainly a salient factor in his offending. However, even moderate use may be relevant, as it may facilitate offending by reducing inhibitions that would otherwise prevent offensive behavior. Thus, although evidence of substance abuse indicates that this topic should be an important target of assessment, it should also be determined during interviews if substance use is instrumental in clients' sexual offending.

Physical Problems

The interview is the primary source of information to determine whether referrals for brain dysfunction screening or hormonal assays are necessary. Disturbed sex steroids and disturbances of brain functioning are reasonably uncommon in sexual offenders and, as such, unless a concern is raised by interview, this is not an area commonly assessed. There are, however, some programs that routinely evaluate these aspects of an offender's functioning, and they have found evidence of dysfunction which might otherwise have been missed (Bradford, 1990; Hucker & Bain, 1990; Langevin, 1990). Offenders with these problems, however, are too few to warrant routinely assessing this aspect of their functioning, given the limited resources of most programs.

Relapse-Related Issues

There are few measures to assess the relevant issues in this area, and yet the offender's ability to identify his offense cycle and the situations that place him at risk to reoffend are thought to be important in avoiding post-treatment relapse. Victim seeking and grooming, as well as the offender's emotional states and current stress, must all be recognizable as risk factors to the offender by the end of treatment in order for him to protect himself from reoffending. MacDonald and

Pithers (1989) used self-monitoring by the offenders to determine the situations or circumstances that increased their risk to reoffend. Miner, Day, and Nafpaktitis (1989) have developed a Situational Competency Test to estimate how well offenders will cope in a high-risk situation. In addition, engaging in high-risk behaviors and the strength of temptation elicited by these behaviors, as well as the confidence the offender has in his ability to resist these temptations and the availability of skills to cope with risky situations, are four features related to potential relapse described by Hall (1989) in his measures of self-efficacy.

Intervention

Treatment for child molesters has grown considerably in the past 20 years. Therapy for these offenders has been offered in various settings and for an increased range of specific populations (Marshall, Fernandez, Hudson, & Ward, 1998; Schwartz & Cellini, 1997). The content of these programs has also been expanded from the original emphasis on deviant sexuality and social skills to include cognitive functioning, relationship issues, empathy, and relapse prevention strategies. While there is some controversy over the effectiveness of treatment (see the debate between Quinsey, Harris, Rice, & Lalumière [1993], Marshall [1993], and Marshall & Pithers [1994]), when treatment is effective, it reduces future victimization and saves the taxpayers considerable money (Marshall, 1992; Prentky & Burgess, 1991).

Although individual (i.e., one-on-one) work is usually provided as an adjunct, the majority of cognitive behavioral programs deliver treatment primarily via group therapy. Within this context, therapists challenge offenders in a firm but supportive manner (Kear-Colwell & Pollock, 1997; Marshall, 1996b). As we have seen, child molesters are characteristically low in self-esteem, and this seriously hinders behavior change (Marshall, Anderson, & Champagne, 1996). Thus, the overall approach to treatment encourages change while displaying a respect for the client's dignity and strengths.

Acceptance of Responsibility

Offenders are required to give a detailed account of their offense including the thoughts, feelings, and behaviors in which they engaged. These accounts are challenged by the therapist and by each other participant. When the view expressed by other participants collides with the target offender's claim of innocence, the therapist uses this opportunity to illustrate the inappropriateness and unacceptability of such a response.

The processes of disclosure and challenge are repeated until a satisfactory account is given, or until it is evident that no further progress will be made. In those cases, the offender is suspended from the program and apprised of the consequences (e.g., parole will likely be denied or revoked). If the suspended client subsequently says he has decided to be more forthcoming, he is allowed to reenter treatment.

Cognitive Distortions

Through the processes involved in acceptance of responsibility, the distorted beliefs, perceptions, and thoughts of offenders are also challenged, again by both the therapist and the other group participants. In a sense, this is challenging their attempts to minimize responsibility, so the distinction between cognitive distortions and refusal to accept full responsibility is essentially arbitrary. The same therapeutic processes are involved and the same sort of resistance on the part of the offender is apparent.

Empathy

We have conceptualized empathy as an unfolding process of four stages: (1) emotional recognition; (2) seeing the situation from the victim's perspective; (3) feeling distress over the victim's suffering; and (4) taking some action to make amends (Marshall, Hudson, Jones, & Fernandez, 1995). Accordingly, as a first step, offenders are trained to recognize emotional states in themselves and in others. They describe an emotionally distressing experience from their past, allowing their emotions to be expressed as vividly as possible. Other participants are then required to identify the emotions displayed and report what feelings they had while listening to the account. Next, each participant is asked to indicate what distress and problems might befall a victim of child sexual abuse. When these responses are all recorded, each offender is required to indicate which ones apply to his victim. If a client has trouble doing this, role-play enactments of some aspects of his offense may assist him in seeing things from the victim's point of view. Each client then writes a hypothetical letter from the victim to himself expressing the victim's feelings and problems arising from the offense. Typically, this letter has to be written several times before it represents a reasonable account of the victim's suffering. The offender then writes a hypothetical response to the victim outlining his recognition of the victim's problems, his regret for having caused pain, and his intention to do everything he can to ensure that he does not do it again.

Social Functioning

Training in social skills typically includes teaching child molesters to be more assertive, to have greater control over their anger, to be better conversationalists, to be less anxious, and, most importantly, to be able to develop good quality adult relationships. Most approaches to these deficits employ a diversity of psychoeducational techniques such as role-play, modeling, videotape feedback, and social reinforcement shaping (Green, 1995). Our primary target in this component has been relationship skills. We have developed a specific module to enhance intimacy and reduce loneliness (Marshall, Bryce, Hudson, Ward, & Moth, 1996).

Deviant Fantasies

No doubt, all child molesters at least occasionally entertain sexual thoughts or fantasies of children, even if only at the time they are actually abusing a child. How important these fantasies are in triggering offenses or in maintaining deviant patterns of behavior, is another question. However, certainly a substantial number of child molesters experience repeated fantasies of sexually abusing children (Abel, Becker, Cunningham-Rathner, Mittelman, & Rouleau, 1988; Marshall, Barbaree, & Eccles, 1991). For those offenders who are plagued by persistent deviant fantasies, the following procedures appear to be helpful in reducing both the intensity and frequency of these fantasies.

Typical behavioral methods include covert sensitization and masturbatory reconditioning. Covert sensitization, which involves imagining enacting the deviant behavior followed by imagining dreadful consequences, is still popular, although the evidence in support of its utility remains weak (Quinsey & Earls, 1990). Laws and Marshall (1991) reviewed the evidence on masturbatory reconditioning procedures and concluded that the evidence best supported a combination of directed masturbation (i.e., instructing the client to masturbate to appropriate fantasies) followed by satiation (i.e., having the client rehearse deviant fantasies in the refractory period after orgasm).

Because these behavioral techniques do not always work, most programs also use pharmacological interventions. Antiandrogens, given in appropriate doses, can provide sufficient control to the offenders, decreasing deviant fantasies, and increasing appropriate responses (Bradford & Pawlak, 1993). Similarly, the serotonin-reuptake-inhibitors, such as fluoxetine, sertraline, or buspirone, appear to provide some sexual offenders with control over their deviant thoughts (Federoff, 1993).

Relapse Prevention

Relapse prevention provides an integrative way of viewing all treatment components. Offenders are told that each component of treatment provides them with the personal knowledge and skills to avoid future reoffending. Relapse prevention also provides specific strategies for identifying and avoiding future risks, or dealing with them should they inadvertently arise (Pithers, 1990).

While there are quite complex ways to put relapse prevention into therapeutic practice (e.g., training offenders in the language of relapse prevention, teaching them how to control the problem of immediate gratification, or how to abort the abstinence violation effect), essentially offenders are trained to: (1) identify the factors (both distal and proximal) in their offense cycle and the associated high-risk situations; (2) develop plans that are aimed at avoiding or dealing with risks; and (3) generate a list of internal and external signs that might warn themselves or others that they are returning to pretreatment risk levels.

Other Issues

Other issues that are characteristically dealt with in treatment include the following: substance abuse, sex education, marital counseling, parenting skills, personal victimization, and stress management. Approaches to these issues follow strategies developed in those fields that specifically deal with such problems. However, not all programs include all of these components, and it is not presently clear whether it is necessary to include all of these in child-molester-specific treatment.

Case Illustration

It is impossible in the space available to take the reader through all the steps in our treatment program for a single client. To illustrate particular issues, we will give the example of a client dealing with limited aspects of our program.

Gary was a 38-year-old single male convicted of sexually abusing a 13-year-old girl over a period of 18 months while he was having an on-again-off-again relationship with the girl's mother. He was seen in our prison program.

Gary initially presented as defensive and somewhat hostile, and he repeatedly denigrated himself throughout the pretreatment evaluation process. At assessment, Gary scored low on self-esteem and intimacy measures, high on a measure of minimization, and expressed a lack of empathy for his victim. Gary admitted to using alcohol and marijuana to excess throughout the time that he was offending, although he agreed somewhat reluctantly that he did on occasion molest the girl when he was sober. On most other measures, Gary looked normal. Consequently, the primary focus in treatment was on issues of taking responsibility, recognizing harm, enhancing self-esteem, developing better relationship skills, outlining his offense cycle, and generating relapse prevention plans.

Whenever Gary was challenged in the early stages of treatment, he would respond defensively, and he clearly resented and felt threatened by the challenges.

> QUESTION:[1] You said that the girl often walked from the bathroom to her bedroom with only a towel wrapped round her. Why is this important?
>
> GARY: She was obviously trying to attract my attention.
>
> QUESTION: Why do you think that?
>
> GARY: I could just tell.
>
> QUESTION: But it seems reasonable for someone in their own house, in the presence of a man who is supposed to be acting as a father, to do this. Particularly when it is a quite young person.
>
> GARY: See. You're doing it again. You're attacking me. Why does everyone think I'm lying?

QUESTION: We are not suggesting you're lying; we are simply trying to get you to see that your interpretation of what the young girl was doing might be wrong.

GARY: No you're not. You're trying to force me to say that she had nothing to do with trying to get me to have sex with her.

QUESTION: Well, we're not trying to force you, Gary. We're just trying to get you to see it from a different perspective. Let's try a different approach. Suppose I told you I had just met a young, glamorous and famous movie star, and that she smiled at me when I said hello. What would you say if I claimed that her smile meant she was sexually interested in me? Remember, I am over 60 years of age and not exactly of dashing appearance.

GARY: I'd say you were full of shit.

QUESTION: Exactly. But that doesn't mean that I didn't, at the time, believe it. Right?

GARY: Yeah, so what?

QUESTION: Well, it's just that we all see the world and the behavior of others in a way that serves our needs at the time. That, however, does not mean that our perspective is correct. It does, however, mean that we are all human and that our perceptions can be wrong. You are not a bad person simply because your perception of the behavior of the girl might be wrong. All of us perceive things in a way that pleases us or excuses our behavior. It's OK to be wrong about these things, but it does take courage to try to see things from another person's perspective.

Gary, of course, did not immediately change his views, but this interchange began a process that, with repeated challenges over time, resulted in him coming to accept that his perceptions were inaccurate and self-serving. Repeatedly pointing out that the processes that govern Gary's behavior are the same as those that govern the behavior of all people, allowed Gary to see that it was not that he was a completely bad person, but that he was primarily a normal person who had committed a bad behavior. This encouraged Gary to have the confidence to distinguish his offensive acts from himself as a whole person, and that made it easier for him to accept that he had made mistakes which he could correct.

Gary also had considerable difficulty accepting that he had caused harm to his victim. It was evident that, for Gary, accepting he had hurt the girl was equivalent to accepting that he was a completely bad person who was irredeemable. This, of course, is not something anyone would readily accept, and it is no surprise that Gary resisted admitting to having harmed the girl. To buttress his claim to not having hurt her, Gary attempted to portray the victim in a bad light. For example, Gary claimed she was a thief and a liar, a school truant, and an underachiever at school. Once she became a teenager, Gary said, the girl's school grades dropped, she began skipping school and lying to her mother about where she had been, and she began to steal money from home.

> QUESTION: Gary, you say the victim began to do these things when she turned 13 years old. Was she all right before that? Did she steal, lie, skip school, or get bad grades when she was younger?
>
> GARY: No. In fact, she was a good girl before she started hanging out with the wrong crowd. I think her friends told her to report me and they helped her make up all the stories about what I did.
>
> QUESTION: But Gary, the changes in behavior you have just described are just the sort of problems that children who are being sexually molested show at exactly that age. What do you think of that?
>
> *(Gary appeared confused over this suggestion and said nothing.)*
>
> QUESTION: Perhaps you might want to think about this until the next session. Here is a little book[2] that might help you see what happens to kids when they are abused. Remember what we talked about before about how people's perceptions, all people that is, are affected by their needs, particularly their need to see themselves as good people? Remember, good people can do bad things. You are not a bad person for hurting the girl because I am sure you didn't mean to, but I think you did hurt her just the same.

Again, this did not eliminate Gary's resistance to the idea that he had caused harm to his victim, but it did begin a process that, over several sessions, led him to accept that he had.

As noted, Gary's relationship with the girl's mother waxed and waned. He reported several previous relationships with women (fortunately, none of whom had young children), all of which had ended either by the woman's infidelity or by her telling him to leave. We asked Gary to describe his relationship with the girl's mother.

> GARY: Well, I was always doing things for her, but she didn't appreciate it.
>
> QUESTION: What sort of things?
>
> GARY: Well, I would always make supper, and I would do the week's shopping on Saturday.
>
> QUESTION: Did your partner not like cooking or shopping?
>
> GARY: Oh yeah, but I insisted on doing them.
>
> QUESTION: Why?
>
> GARY: I wanted to please her.
>
> QUESTION: That's nice, but did she ever complain about it?
>
> GARY: Oh yeah. She often got pissed off that I had cooked things she didn't like.
>
> QUESTION: Then why didn't you let her cook the meals herself at least some of the time?
>
> GARY: I don't know. I guess I wanted her to know that I could look after her.

QUESTION: Were there other things you did that she would liked to have done?

GARY: Well, I always put (the victim) to bed and read her a story. And I took her to school.

QUESTION: Do you think maybe her mother might have liked to do those things?

GARY: Sure. In fact, she seemed to resent it. She once said I was getting between her and her daughter. I can't help it if the girl preferred me.

It was clear from Gary's responses to these and other questions that he took over, against his partner's evident wishes, many of the tasks she wanted to at least share. It was also clear that Gary resented her objections and saw her as ungrateful. He obviously ignored her wishes, and it is little wonder she eventually asked him to leave, even before her daughter reported the abuse. Gary's description of his previous relationships revealed the same pattern of behavior, with his taking arbitrary control of so many functions that his partners, not surprisingly, felt angry toward him. Gary, however, saw himself as a self-sacrificing person that any woman should be grateful to have as a partner. He eventually came to see how it was his "self-sacrificing" behavior that drove women away, and he had to learn a whole new approach to relationships.

Figure 6.1 provides a brief description of Gary's offense cycle. The offense cycle Gary finally produced was more detailed than this, but the Figure captures the essential features. The critical element that is missing, but that Gary included in his final version, is the self-narrative Gary typically engaged in during this process. This narrative essentially involved Gary telling himself that what he was doing was only play, that the girl liked it, that when she asked him to desist it was only what she thought she should say, and that she really desired him sexually.

In response to this offense cycle, Gary generated a set of relapse prevention plans that were aimed at avoiding future risks and in dealing with problems that might arise in the future. Figure 6.2 illustrates some of these plans, and it can be seen that for each problem, Gary generated several responses, some of which were fall-backs if the initial tactic failed. Again, this is a briefer version of Gary's more elaborate relapse prevention plans.

Summary

Child molestation is a serious social problem affecting the lives of many innocent children. Part of an appropriate response has been the development of comprehensive assessment and treatment programs for these offenders in an attempt to ensure that they do not reoffend against more innocent children.

Research over the past 20 years, in particular, has not only revealed the considerable extent and intrusive nature of child molestation, it has also identified characteristics of the offenders that permit both comprehensive assessments and

FIGURE 6.1 Gary's Offense Cycle

Background Factors
1. Poor relationship style:
   a. Takes over too many activities
   b. Doesn't share his feelings
   c. Doesn't listen to or respond to partner's complaints
   d. Is terrified of being alone so rushes into relationships

2. Low self-esteem:
   a. Feels rejected by others
   b. Feels taken advantage of by others
   c. Feels other adults find him sexually unattractive
   d. Feels he is a bad person
   e. Says negative things to himself
   f. Denigrates himself to others

3. Abuses alcohol/drugs:
   a. To make himself feel better
   b. To avoid dealing with problems
   c. To give himself the courage to offend

Steps to Offending

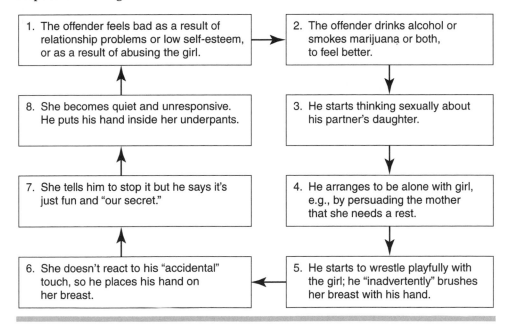

FIGURE 6.2   Gary's Relapse Prevention Plans

1. Poor relationships:
   a. Take time forming a relationship.
   b. Don't enter a live-in relationship until sure of compatibility.
   c. Share feelings and concerns and listen to partner.
   d. Share household chores.
   e. Do not try to take control.
   f. Attend marital counseling.

2. Low self-esteem:
   a. Repeat good qualities to self several times each day.
   b. When feeling low, talk to friends or do something enjoyable.
   c. Avoid trying to win friends by buying them things or by excessively doing things
      for them.
   d. Accept positive feedback from others.

3. Alcohol/drug abuse:
   a. Attend AA regularly.
   b. When urge is strong, talk to support group.
   c. If urge becomes overwhelming, admit self to treatment program.
   d. Arrange to have parole officer administer random drug and alcohol testing.

4. Being with children:
   a. Avoid relationships with women who have young children.
   b. Never be alone with young children.
   c. Escape from situation if inadvertently alone with a child.

5. Sexual attraction to a child:
   a. Use techniques learned in treatment to control fantasies.
   b. Attend treatment upon release.
   c. Report deviant urges to therapist.

treatment. We now know that females and juveniles also molest children, and that
all these offenders share a number of characteristics in common. At the same time,
however, we have learned that child molesters are more like other people than
they are different. No doubt continuing research efforts will reveal more precisely
the nature of those characteristics that distinguish child molesters, as well as additional features that need to be addressed.

Assessment procedures not only tell us what are the specific problems of an
individual offender that need to be addressed in treatment, they also indicate his
or her risk to reoffend. An estimate of an individual's risk to reoffend may direct
treatment, and may assist the courts and parole boards in their decisions about what
to do with a convicted offender. Treatment appears to reduce reoffending and, as
a result, can save some potential victims from suffering and can save society significant sums of money that would otherwise be spent on prosecuting and incar-
cerating the offenders and treating the victims. We look forward to the continued
development of effective treatment and assessment programs for child molesters.

NOTES

1. All questions were asked in the group context and may have been from either one of the therapists (a male and a female) or from one of the other offenders.

2. We provide various books to our clients that illustrate, from the victim's point of view, the harmful effects of sexual abuse. In this case, we gave Gary a book by Woods (1992).

REFERENCES

Abel, G. G. & Becker, J. V. (1985). *Sexual Interest Cardsort.* Atlanta: Behavioral Medicine Laboratory, Emory University.

Abel, G. G., Becker, J. V., & Cunningham-Rathner, J. (1984). Complications, consent, and cognitions in sex between children and adults. *International Journal of Law and Psychiatry, 7,* 89–103.

Abel, G. G., Becker, J. V., Cunningham-Rathner, J., Mittelman, M. S., & Rouleau, J. L. (1988). Multiple paraphilic diagnoses among sex offenders. *Bulletin of the American Academy of Psychiatry and the Law, 16,* 153–168.

Abel, G. G. & Blanchard, E. B. (1974). The role of fantasy in the treatment of sexual deviation. *Archives of General Psychiatry, 30,* 467–475.

Abel, G. G., Gore, D. K., Holland, C. L., Camp, N., Becker, J. V., & Rathner, J. (1989). The measurement of cognitive distortions of child molesters. *Annals of Sex Research, 2,* 135–152.

Abel, G. G., Osborn, C. A., & Twigg, D. A. (1993). Sexual assault through the lifespan: Adult offenders with juvenile histories. In H. E. Barbaree, W. L. Marshall, & S. M. Hudson (Eds.), *The Juvenile Sex Offender* (pp. 104–117). New York: Guilford.

American Psychiatric Association. (1994). *Diagnostic and Statistical Manual of Mental Disorders* (4th ed.). Washington, DC: Author.

Barbaree, H. E. & Marshall, W. L. (1989). Erectile responses amongst heterosexual child molesters, father-daughter incest offenders, and matched nonoffenders: Five distinct age preference profiles. *Canadian Journal of Behavioural Science, 21,* 70–82.

Barbaree, H. E., Marshall, W. L., & Hudson, S. M. (Eds.). (1993). *The Juvenile Sex Offender.* New York: Guilford.

Barbaree, H. E. & Peacock, E. J. (1995). Phallometric assessment of sexual preferences as an investigative tool in cases of alleged child sexual abuse. In T. Ney (Ed.), *Allegations of Child Sexual Abuse: Assessment and Case Management* (pp. 242–259). New York: Brunner/Mazel.

Barnard, G. W., Fuller, A. K., Robbins, L., & Shaw, T. (1989). *The Child Molester: An Integrated Approach to Evaluation and Treatment.* New York: Brunner/Mazel.

Bradford, J. M. W. (1990). The antiandrogen and hormonal treatment of sex offenders. In W. L. Marshall, D. R. Laws, & H. E. Barbaree (Eds.), *Handbook of Sexual Assault: Issues, Theories, and Treatment of the Offender* (pp. 297–310). New York: Plenum.

Bradford, J. M. W. & Pawlak, A. (1993). Double-blind placebo crossover study of cyproterone acetate in the treatment of the paraphilias. *Archives of Sexual Behavior, 22,* 383–402.

Bumby, K. M. (1996). Assessing the cognitive distortions of child molesters and rapists: Development and validation of the MOLEST and RAPE scales. *Sexual Abuse: A Journal of Research and Treatment, 8,* 37–54.

Bumby, K. M., Langton, C., & Marshall, W. L. (1997). *Shame and Guilt in Sex Offenders.* Submitted for publication.

Check, V. J. (1984). *The Hostility Toward Women Scale.* Unpublished doctoral dissertation, University of Manitoba, Winnipeg.

Cohen, M., Seghorn, T., & Calmus, W. (1969). Sociometric study of the sex offender. *Journal of Abnormal Psychology, 74,* 249–255.

Committee on Sexual Offenses Against Children and Youths. (1984). *Report on the Committee on Sexual Offenses Against Children and Youths, Vol. 1-11, and Summary* (Badgley Report, Cat. No. Vol. 1-11: J2-50/1984/E; Summary: H74-13/1984-1E). Ottawa: Department of Health and Welfare.

Crawford, D. A. & Allen, J. V. (1979). A social skills training programme with sex offenders. In M. Cook & G. Wilson (Eds.), *Love and Attraction* (pp. 527–536). New York: Pergamon.

Davis, G. E. & Leitenberg, H. (1987). Adolescent sex offenders. *Psychological Bulletin, 101,* 417–427.

Dhawan, S. & Marshall, W. L. (1996). Sexual abuse histories of sexual offenders. *Sexual Abuse: A Journal of Research and Treatment, 8,* 7–15.

Federoff, J. P. (1993). Serotonic drug treatment of deviant sexual interests. *Annals of Sex Research* 6, 105–121.

Fernandez, Y. M., Marshall, W. L., Lightbody, S., & O'Sullivan, C. (1997). *The Child Molester Empathy Measure.* Submitted for publication.

Finkelhor, D. (1979). *Sexually Victimized Children.* New York: Free Press.

Finkelhor, D. & Lewis, I. (1988). An epidemiologic approach to the study of child molestation. *The Annals of the New York Academy of Science,* 528, 64–67.

Finkelhor, D. & Russell, D. H. (1984). Women as perpetrators. In D. Finkelhor (Ed.), *Child Sexual Abuse: New Theory and Research* (pp. 98–115). New York: Free Press.

Flannery, R. B. & Wieman, D. (1989). Social support, life stress, and psychological distress: An empirical assessment. *Journal of Clinical Psychology,* 45, 867–872.

Frenzel, R. R. & Lang, R. A. (1989). Identifying sexual preferences in intrafamilial and extrafamilial child sexual abusers. *Annals of Sex Research,* 2, 255–275.

Freund, K. (1981). Assessment of pedophilia. In M. Cook & K. Howells (Eds.), *Adult Sexual Interest in Children* (pp. 139–179). London: Academic.

Freund, K., Watson, R. J., & Dickey, R. (1991). Sex offenses against female children perpetrated by men who are not pedophiles. *Journal of Sex Research,* 28, 409–423.

Garlick, Y., Marshall, W. L., & Thornton, D. (1996). Intimacy deficits and attribution of blame among sexual offenders. *Legal and Criminological Psychology,* 1, 251–258.

Graham, J. R. (1993). *MMPI-2: Assessing Personality and Psychopathology.* New York: Oxford University Press.

Green, R. (1995). Psycho-educational modules. In B. K. Schwartz & H. R. Cellini (Eds.), *The Sex Offender: Corrections, Treatment and Legal Practice* (pp. 13.1–13.10). Kingston, NJ: Civic Research Institute.

Hall, R. L. (1989). Self-efficacy ratings. In D. R. Laws (Ed.), *Relapse Prevention with Sex Offenders* (pp. 137–146). New York: Guilford.

Hanson, R. K. (1997). Invoking sympathy: Assessment and treatment of empathy deficits among sexual offenders. In B. K. Schwartz & H. R. Cellini (Eds.), *The Sex Offender: New Insights, Treatment Innovations and Legal Developments* (Vol. 11, pp. 1:1–1:12). Kingston, NJ: Civic Research Insititute.

Hanson, R. K. & Bussière, M. (1997). *Predictors of Sex Offender Recidivism: A Meta-Analysis.* Report to the Solicitor General of Canada, Ottawa.

Hanson, R. K., Gizzarelli, R., & Scott, H. (1994). The attitudes of incest offenders: Sexual entitlement and acceptance of sex with children. *Criminal Justice and Behavior,* 21, 187–202.

Hanson, R. K. & Slater, S. (1988). Sexual victimization in the history of child sexual abusers: A review. *Annals of Sex Research,* 1, 485–499.

Hare, R. D. (1991). *Manual for the Revised Psychopathology Checklist.* Toronto: Multi-Health Systems.

Harrison, H. (1993). Female abusers: What children and young people have told Childline. In M. Elliott (Ed.), *Female Sexual Abuse of Children* (pp. 89–92). New York: Guilford.

Haugaard, J. J. (1987). *The Consequences of Child Sexual Abuse: A College Survey.* Unpublished manuscript, University of Virginia, Charlottesville.

Haugaard, J. J. & Emery, R. E. (1989). Methodological issues in child sexual abuse research. *Child Abuse and Neglect,* 13, 89–100.

Hildebran, D. & Pithers, W. D. (1989). Enhancing offender empathy for sexual-abuse victims. In D. R. Laws (Ed.), *Relapse Prevention with Sex Offenders* (pp. 236–243). New York: Guilford.

Horley, J. (1988). Cognitions of child sexual abusers. *Journal of Sex Research,* 25, 542–545.

Horley, J. & Quinsey, V. L. (1995). Child molesters' construal of themselves, other adults, and children. *Journal of Constructivist Psychology,* 8, 193–211.

Howells, K. (1978). Some meanings of children for pedophiles. In M. Cook & G. Wilson (Eds.), *Love and Attraction* (pp. 57–82). London: Pergamon.

Hucker, S. J. & Bain, J. (1990). Androgenic hormones and sexual assault. In W. L. Marshall, D. R. Laws, & H. E. Barbaree (Eds.), *Handbook of Sexual Assault: Issues, Theories and Treatment of the Offender* (pp. 93–102). New York: Plenum.

Kanner, A. D., Coyne, J. C., Schafer, C., & Lazarus, R. S. (1981). Comparison of two modes of stress management: Daily hassles and uplifts versus major life events. *Journal of Behavioral Medicine,* 4, 1–39.

Kear-Colwell, J. & Pollock, P. (1997). Motivation or confrontation: Which approach to the child sex offender. *Criminal Justice and Behavior,* 24, 20–33.

Knopp, F. A. (1986). Introduction. In E. Porter (Ed.), *Treating the Young Male Victim of Sexual*

Assault (pp. 1–4). Brandon, VT: Safer Society Press.

Knopp, F. H., Freeman-Longo, R. E., & Stevenson, W. (1992). *Nationwide Survey of Juvenile and Adult Sex-Offender Treatment Programs.* Orwell, VT: Safer Society Press.

Lalumière, M. L. & Quinsey, V. L. (1991). Polygraph testing of child molesters: Are we ready? *Violence Update, 1,* 3–11.

Lang, R. A., Black, E. L., Frenzel, R. R., & Checkley, K. L. (1988). Aggression and erotic attraction toward children in incestuous and pedophilic men. *Annals of Sex Research, 1,* 417–441.

Langevin, R. (1983). *Sexual Strands: Understanding and Treating Sexual Anomalies in Men.* Hillsdale, NJ: Erlbaum.

Langevin, R. (1990). Sexual anomalies and the brain. In W. L. Marshall, D. R. Laws, & H. E. Barbaree (Eds.), *Handbook of Sexual Assault: Issues, Theories, and Treatment of the Offender* (pp. 103–113). New York: Plenum.

Langevin, R. (1991). A note on the problem of response set in measuring cognitive distortions. *Annals of Sex Research, 4,* 287–292.

Langevin, R. & Lang, R. A. (1990). Substance abuse among sex offenders. *Annals of Sex Research, 3,* 397–424.

Langton, C. & Marshall, W. L. (1997). *Cognitive Distortions in Sexual Offenders.* Unpublished manuscript, Queen's University, Kingston, Ontario, Canada.

Laws, D. R. & Marshall, W. L. (1991). Masturbatory reconditioning: An evaluative review. *Advances in Behaviour Research and Therapy, 13,* 13–25.

Lawson, J. S., Marshall, W. L., & McGrath, P. (1979). The Social Self-Esteem Inventory. *Educational and Psychological Measurement, 39,* 803–811.

Levin, S. M. & Stava, L. (1987). Personality characteristics of sex offenders: A review. *Archives of Sexual Behavior, 16,* 57–79.

MacDonald, R. K. & Pithers, W. D. (1989). Self-monitoring to identify high-risk situations. In D. R. Laws (Ed.), *Relapse Prevention with Sex Offenders* (pp. 96–104). New York: Guilford.

Maletzky, B. M. (1991). *Treating the Sexual Offender.* Newbury Park, CA: Sage.

Marshall, W. L. (1989). Invited essay: Intimacy, loneliness and sexual offenders. *Behaviour Research and Therapy, 27,* 491–503.

Marshall, W. L. (1992). The social value of treatment with sexual offenders. *Canadian Journal of Human Sexuality, 1,* 109–114.

Marshall, W. L. (1993). The treatment of sex offenders: What does the outcome data tell us? A reply to Quinsey et al. *Journal of Interpersonal Violence, 8,* 524–530.

Marshall, W. L. (1996a). Psychological evaluation in sexual offence cases. *Queen's Law Journal, 21,* 499–514.

Marshall, W. L. (1996b). The sexual offender: Monster, victim, or everyman? *Sexual Abuse: A Journal of Research and Treatment, 8,* 317–335.

Marshall, W. L. (1997). Pedophilia: Psychopathology and theory. In D. R. Laws & W. O'Donohue (Eds.), *Handbook of Sexual Deviance: Theory and Application* (pp. 152–174). New York: Guilford.

Marshall, W. L., Anderson, D., & Champagne, F. (1996). The importance of self-esteem in sexual offenders. *Psychology, Crime and Law, 3,* 81–106.

Marshall, W. L. & Barbaree, H. E. (1990). An integrated theory of sexual offending. In W. L. Marshall, D. R. Laws, & H. E. Barbaree (Eds.), *Handbook of Sexual Assault: Issues, Theories, and Treatment of the Offender* (pp. 257–275). New York: Plenum.

Marshall, W. L., Barbaree, H. E., & Christophe, D. (1986). Sexual offenders against female children: Sexual preferences for age of victims and type of behaviour. *Canadian Journal of Behavioural Science, 18,* 424–439.

Marshall, W. L., Barbaree, H. E., & Eccles, A. (1991). Early onset and deviant sexuality in child molesters. *Journal of Interpersonal Violence, 6,* 323–336.

Marshall, W. L., Barbaree, H. E., & Fernandez, Y. M. (1995). Some aspects of social competence in sexual offenders. *Sexual Abuse: A Journal of Research and Treatment, 7,* 113–127.

Marshall, W. L., Bryce, P., Hudson, S. M., Ward, T., & Moth, B. (1996). The enhancement of intimacy and the reduction of loneliness among child molesters. *Journal of Family Violence, 11,* 219–235.

Marshall, W. L. & Christie, M. M. (1981). Pedophilia and aggression. *Criminal Justice and Behavior, 8,* 145–158.

Marshall, W. L., Fernandez, Y. M., Hudson, S. M., & Ward, T. (Eds.). (1998). *Sourcebook of Treatment Programs for Sexual Offenders.* New York: Plenum.

Marshall, W. L. & Hall, G. C. N. (1995). The value of the MMPI in deciding forensic issues in accused sexual offenders. *Sexual Abuse: A Journal of Research and Treatment, 7,* 205–219.

Marshall, W. L., Hudson, S. M., Jones, R., & Fernandez, Y. M. (1995). Empathy in sex offenders. *Clinical Psychology Review, 15,* 99–113.

Marshall, W. L. & Pithers, W. D. (1994). A reconsideration of treatment outcome with sex offenders. *Criminal Justice and Behavior, 21,* 10–27.

McConaghy, N. (1993). *Sexual behavior: Problems and Management.* New York: Plenum.

McFall, R. M. (1990). The enhancement of social skills: An information-processing analysis. In W. L. Marshall, D. R. Laws, & H. E. Barbaree (Eds.), *Handbook of Sexual Assault: Issues, Theories, and Treatment of the Offender* (pp. 311–330). New York: Plenum.

McGuire, R. J., Carlisle, J. M., & Young, B. G. (1965). Sexual deviations as conditioned behavior: A hypothesis. *Behaviour Research and Therapy, 2,* 185–190.

Miller, R. S. & Lefcourt, H. M. (1982). The assessment of social intimacy. *Journal of Personality Assessment, 46,* 514–518.

Miller, W. R. & Rollnick, S. (1991). *Motivational Interviewing: Preparing People to Change Addictive Behavior.* New York: Guilford.

Miner, M. H., Day, D. M., & Nafpaktitis, M. K. (1989). Assessment of coping skills: Development of a situational competency test. In D. R. Laws (Ed.), *Relapse Prevention with Sex Offenders* (pp. 127–136). New York: Guilford.

Mohr, J. W., Turner, R. E., & Jerry, M. B. (1964). *Pedophilia and Exhibitionism.* Toronto: University of Toronto Press.

Moos, R. & Moos, B. S. (1986). *Family Environment Scale Manual.* Palo Alto, CA: Consulting Psychologists.

Murphy, W. D. & Barbaree, H. E. (1994). *Assessments of Sex Offenders by Measures of Erectile Response: Psychometric Properties and Decision Making.* Brandon, VT: The Safer Society Press.

Nichols, H. R. & Molinder, I. (1984). *Multiphasic Sex Inventory Manual.* Tacoma, WA: Nichols & Molinder.

Pithers, W. D. (1990). Relapse prevention with sexual aggressors: A method for maintaining therapeutic gain and enhancing external supervision. In W. L. Marshall, D. R. Laws, & H. E. Barbaree (Eds.), *Handbook of Sexual Assault: Issues, Theories, and Treatment of the Offender* (pp. 343–361). New York: Plenum.

Pithers, W. D., Beal, L. S., Armstrong, J., & Petty, J. (1989). Identification of risk factors through clinical interviews and analysis of records. In D. R. Laws (Ed.), *Relapse Prevention with Sex Offenders* (pp. 77–87). New York: Guilford.

Prentky, R. A. & Burgess, A. W. (1991). Rehabilitation of child molesters: A cost-benefit analysis. *American Journal of Orthopsychiatry, 60,* 108–117.

Prentky, R. A. & Knight, R. A. (1986). Impulsivity in the lifestyle and criminal behavior of sexual offenders. *Criminal Justice and Behavior, 13,* 141–164.

Quinsey, V. L. & Chaplin, T. C. (1988). Penile responses of child molesters and normals to descriptions of encounters with children involving sex and violence. *Journal of Interpersonal Violence, 3,* 259–274.

Quinsey, V. L., Chaplin, T. C., & Carrigan, W. F. (1979). Sexual preferences among incestuous and nonincestuous child molesters. *Behavior Therapy, 10,* 562–565.

Quinsey, V. L. & Earls, C. M. (1990). The modification of sexual preferences. In W. L. Marshall, D. R. Laws, & H. E. Barbaree (Eds.), *Handbook of Sexual Assault: Issues, Theories, and Treatment of the Offender* (pp. 279–295). New York: Plenum.

Quinsey, V. L., Harris, G. T., & Rice, M. E. (1995). Actuarial prediction of sexual recidivism. *Journal of Interpersonal Violence, 10,* 85–105.

Quinsey, V. L., Harris, G. T., Rice, M. E., & Lalumière, M. L. (1993). Assessing treatment efficacy in outcome studies of sex offenders. *Journal of Interpersonal Violence, 8,* 512–523.

Quinsey, V. L., Lalumière, M. L., Rice, M. E., & Harris, G. T. (1995). Predicting sexual offenses. In J. C. Campbell (Ed.), *Assessing Dangerousness: Violence by Sexual Offenders, Batterers, and Child Abusers* (pp. 114–137). Thousand Oaks, CA: Sage.

Rathus, S. A. (1973). A 30-item schedule for assessing assertive behaviour. *Behavior Therapy, 4,* 398–406.

Reed, R. S. & Kenning, M. K. (1987, July). *The Prevalence of Child Sexual Abuse among a Midwestern College Population.* Paper presented at the Third Annual Symposium on Family Violence. Durham, NH.

Risin, L. I. & Koss, M. P. (1987). The sexual abuse of boys: Prevalence and descriptive characteristics of childhood victimizations. *Journal of Interpersonal Violence, 2,* 309–323.

Roberts, R. E., Abrams, L., & Finch, J. R. (1973). Delinquent sexual behavior among adolescents. *Medical Aspects of Human Sexuality, 7,* 162–183.

Russell, D. E. H. (1984). *Sexual Exploitation: Rape, Child Sexual Abuse, and Workplace Harassment.* Newbury Park, CA: Sage.

Russell, D., Peplau, L. A., & Cutrona, C. A., (1980). The Revised UCLA Loneliness Scale. *Journal of Personality and Social Psychology, 39,* 472–480.

Salter, A. C. (1992). Epidemiology of child sexual abuse. In W. O'Donohue & J. H. Gear (Eds.), *Sexual Abuse of Children: Theory and Research* (Vol. 1, pp. 108–138). Hillside, NJ: Erlbaum.

Schwartz, B. K. & Ceiling, H. R. (Eds.). (1997). *The Sex Offender: New Insights, Treatment Innovations and Legal Developments* (Vol. 11). Kingston, NJ: Civic Research Institute.

Segal, Z. V. & Marshall, W. L. (1985). Heterosexual social skills in a population of rapists and child molesters. *Journal of Consulting and Clinical Psychology, 53,* 55–63.

Seidman, B. T., Marshall, W. L., Hudson, S. M., & Robertson, P. J. (1994). An examination of intimacy and loneliness in sex offenders. *Journal of Interpersonal Violence, 9,* 518–534.

Selzer, M. L. (1971). The Michigan Alcoholism Screening Test: The quest for a new diagnostic instrument. *American Journal of Psychiatry, 127,* 1653–1658.

Serin, R. C., Malcolm, P. B., Khanna, A., & Barbaree, H. E. (1994). Psychopathy and deviant sexual arousal in incarcerated sexual offenders. *Journal of Interpersonal Violence, 9,* 3–11.

Skinner, A. H. (1982). The Drug Abuse Screening Test. *Addictive Behaviors, 7,* 363–371.

Speilberger, C. D. (1988). *State-Trait Anger Expression Inventory: Professional Manual, Research Edition.* Odessa, FL: Psychological Assessment Resources.

Stermac, L. E., Segal, Z. V., & Gillis, R. (1990). Social and cultural factors in sexual assault. In W. L. Marshall, D. R. Laws, & H. E. Barbaree (Eds.), *Handbook of Sexual Assault: Issues, Theories, and Treatment of the Offender* (pp. 143–159). New York: Plenum.

Ward, T., Hudson, S. M., & Marshall, W. L. (1995). Cognitive distortions and affective deficits in sex offenders: A cognitive deconstructionist interpretation. *Sexual Abuse: A Journal of Research and Treatment, 7,* 67–83.

Watson, D. & Friend, R. (1969). Measurement of social evaluative anxiety. *Journal of Consulting and Clinical Psychology, 33,* 448–457.

Williams, L. M. & Finkelhor, D. (1990). The characteristics of incestuous fathers: A review of recent studies. In W. L. Marshall, D. R. Laws, & H. E. Barbaree (Eds.), *Handbook of Sexual Assault: Issues, Theories, and Treatment of the Offender* (pp. 143–159). New York: Plenum.

Woods, G. (Ed.). (1992). *Voices: A Collection of Writings by Survivors of Sexual Abuse.* Belleville, Ontario: Community Mental Health Programs of Hastings and Prince Edward Counties.

Wormith, J. S. & Hanson, R. K. (1992). The treatment of sexual offenders in Canada: An update. *Canadian Psychology, 33,* 180–198.

Wyatt, G. E. (1985). The sexual abuse of Afro-American and White-American women in childhood. *Child Abuse and Neglect, 9,* 507–519.

7

Incest

KATHRYN KUEHNLE
University of South Florida

MICHAEL GAMACHE
University of South Florida

MARTHA COULTER
University of South Florida

Case Illustrations: Types of Incest

Role Distortion

When she was 5 years old, following the death of her mother, Brandi began to sleep with her father. She was 6 years old when her father began to teach her how to stroke his genitals. Over the course of her childhood, Brandi was used as her mother's replacement, and the sexual abuse progressed to intercourse. Brandi cooked for her father and kept house. At age 12, she was driving the family car to the grocery store to shop. She kept herself at a distance from any potential female or male friends. While living with her father, she never disclosed her sexual abuse to anyone. Brandi ran away when she was 14 years old, following the remarriage of her father. Brandi now resides in a foster home with eight other adolescents.

Sibling Abuse

Donesha's parents worked long hours at their family grocery store and left their children at home to care for themselves. Donesha was 7 years old when her oldest brother, who was five years her senior, raped her in the basement of their home while two of his friends watched. Over the course of her childhood, her oldest brother frequently engaged her in sexual activity and taught his younger brother to have sex with Donesha. Donesha was impregnated by her youngest brother when he was 17 years and she was 13 years old. The fetus was aborted. Donesha's father and mother were aware that their son was the father of the baby, and that both of their sons were sexually involved with their daughter. However, the parents did nothing to protect their daughter from the sexual abuse prior to or following the abortion. When Donesha was 15 years old, she was again impregnated by her brother and gave birth to a male child who was placed for adoption.

Intergenerational Abuse

Emily's stepfather repeatedly engaged her in fellatio from the first year he moved in with Emily's mother. The sexual abuse occurred from the time that Emily was age 10 years until Emily was 15 years old. At age 15 years, Emily threatened her step-father that if he continued to abuse her she would reveal the sexual abuse. Subsequently, the abuse terminated. Emily grew up believing that her stepfather's sexual impulses were confined to her, until her 9-year-old daughter disclosed that her step-grandfather had made her perform fellatio.

Description of the Problem

Disciplinary Definition

Child sexual abuse is one of four categories of child maltreatment, and may include incest, sexual assault by a relative or stranger, fondling of genital areas, exposure to indecent acts, sexual rituals, or involvement in child pornography (National Research Council, 1992). The previously described cases reflect the many different ways in which incest can occur. Incest refers to sexual abuse that is per-petrated by family members, such as the biological father who sexually abused Brandi, or the biological brothers who sexually abused Donesha, in the preceding examples.

The meaning of the word *incest* can be confusing because it is shared by anthropologists and child sexual abuse researchers who utilize different defini-tions of this word (Finkelhor, 1984). Anthropologists use the term *incest* to include violation of marriage rules between blood relatives, regardless of age, and are pri-marily concerned with the meaning of marriage and sexual intercourse among blood kin. An anthropological definition of incest is adopted in common law, which defines incest as a crime involving "sexual intercourse or cohabitation between a man and woman who are related to each other within the degrees [of family relation] wherein marriage is prohibited" (Black, 1979, p. 685).

In contrast to the focus of anthropologists, sexual abuse researchers are inter-ested in explaining deviant sexual behavior between adults and dependent chil-dren within families whose members may be related by blood or social contract (e.g., marriage, cohabitation). Unlike anthropologists, sexual abuse researchers have little interest in consentive intercourse that occurs between adults related by blood (Finkelhor, 1986). As a result, in order to clarify definitions within the psy-chological literature, the term *intrafamilial sexual abuse* is now used interchangeably with the term *incest*. The terms *intrafamilial sexual abuse* and *incest* are defined by sexual abuse researchers as "sexual acts, which may or may not include intercourse, between members of a family other than a husband and wife" (Becker, 1994, p. 176). In this chapter, the term *incest* will be consistent with the definition used by child sexual abuse researchers.

Definitions Found in State Statutes

Every state has statutes that define children as incapable of providing informed consent to sexual interactions perpetrated by adult family or nonfamily members. Illegal sexual interactions, for which children do not have the maturity to provide consent, include activities of contact and noncontact, such as fondling, oral sex, intercourse, and involvement in pornography.

State courts have two major divisions in which a sexually abused child may be involved: the criminal justice system and the civil justice system, including family juvenile courts. With respect to states' legal definitions of sexual abuse, there are three different functions for which child sexual abuse is typically defined: (1) criminal prosecution; (2) determination of dependency based on abuse or neglect; and (3) identification of cases that professionals are required to report to state authorities. Whether the child victim's abuse was incestuous is paramount in juvenile and family courts where a judge will determine if it is safe to leave the child within his or her parents' care.

Regarding criminal prosecution and mandated reporting of children suspected to be sexually abused, some states do not legally distinguish, by definition, sexual abuse that occurs inside from sexual abuse that occurs outside of the family unit. For example, when the victim is a young child, child sexual abuse may be criminally prosecuted under sexual battery statutes that define sexual abuse by the sexual acts, with the identity of the perpetrator and the perpetrator's relationship with the child perhaps only relevant during the sentencing phase. If the child's sexual abuse is perpetrated by a blood relative, in many states, the perpetrator may be charged with several crimes. For example, a perpetrator could be charged with sexual battery (e.g., oral, vaginal, or anal penetration on a child by a person over the age of 18 years) and incest (e.g., penetration of the child's vagina by her biological father's penis).

Assigning Responsibility

Our society holds there are a number of inaccurate beliefs about child sexual abuse. These inaccurate beliefs include misconceptions about what causes an individual to sexually abuse a child, the victim's responsibility for the sexual abuse, and the mother's collusion with the perpetrator in the sexual abuse of her children. A child sex offender may blame his sexual involvement with a child on the child's seductiveness, his wife's emotional distance, the effect of alcohol and drugs, or the stress of poverty. While incest often occurs in the presence of multiple problems within a family or social environment, such as substance abuse and poverty, none of these elements are ever considered to be the cause of offenders' sexual activity with children.

While perpetrators may blame their victims for their sexual relationship, stating that the child seduced them or did not tell them to stop, all states identify young children as incompetent to consent to sexual activity with adults. The majority of states identify age 18 as the age of consent to have sex with an adult (Myers, 1997).

Perpetrators are not helpless victims of seductive children; rather, most offenders who sexually abuse children plan their abuse by grooming their victims (Salter, 1995). *Grooming* is the gradual movement from inappropriate minor touching to more serious abuse, such as intercourse. In one study, approximately three quarters of incestuous fathers believed that building a relationship of trust with their intended child victim decreased their chances of exposure (Warner-Kearney, 1987).

Many children who are victims of sexual abuse have specific personality characteristics and/or family risk factors that make them vulnerable to the manipulations of sex offenders. Children who are socially isolated, have few friends, and are in need of affection, approval, and attention, are at increased risk for sexual abuse (Berliner & Conte, 1990; Finkelhor, 1984).

Children living in families characterized by poor family relationships and unavailable parents are also at increased risk for sexual victimization (Paveza, 1988; Sirles & Franke, 1989). For example, living with a father who holds rigid beliefs about the subordination of women or within a home that is absent a biological father increases risk. Moreover, risk increases when a daughter lives with a mother who is emotionally unavailable or chronically ill. One of the strongest risk factors for girls is the temporary or permanent separation from their mother at some time during their development (Finkelhor, 1984).

Children who are emotionally needy and do not have an available nurturing mother and father may be more susceptible to the manipulations of sexual predators who are quick to spot the vulnerabilities of these children (Salter, 1995). Finkelhor (1984) suggests that a child who is in need of nurturing, affection, and attention may have difficulty discriminating between affection initiated by an adult, and disguised affection culminating in sexual exploitation.

For several decades, mothers were blamed for having knowledge that their children were sexually victimized and failing to intervene. In some cases, mothers received as much or more of the blame for their children's sexual abuse than did the perpetrator. There is little evidence that the majority of mothers residing in incestuous families collude with or protect the perpetrator from discovery. Rather, given the high co-occurrence of child and spouse abuse (see Strauss, Gelles, & Steinmetz, 1980), these mothers also may be victims of the incest offenders.

Salter (1995) proposes that sexual abuse should be conceptualized as a deviant cycle in which there is an interlocking series of thoughts, feelings, and behaviors that culminate in the offender sexually abusing the child. While child victims may initiate sexualized affection and some mothers may be withdrawn, from a policy perspective, the responsibility for the sexual abuse of a child lies within the perpetrator and not within the child, mother, or dysfunctional family dynamics.

Effects of Child Sexual Abuse

Although sexual abuse is perpetrated on children of all ages, there appear to be peaks of greater risk at different stages of development. Rates of child sexual abuse peak at ages 6 to 7 years and 10 to 12 years, with children victimized at more than double the average rate during the preadolescent years (Finkelhor, 1986). Other research indicates an earlier vulnerability, showing the highest risk for sexual abuse of girls to be 3 to 4 years of age (Bronfenbrenner Life Course Center, 1996).

The effects of sexual abuse will depend on a complex matrix of factors including the functioning of the child prior to the abuse (e.g., emotional or behavior problems), the characteristics of the abuse (e.g., noncontact, contact without penetration, contact with violence and penetration), family dynamics (e.g., presence of emotional or physical abuse), the nonoffending caretaker's response to the child's disclosure of abuse (e.g., support, blame, or disbelief), and the child's involvement in the legal system (e.g., removal from the family, testifying against a parent). These variables can be combined in a multitude of ways and interact with a child's personality to create varying long-term psychological outcomes (Friedrich, Urquiza, & Beilke, 1986; Mannarino & Cohen, 1987).

Events of sexual abuse can affect emotional adjustment (e.g., depression, anxiety), behavior (e.g., aggression, withdrawal), interpersonal relationships (e.g., mistrust of people), sexual functioning (e.g., sexual acting out), physical health (e.g., stomachaches, headaches), and cognitive functioning (e.g., concentration problems) (see Kendall-Tackett, Williams, & Finkelhor, 1993). While factors such as family relationships, age, gender, developmental status, and intrinsic strengths and vulnerabilities within the child's personality may influence the impact of the sexual abuse experience, the complex interaction of these factors with abuse is not yet well understood.

Child, Family, and Environment Moderator Variables

Moderator variables are factors that influence the child's long-term outcome. Cicchetti and Rizley (1981) classified these variables as *potentiating factors* (i.e., factors that increase the probability of a negative outcome for the child's long-term development) and *compensatory factors* (i.e., factors that decrease the probability of a negative outcome for the child's long-term development). Both sets of factors are further classified into individual, family, environment, and abuse factors for examining the effect of abuse on the developing child.

Potentiating and compensatory factors include how the child cognitively processes the experience of sexual abuse. Child sexual abuse victims differ in the degree of responsibility they attribute to the perpetrator for the sexual activity and the negative perceptions they have regarding how other people think about them.

The more self-blaming the attributions, and negative the perceptions held by the sexually abused child, the greater the risk for long-term psychological problems (Mannarino, Cohen, & Berman, 1994).

The child's functioning prior to the sexual abuse is also a factor that appears to influence the consequences of the sexual abuse experience. Although research on children's resiliency is not specifically focused on sexually abused children, inferences can be drawn. For example, children who were well adjusted prior to a trauma are better insulated against potentially psychologically damaging events. Children with above-average IQ and positive experiences in school, sports, and artistic endeavors appear to generate feelings of self-esteem and self-efficacy that may act as a protective mechanism (Masten, Best, & Garmezy, 1990; Rutter, 1993; Werner, 1993).

Many children who reside in incestuous families may not have the benefits of these protective mechanisms, because the family environment in which they live is not conducive to the development of above-average IQ, academic excellence, and athletic prowess. Instead, children who live in abusive families are at high risk to develop insecure attachments to their parents, which will greatly influence their cognitive development and social competence (Egeland, Sroufe, & Erickson, 1983; Erickson & Egeland, 1987). Insecurely attached children are more likely than securely attached children to do poorly in school, have deficient problem-solving skills, and demonstrate poor peer relationships, possibly heightening their vulnerability to long-term negative consequences of the sexual abuse experience.

Levels of distress in, and speed of recovery for sexually abused children are related to parental support and maternal disturbance following the child victim's disclosure (Deblinger, McLeer, & Henry, 1990; Runyan, Everson, Edelsohn, Hunter, & Coulter, 1988). Family conflict and lack of parental support are greater predictors of emotional and behavioral problems for sexually abused children than are the specific acts (e.g., fondling, oral sex, intercourse) of the sexual abuse (Finkelhor, 1988; Friedrich et al., 1986). Sexually abused children who have disbelieving parents or parents who blame them for the sexual abuse may feel even greater stigmatization (Finkelhor & Browne, 1985).

Another factor in the sexually abused child's environment that may increase the deleterious effects of the sexual abuse experience is the child's involvement in legal proceedings. Goodman and colleagues (1992) found children involved in court proceedings, compared to those not involved, were slower to recover during the first year following disclosure. Psychological recovery was particularly impeded in children who had to testify on multiple occasions; were afraid of their perpetrators; or testified in a case in which there was no corroborating evidence. Runyan and colleagues (1988) found that children who showed better spontaneous recovery had no involvement in court, or if involved, their testimony was in dependency proceedings.

Epidemiology

Identity of Perpetrators

The majority of child sexual offenders (i.e., 70% to 90%) are known to the child (Finkelhor, 1994). Although the media has provided a great deal of coverage on children who are sexually abused by a father figure, only a small percentage of individuals who sexually abuse children are identified as biological fathers or stepfathers. Gomes-Schwartz, Horowitz, and Cardarelli (1990) found that 19 percent of the children's perpetrators were biological parents, 20 percent were parent figures (i.e., step-, adoptive-, foster-parent, or live-in partner), and 22 percent were relatives. Almost half of the perpetrators lived with their victims. Gomes-Schwartz and her colleagues concluded the physical proximity of the perpetrator and victim play a role in allowing repeated sexual activity to go undiscovered.

In two retrospective studies, when questioned about their sexual abuse experiences when they were children, less than one-fourth of the female adults reported their childhood sexual abuse had been perpetrated by a father figure (Finkelhor, Hotaling, Lewis, & Smith, 1990; Russell, 1983) and none of the adult male respondents reported sexual abuse by a father figure (adult males were not interviewed for the Russell study). Boys are substantially less likely to be victims of incest than girls, with family members composing one-third to one-half of those offenders who sexually abuse girls, and only one-tenth to one-fifth who sexually abuse boys (Finkelhor, 1994).

Unreliable Figures

The true number of children who have been sexually abused is not represented by the number of cases that is reported each year to the various state investigative agencies (Finkelhor & Dziuba-Leatherman, 1994). Professionals debate whether the annual reports made to state authorities underestimate or overestimate the frequency of actual sexual abuse (see Kuehnle, 1996). Because the child victim is typically the only witness, medical evidence is usually absent, and behavioral symptoms can be linked to other causes. Child sexual abuse estimates, based on reports to child protection agencies, have generated the most intense disagreements by professionals and remain the most hotly debated of the child abuse and neglect statistics.

In 1996, the National Committee to Prevent Child Abuse (Lung & Daro, 1997) estimated that there were over 3 million children reported to state child protection services as alleged victims of physical, sexual, and emotional abuse, neglect, and other forms of maltreatment. Approximately 1 million of the 1996 reports were substantiated; 9 percent of the substantiated cases were sexual abuse.

Unsubstantiated cases of abuse include reports that are fabricated (falsely made) or involve insufficient evidence to determine if the report is true or false. Most unsubstantiated cases fall in the latter category. While some research indicates that the rate of false sexual abuse allegations ranges from 5 to 8 percent (see

Barnett, Miller-Perrin, & Perrin, 1996), some authors have argued that this estimate is misleadingly low (Ceci & Bruck, 1995) and a more accurate estimate is 23 to 35 percent (Poole & Lindsay, 1998).

The media coverage of high profile cases involving allegations of incest, such as the Woody Allen case, may create a heightened awareness of the issue of false allegations and a false impression that these cases are even more numerous than even the highest estimates would suggest. Results from several research studies (Elliott & Briere, 1994; Lawson & Chaffin, 1992; Sorenson & Snow, 1991) support the view that national figures, based on reports to state investigative agencies, most likely represent underestimates of true cases of child sexual abuse rather than inflated estimates based on false accusations.

Parents' Influence on Disclosure

There are a number of factors that impact children's disclosures of their participation in events of sexual abuse. One important factor is the child's relationships with his or her parents, especially if the abuse occurs within the child's family.

Some child victims of sexual abuse, when interviewed by child protection investigators, will not disclose their sexual abuse (Lawson & Chaffin, 1992; Sorenson & Snow, 1991). Misguided loyalty, confused morals, or fear of the consequences for themselves and/or the perpetrator are a few of the reasons that children do not reveal their abuse. In one study, the majority of the child sexual abuse victims would not have been identified if not for the presence of a venereal disease (Lawson & Chaffin, 1992).

A child's denial of or refusal to talk about his or her sexual abuse with authorities might lead a mother to conclude that her child was not abused. However, in many cases, the mother's disbelief is the primary source of the child's unwillingness to talk to authorities. Several investigators found that in over 50 percent of the cases in which there was strong evidence of sexual abuse and no disclosure by the child to state investigators, the children had disbelieving mothers (Elliott & Briere, 1994 Lawson & Chaffin, 1992; Sorenson & Snow, 1991).

The perpetrator's relationship with the child also influences whether the child will disclose the sexual abuse. The more closely related the child is to the perpetrator, the less likely is the child to tell anyone about his or her sexual abuse. In one study (Gomes-Schwartz et al., 1990) over one-half of the child victims who were sexually abused by a natural parent revealed their abuse to no one, and 40 percent kept their secret when the perpetrator was a relative.

As the biological connection between the perpetrator and the child victim becomes increasingly distant, the child victim shows a greater willingness to reveal the sexual abuse. For example, Gomes-Schwartz and colleagues (1990) found that when the perpetrator was a step-parent, approximately one-fourth of the children kept their sexual abuse a secret. The immediate reporting of sexual abuse by the child was most frequent when the perpetrator was not a family member and the abuse did not involve intercourse, penetration, or aggression to gain the child's compliance. Children primarily resist disclosing their involvement in sex because of fear that they will lose the affection of the offender, be blamed for the abuse, or be harmed.

Professionals' Failure to Report

Professionals disregard of mandated reporting laws has also added to lower national estimates of abused children. According to the National Incidence Study (Sedlak, 1991), professionals who were legally mandated to report known cases or suspicions of abuse and neglect failed to report approximately 40 percent of the alleged child sexual abuse cases they encountered. Some professionals may disregard mandated reporting laws because they believe the family can resolve their problems without state intervention and that the state investigative process may harm the family. In many cases, this is a naive assumption resulting in the child's continued abuse, especially if the perpetrator is living in the child's home.

Characteristics of the Offender

Adult Perpetrators

Approximately 90 percent of the individuals who molest children are male (Finkelhor, 1984; Finkelhor et al., 1990; Gomes-Schwartz et al., 1990; Russell, 1983). Female perpetrators are more common than previously suspected, although far fewer than male perpetrators (Elliott, 1993; Lawson, 1993). Incestuous female perpetrators may be accomplices to their male mates, or act independently.

Although sex offenders are a heterogeneous group, representing all ethnic, racial, socioeconomic groups, and vocations, perpetrators have several factors in common, such as deviant sexual arousal to children (Laws & Marshall, 1990) and cognitive distortions that allow them to rationalize and defend their sexually deviant behavior (Abel et al., 1989; Hayashino, Wurtele, & Klebe, 1995). Many child sex offenders may show antisocial thinking and engage in nonsexual crimes (Abel, Mittelman, & Becker, 1985; Weinrott & Saylor, 1991; Williams & Finkelhor, 1990). Although incest offenders report engaging in fewer nonsexual crimes (e.g., aggravated assault, use of hard drugs, shoplifting, supplying drugs to minors, spouse abuse) than rapists or extrafamilial offenders, many report participation in these offenses (Weinrott & Saylor, 1991).

Classification systems attempt to create definitive categories, such as extrafamilial, intrafamilial, or rapist. However, the majority of child molesters are found to belong to more than one category, with large numbers of incest offenders also belonging in the category of extrafamilial molesters. Weinrott and Saylor (1991) found one-half of incest offenders admitted to child sexual abuse outside of their home, none of which had been discovered. Abel and his colleagues (1988) reported that 49 percent of incest offenders who molested girls within the family also molested girls outside of the family. Moreover, of those who molested boys within the family, 61 percent also molested females, and 68 percent molested males outside of the family. These findings support the observation by Becker (1994) that, "child molesters may engage in incestuous, as well as nonincestuous abuse, and may target children of both genders" (p. 178).

Men who engage children in sex, including those who sexually abuse their own children, often show other types of sexual deviance. In a review of the research on sex offenders' paraphilias, Salter (1995) noted significantly high rates of crossover from the sex offender's identified sexual deviancy to other paraphilias (e.g., pedophilia, rape, exhibitionism, voyeurism, sadism, frottage). For example, Abel and colleagues (1985) reported that 51 percent of rapists had also committed child molestation, 17 percent of child molesters had raped, 3 percent of the child molesters and rapists were exhibitionists, and 14 percent of child molesters were voyeurs.

Over 80 percent of extrafamilial and 70 percent of incest offenders were found by Abel and Rouleau (1990) to have more than one paraphilia. Abel and colleagues (1988) found 9 percent of the incest offenders had over 10 paraphilias. Salter argues, "The data on multiple paraphilias and on nonsexual crimes committed by incest offenders challenges the widespread assumption that incest offenders are somehow different from other sex offenders" (1995, p. 23).

Adolescent Perpetrators

Although father-daughter incest is the most widely documented form of incest, brother-sister incest is considered by some experts to be the most common form (Loredo, 1982). While sexual play by siblings of approximately the same developmental level is not considered sexual abuse, sexual activity between children who differ between 3 to 5 years in age is considered to be abuse. When there is a large discrepancy between the age and relative power status of the siblings, the sexual interaction between siblings has dynamics similar to parent-child incest (Finkelhor, 1980).

Adolescents represent a substantial proportion of those individuals who perpetrate child sexual abuse (Finkelhor, 1979; Gomes-Schwartz et al., 1990). In the past, adolescents who molested children were identified as acting out normal sexual experimentation. Juvenile offenders are no longer identified as exhibiting normal sexual development but, instead, are considered to have serious sexual problems and to be at risk to develop into adult sexual predators who will continue to sexually abuse children (Abel et al., 1985; Abel, Osborn, & Twigg, 1993).

The majority of juvenile offenders' victims are relatives and friends, with relatives constituting between 6 percent to 40 percent of the victims (see Barbaree, Hudson, & Seto, 1993). Adolescent incest offenders may be brothers, step-brothers, or cousins who have easy access to the young children in their homes or extended family members' homes. Typically, the majority of victims are female and under the age of 12 years (Awad, Saunders, & Levene, 1984; Fehrenbach, Smith, Monastersky, & Deisher, 1986). As the age of the victim decreases, the number of male victims increases (Awad & Saunders, 1989).

Adolescent sex offenders are also frequently victims of sexual abuse, with victimization figures ranging from 19 to 81 percent (Becker, Kaplan, Cunningham-Ruthner, & Kavoussi, 1986; Fehrenbach et al., 1986; Friedrich & Luecke, 1988; Longo, 1982). Knight and Prentky (1993) found that adult child molesters who had juvenile sex offense histories were more frequently sexually abused as children than adult offenders, who did not have histories of juvenile offenses. Moreover, adult rapists who had histories of juvenile offenses more frequently came from families in which sexually deviant or abusive behavior was directed at other family members.

Abel and his colleagues found 40 percent of the male-oriented incest offenders, 25 percent of the female-oriented incest offenders, and 40 percent of the female-oriented extrafamilial offenders developed their deviant sexual arousal pattern prior to the age of 18. Male-oriented pedophiles have the earliest onset of deviant sexual arousal, with over half of this group developing their deviant sexual interest by age 16 (Abel et al., 1985; Abel & Rouleau, 1990).

Assessment

Assessment of whether a child is a victim of sexual abuse or an individual is a sex offender is a complicated task. Evaluators who are experts in child sexual abuse or have expertise with adolescent and adult sex offenders do not generally hold dual expertise. Therefore, evaluators who conduct assessments of child victims do not typically assess offenders and those who evaluate sex offenders rarely conduct evaluations with child victims.

Assessment of the Perpetrator

The history of sex offender assessment is dominated by many years of unsuccessful efforts to establish an offender profile. Extensive research has been conducted using relatively popular instruments, such as the Minnesota Multiphasic Personality Inventory (MMPI), to answer two pressing questions: (1) How are sex offenders (or more narrowly, incest offenders) different than nonsex offenders? and (2) Can psychological instruments differentiate guilty perpetrators from the innocent accused? Because sex offenders are a heterogeneous group and the psychological factors contributing to deviancy are complex, this line of research has not been fruitful (Abel et al., 1985; Becker and Quinsey, 1993; Nichols & Molinder, 1984).

The aggressive, but generally naive and unsuccessful, pursuit of these two objectives caused many clinicians to conclude that the role of psychological assessment in the evaluation and treatment of sex offenders was insignificant and altogether unnecessary. The rejection of psychological assessment techniques was further facilitated by the incompetent and unethical actions of a select few clinicians who conducted assessments of accused or convicted sex offenders, pronouncing them psychologically healthy, and thereby discouraging prosecution or treatment interventions.

Recent research, particularly during the last decade, has helped to redefine and slowly reestablish the role of psychological assessment in the evaluation of sexual deviancy. By distancing themselves from the task of differentiating offender from nonoffender, and refocusing on the identification of the key thoughts, beliefs and behaviors that are important in understanding the individual offender, mental health professionals are beginning to reshape the offender assessment landscape. Consistent with recent research developments, the purpose of sex offender assessment can be conceptualized as addressing two needs: the prediction of recidivism and treatment planning.

Risk assessment of recidivism may occur at the time of sentencing, or when a sex offender's criminal sanctions have expired. With respect to sentencing, progressive judiciary have recognized the inability of clinicians to assess offender or nonoffender determinations, while recognizing the value of utilizing clinicians to formulate sentencing plans, community sanctions, and special conditions aimed at minimizing recidivism and reducing threat to the community.

Risk assessment for recidivism may also occur pending an offender's release from incarceration. Currently, the courts and the community at large have become increasingly concerned with the subset of offenders who are so fixated and preoccupied with deviant sexual thoughts and urges that their offense behavior is chronic, habitual, and accounts for a disproportionate percentage of victims. Several studies have established the predictive validity of specific assessment methods for evaluating this type of predatory or recidivistic behavior (Prentky, Knight, & Lee, 1997; Quinsey, Rice, & Harris, 1995; Witt, DelRusso, Oppenheim, & Ferguson, 1996).

In addition to recidivism prediction, current employment of sex offender assessment is for treatment planning. As theoretically sound models for treatment of offenders are created and tested, the use of psychological testing and assessment can be expected to increase (Hall, 1995). Assessment has utility in matching individual offender characteristics with specific forms of intervention.

When assessment is used as an aide in the prediction of recidivism and treatment, two types of approaches are commonly employed. These are the psychophysiological and psychometric assessment approaches. The first of these, psychophysiological assessment, has generated much professional attention and controversy.

One type of psychophysiological assessment technique specific to sexual deviancy is the penile plethysmograph. This device is composed of a mechanical strain gauge attached to the base of the penis. This gauge interfaces with computer recording equipment to measure sexual arousal. By varying the stimulus material along such dimensions as age, sex, and violent content, it is possible to establish an arousal profile for individual offenders (Abel, Huffman, Warberg, & Holland, 1998). The arousal profile has been used in confronting denial, in formulating treatment plans, and in measuring the effectiveness of treatment designed to extinguish or diminish the deviant arousal patterns. The plethysmograph has been criticized by some professionals as unreliable, subject to intentional distortion, and intrusive.

Moreover, problems with the employment of this device have included the ethical problems in the presentation of stimuli that include pictures of nude children.

The polygraph is another example of a psychophysiological assessment device, although it is not specific to sexual deviancy. There has been a recent resurgence of interest and enthusiasm in utilizing this traditional law-enforcement methodology with sex offenders, despite its continued inadmissibility in most judicial proceedings. As with other sex offender assessment techniques, the use of the polygraph has shifted away from determinations of guilt or innocence. It is currently considered by some experts (Salter, 1995) to be a crucial component of a thorough sex offender assessment. The polygraph is believed to have particular utility as an aide in overcoming offender denial, documenting treatment-induced changes, and monitoring continued deviant sexual behavior, fantasies, or arousal. In some locales, the courts or probation officials have mandated routine polygraph testing as part of the ongoing supervision of all sex offenders.

The second assessment approach, psychometric assessment, has focused on elucidating case-specific, individual psychological characteristics of sex offenders. Offenders are a heterogeneous population and have diverse characteristics, despite specific sex offender classifications (e.g., incest offenders).

Psychometric techniques employed in sex offender assessments can be classified as evaluating one or more of three areas: sexual arousal, psychopathology, and cognitive style. One example of a psychometric technique used to assess sexual arousal is the Abel Assessment for Sexual Interest (Abel, 1997). The Abel is a computerized instrument that is designed to identify sexual interest through measurement of the duration of time an offender spends processing or viewing pictures of adults, teens, and children. Unlike the stimulus material typically used in phallometric assessment, the pictures utilized in this test are not sexually explicit. The test has greater practicality than the penile plethysmograph because it does not require handling of sexual organs. Preliminary research by Abel and colleagues (1998) shows that stimulus-specific measures from visual reaction time correlate with the corresponding category of the offender's sexual behavior in three of four categories measured: female children under 14 years old, male children under 14 years old, and adolescent males. Significant correlations were not found for adolescent females.

Psychometric techniques utilized to assess the presence of comorbid psychopathology and specific personality characteristics include personality instruments, such as the MMPI-2 and the Rorschach (Comprehensive System). These instruments are used to identify personality characteristics that may influence the onset, progression, or control of sexual deviancy. For example, research has identified insecure attachment (Ward, Hudson, & Marshall, 1996), low self-esteem (Marshall, 1997), intimacy problems (Bumby & Hansen, 1997), and affective dyscontrol (Hall, 1995) as factors and personality characteristics exhibited by some sex offenders. While these characteristics are not specific to sex offenders, careful assessment for these types of problems is important in establishing an individualized and theoretically sound treatment plan (Hall, 1995).

Psychometric techniques have also included cognitive assessment measures as a third area in the identification and treatment of sexual deviancy. Cognitive measures have utility in the assessment of an individual's ability to show compassion for the vulnerability of children and women. This area of inquiry has importance based on research suggesting that offenders' sexual deviancy is associated with an inability to empathize with the victims or take their perspective (Hanson & Scott, 1995). Cognitive assessment measures also may help to identify forms of distorted thinking (e.g., "I didn't hurt her; I was educating her about sex") that enable the offender to initiate or continue deviant sexual behavior despite awareness of the illegality of their actions (Bumby, 1996).

A final area for discussion in the evaluation of sex offenders is actuarial assessment. Conclusions, using this method of assessment, rest on empirically established relationships between data and the behavior of interest, rather than on subjective observations and redundant clinical experience (Dawes, Faust, & Meehl, 1989). Actuarial methods (e.g., Hanson, 1997; Sorag, Quinsey, Harris, Rice & Cormier, 1998) have been employed to predict the risk of recidivism in known sex offenders. For example, factors associated with recidivism, such as personality factors (i.e., psychopathy and strength of illegal sexual interest), environmental factors (i.e., involvement in treatment and availability of supportive environment), paraphilias, number of prior sexual offenses, (Prentky et al., 1997; Quinsey et al., 1995; Witt et al., 1996), are combined in regression equations. The actuarial method, based on the statistical analyses of these variables, has been found to be significantly better than chance or clinical judgment in predicting recidivism among sex offenders.

Assessment of the Victim

Assessment of the alleged child victim is also a complicated task. Similar to the absence of psychometrically sound tests that can identify sex offenders, there are no tests that can determine whether a child is the victim of sexual abuse.

In an attempt to increase the accuracy of professional judgment in child sexual abuse cases, two models have been relied upon. These are the standards and indicator models (see Berliner & Conte, 1993). The first of these, the standards model, delineates expectations for the conduct of professionals who evaluate allegations of child sexual abuse. Within this model, guidelines, based on available scientific research and the current state of clinical practice, have been promulgated by several national organizations (American Academy of Child and Adolescent Psychiatry, 1997; American Professional Society on the Abuse of Children, 1997). According to the standards model, the collection of collateral information and documentation of information are of great importance.

Within the standards model, the expertise and skill of the interviewer is the primary focus and viewed as critical for the collection of accurate information from children alleged to have been sexually abused. Because admission of sexual abuse by the perpetrator is rare, the interviewer's skill in accessing information through the child's narrative report becomes a critical factor for determining the veracity of the allegation.

Interviewers are challenged by the fact that very young children may provide limited information to open ended and nondirected questions or may be susceptible to interviewer influence, including pre- and post-event suggestions (Bruck, Ceci, Francoeur, & Barr, 1995; Ceci, Huffman, Smith, & Loftus, 1994; Leichtman & Ceci, 1995). Interviewers are also challenged by older children who may not disclose experiences of sexual abuse because of embarrassment, guilt, or misguided loyalty (Saywitz, 1995; Saywitz, Goodman, Nicholas, & Moan, 1991).

While the standards model focuses on practice procedures, the indicator model focuses on discriminating variables that can be used for classification of cases. This model structures the assessment to explore casual links between sexual abuse and psychological or behavioral symptoms. Attempts are made to identify verbal, emotional, and behavioral characteristics that differentiate sexually abused from nonsexually abused children.

However, because sexually abused children are a heterogeneous group, their responses to the experience of sexual abuse will vary. Thus, there are problems in applying lists of criteria to sexually abused children who have different cognitive abilities, personalities, coping styles, and experiences. Further, because of the similarity of symptoms caused by other traumas and/or consequences that are associated with family or social problems, it is difficult to determine causal links between sexual abuse and psychological or behavioral symptoms.

Standardized tests, including parent-report and self-report measures, are utilized by some evaluators when conducting child sexual abuse evaluations. For example, problem behavior rating scales are used to identify emotional and behavior problems exhibited by the child, as observed by the parent. However, these general behavior rating scales lack specificity and sensitivity for evaluating sexually abused children. Although fears, dissociative behavior, and behavior problems occur more frequently with sexually abused children than their nonabused peers, many victims show no significant behavior problems on broad-based child behavior rating scales (Kendall-Tackett et al., 1993).

Due to the lack of predictive diagnostic validity of behavior rating scales in assessing sexual abuse, several instruments were developed specifically for evaluating child sexual abuse. Two such instruments, with solid psychometric properties, are the Child Sexual Behavior Inventory ([CSBI] Friedrich, 1997) and the Trauma Symptom Checklist for Children ([TSCC] Briere, 1996).

The CSBI, is a parent-report measure, standardized on 2- to 12-year-old children, which measures a wide variety of sexual behaviors related to sexual interest, gender role behavior, self-stimulation, sexual knowledge, sexual intrusiveness, exhibitionism, voyeuristic behavior, and boundary issues (Friedrich, 1997; Friedrich et al., 1996; Friedrich et al., 1992). The three scales that have clinical utility are the CSBI Total (overall level of sexual behavior), Developmentally Related Sexual Behavior (sexual behaviors that can be viewed as normative for the child's age and gender), and Sexual Abuse Specific Items (sexual behaviors that can be viewed as relatively atypical for the child's age and gender). This instrument was developed from research showing inappropriate sexual behavior to consistently occur at a higher frequency with sexually abused children (Friedrich et al., 1986).

The second instrument, the Trauma Symptom Checklist for Children, is a 54-item child self-report measure, standardized on 8- to 18-year-olds (Briere, 1996). This instrument measures a number of symptoms related to traumatic events including sexual concerns, posttraumatic stress, dissociation, anxiety, depression, and anger. Sexual abuse has been related to higher TSCC scores (Lanktree & Briere, 1995; Lanktree, Briere, & deJonge, 1993).

Although both of these instruments have solid psychometric properties, neither instrument can determine whether a child has experienced the event of sexual abuse. These instruments may be sensitive to, but not specific to the impact of sexual abuse.

Nonstandardized techniques utilized by some evaluators in child sexual abuse assessments include children's drawings and doll play. To date, satisfactory reliability and validity of Human Figure Drawings and drawing tasks such as the House-Tree-Person or Kinetic Family Drawing have not been established (Weiner & Kuehnle, 1998). Moreover, there are no known behaviors demonstrated with dolls by children that are definitive markers of sexual abuse. As noted by Kuehnle (1998), specific behavioral and emotional symptoms, interactions with anatomical dolls, or genitalia drawn on human figures cannot be used to form cause and effect associations between the response and the occurrence of an event, such as sexual abuse.

While there is no single test, marker, or mathematical equation for determining whether a child has experienced sexual abuse, the empirical data, historical information, test results, and children's statements must all be evaluated against a complex matrix of interrelated factors (Kuehnle, 1998). Certain factors may be given greater weight than others, based on behavior base rates and corroborating evidence. For example, a 3-year-old female spontaneously requesting to "lick my pussy like daddy does," while initiating specific adult sexual acts, such as fellatio and cunnilingus, is so unusual within a nonsexually abused child population, the statement and behaviors should be weighted more heavily than statements derived from a structured interview or nonsexual behaviors associated with trauma in general. Moreover, a latency-age child's spontaneous disclosure identifying a loved uncle as an abuser is given greater weight than the repeatedly interrogated 2-year-old disclosing sexual abuse by his father.

Case Illustration

This case illustration will show the process of a child victim's engagement by both the incest offender and the multifaceted system that is organized within each state to intervene in child sexual abuse cases. The case presentation will focus on father-daughter incest.

Grooming

Grooming is a process in which the offender develops a relationship with his or her intended child victim and desensitizes the child to increasingly overt sexual acts.

Lesli had a close relationship with her father. Her father worked nights as a foreman and took care of Lesli in the early morning and afternoon when her mother was at work. Lesli and her father fished and swam together on weekends. The family attended church every Sunday; church members observed the family to be good Christians and Lesli's father to be a responsible husband and father.

When Lesli was 6 years old, her father began grooming her for a sexual relationship. Initially, Lesli was brought into her father's bed after Lesli's mother left for work. Father and daughter would lie nude together while Lesli watched cartoons. Over the next year, the father began to engage Lesli in French kissing and show Lesli his erect penis during their early morning cartoon time. By the age of 7, Lesli was playing a touching game with her father, in which her father had identified his penis as a magic wand. By the age of 10, Lesli's sexual abuse included fellatio, cunnilingus, digital vaginal penetration, and attempted intercourse. Intercourse had been unsuccessful because of Lesli's small vaginal opening. Lesli's father had instructed Lesli not to tell anyone about their sexual activity, informing her that they had a special relationship which other people would not understand. Lesli was told if others found out, her father would be taken away from her and sent to jail.

Disclosure

Disclosures by the victim may be an intentional or nonintentional disclosure. A nonintentional disclosure occurs when the child does not reveal his or her abuse to seek assistance from authorities. Accidental disclosure of abuse may occur through medical evidence, disclosure by an eye witness, or disclosure by a confidant of the victim.

While spending the night together, 11-year-old Lesli told her best friend, Katrina, about her father touching her vagina and breasts. She further informed Katrina that her father had recently tried to put his penis inside of her vagina. Lesli swore Katrina to secrecy, telling her that her father had warned her he would go to jail if she told anyone. Several days later, after worrying about her friend, Katrina told her mother about Lesli's disclosure.

Notification and Investigation

Each state has laws that mandate the time lapse between when a report is received by authorities and when the investigation must commence. In many states, child protection investigators and law-enforcement officers work as a team during the initial interviews of the alleged victim and perpetrator.

The morning Katrina's mother was informed of Lesli's statements, she telephoned the state child abuse reporting agency and notified authorities of Lesli's disclosure to her daughter. By late morning, a child protection investigator, accompanied by a law-enforcement official, arrived at Lesli's school to conduct an interview with Lesli. At that time, Lesli affirmed her sexual victimization and tearfully disclosed information that was consistent with what she had reported to Katrina.

Following their interview with Lesli, the state investigator and police officer interviewed Lesli's mother, at her home, and Lesli's father, at his place of employment. When interviewed by the authorities, the mother became angry and informed the investigators that the allegation was a lie, and that Lesli had a history of fabricating stories. Lesli's father, upon questioning, also vehemently denied the abuse allegation, stating that Lesli was mad at him for grounding her and concluded that she fabricated the allegation to get back at him.

After her initial interview, Lesli underwent a medical examination; the medical findings were consistent with penetration. Despite the parents' claims that the father was innocent, authorities substantiated the allegation and Lesli's father was arrested.

Placement

Following a substantiated allegation of sexual abuse involving incest, authorities must immediately determine the safety of the child. If the nonoffending caretaker is found to be unsupportive to the child or shows disbelief of the allegation, alternative placements with relatives or foster parents are considered.

Based on the mother's lack of support for her daughter, authorities placed Lesli in the temporary custody of her maternal grandmother who lived in a town approximately 80 miles from Lesli's home. This move required Lesli to transfer schools and lose contact with her parents and friends.

Further Evaluation

Prior to the filing of formal criminal charges, the alleged child victim, in some counties, undergoes a more formal videotaped forensic interview. The alleged perpetrator may also be asked to take a polygraph.

Several days after her initial interview by authorities, Lesli underwent a videotaped interview by specialists, trained in interviewing children. During the taped interview, Lesli recanted her allegation. The father was administered a polygraph which he failed.

Criminal Charges and Prosecution

Based on the evidence provided to them by law enforcement, the state attorney's office makes a decision on whether there is enough evidence to proceed in a court of law with the prosecution of an alleged case of child sexual abuse

Although Lesli did not want criminal charges filed against her father, the state prosecutor filed formal charges. The father's first court appearance took place the morning following his arrest, where bail was set and the father was ordered to have no contact with his daughter. Later in the day, after Lesli's mother posted bail, the father was released from jail.

At a preliminary hearing, two weeks following the father's release from jail, the judge determined that the evidence of guilt, based on medical findings, Lesli's initial statements to investigators, and Katrina's statements, was sufficient for the case to proceed to formal trial.

Treatment Intervention for the Victim

Among other factors, treatment planning must be based on the victim's age; social, emotional, and cognitive functions; and willingness to become involved in therapy.

A psychological evaluation conducted on Lesli, after she was placed with her grandmother, showed Lesli was depressed and anxious. Test results indicated that she had many negative perceptions and attributions of self-blame. Because of her reticence to talk about the sexual abuse perpetrated by her father, Lesli was placed in individual therapy, rather than group therapy. Therapy initially focused on the trauma following her disclosure, including the loss of her parents, neighborhood, friends, and teachers.

During a six-month period of time, therapy was unsuccessful with Lesli. She remained highly symptomatic and frequently reported to her therapist that she wished she could go home. Because of Lesli's continued denial of sexual abuse and the ongoing criminal proceedings, Lesli's therapist did not focus treatment on Lesli's sexual victimization.

Lesli was allowed supervised visitation with her parents, with the grandmother as the acting supervisor. Over an 11-month time period, Lesli's parents participated in one visit with their daughter.

Determination of Guilt

The majority of child sexual abuse cases, in which criminal charges are filed, do not go to formal trial. Instead these cases are typically settled through a plea bargain process in which the state attorney and defense attorney renegotiate the severity of the criminal charges and the punishment for the offender.

After a six-month period of time, during which Lesli was deposed and questioned by the attorneys twice, the father's attorney initiated a plea negotiation with the prosecutor. Because Lesli remained firm in her recantation of sexual abuse during her depositions, and sex offender treatment was not contraindicated for the father, the prosecutor was willing to plea bargain. Eventually, the defense and prosecuting attorneys agreed that the father would plead guilty to a less serious criminal charge of sexual abuse, a charge that did not involve admission of penetration. Further agreement involved the father's placement on probation, successful completion of an outpatient specialized sex offender treatment program rather than prison, and annual testing to monitor treatment progress. This testing was mandated to include the Abel Assessment for Sexual Interest, in order to monitor intervention success for decreasing sexual attraction to children. A polygraph was also mandated, specifically targeted to assess violation of probation and/or commission of additional sexual offenses unidentified while on probation.

Offender Treatment

A requirement for the provision of treatment by the majority of nationally recognized sex offender treatment programs is the sex offender's admission of the sexual abuse.

Lesli's father entered a sexual offender treatment program 11 months after Lesli's disclosure to Katrina. This program was a two-year group therapy program with a criterion-based cognitive-behavioral intervention design. The father was also placed on antidepressant medication for help in controlling his obsessive and intrusive sexual thoughts and compulsive behaviors.

During the father's first group therapy session, he reported to the therapist and other group members that he was not a sex offender, but had only admitted guilt in court on the advice of his attorney. The therapist informed the father that the group was for the treatment of sex offenders, if he was not a sex offender he could not remain in the group. The father was given a limit of three sessions to determine if he would return to court to plead his innocence or commit himself to treatment by admitting guilt. At his third session, the father admitted that he sexually abused Lesli and, over the course of treatment, admitted to molesting two other children who were not family members.

Summary

Incest is the sexual involvement of a child under the age of 18 by an adult or adolescent family member who is at least 3 to 5 years older than the victim. An exception to this age differential is child sexual abuse that involves developmentally disabled victims or the use of force, whereupon the chronological age differential may be zero. The actual number of child victims of sexual abuse is unknown. Surveys conducted to assess the number of child sexual abuse reports documented by state child protection services suggest the number is over 300,000 annually. Self-report surveys of adults who disclose having experienced sexual victimization during childhood show even higher figures, ranging from 7 to 62 percent for females and 3 to 16 percent for males in the general population.

The majority of individuals who molest children are male; however, female perpetrators are more common than previously estimated. Approximately 10 percent of individuals who molest children are female. From 25 to 50 percent of child sex offenders develop their deviant sexual arousal pattern prior to the age of 18. Male-oriented pedophiles have the earliest onset of deviant sexual arousal. Classification categories of sex offenders are not as distinct as previously believed. There is a high rate of crossover from the sex offenders' identified sexual deviancy to other paraphilias, with the majority of incest offenders having more than one paraphilia. These data suggest that incest offenders are not different from other sex offenders.

Although a large percentage of child sexual offenders live with their victims, the majority are not father figures. Less than one-fourth of the perpetrators of girls are found to be biological fathers, and the percentage of perpetrators who are biological fathers to their male victims is even lower. Moreover, compared to girls, boys are much less likely to be victims of sexual abuse by any relative.

Assessment of child sexual abuse allegations is a complicated task. Perpetrators rarely admit to sexually abusing a child, and there typically is little corroborating evidence, such as an eye witness or medical evidence. There do not exist any instruments at this time that can prove an individual has sexually abused a child or that a child was the victim of sexual abuse. However, there are several instruments developed for assessment of sexual offenders that show promise in determining sexual deviant interest in children. Currently, children's spontaneous statements and narratives evaluated against a matrix of historical information remain the critical factors in determining whether a child is a victim of sexual abuse.

REFERENCES

Abel, G. G. (1997). *The Abel Assessment for Sexual Interest*. Atlanta: Author.

Abel, G. G., Becker, J. V., Cunningham-Rathner, J., Mittelman, M., & Rouleau, J. L. (1988). Multiple Paraphilic Diagnoses among Sex offenders. *Bulletin of the American Academy of Psychiatry and the Law, 16*, 153–168.

Abel, G. G., Gore, D. K., Holland, C. L., Camp, N., Becker, J. V., & Rathner, J. (1989). The measurement of the cognitive distortions of child molesters. *Annals of Sex Research, 2*, 135–153.

Abel, G. G., Huffman, J., Warberg, R. & Holland, C. L. (1998). Visual reaction time and plethysmography as measures of sexual interest in child molesters. *Sexual Abuse: A Journal of Research and Treatment, 10(2)*, 81–95.

Abel, G. G., Mittelman, M. S., & Becker, J. V. (1985). Sex offenders: Results of assessment and recommendations for treatment. In M. R. Ben-Aron, S. J. Huckle, & C. D. Webster (Eds.), *Clinical Criminology: The Assessment and Treatment of Criminal Behavior* (pp. 191–205). Toronto: M & M Graphic.

Abel, G. G., Osborn, C. A., & Twigg, D. A. (1993). Sexual assault through the life span: Adult offenders with juvenile histories. In H. E. Barbaree, W. L. Marshall, & S. M. Hudson (Eds.),

The Juvenile Sex Offender (pp 104–117). New York: Guilford.

Abel, G. & Rouleau, J. L. (1990). The nature and extent of sexual assault. In W. L. Marshall, D. R. Laws, & H. E. Barbaree (Eds.), *Handbook of Sexual Assault: Issues, Theories, and Treatment of the Offender* (pp. 9–21). New York: Plenum.

American Academy of Child and Adolescent Psychiatry. (1997). Practice parameters for the forensic evaluation of children and adolescents who may have been physically or sexually abused. *Journal of the American Academy of Child & Adolescent Psychiatry, 36*, 423–444.

American Professional Society on the Abuse of Children. (1997). *Practice Guidelines: Use of Anatomical Dolls in Child Sexual Abuse Assessment. (2nd ed.)* Chicago: Author.

Awad, G. A. & Saunders, E. (1989). Adolescent child molesters: Clinical observations. *Child Psychiatry and Human Development, 19*, 195–206.

Awad, G. A., Saunders, E., & Levene, J. (1984). A clinical study of male adolescent sex offenders. *International Journal of Offender Therapy and Comparative Criminology, 28*, 105–116.

Barbaree, H. E., Hudson, S. M., & Seto, M. C. (1993). Sexual assault in society: The role of the juvenile offender. In H. E. Barbaree, W. L. Marshall, & S. M. Hudson (Eds.), *The Juvenile Sex Offender* (pp. 104–117). New York: Guilford.

Barnett, O. W., Miller-Perrin, C. L., & Perrin, R. D. (1996). *Family Violence Across the Life Span.* Thousand Oaks, CA: Sage.

Becker, J. V. (1994). Offenders: Characteristics and treatment. *The Future of Children, 4,* 176–197.

Becker, J. V., Kaplan, M. S., Cunningham-Ruthner, J., & Kavoussi, R. J. (1986). Characteristics of adolescent incest sexual perpetrators: Preliminary findings. *Journal of Family Violence 1,* 85–97.

Becker, J. V. & Quinsey, V. L. (1993). Assessing suspected child molesters. *Child Abuse and Neglect, 17,* 169–174.

Berliner, L. & Conte, J. R. (1990). The process of victimization: The victim's perspective. *Child Abuse & Neglect, 14,* 29–40.

Berliner, L. & Conte, J. R. (1993). Sexual abuse evaluations: Conceptual and empirical obstacles. *Child Abuse & Neglect, 17,* 111–125.

Black, H. C. (1979). *Black's Law Dictionary.* St. Paul, MN: West.

Briere, J. (1996). *The Trauma Symptom Checklist for Children (TSCC) Professional Manual.* Odessa, FL: Psychological Assessment Resource, Inc.

Bronfenbrenner Life Course Center. (1996). Who are the victims? *Bronfenbrenner Life Course Center Issue Brief, 1,* 1–4.

Bruck, M., Ceci, S. J., Francoeur, E., & Barr, R. (1995). Anatomical detailed dolls do not facilitate preschoolers' reports of a pediatric examination involving genital touching. *Journal of Experimental Psychology: Applied, 1,* 95–99.

Bumby, K. M. (1996). Assessing the cognitive distortions of child molesters and rapists: Development and validation of the MOLEST and RAPE scales. *Sexual Abuse: Journal of Research and Treatment, 8,* 37–54.

Bumby, K. M. & Hansen, D. J. (1997). Intimacy deficits, fear of intimacy, and loneliness among sexual offenders. *Criminal Justice & Behavior, 24,* 315–331.

Ceci, S. J. & Bruck, M. (1995). *Jeopardy in the courtroom.* New York: American Psychological Association.

Ceci, S. J., Huffman, M. L., Smith, E., & Loftus, E. F. (1994). Repeatedly thinking about non-events: Source misattributions among preschoolers. *Consciousness and Cognition, 3,* 388–407.

Cicchetti, D. & Rizley, R. (1981). Developmental perspectives on the etiology, intergenerational transmission, and sequelae of child maltreat-

ment. *New Directions for Child Development, 11,* 31–55.

Dawes, R. M., Faust, D., & Meehl, P. E. (1989). Clinical versus actuarial judgment. *Science, 238,* 1556–1557.

Deblinger, E., McLeer, S. V., & Henry, D. (1990). Cognitive behavioral treatment for sexually abused children suffering post-traumatic stress: Preliminary findings. *Journal of American Academy of Child and Adolescent Psychiatry, 29,* 747–752.

Egeland, B., Sroufe, L. A., & Erickson, M. F. (1983). Developmental consequences of different patterns of maltreatment. *International Journal of Child Abuse, 7,* 459–469.

Elliott, D. M. & Briere, J. (1994). Forensic sexual abuse evaluations of older children: Disclosures and symptomatology. *Behavioral Science and the Law, 12,* 261–277.

Elliott, M. (1993). *Female Sexual Abuse of Children.* New York: Guliford.

Erickson, M. F. & Egeland, B. (1987). Developmental view of the psychological consequences of maltreatment. *School Psychology Review, 16,* 156–168.

Fehrenbach, P. A., Smith, W., Monastersky, C., & Deisher, R. W. (1986). Adolescent sexual offenders: Offender and offense characteristics. *American Journal of Orthopsychiatry, 56,* 225–233.

Finkelhor, D. (1979). *Sexually Victimized Children.* New York: Free Press.

Finkelhor, D. (1980). Sex among siblings: A survey on prevalence, variety, and effects. *Archives of Sexual Behavior, 9,* 171–194.

Finkelhor, D. (1984). *Child Sexual Abuse: New Theory and Research.* New York: Free Press.

Finkelhor, D. (1986). *A source book on child sexual abuse.* Beverly Hills, CA: Sage.

Finkelhor, D. (1988). The trauma of sexual abuse. In G. E. Wyatt & G. J. Powell (Eds.), *Lasting Effects of Child Sexual Abuse* (pp. 61–82). Newbury Park, CA: Sage.

Finkelhor, D. (1994). Current information on the scope and nature of child sexual abuse. *The Future of Children, 4,* 31–53.

Finkelhor, D. & Browne, A. (1985). The traumatic impact of child sexual abuse: A conceptualization. *American Journal of Orthopsychiatry, 55,* 530–541.

Finkelhor, D. & Dziuba-Leatherman, J. (1994). Children as victims of violence: A national survey. *Pediatrics, 94,* 413–420.

Finkelhor, D., Hotaling, G., Lewis, I. A., & Smith, C. (1990). Sexual abuse in a national survey of adult men and women: Prevalence, characteristics, and risk factors. *Child Abuse and Neglect, 14,* 19–28.

Friedrich, W. N. (1997). *Child sexual behavior inventory manual.* Odessa, FL: Psychological Assessment Resource, Inc.

Friedrich, W. N., Berliner, L., Cohen, J., Damon, L., Bulter, J., & Shafran, C. (1996). *Normative Sexual Behaviors-CSBI-3.* Unpublished paper presented at Trauma and Memory: An International Research Conference, Durham, NH.

Friedrich, W. N., Grambsch, P., Damon, L., Hewitt, S. K., Koverola, C., Lang, R. A., Wolfe, V., & Broughton, D. (1992). Child sexual behavior inventory: Normative and clinical contracts. *Psychological Assessment, 4,* 303–311.

Friedrich, W. N. & Luecke, W. J. (1988). Young school-age sexually aggressive children. *Professional Psychology Research and Practice, 19,* 155–164.

Friedrich, W. N., Urquiza, A. J., & Beilke, R. L. (1986). Behavior problems in sexually abused young children. *Journal of Pediatric Psychology, 11,* 47–57.

Gomes-Schwartz, B., Horowitz, J. M., & Cardarelli, A. P. (1990). *Child Sexual Abuse: The Initial Effects.* Newbury Park, CA: Sage.

Goodman, G. S., Taub, E. P., Jones, D. P. H., England, T., Port, L. K., Rudy, L., & Prado, L. (1992). Testifying in criminal court. *Monograph of the Society for Research in Child Development, 57,* 1–141.

Hall, G. C. N. (1995). The preliminary development of theory-based community treatment for sexual offenders. *Professional Psychology: Research and Practice, 26,* 478–483.

Hanson, R. K. (1997). *The Development of a Brief Accuarial Risk Scale for Sexual Offense Recidivism.* Ottawa Ontario, Canada: Department of Solicitor General Canada.

Hanson, R. K. & Scott, H. (1995). Assessing perspective-taking among sexual offenders, nonsexual criminals, and nonoffenders. *Sexual Abuse: Journal of Research and Treatment, 7,* 259–277.

Hayashino, D. S., Wurtele, S. K., & Klebe, K. J. (1995). Child molesters: An examination of cognitive factors. *Journal of Interpersonal Violence, 10,* 106–116.

Kendall-Tackett, K. A., Williams, L. M., & Finkelhor, D. (1993). Impact of sexual abuse on children: A review and synthesis of recent empirical studies. *Psychological Bulletin, 113,* 164–180.

Knight, R. A. & Prentky, R. A. (1993). Exploring characteristics for classifying juvenile sex offenders. In H. E. Barbaree, W. L. Marshall, & S. M. Hudson (Eds.), *The Juvenile Sex Offender* (pp. 104–117). New York: Guilford.

Kuehnle, K. (1996). *Assessing Allegations of Child Sexual Abuse.* Sarasota, FL: Professional Resource Press.

Kuehnle, K. (1998). Child sexual abuse evaluations: The scientist-practitioner model. *Behavioral Science and the Law, 16,* 5–20.

Lanktree, C. B. & Briere, J. (1995). *Early Data on the New Sexual Concerns and Dissociation Subscales of the TSCC.* Unpublished manuscript, Department of Psychiatry, University of Southern California School of Medicine.

Lanktree, C. B., Briere, J., & deJonge, J. (1993, August). *Effectiveness of Therapy for Sexually Abused Children: Changes in Trauma Symptom Checklist for Children TSCC Scores.* Paper presented at the meeting of the American Psychological Association, Toronto, Canada.

Laws, D. R. & Marshall, W. L. (1990). A conditioning theory of the etiology and maintenance of deviant sexual preferences and behavior. In W. L. Marshall, D. R. Laws, & H. E. Barbaree (Eds.), *Handbook of Sexual Assault: Issues, Theories, and Treatment of the Offender* (pp. 209–229). New York: Plenum.

Lawson, C. (1993). Mother-son sexual abuse: Rare or underreported? A critique of the research. *Child Abuse and Neglect, 17,* 261–269.

Lawson, L. & Chaffin, M. (1992). False negatives in sexual abuse disclosure interviews. *Journal of Interpersonal Violence, 7,* 532–542.

Leichtman, M. D. & Ceci, S. J. (1995). The effects of stereotypes and suggestions on preschoolers reports. *Developmental Psychology, 31,* 568–578.

Longo, R. E. (1982). Sexual learning and experience among adolescent sexual offenders. *International Journal of Offender Therapy and Comparative Criminology, 27,* 150–155.

Loredo, C. (1982). Sibling incest. In S. M. Sgroi (Ed.), *Handbook of Clinical Intervention in Child Sexual Abuse* (pp. 177–189). Lexington, MA: Lexington Books.

Lung, C. T. & Daro, D. (1997). *Current Trends in Child Abuse Reporting and Fatalities: The Results of the 1996 Annual 50 State Survey.* Chicago, IL: National Committee to Prevent Child Abuse.

Mannarino, A. P. & Cohen, J. (1987). *Psychological Symptoms of Sexually Abused Children.* Paper presented at the Third National Family Violence Research Conference, Durham, NH.

Mannarino, A. P., Cohen, J. A., & Berman, S. R. (1994). The children's attributions and perceptions scale: A new measure of sexual abuse-related factors. *Journal of Clinical Child Psychology, 23,* 204–211.

Marshall, W. L. (1997). The relationship between self-esteem and deviant sexual arousal in non-familial child molesters. *Behavior Modification, 21,* 86–96.

Masten, A. S., Best, K. M., & Garmezy, N. (1990). Resilience and development: Contributions from the study of children who overcome adversity. *Development and Psychopathology, 2,* 425–444.

Myers, E. B. (1997). *A Mother's Nightmare—Incest.* Thousand Oaks, CA: Sage.

National Research Counsel. (1992). *Understanding Child Abuse and Neglect.* Washington, DC: National Academy.

Nichols, H. R. & Molinder, I. (1984). *Multiphasic Sex Inventory Manual.* Tacoma, WA: Authors.

Paveza, G. J. (1988). Risk factors in father-daughter child sexual abuse: A case control study. *Journal of Interpersonal Violence, 3,* 290–306.

Poole, D. A. & Lindsay, D. S. (1998). Assessing the accuracy of young children's reports: Lessons from the investigation of child sexual abuse. *Journal of Applied and Preventive Psychology, 7,* 1–26.

Prentky, R. A., Knight, R. A., & Lee, A. F. (1997). Risk factors associated with recidivism among extrafamilial child molesters. *Journal of Consulting & Clinical Psychology, 65,* 141–149.

Quinsey, Z. L., Harris, G., Rice, M., & Cormier, C. (1998). *Violent Offenders: Appraising and Managing Risk.* Washington, DC: American Psychological Association.

Quinsey, Z. L., Rice, M. E., & Harris, G. T. (1995). Actuarial prediction of sexual recidivism. *Journal of Interpersonal Violence, 10,* 85–105.

Runyan, D. K., Everson, M. D., Edelsohn, G. A., Hunter, W. M., & Coulter, M. L. (1988). Impact of legal intervention on sexually abused children. *Journal of Pediatrics, 113,* 647–653.

Russell, D. E. (1983). The incidence and prevalence of intrafamilial and extrafamilial sexual abuse of female children. *Child Abuse and Neglect, 7,* 133–146.

Rutter, M. (1993). Resilience: Some conceptual considerations. *Journal of Adolescent Health, 14,* 626–631.

Salter, A. C. (1995). *Transforming Trauma: A Guide to Understanding and Treating Adult Survivors of Child Sexual Abuse.* Thousand Oaks, CA: Sage.

Saywitz, K. J., Goodman, G. S., Nicholas, G., & Moan, S. (1991). Children's memories of physical examinations that involve genital touch: Implications for reports of child sexual abuse. *Journal of Consulting and Clinical Psychology, 59,* 682–691.

Sedlak, A. J. (1991). *National Incidence and Prevalence of Child Abuse and Neglect: 1988—Revised Report.* Rockville, MD: Westat.

Sirles, E. A. & Franke, P. J. (1989). Factors influencing mothers' reactions to intrafamily sexual abuse. *Child Abuse and Neglect, 13,* 131–139.

Sorenson, T. & Snow, B. (1991). How children tell: The process of disclosure in child sexual abuse. *Child Welfare, 70,* 3–15.

Strauss, M. A., Gelles, R. J., & Steinmetz, S. K. (1980). *Behind Closed Doors: Violence in the American Family.* Garden City, NY: Anchor/Doubleday.

Ward, T., Hudson, S. M., & Marshall, W. L. (1996). Attachment style in sex offenders: A preliminary study. *Journal of Sex Research, 33,* 17–26.

Warner-Kearney, D. (1987, February). *The Nature of the Grooming Behavior Used by Sexual Offenders in Father-Daughter Incest.* Paper presented at the Western Criminology Association, Las Vegas, NV.

Weiner, I. & Kuehnle, K. (1998). Projective assessment of children and adolescents. In M. Hersen & A. Bellak (Eds.), *Comprehensive Clinical Psychology,* (Vol. 3). Tarrytown, NY: Elsevier Science.

Weinrott, M. R. & Saylor, M. (1991). Self-report of crimes committed by sex offenders. *Journal of Interpersonal Violence, 6,* 286–300.

Werner, E. E. (1993). Risk, resilience, and recovery: Perspectives from the Kauai Longitudinal Study. *Development and Psychopathology, 5,* 503–515.

Williams, L. & Finkelhor, D. (1990). The characteristics of incestuous fathers: A review of recent studies. In W. L. Marshall, D. R. Laws, & H. E. Barbaree (Eds.), *Handbook of Sexual Assault: Issues, Theories, and Treatment of the Offender* (pp. 231–255). New York: Plenum.

Witt, P. H., DelRusso, J., Oppenheim, J. & Ferguson, G. (1996). Sex offender risk assessment and the law. *Journal of Psychiatry and Law, 24,* 343–377.

8 Partner Abuse

SHARI FELDBAU-KOHN
State University of New York at Stony Brook

K. DANIEL O'LEARY
State University of New York at Stony Brook

JULIE A. SCHUMACHER
State University of New York at Stony Brook

Rachel and Tony were experiencing conflict in their relationship over the discipline of their two young children. Tony felt that it was important to tell their children what to do and to punish them if they did not follow instructions. Rachel believed that because the children were still young (2 and 4 years old) it was important to work with them and explain to them what needed to be done as often as necessary. One day Rachel was in the bedroom with their older son happily helping him clean his room, when Tony came home from work after having a particularly stressful day. When he walked into the house and heard Rachel helping their son cleaning his room Tony became furious. He quickly walked toward the bedroom wondering why Rachel would purposely hurt him by going against his wishes. By the time he reached the door to his son's room, Tony was so angry that he grabbed his wife, knocking his son over in the process, shook her and pushed her into the wall, continuously yelling at her for breaking "his" rules.

Definition

The story of Rachel and Tony is an account of a violent incident reported to the first author during a marital therapy session. Rachel's experience is just one of the many forms of violence experienced by women in abusive relationships. Physical aggression toward a partner includes acts ranging in severity from pushing, grabbing, and shoving to incidents such as slapping, hitting, kicking, beating, and using a weapon. In 1994, the *Diagnostic and Statistical Manual of Mental Disorders (DSM-IV)* (American Psychiatric Association, 1994), a reference work which outlines all psychiatric and psychological disorders, recognized partner abuse as a disorder, and added a new diagnostic category, "Problems Related to Abuse or

Neglect." Partner abuse refers to acts of physical aggression occurring more than once a year, including but not limited to pushing, shoving, slapping, and hitting. An act of aggression meets the definition of partner abuse, regardless of whether or not it results in physical injury requiring medical attention; however *all* acts that cause physical injury requiring medical attention meet the definition of partner abuse. O'Leary and Jacobson (1997) indicate that acts which result in the victim being constantly afraid of the perpetrator of aggression, including threats ("I'll kill you") and intimidation (e.g., punching a wall next to a victim's head), also fall under the definition of partner abuse. Men and women from 18 to 25 years of age are the most likely to be involved in abusive relationships. The likelihood of partner violence decreases with age.

This chapter will include information about the prevalence of partner aggression among couples who are dating and those who are married. Among married couples, information is broken down into couples responding to a national survey, and those seeking marital therapy. The chapter will also cover information about the assessment of partner aggression, risk factors for partner abuse, as well as correlates of victimization. Finally, the chapter will discuss issues related to the prevention and treatment of partner abuse.

Prevalence

The term *prevalence* refers to the total number of cases of a disorder in the population at any given time. When we discuss prevalence in this chapter we will be referring to point prevalence and lifetime prevalence. Unless otherwise specified, the term *prevalence* will refer to point prevalence. For the purposes of this chapter, *point prevalence* will refer to the amount of partner aggression that has occurred in the past year (unless otherwise specified). On the other hand, the term *lifetime prevalence,* refers to any aggression that has occurred during a person's entire life.

Dating Couples

Over the past two decades, it has become increasingly apparent that many thousands of American adolescents and young adults experience violence in their dating relationships. In fact, a recent study revealed that in certain high schools, as many as 57 percent of the students are currently or have been involved in violent relationships either as victims or perpetrators (Avery-Leaf, Cascardi, & O'Leary, 1994). Surveys of college students reveal that violence is very common in college dating relationships as well. When asked about their dating histories, up to 65 percent of college students report that they have been involved in an aggressive dating relationship at some time in their lives (Arias, Samios, & O'Leary, 1987; Bookwala, Frieze, Smith, & Ryan, 1992; Breslin, Riggs, O'Leary, & Arias, 1990; Makepeace, 1981). These percentages attest to the fact that a sizable number of young men and women are slapped, pushed, kicked, or otherwise aggressed against by their dating partners and/or perpetrate such acts of aggression against their dating partners during high school and college.

Population of Married Couples Community

Due to its private nature, marital violence is rarely discussed. Therefore, it is surprising to learn how often it actually occurs. Approximately 12 percent of 2,000 married or cohabiting women in the United States taking part in a national survey reported that they had been physically aggressed against by their partner in the past year (Straus & Gelles, 1990). Most women reported experiencing aggression, such as pushing, grabbing, and shoving. However, about 5 percent of these women reported experiencing much more severe aggression, including being beaten up, or having a knife or gun used against them. Lifetime prevalence of physical aggression against a partner is obviously much higher. Over the course of a lifetime, about one-third of all married or cohabiting women will experience some form of physical aggression by their partners and 10 percent of these women will face severe aggression toward them during their lifetime (Straus & Gelles, 1990). Of nine women, at least three will experience physical aggression by their partners at some point in their lifetime, and at least one will be beaten, threatened with a knife or gun, or actually have a knife or gun used on her. A vision such as that one illustrates the severity of the problem. Another indication of the severity of the problem is the finding that some women are murdered by their romantic partner. Browne and Williams (1993) have reported that women are more likely to be murdered by their partners than anyone else.

Population of Married Couples Clinic

As one might expect, among couples seeking marital therapy, rates of aggression are higher than they are in community samples. For instance, O'Leary, Vivian, and Malone (1992) found that among 132 couples seeking treatment at a marital clinic, 53 percent of women reported some physical aggression and 21 percent of these women reported experiencing severe physical aggression during the preceding year. Cascardi, Langhinrichsen, and Vivian (1992) found that at least 71 percent of couples seeking general marital therapy reported at least one act of physical violence in the past year. Roughly speaking, between 50 to 70 percent of those couples experiencing marital discord, also experienced physical aggression in their relationship.

Assessment

How can partner abuse be measured? It might seem like there is an obvious answer: Just ask the couple if there is any partner aggression. Unfortunately, for a number of reasons, the issue of assessment of partner abuse is much more complicated. For example, a victim of partner abuse may be unwilling to report her partner's aggression for a number of reasons, including the possibility that she may be fearful of the repercussions, concerned as to how the consequences may affect her partner, or she may even be too embarrassed. Furthermore, many people may not see relationship aggression as a problem and therefore do not see any point in mentioning it. For example, in the above mentioned marital clinic sample, 53 percent of women reported some aggression in the previous year, but when asked to write about problems in the relationship, only 6 percent indicated that physical aggression was a problem (O'Leary et al., 1992). Therefore, it is very important to use a measure that will directly assess the presence of physical violence in a relationship. The most common assessment measure of physical aggression against a partner is the Conflict Tactic Scale (CTS) (Straus, 1979) and its many modifications (e.g., Cascardi et al., 1992; Pan, Neidig, & O'Leary, 1994; Straus, Hamby, Boney-McCoy, & Sugarman, 1996). The CTS is a self-report and partner-report measure. That is, the CTS asks each person about his/her own acts of aggression, as well as their partner's aggressive acts. For example, the CTS would ask a woman if she had slapped her partner in the past year. It would then ask if her partner slapped her in the past year. When both husbands and wives are asked about aggression in their relationship, a number of researchers have found that there is some agreement between the partners' reports (e.g., Cantos, Neidig, & O'Leary, 1994), but clearly there is significant disagreement as well (e.g., Arias & Beach, 1987). Both husbands and wives tend to underestimate their own use of violence relative to their partners' reports, but husbands seem to be more likely to make such underestimates, particularly when they are reporting severe violence. Unfortunately, at times it is only possible to obtain one partner's report of the aggression. In order to deal with this issue, correction factors of partner-reports of physical aggression based only on self-reports have recently been developed (Heyman & Schlee, 1997). These correction factors could be used to adjust self-report scores slightly upward to correct for underestimates.

In addition to which questions one asks, it is also important where and how one ask them. At times, it is necessary to assess for partner aggression over the phone. It is important to be sure the person one is speaking with will not be placed in danger by responding to your questions (e.g., her abusive partner could be next to her at the time you are assessing for his aggression against her). In addition, it is advisable to also administer an individual interview to assess the presence and context of the aggression (O'Leary & Jacobson, 1997). For example, if a spouse felt responsible for an aggressive action, she may be less likely to report her husband's aggression. If she were alone in a face-to-face meeting with an interviewer, she might feel better about disclosing the violent episode, feeling she would at least be able to explain away her husband's abuse. In any case, it is always important for a clinician to try to understand the context of aggressive incidents, to assess the level of fear of the partner, and to assess the need for assisting the woman in developing a safety plan. (Safety plans will be discussed later in this chapter.)

Are Wives Aggressive toward Their Husbands?

According to nationally representative samples, the rate of husband-to-wife aggression (typically lower levels of aggression, including pushing, grabbing, and shoving) is approximately equal to rates of physical aggression of wives toward their husbands (Straus & Gelles, 1986). Cascardi and colleagues (1992) found that of couples seeking marital therapy, 85 percent of those reporting any violence in their relationship described such aggression as bidirectional (i.e., both partners were aggressive). This, however, can be a misleading statistic. As you may recall, one of the criteria for a diagnosis of partner abuse is the resulting injury an aggressive act may produce, and/or the resultant feeling of fear and intimidation. Wives report experiencing more negative consequences of partner aggression than husbands (Cantos et al., 1994). In a nationally representative sample surveyed by Stets and Straus (1990), 3 percent of women experiencing abuse by her spouse reported needing medical attention, whereas only 0.4 percent of men reported the same. In a sample of couples seeking treatment at a marital clinic, approximately 15 percent of wives who had experienced physical aggression from their husbands reported experiencing serious physical injuries (e.g., broken teeth, broken bones, injuries to sensory organs). These percentages are in sharp contrast to reports from men. Only 2 percent of the men experienced serious physical injury from their partner's physical aggression (Cascardi et al., 1992). Furthermore, even men who report that their wives engage in unilateral (i.e., one-sided) physical aggression against them, in general, do not report that they fear their wives (Wilson et al., 1996). Therefore, although aggression by women toward their partners does occur, it is important to keep in mind that for the most part, the resultant injury and impact is much more severe for women than for men. Based on these and similar findings, it is recommended that multidimensional assessments of aggression (i.e., assessments that measure context, injury, and impact of the aggression, in addition to frequency) be implemented (Vivian & Langhinrichsen-Rohling, 1996). The rest of this chapter will focus on husband-to-wife physical aggression.

Risk Factors for Perpetration of Partner Aggression

Risk factors are those characteristics or variables that make it more likely that someone who possesses these characteristics or variables, rather than someone selected from the general population, will develop a particular disorder or experience a particular outcome. For example, if we surveyed your class, we would probably find that not reading this textbook is a risk factor for getting a poor grade in this course. That is, those in the class who do not read the textbook are more likely to get an "F" in this course than the average student in this class. Although in that particular instance, we would probably say that not reading the textbook is causally related to getting a poor grade in the course, *risk factors are not necessarily causally related to outcomes*. To say that something is a risk factor for a particular outcome only means that it is a characteristic associated with increased probability of having that outcome.

There is a large body of research on risk factors for perpetration of partner aggression, particularly among males. For reasons discussed earlier in this chapter there has been very little research on female-perpetrated partner aggression, and not much is known about the risk factors for that type of aggression. As a result, this section will focus on risk factors for perpetration of partner aggression by men.

Demographic Variables.   Certain demographic factors, such as age, social class, and race are risk factors for partner aggression. As mentioned earlier, as men age, their risk of engaging in partner aggression decreases. That means that being young is a risk factor for partner aggression. Pan, Neidig, and O'Leary (1994) surveyed 11, 870 men in the military, and found that for every 10 years increase in age, a man's risk of engaging in mild partner aggression was decreased by 19 percent, while his risk of engaging in severe partner aggression decreased by 29 percent. In other words, a 30-year-old man is 29 percent less likely to hit, kick, or beat his partner than a 20-year-old man is.

The term *socioeconomic status (SES)* refers to a composite of variables that represents an individual's overall social standing and wealth. SES often includes educational attainment, employment status, occupational attainment, and annual income. In the case of married couples, it often includes measures of a spouse's standing as well as one's own. Overall, the literature suggests that having lower SES—that is, being less educated, having a lower income, or living in poverty, and being employed in a lower-prestige occupation (e.g., blue collar versus white collar)—is associated with increased risk for partner aggression (Kantor & Straus, 1987; McCloskey, 1996; O'Leary & Curley, 1986; Pan, Neidig, & O'Leary, 1994). Race and ethnicity are two other demographic characteristics that have been investigated as risk factors for partner aggression. Research has shown that rates of partner aggression may be slightly higher among men who identify racially as Black (Cazanave & Straus, 1990), ethnically as Hispanic (Straus & Smith), or otherwise identify as non-White (Leonard & Blane, 1992). However, individuals belonging to minority groups often have other characteristics that are risk factors for partner aggression, such as lower income and lower occupational prestige. Kantor, Jasinski, and Aldarondo (1994) used a statistical technique to examine the risk associated with being Hispanic over and above age and SES. They found that Hispanic ethnicity did not predict aggression when age and SES were controlled. This suggests that race and ethnicity are probably not key risk factors for partner aggression, but rather that they are associated with partner aggression because of their association with other key risk factors, such as socioeconomic status.

It is important to note that each of the demographic variables mentioned increases the risk for partner aggression only slightly. Partner aggression is a problem that does not discriminate. There are no racial, social, or age groups that are unaffected by partner aggression.

Witnessing or Experiencing Violence as a Child.   Many men who engage in acts of aggression against a romantic partner report that they grew up in violent homes. Being physically, emotionally, or sexually abused by parents or caretakers and/or witnessing physical or verbal abuse between one's parents during childhood are risk factors for partner aggression (Barnett & Fagan, 1993; O'Leary & Curley, 1986; Widom, 1989). Recent evidence also suggests that being victimized by siblings during childhood is associated with increased risk for partner aggression (Brennan, Schumacher, Shaver, & Clark, 1998). Men who experience aggression at the hands of their parents or siblings or witness aggression between their parents as children may learn that aggression is the way to deal with problems with loved ones (Bandura, 1978; Huesmann, 1988), and may not learn more effective ways of solving these problems, such as discussing issues calmly. This can lead to development and perpetuation of a *cycle of violence* in which adults who were raised in violent homes, raise their own children in violent homes. Their children, in turn, raise their own children in violent homes, and so on (Widom, 1989).

Psychological Factors.   Many psychological factors are associated with greatly increased risk for partner aggression. Men who engage in partner aggression tend to obtain high scores on measures of anger and hostility (Dutton, Starzomski, & Ryan, 1996; Maiuro, Cahn, Vitaliano, & Wagner, 1988). Aggressive men may also behave less assertively with their partners than nonaggressive men (O'Leary & Curley, 1986; Rosenbaum & O'Leary, 1981). Broadly speaking, assertiveness can be defined as the ability to confidently and appropriately express one's feelings, particularly as it relates to refusing requests from others, making requests of others, or initiating contact with others. Failure to behave assertively often results in resentment and hostility directed at individuals with whom assertiveness would have been appropriate. For example, a man who is not assertive enough to say no when his wife asks him to go shopping with her, may later resent his wife and feel that she took advantage of him by asking him to go shopping. Low self-esteem (Neidig, Friedman, & Collins, 1986), jealousy (Dutton, vanGinkel, & Landolt, 1996), and need for power and control (Prince & Arias, 1994) are additional psychological factors that increase risk for aggression.

Having a psychological disorder, particularly a personality disorder, is also a strong risk factor for partner aggression (Murphy, Meyer, & O'Leary, 1993). Depression is another psychological disorder that is associated with increased risk for partner aggression (Feldbau-Kohn, Heyman, & O'Leary, 1998; Murphy et al., 1993; Pan et al., 1994). Men who engage in partner aggression are also more likely to have alcohol problems (Barnett & Fagan, 1993; Heyman, O'Leary, & Jouriles, 1995; Leonard & Senchak, 1996; Schumacher & O'Leary, 1998), and drug problems (Kantor & Straus, 1987; Murphy et al., 1993; Pan et al., 1994). Finally, having a borderline personality organization has been correlated with perpetration of partner aggression, and it is predictive of regression following treatment (Dutton, Starzomski, & Ryan, 1996).

Relationship Variables.   Relationship factors can also increase risk for partner aggression. Men who report that they are unhappy or dissatisfied in their relationships or that they disagree and argue a lot with their partners are more likely to engage in partner aggression (O'Leary & Curley, 1986; Pan, Neidig, & O'Leary, 1994; Rosenbaum & O'Leary, 1981). In fact, marital discord or dissatisfaction is one of the largest risk factors for partner aggression. In addition, men who are verbally or psychologically aggressive toward their partners are also more likely to engage in physical aggression (Dutton, Starzomski, & Ryan, 1996).

Correlates of Victimization

In addition to the numerous factors associated with the perpetration of partner violence, a large number of negative ramifications related to being abused have been found. We turn to these now.

Psychological

Abused women are more likely to report feeling fearful than nonabused women (Russel, Lipov, Phillips, & White, 1989). Women involved in aggressive relationships are also likely to feel helpless (Walker, 1979), which often leads to anxiety and depression (Shepherd, 1990). Depression is also a common consequence of being physically aggressed on by an intimate partner (e.g., Cascardi et al., 1992). For example, when compared to women who were not abused, abused women were four-times more likely to be depressed and to attempt suicide (Straus & Smith, 1990). Furthermore, depression that results from partner abuse can also lead to its own maladaptive consequences. Another consequence of experiencing partner violence is stress (Barnett, Miller-Perrin, & Perrin, 1997). According to Barnett and colleagues (1997), ongoing stress is likely to contribute to anxiety, anger, aggression, and depression. Stress is also likely to lead to physical illness (Koss, Koss, & Woodruff, 1991). Another consequence of physical abuse against an intimate partner is posttraumatic stress disorder (PTSD) (American Psychiatric Association, 1987). This disorder, is characterized by persistent reexperiencing of traumatic events, avoidance of stimuli associated with the traumatic events, and symptoms of increased arousal (e.g., difficulty sleeping and concentrating). Researchers investigating samples of battered women have found that between 45 to 60 percent have experienced PTSD symptoms (Houskamp & Foy, 1991; Saunders, 1994). Decreased self-efficacy and low self-esteem are also common results of partner aggression (Cascardi & O'Leary, 1992). Partner abuse also negatively affects wives' reports of marital satisfaction (Buaserman & Arias, 1992). That is, women abused by their husbands are more likely to report lower marital satisfaction than those not in abusive relationships. Although findings have been mixed (see Orava, McLeod, & Sharpe, 1996), a few studies have concluded that women in partner-violent relationships may suffer from cognitive impairments. For example, in their study of battered women, women in therapy for anxiety and depression, and women who were neither abused or in therapy, Getter and Nowinski (1981) found that abused women had more difficulty solving everyday problems than the women in the other two groups. Other researchers (e.g., Bard & Sangrey, 1986; Barnett et al., 1997; Dobson & Dobson, 1981; Launius & Jensen, 1987; Lanius & Lindquist, 1988; Nurius, Furrey, & Berliner, 1992) have reported similar finding of cognitive impairments (e.g., poor problem-solving and coping ability) experienced by battered women.

Physical

Partner aggression often leads to physical injury and sometimes death. If attacked, a woman is more likely to be injured by an intimate partner than by a stranger (Bachman & Saltzman, 1996). In a nationally representative community sample, 3 percent of women reporting aggression by their partners needed medical attention. In a clinical sample of 93 couples, 40 percent of wives who had been the victims of partner violence in the past year had received superficial bruises, 17 percent had suffered serious bruises, and 13 percent reported broken bones, broken teeth, or damage to sensory organs (Cascardi et al., 1992). Similar findings from their community-based family practice clinic were reported by Hamberger, Saunders, and Hovey (1992). One of the most common causes of death for young women is aggression by her husband or boyfriend. According to Browne and Williams (1993) about 2,000 women are killed each year by their partners or ex-partners.

Societal Costs

Due to the private nature of partner abuse, estimating the monetary cost to society has been rather difficult. However, it is known that approximately 12 to 50 percent of women who seek treatment in an emergency room are there because of injuries incurred during a violent attack from their spouse (Abbott, Johnson, Koziol-McClain, & Lowenstein, 1995). The costs of arresting and processing perpetrators of partner violence are very high. For example, in just one year, police, court, and detention costs for partner aggression in New York City were $41 million (Zorza, 1994).

Why Do Battered Women Stay?

Of all the questions asked about partner abuse, this is probably the most frequent. It would seem that a logical solution to problems with partner abuse would be to just exit the relationship. While educating high school and college students, as well as community groups about domestic violence, one often hears many women at these presentations say things such as "If my boyfriend ever did that to me, I'd leave him." As complicated an issue as partner abuse is, reasons women stay in these relationships are just as complicated. According to Strube (1988) there are many reasonable explanations why a women would choose to remain in an abusive relationship. Strube (1988) contends that it may not be safe for her to exit the relationship. For example, her leaving may anger her husband even more, and he may be even more likely to threaten and harm her or someone she cares about (e.g., her family). A second reason a woman may choose to stay may be because she does not have the financial means to leave. This point will be discussed in greater detail later in this chapter. Finally, it is difficult to leave a bad marriage, whether it is abusive or not; therefore, the response may not be atypical to women in general making a decision to leave their partners. Given these findings, maybe a more constructive way to ask the question "Why do women stay in abusive relationships?" is "Why is it so hard for women to leave these abusive relationships?"

Prevention

As partner aggression becomes more of a national and international priority (Marwick, 1998), attempts to prevent this type of aggression increase. Curricula designed to increase awareness about partner aggression, change attitudes about partner aggression, teach alternative strategies to physical aggression as a means of resolving conflict, and increase help-seeking behavior among those students already involved in aggressive relationships, are becoming more commonplace in high schools (Avery-Leaf, Cascardi, O'Leary, & Slep, 1996; Jaffe, Suderman, Reitzel, & Killip, 1992; Lavoie, Vezina, Piche, & Boivin, 1995). These types of programs appear to have an impact on the attitudes and behaviors of high school students, although long-term follow-ups are necessary to determine if such programs have a lasting impact.

Treatment

When working with a violent couple, the safety of the woman must be addressed first. An immediate discussion with the wife about a safety plan (e.g., local resources, legal options, a way to get out of the house safely, and a place to go for refuge) is important in many cases. There are a number of ways to treat partner abuse. Treatment can take the form of counseling; focusing on the husband, the wife, or both; in group, or individual formats. Other forms of intervention include community-level interventions (e.g., shelters), encouraging economic independence, pharmacological treatments, and interventions by the criminal justice system (e.g., arrest). Regardless of the therapeutic modality (i.e., type of therapy), cessation of the aggression must be a priority. Ironically, this is not always the priority of the couple presenting for therapy. As mentioned earlier, even couples experiencing violence do not report such violence when asked to identify problems in their relationship (O'Leary et al., 1992).

Educational and Psychological Interventions

The following section will discuss different formats of programs designed to treat partner violence, including programs for men, programs for women, and couples' programs. If a couple presents for therapy, and it is decided that the treatment focus will be on the aggression in the relationship, it is important for the therapist to use information from the assessment to determine if the individual or if the couple should receive some intervention. There are a number of advantages and disadvantages to each form of approach.

Many of the available treatment programs for partner abuse have been derived from cognitive-behavioral theories of husband-to-wife violence (e.g., Edelson & Syers, 1990; Hamberger & Lohr, 1989). A large number of programs for men have come out of a feminist approach to the treatment of partner aggression (e.g., EMERGE, 1980). Although less common, there are a number of programs designed to treat partner-abusive men that are derived from other theoretical perspectives, including insight-oriented approaches (e.g., Saunders, 1996; Snyder & Wills, 1991).

Programs for Men.   Many programs for men (also known as gender-specific programs) have been influenced by a feminist approach. This perspective views battering as a means of controlling and oppressing women. Followers of this orientation believe that men must learn not to "choose" violence toward their partners (e.g., EMERGE, 1980). In cognitive-behavioral oriented groups, treatment typically focuses on cessation of the physical and psychological aggression through such techniques as anger management and conflict management. In addition, such groups usually attend to the feelings men have while engaging in their aggressive acts (see Adams & McCormick, 1982; Caesar & Hamberger, 1989)

Programs for Women.   It is important to remember that programs for women (also known as gender-specific programs) are not "treating" the women for being abused (Tutty, Bidgood, & Rothery, 1993). These programs usually focus on decreasing self-blame and on helping women become aware of alternatives to the abusive relationship. Other components of women's treatment include teaching them to recognize characteristics of abusive relationships, helping them to understand the emotional effects of violence, and teaching them ways to control their reactions to negative events (O'Leary, Heyman, & Neidig, 1998). Reasons to conduct individual instead of couples treatment include (1) the victims would probably not feel comfortable expressing themselves in a couples format for fear of retaliation from spouses; (2) if the treatment included husbands and wives, wives might believe they were partly responsible for the aggression perpetrated against them; and (3) it may be difficult to accurately assess a woman's motivation to continue the relationship with her spouse present (Bograd, 1984; Ganely, 1981; Margolin & Burman, 1993; Pence & McMahon, 1996). There are also advantages to conducting couples therapy in addition to, or in place of an individual intervention. Some of the advantages of couples therapy include (1) changing the interactional patterns that typically precede aggression; and (2) teaching both partners the same techniques and information so they are sure of the therapist's conceptualization of the problem (e.g., the wife is not responsible for the aggression) and they can both implement the various techniques (e.g., Heyman & Neidig, 1997; Margolin & Burman, 1993). Although there seems to be theoretical reasons for choice of therapeutic format, there is no clear evidence about whether couples therapy is better or if individual therapy is more appropriate. It is generally accepted that couples therapy may be indicated if aggression is in the past or is relatively "mild" and infrequent, and the wife does not fear her husband, and is not in any serious danger (O'Leary,

Heyman, & Neidig, 1998). In addition, other researchers (Vivian & Langhinrichsen-Rohling, 1996) contend that if couples present for treatment with truly mutual and mild aggression, a couples format may be the best way to address marital and individual issues related to the aggression.

Programs for Couples. Couples group formats (also known as conjoint programs) focus on how each partner may be contributing to escalation of physical aggression—that is, a focus on each partner's role in allowing a relatively calm discussion to get out of hand. Specifically, many programs focus on helping spouses to eliminate any physical and psychological aggression, to accept responsibility for escalation of anger interchanges, to recognize and control self-angering thoughts, to communicate better, to increase positive activities, and to understand that each partner is entitled to be treated with respect (O'Leary et al., 1998). As mentioned, conjoint formats are certainly more controversial than gender-specific groups. Recent studies have investigated the effectiveness of such programs and have found outcomes to be positive (e.g., Brannen & Rubin, 1996; O'Leary et al., 1998).

Community-Level Interventions

Community-level interventions include services, such as shelters, safe homes, and advocacy. According to a recent survey by Plichta (1996), there are approximately 1,800 programs, including 1,200 shelters for battered women in the United States. Although it does not "fix" the problem, shelters and safe homes give the victim of partner abuse an alternative to remaining in the violent relationship. According to Dutton-Douglas (1991), the most important aspect of any shelter program is to help women make plans for their safety. Shelter counseling programs can help a woman feel less isolated, and possibly begin to think differently about her situation (Gelles, 1976). Public education and changing societal norms are also a big part of the "shelter movement." Women can also receive therapy and counseling services during their stay at the shelter. A safe home network, on the other hand, relocates women and children to a host family for up to three months. Although there are few data on the number of women that take advantage of these community-level interventions, it appears that services are inadequate to meet the needs of the women seeking them (O'Sullivan, Wise, & Douglass, 1995).

Encouraging Economic Independence

According to Strube (1988), financial dependency is one of the reasons women stay in abusive relationships. Take the scenario of a woman married to a wealthy doctor who is aggressive toward her. The couple decided together, years earlier, that she would stay home and raise their children, while the husband earned a comfortable salary. She may be terribly upset by the abuse she experiences, but each time she thinks of leaving him, the alternative seems even more dismal. That is, without her husband, she would never be able to afford the life she is accustomed to, and even worse, she may not even be able to support her two children. Therefore, when she thinks of her alternative, she may be more inclined to withstand the aggression than leave her husband and face the unknown. Therefore, having the financial means to leave an abusive relationship will play an important role in abused women's freedom from victimization (Barnett et al., 1997). If a woman is not economically dependent on her partner, she will be in a better position to leave her partner if violence continues. Furthermore, Gelles (1976) believes that having a job removes a battered woman's isolation, which may enable her to gain a different perspective on her situation. Therefore, aiding women in abusive relationships to obtain welfare benefits, and preparing them for employment is critical (Dutton-Douglas, 1991).

Pharmacological Treatments

Recently, researchers have been looking toward a biomedical prospective in an effort to learn more about and respond to partner violence (American Medical Association, 1992b). That is, there has been an effort to see if there are chemicals in the body of aggressive men that would react positively to medication. According to Maiuro and Avery (1996) a number of studies have suggested that selective serotonin reuptake inhibitors (SSRIs) may be effective in treating behavioral emotional features found in partner violent men.

Criminal Justice System

Arrest.   Implementation of a mandatory arrest policy for perpetrators of partner violence, and the mandatory arrest of victims have proved to be controversial topics. For example, if a woman calls the police in an effort to end her husband's violent attack, or if anyone witnessing the violence notifies the police, the police are mandated to arrest the perpetrator, and in some cases, the victim as well. Otherwise, the police may be called to the scene only to be turned away by a victimized spouse who chooses not to have her husband arrested. Researchers, including Berk (1993) believe that arrest is not superior to a variety of other criminal justice interventions, but it may not be any worse. Therefore, he feels that unless there are legal, ethical, or practical reasons to choose another intervention, arrest should remain an option. Other researchers feel that arrest is not an appropriate solution. For example, Buzawa and Buzawa (1993) have pointed out that studies have failed to show an association between arrest and the deterrence of further violence. Furthermore, Sherman (1992a) reported that when arrest is followed by a rapid release, it actually enhances violence. In addition, other studies have confirmed that any deterrent value of arrest is only of short-term value. It has also been documented that some women do not prefer arrest of their partner for a number of reasons (Smith & Klein, 1984). Some women are aware of the increased risk of abuse when their partners return; some are afraid of the financial ramifications that may be incurred as a result of their partner's arrest. Furthermore, some believe that arrest policies may not have sensitized police to victims' needs (Buzawa & Buzawa, 1993). For example, some people feel that police seem more concerned with liability and political pressures than with victims' needs. There also seems to be an increase in dual arrests. Buzawa and Buzawa (1993) believe that this may be a function of coercing the victim to drop charges or else she will be arrested as well. More recently, police departments and courts have been creating special units and/or have been trained to deal with domestic violence (A. Rosenbaum, personal communication, November, 1997). In any case, at present, the data on whether arrest is beneficial or detrimental is still mixed, but it is a policy that is now implemented quite routinely.

Restraining Orders. A restraining order empowers the police to remove an aggressive partner from a couple's home and to arrest him for a violation if they are called by a potential victim or friend of the victim. In theory, a restraining order should protect a woman from her abusive partner and keep her safe, but this is not always a reality (Kelilitz, 1994). For example, a study of 350 restraining orders issued in Boulder and Denver, Colorado, revealed that violent reoffending occurred in 29 percent of the cases (Harrell, Smith, & Newmark, 1993). There are a number of reasons restraining orders can, at times, be ineffective. For example, a limited protective order (e.g., one that allows visitation of their children by the abuser; one that orders a couple into couples counseling) does not enable a woman to easily remove herself from a negative situation (Hansen, Harway, & Cervantes, 1991).

Different Causes for Different Levels of Partner Aggression. It is important to realize that there are different causes and different levels of severity of partner violence. Therefore, the most appropriate intervention typically depends on the level and severity of the partner abuse. For example, causes of dating violence, which is a very common problem among high school students, are likely different than the cause of severe beating of a partner. Similarly, the causes of initial slapping incidents in early marriage are likely to be different from repeated slapping incidents that escalate into pushing and kicking. For example, based on our own research, we know that drug and alcohol use are important risk factors for severe abuse, but not for mild to moderate levels of partner aggression. Given that there are different causes for different levels of partner aggression, it is necessary to be able to offer a wide variety of interventions that fit the needs of a particular population. More specifically, conjoint therapy may be most appropriate with psychological and occasional physical aggression. Gender-specific treatments appear to be best suited for the more severe partner abuse.

Summary

Prevalence

As many as 57 percent of high school students will experience dating violence by the time they graduate. As many as 65 percent of college students have experienced some form of dating violence. Based on a national survey, about 12 percent of women are abused by their partners each year, and 5 percent are severely abused. Between one-half and two-thirds of women seeking marital therapy have reported experiencing at least one act of partner aggression in the past year. About one-quarter of these women report experiencing severe violence. Although surveys have shown that men and women are equally likely to engage in "mild" forms of partner aggression, women are much more likely to be injured.

Risk Factors

Demographic Variables.   Younger men are more likely to engage in partner abuse. The literature suggests that being less educated, having a lower income or living in poverty, and having a low-prestige occupation increase the likelihood of engaging in partner aggression.

Witnessing or Experiencing.   Experiencing physical, emotional, or sexual abuse by parents or caretakers, or witnessing verbal or physical aggression between one's parents in childhood are risk factors for partner aggression.

Psychological Factors.   Men who have high scores on measures of anger or hostility, increased depressive symptomatology, difficulties being assertive and/or low self-esteem are at risk for partner aggression. In addition, men who experience jealousy, have a need for power and control, and/or have a personality disorder are more likely to be aggressive toward their partners.

Relationship Variables.   Men who are unhappy or unsatisfied in their relationships are more likely to engage in partner abuse. Furthermore, men who are verbally aggressive toward their partners are also at risk for partner abuse.

Prevention and Treatment

Prevention.   Curricula designed to increase awareness about partner aggression, change attitudes about partner aggression, teach alternative strategies to physical aggression as a means of resolving conflict, and increase help-seeking behavior among those students already involved in aggressive relationships are becoming more commonplace in high schools. In addition, there is evidence that some programs change attitudes regarding violence.

Intervention.   There are a number of ways to treat partner abuse. Treatment can take the form of counseling, focusing on the husband, the wife, or both, in group or individual formats. Other forms of treatment include community-level interventions, encouraging economic independence, pharmacological treatments, and interventions by the criminal justice system. Regardless of the type of therapy, cessation of the aggression is always a priority.

REFERENCES

Abbott, J. R., Johnson, J., Koziol-McClain, J., & Lowenstein, S. R. (1995). Domestic violence against women: Incidence and prevalence in an emergency room population. *Journal of the American Medical Association, 273,* 1763–1767.

Adams, D. C. & McCormick, A. J. (1982). Men unlearning violence: A group approach based on the collective model. In M. Roy (Ed.), *The Abusive Partner* (pp. 170–179). New York: Van Nostrand Reinhold.

American Medical Association. (1992). *Diagnostic and Treatment Guidelines on Domestic Violence.* Chicago: Author.

American Psychiatric Association. (1987). *Diagnostic and Statistical Manual of Mental Disorders* (3rd ed. rev.). Washington, DC: American Psychiatric Association.

American Psychiatric Association. (1994). *Diagnostic and Statistical Manual of Mental Disorders* (4th ed.). Washington, DC: American Psychiatric Association.

Arias, I. & Beach, S. H. (1987). Validity of self-reports of marital violence. *Journal of Family Violence, 2,* 139–142.

Arias, I., Samios, M., & O'Leary, K. D. (1987). Prevalence and correlates of physical aggression during courtship. *Journal of Interpersonal Violence, 2,* 82–90.

Avery-Leaf, S., Cascardi, M., & O'Leary, K. D. (1994). *Efficacy of a dating violence prevention program.* Poster presented at the 102nd annual meeting of the American Psychological Association, Los Angeles, CA.

Avery-Leaf, S., Cascardi, M., O'Leary, K. D., & Slep, A. M. S. (1996). *The Prevention of Dating Violence: The Short-Term Impact of a Five Session Curriculum on Dating Aggression and Attitudes Justifying Violence.* Poster presented at the 30th annual meeting of the Association for the Advancement of Behavior Therapy, New York.

Bachman, R. & Saltzman, L. E. (1996). *Violence Against Women: Estimates from the Redesigned Survey* (Bureau of Justice Statistics special report). Rockville, MD: U.S. Department of Justice. (NJC No. 154348)

Bandura, A. (1978). Social learning theory of aggression. *Journal of Communication,* Summer, 12–29.

Bard, M. & Sangrey, D. (1986). *The Crime Victims Book* (2nd. ed.). New York: Brunner/Mazel.

Barnett, O. W. & Fagan, R. W. (1993). Alcohol use in male spouse abusers and their female partners. *Journal of Family Violence, 8,* 1–25.

Barnett, O. W., Miller-Perrin, C. L., & Perrin, R. D. (1997). *Family Violence Across the Lifespan: An Introduction.* Thousand Oaks, CA: Sage.

Berk, R. A. (1993). The scientific evidence is not conclusive. In R. J. Gelles & D. R. Loseke (Eds.), *Current Controversies on Family Violence* (pp. 337–356). Newbury Park, CA: Sage.

Bograd, M. (1984). Family systems approach to wife beating: A feminist critique. *American Journal of Orthopsychiatry, 54,* 558–568.

Bookwala, J., Frieze, I. H., Smith, C., & Ryan, K. (1992). Predictors of dating violence: A multivariate analysis. *Violence and Victims, 7,* 297–311.

Brannen, S. J. & Rubin, A. (1996). Comparing the effectiveness of gender-specific groups in a court-mandated spouse abuse treatment program. *Research in Social Work Practice, 6,* 405–424.

Brennan, K. A., Schumacher, J. A., Shaver, P. R., & Clark, C. L. (1998). *From Brady Bunch to Brady Punch: Connections Between Sibling Victimization and Later Dating Violence.* Poster presented at the meeting of the International Society for the Study of Personal Relationships, Saratoga Springs, NY.

Breslin, F. C., Riggs, D. S., O'Leary, K. D., & Arias, I. (1990). Family precursors: Expected and actual consequences of dating aggression. *Journal of Interpersonal Violence, 5,* 247–258.

Browne, A. & Williams, K. R. (1993). Gender, intimacy, and lethal violence: Trends from 1976–1987. *Gender and Society, 7,* 78–98.

Buaserman, S. A. K. & Arias, I. (1992). Relationships among relational investments, marital satisfaction, and marital commitment in domestically victimized and non-victimized wives. *Violence and Victims, 7,* 287–296.

Buzawa, E. C. & Buzawa, C. G. (1993). The scientific evidence is not conclusive. In R. J. Gelles & D. R. Loseke (Eds.), *Current Controversies on Family Violence* (pp. 337–356). Newbury Park, CA: Sage.

Caesar, P. L. & Hamberger, L. K. (Eds.). (1989). *Treating Men Who Batter: Theory, Practice and Programs.* New York: Springer.

Cantos, A. L., Neidig, P. H., & O'Leary, K. D. (1994). Injuries of women and men in a treatment program for domestic violence. *Journal of Family Violence, 9,* 113–124.

Carden, A. D. (1994). Wife abuse and the wife abuser: Review and recommendations. *Counseling Psychologist, 22,* 539–582.

Cascardi, M. C., Langhinrichsen, J., & Vivian, D. (1992). Marital aggression: Impact, injury, and health correlates for husbands and wives. *Archives of Internal Medicine, 152,* 1178–1184.

Cascardi, M. C. & O'Leary, K. D. (1992). Depressive symptomatology, self-esteem and self-blame in battered women. *Journal of Family Violence, 9,* 249–259.

Cazanave, N. A. & Straus, M. A. (1990). Race, class, network embeddedness, and family violence: A search for potent support systems. In M. A. Straus & R. J. Gelles (Eds.), *Physical Violence in American Families* (pp. 321–339). New Brunswick, NJ: Transaction.

Dutton, D. G., Starzomski, A., & Ryan, L. (1996). Antecedents of abusive behavior in wife assaulters. *Journal of Family Violence, 11,* 113–132.

Dutton, D. G., van-Ginkel, C., & Landolt, M. A. (1996). Jealousy, intimate abusiveness, and intrusiveness. *Journal of Family Violence, 11,* 411–423.

Dutton-Douglas, M. A. (1991). Counseling and shelter services for battered women. In M. Steinman (Ed.), *Woman Battering: Policy Responses* (pp. 113–130). Cincinnati, OH: Anderson.

Edelson, J. L. & Syers, M. (1990). The relative effectiveness of group treatments for men who batter. *Social Work Research and Abstracts, 26,* 10–17.

EMERGE. (1980). *Do You Feel Like Beating Up on Somebody?* Boston: Author.

Feldbau-Kohn, S., Heyman, R. E., & O'Leary, K. D. (1998). Major depressive disorder and depressive symptomatology as predictors of husband to wife physical aggression. *Violence and Victims.*

Ganely, A. L. (1981). *Court-Mandated Counseling for Men Who Batter: A Three Day Workshop for the Mental Health Professional* [Participants manual]. Washington, DC: Center for Women's Policy Studies.

Gelles, R. J. (1976). Abused wives: Why do they stay? *Journal of Marriage and the Family, 38,* 659–668.

Getter, H. & Nowinski, J. (1981). A free response test of personal effectiveness. *Journal of Personality Assessment, 45,* 301–308.

Hamberger, L. K. & Lohr, J. M. (1989). Proximal causes of spouse abuse: A theoretical analysis for cognitive-behavioral interventions. In P. L. Caeser & L. K. Hamberger (Eds.), *Treating Men Who Batter: Theory, Practice, and Programs* (pp. 53–76). New York: Springer.

Hamberger, L. K., Saunders, D. G., & Hovey, M. (1992). The prevalence of domestic violence in community practice and rate of physical injury. *Family Medicine, 24,* 283–287.

Hansen, H., Harway, M., & Cervantes, N. (1991). Therapists' perceptions of severity in cases of family violence. *Violence and Victims, 6,* 225–235.

Harrell, A. D., Smith, B., & Newmark, S. (1993). *Court Processing of Restraining Orders for Domestic Violence Victims.* Washington, DC: Urban Institute.

Heyman, R. E. & Neidig, P. H. (1997). Physical aggression couples treatment. In W. K. Halford & H. J. Markamn (Eds.), *Handbook of Marriage and Couples Intervention.* New York: Wiley.

Heyman, R. E., O'Leary, K. D., & Jouriles, E. N. (1995). Alcohol and aggressive personality styles: Potentiators of serious physical aggression against wives? *Journal of Family Psychology, 9,* 44–57.

Heyman, R. E. & Schlee, K. A. (1997). Toward a better estimate of the prevalence of partner abuse: Adjusting rates based on the sensitivity of the Conflict Tactics Scale. *Journal of Family Psychology, 11,* 332–338.

Holtzworth-Munroe, A., Beatty, S. B., & Anglin, K. (1995). The assessment of marital violence: An introduction for the marital therapist. In N. S. Jacobson & A. S. Gurman (Eds.), *Clinical Handbook of Couple Therapy.* New York: Guilford.

Houskamp, B. M. & Foy, D. W. (1991). The assessment of post-traumatic stress disorder in battered women. *Journal of Interpersonal Violence, 6,* 367–375.

Huesmann, L. R. (1988). An information processing model for the development of aggression. *Aggressive Behavior, 14,* 13–24.

Jaffe, P. G., Suderman, M., Reitzel, D., & Killip, S. M. (1992). An evaluation of a secondary school primary prevention program in intimate relationships. *Violence and Victims, 7,* 129–146.

Kantor, G. K., Jasinski, J. L., & Aldarondo, E. (1994). Sociocultural status and incidence of marital violence in Hispanic families: Special Issue: Violence against women of color. *Violence and Victims, 9,* 207–222.

Kantor, G. K. & Straus, M. A. (1987). The "drunken bum" theory of wife beating. *Social Problems, 34,* 213–230.

Kelilitz, S. L. (1994). Legal report—Civil protection orders: A viable system tool for deterring family violence. *Violence and Victims, 9,* 79–84.

Koss, M. P., Koss, P., & Woodruff, W. J. (1991). Deleterious effects of criminal victimization on women's health and medical utilization. *Archives of Internal Medicine, 151,* 342–357.

Launius, M. H. & Jensen, B. L. (1987). Interpersonal problem-solving skills in battered, counseling, and control women. *Journal of Family Violence, 2,* 151–162.

Launius, M. H. & Lindquist, C. U. (1988). Learned helplessness, external locus of control, and passivity in battered women. *Journal of Interpersonal Violence, 3,* 307–318.

Lavoie, F., Vezina, L., Piche, C., & Boivin, M. (1995). Evaluation of a prevention program for violence in teen dating relationships. *Journal of Interpersonal Violence, 10,* 516–524.

Leonard, K. E. & Blane, H. T. (1992). Alcohol and marital aggression in a national sample of young men. *Journal of Interpersonal Violence, 7,* 19–30.

Leonard, K. E. & Senchak, M. (1996). Prospective prediction of husband marital aggression within newlywed couples. *Journal of Abnormal Psychology, 105,* 369–380.

Maiuro, R. D. & Avery, D. H. (1996). Psychopharmacological treatment of aggressive behavior: Implications for domestically violent men. *Violence and Victims, 11,* 239–261.

Maiuro, R. D., Cahn, T. S., Vitaliano, P. P., & Wagner, B. C. (1988). Anger, hostility, and depression in domestically violent versus generally assaultive men and nonviolent control subjects. *Journal of Consulting and Clinical Psychology, 56,* 17–23.

Makepeace, J. M. (1981). Courtship violence among college students. *Family Relations, 30,* 97–102.

Margolin, G. & Burman, B. (1993). Wife abuse vs. marital violence: Different terminologies, explanations and solutions. *Clinical Psychology Review, 13,* 59–73.

Marwick, C. (1998). Domestic violence recognized as world problem. *Journal of the American Medical Association, 279,* 1510.

McCloskey, L. A. (1996). Socioeconomic and coercive power within the family. *Gender and Society, 10,* 449–463.

Murphy, C. M., Meyer, S. L., & O'Leary, K. D. (1993). Family of origin violence and MCMI-II psychopathology among partner assaultive men. *Violence and Victims, 8,* 165–176.

Neidig, P. H., Friedman, D. H., & Collins, B. S. (1986). Attitudinal characteristics of males who have engaged in spouse abuse. *Journal of Family Violence, 1,* 223–233.

Nurius, P. S., Furrey, J., & Berliner, L. (1992). Coping capacity among women with abusive partners. *Violence and Victims, 7,* 229–243.

O'Leary, K. D. & Curley, A. D. (1986). Assertion and family violence: Correlates of spouse abuse. *Journal of Marital and Family Therapy, 12,* 281–289.

O'Leary, K. D., Heyman, R. E., & Neidig, P. H. (in press). Treatment of Wife Abuse: A Comparison of Gender-Specific and Couples Approaches. *Behavior Therapy.*

O'Leary, K. D. & Jacobson, N. S. (1997). Partner relational problems with physical abuse. In *DSM-IV Sourcebook*, (Vol. III, pp. 673–692). Washington, DC: American Psychiatric Association.

O'Leary, K. D., Vivian, D., & Malone, J. (1992). Assessment of physical aggression against women in marriages: The need for multimodal assessment. *Behavioral Assessment, 14,* 5–14.

Orava, T. A., McLeod, P. J., & Sharpe, D. (1996). Perceptions of control, depressive symptomatology, and self-esteem of women in transition from abusive relationships. *Journal of Family Violence, 11,* 167–186.

O'Sullivan, C., Wise, J., & Douglass, V. (1995). *Domestic Violence Shelter Residents in New York: Profile, Needs, and Alternatives to Shelter.* Paper presented at the 4th International Family Violence Conference, Durham, New Hampshire.

Pan, H. S., Neidig, P. H., & O'Leary, K. D. (1994). Predicting mild and severe husband-to-wife physical aggression. *Journal of Consulting and Clinical Psychology, 62,* 975–981.

Pence, E. & McMahon, M. (1996). Replying to Dan O'Leary. *Journal of Interpersonal Violence, 11,* 452–455.

Pesce, C. (1990, October 4). Intimates hope for freedom to start over. *USA Today,* p. 1.

Plichta, S. B. (1996). Violence and abuse: Implications for women's health. In M. M. Falik, E. Collins, & K. Scott (Eds.), *Women's Health: The Commonwealth Fund Survey.* Baltimore, MD: Johns Hopkins University Press.

Prince, J. E. & Arias, I. (1994). The role of perceived control and the desirability of control among abusive and nonabusive husbands. *American Journal of Family Therapy, 22,* 126–134.

Rosenbaum, A. R. & O'Leary, K. D. (1981). Marital violence: Characteristics of abusive couples.

Journal of Consulting and Clinical Psychology, 49, 63–71.

Russel, M. N., Lipov, E., Phillips, N., & White, B. (1989). Psychological profiles of violent and non-violent maritally distressed couples. *Psychotherapy, 26,* 81–87.

Saunders, D. G. (1994, November). *Cognitive-Behavioral and Process-Psychodynamic Treatments for Men Who Batter: Interactions Between Offenders Traits and Treatments.* Paper presented at the Association for the Advancement of Behavior Therapy.

Saunders, D. G. (1996). Feminist-cognitive-behavioral and process psychodynamic treatments for men who batter: Interaction of abuser traits and treatment models. *Violence & Victims, 11,* 393–414.

Schumacher, J. A. & O'Leary, K. D. (1998). *A Glass Half Empty or Half Full?: Alcohol as a Risk Factor for Partner Aggression.* Manuscript submitted for publication.

Shepherd, J. (1990). Victims of personal violence: The relevance of Symonds' model of psychological response and loss theory. *British Journal of Social Work, 20,* 309–332.

Sherman, L. W. (1992). The influence of criminality on criminal law: Evaluating arrests for misdemeanor domestic violence. *Journal of Criminal Law and Criminology, 85,* 901–945.

Smith, D. & Klein, J. (1984). Police control of interpersonal disputes. *Social Problems, 31,* 468–481.

Snyder, D. K. & Wills, R. M. (1991). Long-term effectiveness of behavioral versus insight oriented marital therapy: A four-year follow-up study. *Journal of Consulting and Clinical Therapy, 59,* 138–141.

Stets, J. E. & Straus, M. A. (1990). Gender differences in reporting marital violence and its medical and psychological consequences. In M. A. Straus & R. J. Gelles (Eds.), *Physical violence in American Families: Risk Factors and Adaptations to Violence in 8,145 Families* (pp. 151–166). New Brunswick, NJ: Transaction.

Straus, M. A. (1979). Measuring intrafamily conflict and violence: The Conflict Tactics (CT) Scale. *Journal of Marriage and the Family, 41,* 75–78.

Straus, M. A. & Gelles, R. J. (1986). Societal change and change in family violence from 1975 to 1985 as revealed by two national surveys. *Journal of Marriage and the Family, 48,* 465–479.

Straus, M. A. & Gelles, R. J. (1990). How violent are American families?: Estimates from the national family violence resurvey and other studies. In M. A. Straus & R. J. Gelles (Eds.), *Physical Violence in American Families: Risk Factors and Adaptions to Violence in 8,145 Families.* New Brunswick, NJ: Transaction.

Straus, M. A., Hamby, S. L., Boney-McCoy, S., & Sugarman, D. B. (1996). The revised conflict tactic scales (CTS2): Development and some preliminary psychometric data. *Journal of Family Issues, 17,* 283–316.

Straus, M. A. & Smith, C. (1990). Violence in Hispanic families in the United States: Incidence rates and structural interpretations. In M. A. Straus & R. J. Gelles (Eds.), *Physical Violence in American Families* (pp. 341–367). New Brunswick, NJ: Transaction.

Strube, M. J. (1988). The decision to leave an abusive relationship: Empirical evidence and theoretical issues. *Psychological Bulletin, 104,* 236–250.

Tutty, L. M., Bidgood, B. A., & Rothery, M. A. (1993). Support groups for battered women: Research on their efficacy. *Journal of Family Violence, 8,* 325–343.

Vivian, D. & Langhinrichsen-Rohling, J. (1996). Are bi-directionally violent couples mutually victimized? A gender sensitive comparison. In L. K. Hamberger & C. Renzetti (Eds.), *Domestic Partner Abuse.* New York: Springer.

Walker, L. E. (1979). *The Battered Woman.* New York: Harper & Row.

Walker, L. (1989*). Terrifying love: Why battered women kill and how society responds.* New York: Harper & Row.

Widom, C. S. (1989). Does violence beget violence? A critical examination of the literature. *Psychological Bulletin, 106,* 3–28.

Wilson, G. T., Nathan, P. E., O'Leary, K. D., & Clark, L. A. (1996). *Abnormal Psychology: Integrating Perspectives.* Needham Heights, MA: Simon & Schuster.

Zorza, J. (1994). Women battering: High costs and the state of the law [Special issue]. *Clearinghouse Review, 28,* 383–395.

9 Elder Abuse

ROSALIE S. WOLF

UMass Memorial Health Care, Worcester, Massachusetts

Description of the Problem

Elder abuse is not a new phenomenon. Since ancient times, writings have recorded the intergenerational and marital conflict that occurs within family life. As a social problem, however, elder abuse is barely in its adolescence. First mentioned in a British medical journal as "granny battering" in 1975 (Burston), it has captured the attention of nations throughout the world.

Case Illustrations

The examples below, taken from elder abuse projects, illustrate the various types of abuse and relationships among victims and perpetrators and the contextual issues associated with elder mistreatment.

Case A. According to Mrs. A (77 years old), her husband came from a dysfunctional family who neglected him. He had always been very abusive to her physically and psychologically. He began during their honeymoon when he pretended to have fallen out of a five-story window, but was hiding under the bed. He took great pleasure in playing cruel tricks and scaring her.

A very well-educated couple, Mr. A taught at prestigious colleges. He took great pride in his work, but had difficulties starting in new positions. Changes were difficult for him. He displayed bad temper only toward his wife. To others, Mr. A was charming. Although he never abused his children, he was unable to show or give affection to them. All three children received excellent educations and seemed to have been spared physical abuse.

The interview with the case worker took place outside the home because Mrs. A feared bringing people there. She was very passive, but evidently cared for her husband. Over the years, she was able to hide the bruises. Mr. A used alcohol moderately, but never in relation to the abuse. He did have periods during which he attempted suicide, was once hospitalized in a psychiatric ward. However, he was able to function well at work and seemed to have been successful until retirement when he became more violent toward his wife. Mrs. A stated that her husband always needed a very structured life; he had a very low tolerance for frustration. Since retirement 10 years before, the violence has increased. She felt that he wanted to punish her for having a nice, supportive family. He was very critical and very jealous of them.

Case B.   Mrs. B (mother, 85 years old) in her early adulthood harbored dreams of stardom in Hollywood and traveled there, managing to get bit parts in the movies. An early marriage put her dreams on hold, especially due to her husband's chronic alcoholism.

The family consisted of two sons, one of whom was 14 years younger than the other; the younger son was the alleged perpetrator of financial abuse. The father passed away from alcohol-related causes about 8 years earlier. Family dysfunction was the norm. Money was almost nonexistent. Beautiful, antique furniture was sold off piece by piece until the family was reduced to two twin beds that were shared with an incontinent, terminally ill father. When the situation deteriorated to the point that there was no money for food, the mother would request financial aid from a welfare agency (private) that provided assistance as long as it could.

The younger son, the perpetrator, grew up in this abusive environment, as an isolated, insecure, and withdrawn individual who only emerged when drinking. He admitted to having an alcohol problem. Mrs. B recognized the predictable pattern that her son was pursuing.

Case C.   Mrs. C, 81 years old, had heart surgery to repair two valves, entered a nursing home for recuperation where she remained for a few months, and then asked to return home. She was independent in feeding, but needed assistance with other activities of daily living. Mr. C was faced with the task of being her primary caregiver, which he was not always able to do, partly because of his alcohol abuse. He often became verbally abusive. He also had unrealistic expectations concerning his wife's condition, anticipating that she would improve to the point where he would no longer need to handle the caregiving responsibilities.

Mr. C believed that his wife was capable of doing more for herself (walking, standing, cooperating with the physical therapist), but was not trying hard enough. There was some discrepancy among the medical staff that cared for Mrs. C as to her restorative potential. In the previous six months, Mr. C slapped her on two different occasions when he became frustrated, once when he was transferring her from the bed to a wheel chair and her legs weakened, resulting in her falling. Despite being overwhelmed with caregiving, Mr. C refused to purchase full-time help even though his son said that he could well afford it.

Mr. and Mrs. C have one son who is remarried and lives some distance away. He had three daughters with his first wife. Ten years previous, one of the girls at a young age was brutally murdered. He may have still been grieving over the situation. Mrs. C appeared to have some unresolved conflicts; her husband's drinking problem did not help matters.

Such situations as those described above may or may not have come to the attention of the authorities or private agencies earlier in this century, but if they had, the cases certainly were not labeled *elder abuse*. As a social problem, elder abuse is very much a legacy of the political climate of the 1960s and 1970s, shaped by forces within the public welfare, aging, and family violence establishments.

Historical Developments

A Public Welfare Issue

Concern about the mistreatment of older persons as a public policy issue first appeared in the 1962 Public Welfare amendments to the Social Security Act. The legislation allocated funds to the states on a 75–25 matching basis for the purpose of providing an array of services (known as protective services) to meet the social, psychological, medical, and legal needs of:

> those who, because of physical or mental limitations are unable to act in their own behalf; are seriously limited in the management of their affairs; are neglected or exploited; or, living in unsafe or hazardous conditions (DC Department of Public Welfare, 1967, p. 12).

Several years later, the government funded a series of demonstration projects to determine the nature, need, clients, and effectiveness of this approach (U.S. DHEW, 1966). Although the projects furnished for the first time, information on many aspects of protective service delivery, serious questions about program effectiveness were raised. The Benjamin Rose Institute, using an experimental-control designed study, found that the intervention (protective services) neither prevented deterioration of their clients nor improved their mental and physical status, but did increase the likelihood of institutionalization and possible risk of death (Blenkner et al., 1971). At two other sites only one-third of the cases were closed because of successful intervention. Also, more than one-third of the workers rated the program negatively, because they failed to meet client needs or provide adequate services (Anetzberger, 1994). Despite the experience and findings of these demonstration projects, the proponents for the expansion of protective services were successful in the passage of Title XX of the Social Security Act in 1974, which mandated and funded protective services for all adults 18 years and older, without regard for income.

By 1977, most states had established adult protective services units (APS) in their public welfare (human services) departments, or contracted with other public or private entities to provide the services. A few states had passed specific adult protective services legislation. For several reasons, perhaps because of the questionable effectiveness of the intervention, the high cost of providing the services, the potential for infringement of civil rights, and the stigma of public welfare, the program was criticized by professionals and the public alike, and further development came to a halt (Anetzberger, 1994).

However, within a few years, the fate of adult protective services changed. Testimony about *parent battering* before a Congressional subcommittee hearing on family violence in 1977 became a headline issue. Aging advocates within Congress seized on to elder abuse as a cause with emotional and political appeal and scheduled a series of Congressional hearings and investigations (U.S. Select Committee on Aging, 1979; 1981). Because these types of cases were being seen by adult protective services programs, a new system to handle elder abuse cases was unnecessary. The states responded by amending their child protection laws to include adults, or passing new ones specifically for elders, often, modeling them after their child abuse laws. This reconceptualization of the problem of elder mistreatment from "adult in need of protective services" to "victims of elder abuse, neglect, and exploitation" breathed new life into the protective services movement.

An Aging Issue

As an aging issue, elder abuse was viewed within the context of caregiving. The victim was portrayed as a very old, physically and or cognitively impaired elder (usually a mother) under the care of a family member (usually a daughter) who, because of heavy caregiving demands, other immediate family and job responsibilities, became abusive or neglectful. It was this picture of elder abuse that resonated with the Congress and especially the media.

Within the Congress, a campaign was mounted to pass an elder abuse act similar to the Child Abuse Prevention Act, which established the National Center on Child Abuse and Neglect (NCCAN). A bill for a National Center on Elder Abuse was filed in 1981 and refiled in successive Congresses, but never received enough votes to be reported out of committee. As a compromise in 1989, proponents added an amendment to the reauthorized Older Americans Act, which would allocate a small amount of funds for elder abuse preventive services to each of the more than 600 area agencies on aging, the first public policy initiative on elder abuse. Three years later, when it again appeared that the National Center Bill would fail to garner enough votes, the advocates agreed to have it included as an amendment to the 1992 re-authorized Older Americans Act. The National Center was to be a national clearinghouse, to disseminate information, provide technical assistance and training, and promote research. The mandate to establish the National Center was given to the Administration on Aging. Although it was a hard won victory for the supporters, the National Center on Elder Abuse fell far short of the NCCAN in scope and funding.

A Family Violence Issue

Clearly, the child abuse model had a profound effect on how elder abuse was conceptualized in the early years of the field, and the response to it. The commonly accepted and media-promoted view of elder abuse as a consequence of caregiving stress was very much related to the child abuse model. Both dealt with dependent victims, sometimes overly demanding, who required care and attention. The analogy extended even further. Because no model statute existed, the child abuse law, with its mandatory reporting of suspected cases, became the prototype for legislation in three-fourths of the states.

At the same time that the limitations of the child abuse model in explaining elder abuse became apparent, community surveys were showing that spouse abuse was more prevalent than abuse by adult children. Despite the fact that much of elder abuse is partner abuse, there was little recognition of the elder victim on the part of the domestic violence movement until the 1990s (AARP, 1992). In part, such lack of awareness was a result of the distinctly different origins of the two movements. One was a grass roots effort, antiprofessional, and strongly feminist, while the other was professionally motivated mainly by social workers. Also, the early formulation of elder abuse as caregiver stress did not fit within the paradigm of the battered women's movement.

Efforts on the part of the American Association of Retired Persons Women's Initiative Department, the Older Women's League (U.S. Senate Special Committee on Aging, 1994), the Administration on Aging, and others resulted in opening a dialogue between the two groups. Inclusion of elder abuse within the family violence framework transformed it into a public health and criminal justice issue. While some people regret the medicalization and criminalization of the problem, greater awareness and interest in it by medical, legal, law-enforcement personnel and domestic violence advocates have helped to legitimate the movement to the degree that was not possible when elder abuse was regarded exclusively as a public welfare or social service issue.

Definitions

From the earliest days, definitions ascribed to elder abuse have been confusing. Although there is a consensus about the broad categories—physical, psychological (emotional), and financial abuse—there is less agreement as to what the terms represent. Even more perplexing is the inclusion of neglect under the rubric of elder abuse. More appropriate, perhaps, is the more inclusive term of *elder mistreatment* or *elder maltreatment*.

To clarify the relations among the various types of elder victimization, Hudson (1991) undertook a Delphi study involving over 100 researchers, practitioners, educators, and policy-makers working in the field of elder mistreatment. The results are a five-level taxonomy using *violence involving older adults* as the overarching theme. Level II in the classification schema describes the relationship of victim to perpetrator and consists of three categories: self-mistreatment, elder mistreatment, and crime by strangers. Elder mistreatment is further subdivided in terms of the nature of the relationship, which can be either a person/social or a business/professional one. Level III refers to the manner in which elder mistreatment is perpetrated, either by commission (abuse) or omission (neglect). The motivation behind the act of mistreatment becomes the Level IV classification principle: whether it is intentional or unintentional. Level V refers to the types of mistreatment: physical, psychological, social, and financial.

From the taxonomy, Hudson developed the following definition that will serve as the focus of this chapter:

> Elder mistreatment is destructive behavior which is directed toward an older adult, occurs within the context of a relationship denoting trust, and is of sufficient intensity and/or frequency to produce harmful physical, psychological, social, and/or financial effects of unnecessary suffering, injury, pain, loss, and/or violation of human rights and decreased quality of life for the older adult (p. 166).

It includes acts of commission (abuse) and omission (neglect), both intentional and unintentional. Although such deeds can take place in any setting and by any person, for the purpose of this chapter, they are limited to conflict in the home by family members or persons who have a significant relationship with the older person.

More recently, some researchers have questioned the legal and professional basis for elder mistreatment definitions, suggesting that the older person's perception of the particular behavior may be the salient factor for case identification and intervention (Gebotys et al., 1992; Hudson, 1994). New studies on minority aging populations have revealed the important role that culture plays in determining what is acceptable or unacceptable behavior within the family (Hudson & Carlson, 1997; Moon & Williams, 1993; Tomita, 1995).

Epidemiology

Prevalence

Only four studies on the prevalence of elder abuse have been reported in the literature. The first was a random sample survey of 2,020 community dwelling persons age 65 years and older, living in the Metropolitan Boston area (Pillemer & Finkelhor, 1988). The investigators adapted the method used in two previous national family violence surveys (Straus, 1992) and added questions on neglect. When contacted by telephone, the elders were asked about their experience with three types of maltreatment since reaching the age of 65 years. If not able to respond on the telephone, a face-to-face interview was conducted with the elder or a proxy. The questions dealt with very specific acts of violence and neglect. Sixty-three persons reported being mistreated in at least one or more ways, which translated into a rate of 32 elders per 1,000: 20 per 1,000, physical abuse; 11 per 1,000, verbal aggression (also known as psychological or emotional abuse); and 4 per 1,000, neglect. Applying these figures to the entire United States would produce a total of one million victims. Fifty-eight percent of the perpetrators were spouses (23 husbands and 14 wives); 24 percent were adult children, and 18 percent were other persons (grandchildren, siblings, and boarders).

The second study was a random sample telephone survey of Canadian elders based on the Boston survey methods, to which the category of financial exploitation was added (Podnieks et al., 1990). No attempt was made to collect data from persons with physical and/or cognitive deficits who could not respond on the telephone. The rate of victimization of Canadian elders was 40 per 1,000 elders; financial abuse, 25 per 1,000; verbal aggression, 14 per 1,000; physical violence, 5 per 1,000; and neglect, 4 per 1,000. The total number of victims was 80, but some were subjected to more than one type of abuse. Twenty-four of the 26 perpetrators of verbal aggression were spouses, as were 9 of the 10 perpetrators of physical abuse; perpetrators in the remaining cases were other relatives. No information was furnished about the perpetrators of neglect.

A geriatric medical team in a small, semi-industrialized town in Finland carried out an elder abuse prevalence survey as part of a larger mental health and depression study (Kivelä et al., 1992). Postal questionnaires, interviews, and clinical examinations were utilized to collect the data from 1,225 persons. Those unable to respond to the questionnaire were excluded from the study. The elders were asked three questions: their opinion (yes/no) about types of abuse (physical, psychological, neglect, economic, and sexual); if they knew a person(s) who had been abused since he or she had reached retirement age; and if they themselves had been abused since reaching retirement age. Rather than asking the respondents whether they had been subject to very specific acts of violence or neglect, as was done in the Boston and Canadian studies, the Finnish elder decided on his or her own whether mistreatment had occurred. Fifty-five persons reported having been mistreated. Spouses were perpetrators in 49 percent of the cases; adult children, 18 percent; other relatives, 18 percent; and friends, 15 percent. The rate was 2.5 percent of the men and 7.0 percent of the women for an overall abuse rate of 5.7 percent.

The fourth survey was conducted in Britain (Ogg, 1993). Although the British team wanted to replicate the Boston survey, concern on the part of the government about human subject rights forced them to adopt another approach. A few questions from the Boston survey dealing with acts of physical abuse, verbal aggression, and neglect were added to an annual omnibus survey. Of the 593 individuals 65 years and older interviewed, 32 (5%) reported having been mistreated recently by a close family member; 9 (2%), physically abused; and 9 (2%), neglected. No information about the perpetrators was obtained. Similar to the Canadian and Finnish projects, persons unable to participate because of illness or disability were excluded.

In spite of the fact that the studies were carried out in four different countries using three different methods, the results are fairly consistent. If the proportion of financial abuse found in Canada is added to the rate for Boston, the total is 5.7 percent of elders 65 years and over were subject to physical, verbal, and financial abuse. The range for the four studies is 4.0 to 5.7 percent, a minimum figure, since the more disabled elders were excluded from the study. These numbers can only be used as an estimate because the number of cases identified in all the studies was small, which precluded further analyses beyond obtaining descriptive information.

Incidence

The National Center on Elder Abuse has developed a method for estimating incidence abuse and neglect cases based on the reports received from the 50 states (Tatara, 1993). Because the state reporting systems have different eligibility criteria and definitions, the results can only be considered an approximation. From 1986 there has been a steady increase in the number of reports of domestic elder abuse nationwide: 117,000 in 1986; 140,000 in 1988; 211,000 in 1990; 241,000 in 1994; and 290,000 in 1996. Of the substantiated cases (Tatara, Kuzmeskus, & Duckhorn, 1997), 37 percent involved adult children as perpetrators; 13 percent, spouses; 8 percent, grandchildren; 11 percent, other relatives; and the remaining various categories, including friends, service provider, and unrelated caregivers.

The percentage of spousal and adult children perpetrators among the cases reported to state protective service programs differ dramatically from those found in the prevalence studies where spouse abuse was more than twice as common as abuse by adult children. The difference has been attributed to the fact that abuse is more likely to occur between two people who live together, and many more elders live with their spouses than with their children. The Boston study found that among older persons who lived with their spouses, the rate of abuse was 41 per 1,000; among those who lived with just their children, it was 44 per 1,000.

Undoubtedly, the number of reports is rising, but how much is due to changes in behavior, growing elderly population, and more intensive public awareness efforts is open to conjecture. A national incidence study was conducted with federal support by the National Center (National Center on Elder Abuse, 1998). Although it lacked the rigor of a truly representative national survey, it did provide information about the cases handled by protective services agencies (reported) and those seen by other community organizations and professionals (reported and nonreported). For each substantiated case reported to protective services agencies, four cases were identified in the community that would not have been reported.

Risk Factors

The causes of elder abuse are unknown; that is, there has been no research to date that links one factor or a group of factors to the mistreatment of an older person. The most that can be stated at this time is that there are certain factors (risk factors) that are associated with elder mistreatment. Over the years, a wide array of psychological, sociological, and gerontological factors have been proposed as possible explanations of why family members mistreat their elderly kin. Factors range from caregiver burden to aggression and violence as a way of life in America. Early work on this topic was hampered by small, nonrepresentative samples, reliance on agency records, and lumping all types of abuse cases together. Interviews with victims and perpetrators, surveys of community elders, and utilization of nonabused comparative samples have provided more reliable and valid data, but still the body of work is too small to provide definitive results.

The most likely explanations appear to be (1) the victims' poor mental and/or physical state, which increases their dependency on the abusers (caregivers) and/or decreases their ability to leave an abusive situation; (2) the abusers' dependency on the victims, primarily for financial support, especially housing; (3) the psychological state of the perpetrators (e.g., history of mental illness, history of substance abuse); and (4) family social isolation. So far, there is little empirical evidence that stressful life events and a childhood history of violence, both of which are closely associated with child and spouse abuse, play a role in elder abuse. However, particularly among spouses, prior history of violence in the relationship may be predictive of elder abuse in later life (Lachs & Pillemer, 1995).

Characteristics of the Perpetrator[1]

Relatively little is known about persons who abuse, neglect, or exploit older persons. From the first awareness of elder abuse as a social problem, the emphasis has been on the victim. A review of the state protective services laws very clearly shows that the state elder protective service systems were established to assist victims (Tatara, 1995). Similarly, the intake and assessment forms used by the states contain few items related to the perpetrator. Because only a very small number of cases ever reach the courts for prosecution, information about perpetrators is not very accessible. Often, perpetrators are absent from the home when the case is investigated.

A comparison of 328 cases of elder abuse by type of abuse revealed three distinctive perpetrator profiles (Wolf & Pillemer, 1989). The first exemplified the physical and psychological cases. The perpetrators were more apt to have a history of psychopathology and to be dependent on the victim for financial resources. In these cases, the victims were likely to be in poor emotional health, but relatively independent in the activities of daily living. Since the abusive behavior involved family members who were most intimately related and emotionally connected (spouses or adult children), it is likely that it can be traced to longstanding pathological family dynamics that become more highly charged when the dependency relationship is altered either because of illness (spouses) or financial needs (adult children or grandchildren).

Neglect cases presented a second profile. Unlike the physical-psychological abuse cases, financial dependency or psychological problems were not significant factors in the lives of these perpetrators, but rather the stress of caring for the elder, who was more likely to be widowed, very old, cognitively and functionally impaired, with few if any friends or relatives for social support. The third profile described the financial abuse cases. Financial needs and a history of substance abuse were associated with these perpetrators. The victims were apt to be widowed, without much social support, but functionally and cognitively intact.

These characteristics were confirmed in later case-control studies. Using in-depth interviews with victims (care recipients) and perpetrators (caregivers) in abusive and nonabusive households, researchers were able to show that perpetrators were more apt to abuse alcohol (Bristowe & Collins, 1989; Pillemer, 1986) and to be dependent on the victim for housing and financial support (Pillemer, 1986).

Further evidence of psychopathology as a risk factor for physical/psychological abuse was presented by Anetzberger (1987) in her study of persons who had physically abused their elderly parents. She demonstrated that the mistreatment could be traced to certain pathological personality characteristics of the adult children; the acute stress in their lives and their social isolation; the vulnerability of the elder parents; and to the prolonged and profound intimacy between the adult offspring and the elder parent. Her sample of abusers was categorized into three types. The first group, labeled *hostiles* as the most abusive of the three. They were aggressive, hated authority, were outspoken, and angry at everyone. For them, contact with the elder parent was a very negative experience. The *authoritarians* in the sample were the least likely to have any psychopathology. However, they were rigid in their expectations regarding the elder parent, as well as critical, impatient, and generally unsympathetic to the elder's situation. The third group composed the *dependents,* who were mainly distinguished from the others by their financial dependency on the elder parent.

When a comparison was made of cases involving adult children and spouses as perpetrators (Wolf & Pillemer, 1997), adult children were more likely to commit acts of psychological abuse and neglect, while the spousal perpetrators were more often associated with acts of physical violence. The adult children tended to have money problems, to be financially dependent on their elderly parents, and to have a history of mental illness and alcoholism. The spousal perpetrators were more apt to have committed physical abusive acts, to have medical complaints, and to have experienced a recent decline in physical health. Gender differences have not been explored, although Wolf and Pillemer (1993) found that in cases drawn from a number of elder abuse programs, abusive daughters were more likely to be perpetrators of neglect and to be involved with victims who were more impaired or who had more severe health problems than the abusive sons.

Some of these perpetrator characteristics can be found in the three cases described earlier in the chapter. The first (case A) is a case of long-term spousal abuse that has continued into old age. The second (case B) involves an adult son with alcohol and financial problems, characteristics that correspond to the financial abuse profile cited above. Caregiver stress is the theme of the third case (case C): a spouse with an alcohol problem, overburdened with the care of an infirmed wife, but reluctant to purchase help.

Intervention

Assessment

The state adult protective service agencies remain the backbone of the elder abuse service system. Generally, the state-designated units are responsible for receiving reports of suspected cases of elder mistreatment, screening for potential seriousness, conducting a comprehensive assessment if indicated, and developing a care plan. As soon as the immediate situation is addressed, the case is turned over to other community agencies for ongoing case management and service delivery.

As mentioned earlier, the focus of the adult protective services is on the victim/client. Thus, the goal of assessment, according to one's state manual (Illinois Department on Aging, 1990) is to gather in-depth information on (1) the *client's* situation and functioning level with regard to the environment, physical health, activities of daily living, mental health, and social and economic resources; (2) the capacity of the victim to make decisions about his or her own welfare, and understand the consequences of those decisions; (3) the level of risk to the client; and (4) the need for immediate interventions. Interviewing the perpetrator, if available and/or willing, is part of the process. Except for age, sex, and relationship to the victim, the states require very little, if any, data on perpetrators documented in the case files.

Following the lead of child protective services, some state adult protective services programs have begun to use instruments that monitor the risk of future abuse (Goodrich, 1997). A numerical score of risk is assigned by the case worker to the client, based on a risk factor matrix. The risk factors are scored low risk (i.e., the situation is alleviated with low likelihood of recurring or escalating), medium risk (i.e., potential exists for the situation to continue and possibly escalate), or high risk (i.e., very likely the situation will continue and probably escalate in the future), based on prescribed behaviors and conditions. An analysis of 552 Illinois protective services clients whose cases had been closed showed that the three consistent predictors of cases remaining at high risk involved perpetrator factors (Neale et al., 1996). Yet, in a survey of risk-assessment instruments used by the state agencies, more than two-thirds of the states did not require information on these items (Goodrich, 1997).

Service Delivery

Services to victims of elder abuse and their families are primarily handled through adult protective services case workers who make the arrangements with outside community groups for the requisite services after an assessment of the case and consent of the victim. Although the victim is the APS client, the perpetrator as a family member is also a beneficiary, if available and willing to accept help. On the whole, most APS laws specify the types of services available to these families. Twenty-six different services are listed in the state laws; however, not all in every state. Among them are assessment, psychiatric/medical, legal, mental health, home energy, home health, case management, food/meals, clothing, homemaker/chore, personal care, financial assistance, shelter, and transportation.

In the Wolf, Godkin, and Pillemer study of three model projects on elder abuse (1984), about two-thirds of the cases were referred for social services; one-half, medical services; one-third, mental health; one-fifth, police; and one-seventh, legal services. Of the 328 cases in the study, orders of protection were issued in 15 cases; criminal action taken in 9 cases; involuntary commitment/short-term protective removal carried out in 8 cases; family court appearance in 4 cases; and conservatorship and representative payee obtained in 3 each. A later study that involved 115 cases from four projects indicated that orders of protection were issued in 11 cases; family court appearances in 10 cases; criminal action taken in 6 cases; and guardianship, conservatorship, and representative payee obtained in 6 cases (Wolf & Pillemer, 1993). While it is not possible to generalize from these two studies, the figures reveal that a relatively small number of legal interventions have occurred on behalf of the perpetrators.

Among the state APS programs, the Illinois Department on Aging (1990) has probably taken the most proactive position with regard to perpetrators. Acting within a family systems model, they include in their practice guidelines a set of action steps for intervening with perpetrator types (Proctor et al., 1993). With an abusive/neglectful caregiver, a three-phase plan is used: giving relief or respite for the caregiver; providing education and support regarding the client's disease process and the demands on the caregiver; and carrying out interpersonal conflict resolution with the family. In cases that involve domestic abuse "grown old," the Illinois guidelines recommends a coordinated approach with a domestic violence program—the elder abuse worker providing the aging focus, and the domestic violence counselor handling the abuse dynamics. They suggest working with the victim and with the couple. Intervention with the third type, the dysfunctional perpetrator, may involve substance abuse, mental health, and developmental disabilities issues. The guidelines suggest calling on a counselor trained in the various fields to work with the family.

Nearly half the protective services laws have provisions making elder abuse a misdemeanor or a felony, with fines that range from $500 to $10,000, and imprisonment from 90 days to 10 years. However, civil and criminal prosecution of elder abuse cases have been relatively rare events, often because of the reluctance of the victim to press charges and the criminal justice system to become involved with domestic cases. According to Heisler (1991), whereas traditional methods and approaches for dealing with elder abuse may have discouraged victims and service providers from turning to the criminal justice system for help, new awareness, laws, and procedures enable the system to play a stronger part in deterring further violence, particularly as part of community-wide interdisciplinary efforts. She states that involving the criminal justice system in elder abuse cases has many benefits—it can stop the violence, protect the victim, protect the public, hold the perpetrator accountable, rehabilitate the perpetrator, communicate the societal intent to treat the conduct as a crime, and provide restitution to the victim.

Case Illustrations

Some of the action taken in the cases presented earlier in this chapter is described next.

Case A. The goals for this case were to stop the abuse, empower Mrs. A, and improve her quality of life. A volunteer advocate was assigned to visit Mrs. A on a weekly basis to give emotional support, build up her self-esteem, and possibly, through her presence as an outsider, reduce the potential for abuse. Additionally, Mrs. A was referred to a support group for older battered women.[2]

Six months later, although the physical abuse had lessened because of Mr. A's declining health, Mrs. A was more depressed than at the time of the initial assessment. She viewed abuse as her fate; this was her life. She did not see that she has the power to change, despite the fact that she is financially secure in her own right. Her husband continues to psychologically abuse her. His physical frailty has put an end to his physically abusive acts. He still controls her coming and going. If she wants to leave the house, she has to wait until he is watching television and then escape. From her support group experience, Mrs. A has learned to recognize when tension is building up at home and tries to get away to reduce the risk of abuse. It appears that the abuse will continue until Mr. A dies. Mrs. A does not appear to be waiting for this occurrence, but she is aware of his impending decline. Mrs. A is still at risk of abuse; the case is still open.

Case B. The initial goals for this case were to obtain financial relief and drug counseling for the son, and refer Mrs. B to Al-Anon, so that she would have a better understanding of her son's problem and her role in it. Dealing with the son was the key to the case. It had to be a slow, gradual process, since he had avoided any help for many years to the point of not allowing himself to be seen. He had been living off his mother's SSI check. Extended visits, counseling, and caring for the family were strategies used to gain the trust of the victim and her son. The case worker was able to obtain general assistance and food stamps for the son and a representative payee for Mrs. B, who took charge of her rent, utility, and grocery bill.

Six months later, Mrs. B's financial situation remained grim, but all her bills were paid. The outstanding issue at this point was the son's alcoholism. It took a great deal of effort for him to admit that he might be an alcoholic. He did seem to agree to give Alcoholic Anonymous a try. Although there was some improvement in Mrs. B's life, she remains upset that she does not manage her own financial affairs. She is lonely and frustrated with her son's alcoholism. However, any attempt at sobriety is compromised by her codependency. The financial abuse has been alleviated for the moment, but may present a risk in the future; the case is not closed.

Case C. As the initial action, the case worker contacted the son to talk over options for his parents, and a home health agency about providing ongoing help. Later, discussions were held with Mr. C about his alcohol consumption, alleged abuse, and caregiving tasks. He was given the opportunity to share his version of the situation and to vent some of his frustrations. The case worker did acknowledge to him that the caregiving responsibilities were more than a single person could be expected to carry out. Mr. C finally consented to purchase services to supplement those that were provided through his health insurance. Personal care aides were hired to help the client, thus relieving Mr. C of some responsibilities. Both Mr. C's son and the home health agency monitored the situation on a regular basis. The involvement of home health services, both public and private, alleviated some of the stress. With the presence of an outside agency on a regular basis, Mrs. C was viewed as no longer at risk, and the case was closed.

Case C was perhaps the easiest of the three cases to resolve. The case manager had the assistance of a son, and the husband had the means to hire additional home care attendants. However, counseling was necessary to help the husband come to terms with his wife's functional incapacity and his own physical limitations. The perpetrators in Cases A and B were less approachable. At the same time, the victims were unwilling to involve the police or the criminal justice system. They preferred to remain with the perpetrators, at risk of continued abuse. These cases mirror the findings of the study by Neale and colleagues, which showed that the cases most difficult to change are those involving perpetrators with substance abuse problems, the inability to respond appropriately to stress, and financial dependency on the victims.

Ethical Issues

A number of potential conflicts face practitioners who are treating elder abuse cases. While tangible proof may be obtainable in situations involving physical and financial abuse, evidence of psychological abuse and neglect is far more difficult to verify. Cultural biases and lack of full knowledge about the circumstances involved in a case may lead a worker to conclude, falsely, that abuse has occurred. The instability of the mental and physical status of the victim and/or perpetrator and the dynamics of their relationship may add to uncertainty about the case. In the face of denial by the victim and refusal of services, the worker is brought face-to-face with a dilemma: the interest of the state, professionals, and society in protecting vulnerable persons, and the individual's right to self-determination; in terms of ethical principles, the tension between autonomy and beneficence. To the degree that family caregiving issues are involved, elder mistreatment violates the virtues of care, compassion, benevolence, and respect for parents.

The emphasis on individual safety over client autonomy that was evident a quarter of a century ago is no longer the rule. Today, the client's right to self-determination (i.e., the right to due process, the right to die) are paramount. When a competent, abused, neglected, or exploited person refuses services, the worker has to withdraw from the case, often to the dismay of relatives, friends, neighbors, and other professionals who believe the health and property of the person to be in danger. If a case involves an incompetent individual, court action may be required, often resulting in the client losing all rights.

Summary

Within the United States, it is the federal government that has taken the leadership in framing the issue of elder mistreatment: first in supporting state welfare programs for adults in need of protection; later in alerting the aging establishment and the nation to the reality of elder abuse; and more recently, in declaring elder abuse to be a form of family violence. Yet, it is the states that have the responsibility for delivery of services. Federal funds for protective services have decreased over the years, in spite of an increasing number of abuse reports. The more highly developed state programs must draw on state or county tax revenues. Still, most programs are considered to be underfunded and understaffed.

Although progress has been made in the past twenty years in understanding the nature and scope of the problem, a more solid knowledge base is needed for policy, planning, and practice purposes. Many aspects of the problem still remain unknown, such as, the theoretical underpinnings, actual prevalence, causes, and consequences. Almost no research has been done on the effectiveness of interventions. The legacy of the protective service movement of the sixties and seventies has resulted in state systems that focus on the victims with few resources for perpetrators. When elder abuse was thought to be primarily a result of caregiving stress, helping the caregiver was the treatment of choice. The strong association between the dependency of the perpetrator and physical and financial abuse requires that adult protective services agencies work closely with vocational counseling, job placement, housing assistance, alcohol and drug treatment, mental health, batterers, and financial assistance programs to enable perpetrators to assume independent living.

More attention must be given to primary prevention, beginning with informing the public and training professionals about elder mistreatment, how to recognize the risk factors, and where to turn for help. A closer partnership between the mental health system and substance abuse programs, and elder abuse services is vital, given the high proportion of emotional problems and alcoholism in abusive families. Support groups and training for elders that emphasize elder rights and advocacy, outreach efforts to minority communities, financial management programs, and training for caregivers are other ways of diminishing the potential for abuse and neglect. Mediation and conflict resolution also hold promise as methods of resolving disagreements before they escalate into violence.

Perhaps, the most insidious form of abuse against elders is the negative attitudes that prevail about older persons and the aging process, whether expressed as stereotypes, intergenerational conflict, or glorification of youth. As long as older people are devalued and marginalized by society, they risk being subjected to discrimination by others and robbed of their "power" and self-esteem. Society must change its thinking about aging as a time of dependency and uselessness to one of productivity and social contribution (Moody, 1990). This more positive view of aging is needed to offset the negative bias that has been part of our social consciousness and more recently the political agenda.

N O T E S

1. The term for the person who abuses, neglects, or exploits an older person may be one of several depending on the type of case: caregiver, abuser, perpetrator, or offender. Perpetrator, rather than offender, is used in this discussion.

2. This community had one of the few, if not the only, volunteer advocate program and support group for battered older women in the country at the time.

R E F E R E N C E S

American Association of Retired Persons. (1992). *Abused Elders or Battered Women?* Washington, DC: Author.

Anetzberger, G. J. (1987). *The Etiology of Elder Abuse by Adult Offspring.* Springfield, IL: Charles C. Thomas.

Anetzberger, G. J. (1994). Protective services and long-term care. In Z. Harel & R. Dunkle (Eds.), *Long Term Care: People and Services.* New York: Springer.

Blenkner, M., Bloom, M., & Nielson, M. (1971). A research and demonstration project of protective services. *Casework, 52,* 483–497.

Bristowe, E. & Collins, J. B. (1989). Family mediated abuse of non-institutionalized elder men and women living in British Columbia. *Journal of Elder Abuse and Neglect, 1,* 45–54.

Burston, G. R. (1975, September 3). Granny-battering. *British Medical Journal,* 592.

DC Department of Public Welfare. (1967). *Protective Services for Adults: Report on Protective Services Prepared for the DC Interdepartmental Committee on Aging.* Washington, DC.

Gebotys, R. J., O'Connor, D., & Mair, K. J. (1992). Public perceptions of elder physical mistreatment. *Journal of Elder Abuse and Neglect, 4,* 151–172.

Goodrich, C. S. (1997). Results of a nationwide survey of adult protective services programs: Documentation, assessment, and program outcomes. *Journal of Elder Abuse and Neglect, 9.*

Heisler, C. J. (1991). The role of the criminal justice system in elder abuse cases. *Journal of Elder Abuse and Neglect, 3,* 5–34.

Hudson, M. (1991). Elder mistreatment: A taxonomy with definitions by Delphi. *Journal of Elder Abuse and Neglect, 3,* 1–20.

Hudson, M. F. (1994). Elder abuse: Its meaning to middle-age and older adults. Part II, Pilot results. *Journal of Elder Abuse and Neglect, 6,* 55–81.

Hudson, M. F. & Carlson, J. R. (1997). Elder abuse: Its meaning to caucasians, African-Americans and Native Americans. In T. Tatara (Ed.), *Understanding Elder Abuse Among Minority Populations.* Bristol, PA: Taylor & Francis.

Illinois Department on Aging. (1990). *Elder Abuse Intervention: Guidelines for Practice.* Springfield, IL. Author.

Kivelä, S. L., Köngäs-Saviaro, P., Kesti, E., Pahkala, K., & Ijäs, M. L. (1992). Abuse in old age: Epidemiological data from Finland. *Journal of Elder Abuse and Neglect, 4,* 1–18.

Lachs, M. & Pillemer, K. (1995). Abuse and neglect of elderly persons. *New England Journal of Medicine, 332,* 437–443.

Moody, H. (1990). The politics of entitlement and the politics of productivity. In S. A. Bass, E. A. Kutza, & F. M. Torees-Gil (Eds.), *Diversity in Aging: Challenges Facing Planners and Policymakers in the 1990s.* Glenview, IL: Scott, Foresman.

Moon, A. & Williams, O. (1993). Perceptions of elder abuse and help-seeking patterns among African-American, Caucasian-American, and Korean-American elderly women. *Gerontologist, 33,* 386–395.

National Center on Elder Abuse. (1998). *National Elder Abuse Incidence Study.* Washington, DC: Author.

Neale, A. V., Hwalek, M. A., Goodrich, C. S., & Quinn, K. M. (1996). The Illinois elder abuse system: Program description and administrative findings. *Gerontologist, 36,* 502–511.

Ogg, J. (1993). Researching elder abuse in Britain. *Journal of Elder Abuse and Neglect, 5,* 37–54.

Pillemer, K. (1986). Risk factors in elder abuse: Results from a case control study. In K. A. Pillemer & R. S. Wolf (Eds.), *Elder Abuse: Conflict in the Family.* Dover, MA: Auburn House.

Pillemer, K. & Finkelhor, D. (1988). Prevalence of elder abuse: A random sample survey. *Gerontologist, 28,* 51–57.

Podnieks, E., Pillemer, K., Nicholson, J. P., Shillingon, T., & Frizzell, A. (1990). *National Survey* on *Abuse of the Elderly in Canada: Final Report.* Toronto: Ryerson Technical Institute.

Proctor, J., Hwalek, M., & Goodrich, C. S. (1993). *Improving our Effectiveness in Working with Abusers.* Springfield, IL: Illinois Department on Aging.

Straus, M. (1992). The Conflict Tactics Scales and its critics: An evaluation. In M. A. Straus & R. J. Gelles (Eds.), *Physical Violence in American Families.* New Brunswick, NJ: Transaction.

Tatara, T. (1993). Finding the nature and scope of domestic elder abuse with the use of state aggregate data: Summaries of the key findings of a national survey of state PAS and aging agencies. *Journal Of Elder Abuse And Neglect, 5,* 35–57.

Tatara, T. (1995). *An Analysis of State Laws Addressing Elder Abuse, Neglect, and Exploitation.* Washington, DC: National Center on Elder Abuse.

Tatara, T., Kuzmeskus, L., & Duckhorn, E. (1997). *Elder Abuse in Domestic Settings: Elder Abuse Informational Series No. 3.* Washington, DC: National Center on Elder Abuse.

Tomita, S. K. (1995). An exploration of elder mistreatment among Japanese-Americans within a broad context of conflict: Conditions and consequences. *Dissertation Abstracts International.* (University Microfilms No. 9609796).

U.S. Department of Health, Education and Welfare. (1966). State letter No. 925. Subject: Four model demonstration projects: Services to older adults in the public welfare program. Washington, DC.

U.S. Select Committee on Aging. (1979). *Elder Abuse: The Hidden Problem.* Washington, DC: Government Printing Office.

U.S. Select Committee on Aging. (1981). *Elder Abuse: An Examination of a Hidden Problem.* Washington, DC: Government Printing Office.

U.S. Senate Special Committee on Aging. (1994). *Elder Abuse and Violence Against Midlife and Older Women.* Washington, DC: Government Printing Office.

Wolf, R. S., Godkin, M. A., & Pillemer, K. (1984). *Final Report: Three Model Projects on Elder Abuse.* Worcester, MA: University Center on Aging, University of Massachusetts Medical Center.

Wolf, R. S. & Pillemer, K. A. (1989). *Helping Elder Victims: The Reality of Elder Abuse.* New York: Columbia University Press.

Wolf, R. S. & Pillemer, K. (1993). *The Evaluation of Four Elder Abuse Projects.* Worcester, MA: Institute on Aging, Medical Center of Central Massachusetts.

Wolf, R. S. & Pillemer, K. (1994). What's new in elder abuse programming? Four bright ideas. *Gerontologist, 34,* 126–129.

Wolf, R. S. & Pillemer, K. (1997). Older battered women: Wives and mothers compared. *Journal of Mental Health and Aging, 3.*

10   Sexual Assault

BARRY M. MALETZKY

Oregon Health Sciences University

As a social phenomenon, sexual assault has often been addressed and condemned, but rarely has it been a subject on which social scientists have agreed. Among feminists, students of social learning, and evolutionary biologists, few have no theories; fewer among us, however, have the basic facts on which theory, treatment and, hopefully, prevention must be built. This chapter will review the data that exist on sexual assault and how they may help us provide treatment and prevention strategies. It will focus on males assaulting females, but the phenomenon of female perpetrators will not be ignored. Finally, it will attempt to demonstrate, although imperfectly, how sexual aggressors are treated by presenting actual cases admitted recently to our Sexual Abuse Clinic in the northwestern United States (Maletzky & Steinhauser, 1996).

Description of the Problem

As you read these words, a woman is being raped in this country, probably in your state, possibly in your city. Despite its widespread prevalence, however, we should not lose sight of why sexual assault is a crime in all civilized societies: because it creates victims. A number of studies have assessed women immediately following sexual attacks (Burgess & Holmstrom, 1985) and at longitudinal follow-up (Koss, 1985). Victims commonly describe being terrified during and after the crime; within one week, 94 percent met the criteria for posttraumatic stress disorder, and these symptoms persisted in 47 percent after 3 months (Kirkpatrick, Veronen, & Resnick, 1979). Of 507 victims surveyed by Kilpatrick (1993), 35 percent had also experienced major depression. While many victims partially recover from the initial trauma, a number will continue to bear emotional scars for years, including fear and mistrust, low self-esteem, restriction of activities, sexual dysfunction, and depression (Resnick, 1993). Adolescent victims may be particularly vulnerable (Ageton, 1983).

Credit for recognizing the importance of sexual assault must be given to the feminist movement originating in the 1960s. At that time, almost all jurisdictions defined rape as "illicit carnal knowledge of a woman forcibly and against her will." One of the first achievements of the antirape movement was the Michigan Criminal Sexual Code, subsequently adopted by almost all other states. The code broadened the definition of rape to include additional assaultive acts; extended protection to separated spouses and males; eliminated the requirement of resistance; and restricted use of the victim's sexual history against her (Burgess, 1985). More recently, researchers and the media have begun to accept that other types of sexual coercion comprise a broad category of sexual assault, including date and partner rape and assault, sexual harassment and intimidation, and nonforcible rape of an incapacitated person. While *rape* must be defined legally, *sexual assault* will be broadly interpreted here as the use of force or threat to compel sexual acts. Statutory rape will be arbitrarily excluded, but it should remain clear that the effects of sexual assault honor no age barrier.

By expanding the focus of sexual assault beyond rape, attention is now being directed to coercive sexual behavior that was previously ignored. Garvey (1991) reported that among 347 young female victims, 63 percent of all incidents of sexual assault were perpetrated by dates and partners. Among nearly 1,000 married women, 14 percent reported being raped by their husbands (Russell, 1988). Indeed, Kilpatrick (1993) estimated that twice as many women are raped by partners or acquaintances than by strangers. Our conception of rape is thus rapidly changing from one in which a man assumed a right of sexual access, to one in which a woman has the power to refuse, even if she chose not to yesterday.

Sexual assault of partners visits no lesser damage on its victims than rape by a stranger. For months following an assault by a known perpetrator, victims reported sleep disturbances, nightmares, intrusive thoughts, sexual dysfunction, and guilt (Bowie, Silverman, Kalick, & Edbril, 1990). These assaults occurred more commonly in a home or vehicle and, consequently, led to a perception of fear of familiar places, insecurity, and subsequent mistrust.

However, some victims of acquaintance and partner assaults were unclear that such activity is considered rape. Among college women who experienced assaults that legally qualified as rape, only 27 percent thought they were rape victims (Koss & Deniro, 1989). In a large investigation of female university students, Koss (1985) found that, of the 13 percent who reported experiencing sex against their will, just over half acknowledged it as rape; 60 percent of the victims knew their assailant. It is possible that such confidence rapes are even more rarely reported to authorities than are blitz rapes, which fit the public image of a typical rape case. *Confidence rapes* are characterized by nonviolent interactions between the perpetrator and victim before the intention to assault becomes clear. *Blitz rapes* are surprise attacks by strangers. Although these terms have been proposed to describe the two types of sexual attack usually reported, the clumsier but more descriptive terms *acquaintance or partner rape* and *stranger rape* will be used in this chapter. When a legally defined rape did not occur, *sexual assault* will be substituted.

Whether a victim of acquaintance or partner rape, stranger rape, or sexual assault, most women do not report the crime to authorities. In one study of college women soon after they were raped (Koss, 1985), only 8 percent reported the event; almost half never discussed the attack with anyone. In an Australian study by McConaghy and Zamir (cited in McConaghy, 1993a, p. 277), only 2 percent of Sydney women reported a rape, while at Kent State University only 6 percent reported the assault (Koss & Oros, 1982). Women may hesitate to disclose partly from embarrassment, partly due to the high frequency of being raped by acquaintances and partners, and partly from the recognition that a report may generate nothing other than an investigation. Most men who rape remain at large: Of 1,000 rapes occurring today in North America, 100 will be disclosed by victims, 10 will result in trials, and one offender will be convicted. These startling statistics require us to revise the question of why men rape; it may be far more important to explore the reasons why most men do not.

Epidemiology

The Victims

The largest study examining the prevalence of sexual assault was bravely conceived and reported by Russell (1988). The figure found for rape among a common sample of San Francisco women, 24 percent, compares well with Koss and Deniro's subsequent (1989) sample of American university women, in which 27.5 percent reported experiencing rape or attempted rape, and with a New Zealand sample which found 25.3 percent raped within a similar population (Garvey, 1991). Sorenson, Stein, Siegel, Golding, and Burnam (1987) reported a 16 percent prevalence rate in a large Los Angeles sample. However, in a sample using confidential questionnaires, 22 percent of college women reported being forced to have intercourse on a date (Stuckman-Johnson, 1988).

College women have no monopoly on victimization. Ageton (1983) estimated that the incidence of sexual assault among girls 11 to 17 in the United States was 5 to 7 percent, representing 700,000 to 1 million girls abused annually. Relationships and marriage do not confer immunity: Coercion was common in female students during dating relationships (Waldner-Haugrud & Magruder, 1995). Morever, Yllo, and Finkelhor (1985) estimated that 10 to 14 percent of married women are raped, making sexual assault by husbands the most common form of rape. In Russell's (1988) study it was twice as likely that a woman would be raped by her partner than by a stranger.

Male victims have received attention as well, although prevalence and incidence rates are lower than in females in all studies, usually by two-thirds. Most male victims know their attackers, have a homosexual orientation, are orally and anally penetrated, resist the assault, and are at higher risk than female victims of being beaten (Stermac, Sheridan, Davidson, & Dunn, 1996). Of 346 college males, 21 (6%) reported being raped; no male victim reported the act to the police (Collins, 1994).

Sexual assaults are more common in younger than older female victims. In the Los Angeles study (Sorenson et al., 1987), 19 percent of all victims were 11 to 15 years old; 34 percent were 16 to 20 years old; 15 percent were 21 to 25 years old; and only 12 percent were older than 26 years. In a very large study of 10,000 rape victims throughout the United States, females between the ages of 16 and 35 years were five-times more likely to be raped than women in any other age category (Thornhill & Thornhill, 1990). This age range corresponds to that of a woman's most fecund period, the age at which a woman is most attractive to a male, and suggests that rape is not divorced from reproductive strategies that have evolved in all male primates.

Methodological problems abound in attempts to determine incidence and prevalence data. How one asks the questions, interviewer gender, and perception of confidentiality may all produce shaky pillars in the documentation of sexual assault. Most prevalence studies use questionnaires and surveys; yet, some research indicates that many individuals responding to such instruments actually falsify responses, even when assured of confidentiality (Riggs, Murphy, & O'Leary, 1989). In addition, much of our knowledge is derived solely from reports of white, middle-class college students. In some cases, noncollege samples report a greater likelihood of disclosing sexual aggression than do women in college (Zweig, Barber, & Eccles, 1997). The nature of college females' experiences and how they recall them, and relate them to others, may not be representative of other victim populations.

The Crimes

While we think of it as a sudden, forceful act, rape exists on a continuum of sexually aggressive behavior—from unwanted sexual comments to inappropriate touching, verbal pressure, threat, intimidation, and the use of restraint or brute force. Some perpetrators may also use alcohol or blackmail to increase the chance of sexual success. However, most sexual crimes are nonviolent (Revitch & Schlesinger, 1988) and most victims are coerced by verbal pressure alone (Stuckman-Johnson, 1988).

Stranger rape is likely to be less aggressive than acquaintance and partner rape, perhaps because a weapon is much more often involved (Bowie et al., 1990) and perhaps because victims in these instances resist their attackers less. Acquaintance and partner rape is more often associated with verbal coercion, use of emotional blackmail (such as threats to end the relationship), and is more likely to involve alcohol on the part of both participants (Seto & Barbaree, 1995). Among teenage girls, the frequency of sexual assault appeared heavily dependent on the use of drugs and alcohol and associating with delinquent male peers (Ageton, 1983). Among these teenagers, one-third of the victims experienced at least one further assault within the same year, and the risk of being attacked sexually exceeded the rate for all adolescents by a factor of 3 to 4. Revictimization is common in the adult population also, as is the incidence of alcohol use by the victim as well as the perpetrator (Koss & Gaines, 1993).

Although many victims try to resist (Sorenson et al., 1987), the obstacles to sexual advances are usually mild, involving verbal pleading. Completed rapes were more likely when a woman used only pleading and if her main concern was avoiding rape rather than avoiding harm (Bart & O'Brien, 1984). Of 94 women attacked in Chicago, 51 successfully avoided being raped; their most effective strategy was to flee (Bart & O'Brien, 1984). Over 80 percent of the women who fled avoided rape, as did 70 percent of women who fought their attacker. Although a woman who fought back slightly increased her risk of being handled roughly, remaining passive was no guarantee of humane treatment. Moreover, women who resisted showed less depression, even if they did not avoid the rape. These results have subsequently been confirmed in a sample of 274 women attacked: More forceful resistance led to less severe sexual abuse (Ullman & Knight, 1991).

Sexual assault rates also vary internationally, although the differences might be attributable to the likelihood of reporting. Abramson and Hayashi (1984) found prevalence rates for reported rapes of 34.5 per 100,000 population in the United States; 10.1 in Great Britain; 10.7 in West Germany; 3.2 in France; and 2.4 in Japan. The cultural factors influencing these variations are still being investigated.

In fortunate contrast to popular opinion, there is no evidence that sexual assault is increasing (Kutchinsky, 1991). Assault rates, however, can vary based on definitions of rape and sexual assault. The National Crime Survey and the Uniform Crimes Report have been criticized for grossly underestimating incidence data (Koss, 1993). The variations in reporting methods, and underreporting itself, render national agencies powerless to improve data collection. Recent changes in societal attitudes may partially compensate for this deficiency, as more victims feel a sense of power over their sexuality and an outrage at a gross injustice.

Characteristics of the Offender

Sexually Aggressive Men

Among the hundreds of studies investigating propensity to become sexually assaultive, none has discovered a single characteristic that would allow us to identify a male prone to aggressive sexual activity. Rather, such studies have pointed to a multitude of factors predisposing some men to aggress, although these have focused on easier-to-measure characteristics of the *offender* rather of the *situation*. We do know that rapists are usually young males. The peak of aggressive sexual activity occurs between the ages of 16 and 29 years (Prentky & Knight, 1991). Indeed, 20 percent of all rape is perpetrated by males under the age of 18 (Becker, Harris, & Sales, 1993). While many come from lower socioeconomic urban areas, and a slightly greater proportion are black (Alder, 1984), these demographics represent trends, not certainties.

While no psychological test of itself can predict rape (Marshall & Hall, 1995), some assessment techniques purport to identify males predisposed to sexual aggression. Chief among these, the Burt Rape Myth Acceptance Scale (RMA) (Burt,

1980) tests the acceptance of myths in sexual aggression. Sample true or false questions include: "A woman who goes to the home...of a man on the first date implies she is willing to have sex," "In the majority of rapes, the victim is promiscuous," and "Many women have a subconscious wish to be raped." Burt reported an investigation of more than 500 subjects and concluded that agreement with rape myths identified a subpopulation more accepting of interpersonal violence, sexrole stereotyping, and the belief that male-female relationships were necessarily adversarial (Burt & Katz, 1988). Muehlenhard and Linton (1987) extended these findings to a large university sample. They compared the attitudes of men involved in sexually aggressive behavior with those of nonaggressive men and found a significant correlation between acceptance of rape myths and the likelihood a man would use some aggression to obtain sexual gratification—a finding echoed in more recent work as well (Truman, Tokar, & Fischer, 1996). Most workers have concluded that acceptance of these myths predispose men to rape and conversely, that primary prevention efforts against sexual aggression must be directed at the promotion of sexual relationships as being mutually undertaken and freely chosen.

Few would argue with that premise; however, as with delusions and old wives' tales, some myths may contain elements of truth. Some women (but probably not most) may enjoy being pressured into sex; 15 percent of female medical students reported the experience of being initially coerced into, but then enjoying, sexual activity (Muehlenhard & Cook, 1988), a finding similar to that of a later sample (Byers & Heinlein, 1989). Similarly, some women entertain fantasies of being romantically abducted or overcome and surrendering to a male (Burgess, 1985; Hucker, 1990). Therefore, while acceptance of rape-supportive beliefs must be challenged, labeling them as myths may encourage skepticism and may pressure researchers to abandon promising avenues of study.

Given the association found between rape myth acceptance and propensity to sexual aggression, researchers have attempted to spot other characteristics in populations of males associated with the possible use of sexual coercion. General findings indicate that men more likely to have used sexual aggression or to rate themselves more likely to rape, have accepted traditional gender roles (Truman et al., 1996); used more alcohol (Muehlenhard & Cook, 1988); scored higher on a hypermasculinity profile (O'Donohue, McKay, & Schewe, 1996); were less likely to judge rape as violent (Langley, Beatty, Yost, & O'Neal, 1991); and were less likely to predict a negative outcome for rape (O'Donohue et al., 1996).

Unfortunately, we may know more about the average college male in this area than we do about males who aggress in the real world. Most of the studies cited used convenience samples of university students answering written survey questions as part of their college classes. However, busy students answering impersonal surveys about their historical intimacies may be a step removed from clinical reality. For example, although Malamuth (1988) found that 21 percent of college men not previously reporting sexual aggression would rape if assured they would not be punished, there is no way to know if such men would actually *commit* a rape. Therefore, analogue studies have been devised, at times ingeniously, to test, within appropriate ethical parameters, a male's likelihood to sexually aggress. In a seminal effort, Malamuth (1981) examined the relationship between male subjects' attitudes about aggression and the tendency to deliver electroshock to a female confederate. The data were interpreted as supporting an association between more positive beliefs in aggression and the real-world behavior of aggression toward women—a finding mirrored in later work (Blader, Marshall, & Barbaree, 1988).

However, while delivery of pain to a female subject may be a laboratory analogue of physical aggression, it is not an exact parallel of sexual coercion. Attempting to overcome the obvious physical and ethical restraints in analogue design, Pryor (1987) asked male subjects to teach a female confederate to play golf. The woman rated how sexual each subject's conversation and physical contact with her was. Men who ranked high on a separate scale of sexual harassment engaged in more sexual behavior, supporting the author's belief that some of the men regarded the golf lesson as a legitimate condition for sexual overtures. The ethics of exposing the female confederate to these conditions have been more recently questioned (Hall & Hirschman, 1994).

In another innovative attempt at analogy, Dermen (1990) attempted to simulate aggressive sexual behavior in the laboratory by asking males to show erotic slides to females described as either liking or disliking pornography. This appears to be analogous to the imposition of an unwanted sexual experience on a female. Most male subjects in this and similar studies (Lopez & George, 1992) were usually unwilling to show the slides to unwilling females, but alcohol increased the likelihood they would do so. More ominously, over time *all* the men showed some erotic slides to some women who they were told did not want to see them.

Hall and colleagues have recently improved the sophistication, and reduced the transparency, of analogue studies by using the guise of showing erotic slides to a female confederate in an attempt to distract her from a bogus memory task (Hall & Hirschman, 1994). They found that males who were more supportive of rape myths were more likely to show sexually explicit slides to a woman identified as disliking pornography. As in the Dermen study, *most* males eventually did expose an unwilling female confederate to some pornography, even though they also had a choice of distracting her with autopsy slides.

Do these data mean that most men would sexually aggress if assured immunity? Some authors have suggested that up to 50 percent of men without a history of sexual aggression would do so (Hucker, 1997). Is rape thus on one end of a normally distributed curve of sexual aggression in males, as many have suspected? Put another way, is rape an aberration or an extreme? No data are yet available to answer these often raised questions with certainty, although it appears that most men do not aggress sexually, even in inviting circumstances. If the tendency to aggress sexually is distributed in all males, one would expect to see some evidence of normal male sexual arousal to scenes depicting aggressive sexuality and, indeed, such evidence exists. A number of males without a history of sexual coercion develop erections, as measured by the penile plethysmograph, when shown scenes of aggressive sexual behavior with women (Quinsey & Earls, 1990). It is difficult to know, however, if men are reacting purely to the sexual elements in such scenes. It seems safe to say that *some* men, at least, are not inhibited by scenes of a woman in distress.

If some males are more likely to aggress sexually, are there any distinguishing characteristics to define this group? Certain personality traits, admittedly difficult to measure precisely, appear repeatedly in the literature, and seem to be associated with either a history of sexually aggressive behavior, the self-report of likelihood of acting in a coercive manner, or the imposition of sex on a woman confederate. These include a hypermasculine profile (aggressive behavior, idolizing sports, using alcohol, and involvement in college fraternities) (Riggs & O'Leary, 1996); endorsement of traditional gender-role stereotypes (Truman et al., 1996); and a behavior style marked by dominance and impulsivity (Calhoun, Bernat, Clum, & Frame, 1997). If most men have the potential to rape, and if the vast majority would never be punished if they did, the study of inhibiting factors blocking rape should prove a fruitful area for researchers keen on exploring the future.

Rapists

Men who rape are usually identified by being arrested, convicted, and mandated into a treatment program. Thus, we have never had the opportunity, and possibly never will, to study over 90 percent of this population. However, we know they are similar to the general prison population, being of low socioeconomic status and having erratic school and work histories (Bard et al., 1997). Rapists differ from most sexual offenders, particularly child molesters, in that they are younger (Christie et al., 1979); more likely to have committed a nonsexual crime (Barbaree, Bogaert, & Seto, 1995); have poorer treatment outcomes (Maletzky, 1993; Marques, 1997); show more arousal on the plethysmograph to aggressive sexual scenes (Hall & Hirschman, 1994; Miner, West, & Day, 1995); and can be distinguished on newly developed scales testing cognitive style and thinking distortions (Bumby, 1996).

Because aggression has been linked to testosterone levels in animal research (e.g., Delgado, 1969), attention has been focused on levels of circulating testosterone in humans known to have raped. Although the data differ somewhat, a recent review (Grubin & Mason, 1997) reflected the generally accepted conclusion that androgen levels in human males do not correlate with the likelihood of committing rape. Although early research was briefly provocative (Ehrenkranz, Bliss, & Sheard, 1974; Rada, Laws, & Kellner, 1976), more recent and larger studies have failed to demonstrate a link between elevated testosterone levels and a history of sexual aggression (Bain, Langevin, Dickey, Hucker, & Wright, 1988; Bradford & Maclean, 1984), although its reduction with medications can markedly reduce aggression in such offenders (Maletzky, 1991; Prentky, 1977).

Some studies have suggested that among aggressive offenders, those with central nervous system damage are overrepresented (Berlin & Meinecke, 1981). Sexually anomalous behavior, including sexual aggression, has been noted following brain damage (Galski, Thornton, & Shumsky, 1990; Langevin, 1990). These offenders may comprise a particularly dangerous set of men who rape. While such men may show deficits in impulse control, a large percentage appear attracted to children rather than to aggressive sexuality. It appears unlikely that structural brain damage will prove to be responsible for the majority of sexually aggressive acts, although it may be an important factor in certain individuals.

In an effort to provide clarity to the classification of rapists, Knight and Prentky (1990) developed the most comprehensive taxonomy in recent years. These workers had initially proposed four types of rapists: *compensatory*, making up for deficits in social skills; *exploitative*, taking advantage of a situation; *displaced anger*, intentionally trying to harm or humiliate a victim; and *sadistic*, being aroused by the aggressive elements of sex. They have more recently (Knight & Prentky, 1997) described nine separate subtypes of rapists by further subdividing these basic types based on level of force, impulsivity, aggressive fantasies, and social competence. However, even these diligent workers admit to some difficulty in detecting valid subtypes. The use of force can vary time after time, depending on level of victim resistance, for example. In clinical experience, it is not unusual to encounter rapists who alter their style based on circumstance: One man who had never used excessive force only became violent when his victim began resisting after penetration. Another man who raped only under the influence of alcohol became increasingly aroused to his victims' struggles and began raping even when sober.

Other authors have attempted simpler divisions. Early models echoed feminists' theories about power and the nonsexual aspects of rape (Darke, 1990; Herman, 1990). Seghorn and Cohen (1980) distinguished sexual, aggressive, impulsive, and sexual diffusion rapists; however, it has proven difficult to distinguish rapists based on speculation about motives, which at present cannot be determined scientifically. McConaghy (1993b) has distinguished between blitz (surprise attack by a stranger) and confidence rapes, but overlaps are not uncommon. Many other authors have attempted to cleave the field in two: rapes involving just enough coercion to ensure sexual compliance, and those in which gratuitous violence occurs (Rosenberg, Knight, Prentky, & Lee, 1988). This assumes, however, knowledge of intent and uniform victim resistance—elements not often associated with clinical reality.

Theorists and commentators appear to have ignored the evidence that genetic factors can play a role in predisposition to sexual aggression and rape. It is possible that intergenerational transmission of personality factors—particularly a low threshold for aggression combined with poor impulse control—contributes energy, driving an individual to aggression. In contrast to other areas of psychiatry, comment about these factors is conspicuously absent, perhaps reflecting political bias, which sadly could obscure this potentially fruitful area from more critical view.

It should thus be clear that classifying rape, and rapists, is both a necessary yet incomplete task. This may be partly due to our lack of insight, but also partly due to a misplaced goal. The act of rape may not represent a symptom of an individual's disorder as much as the result of predisposing personality factors (aggression and impulsivity), present state (level of sexual arousal or alcohol), and opportunity (privacy, faith in nondetection). As such, rapists may be more hetero-geneous than other clinical samples of sexual offenders and, if so, their treatment responses would be expected to be more disappointing, especially as they are almost always treated in programs, and with techniques, developed for child molesters, pedophiles, and exhibitionists (Maletzky & Steinhauser, 1996). Perhaps we should not be surprised that the classification of men who rape and, indeed, of the broader category of those who are aggressive sexually, remains for the future. Rape is a behavior, probably not a disease.

Theories of Sexual Assault

No overarching theory, at present, can explain sexual assault; this is not surprising in view of its heterogeneous nature. There have been many attempts, however, to account for the presence of sexually aggressive behavior in humans, from psycho-dynamic theories early in this century, to more fashionable sociopolitical and evo-lutionary views in its last quarter. To be fair, no present-day theorist would limit explanations of sexual assault to a single cause. Most suggest contributions from multiple pathways, but emphasize certain factors as bearing a stronger influence than others. Thus, in the following presentations, positions on etiology will be summarized as belonging to one school of thought or another; however, in reality, all current researchers recognize a variety of contributing factors.

Feminist Theories

As a consequence of increasing awareness of women's issues, the public has gen-erally accepted that rape is motivated to a degree by men's desire to keep women at an economic and political disadvantage. Rape is held by feminist theorists to be an act more of aggression than lust: "*All* sexual assaults are perpetrated to justify the aggressor's desire for, and to enhance feelings of, [male] power" (Darke, 1990, p. 58). Feminists assert that men, in attempts to maintain positions of power in legal, financial, and social domains, have created a patriarchal society that admires strength in males through physical and logical prowess, financial success, and attainment of possessions, and encourages weakness in females through depen-dency, emotional lability, and passivity.

As a corollary of this view, sexual gratification through aggression is second-ary to achieving power through dominance and humiliation of the female victim. A second corollary follows—that all men are potential rapists. If rape were more a po-litical statement than an attempt to obtain sexual gratification, one would expect this to be reflected in the memories reported by victims and offenders alike and, indeed, many clinicians describe statements supporting this view (as reported in Kilpatrick, Veronen, & Resnick, 1979). Women often report feeling dirty and humil-iated following a rape, and that their attacker used more aggression than necessary to achieve sexual gratification. Frequently, offenders admit to adding insult to in-jury by verbally degrading their victims, expressing disgust toward them, or frightening them unnecessarily. Darke (1990) identified, among 68 cases of rape, 43 (63%) in which humiliation appeared to play a prominent role in the assault. Frequently, the men called their victims "slaves" or possessions, entirely under their control.

Epidemiological studies, surveys, and sexual arousal assessments provide some support for the feminist position. In a study of date rapes in 29 U.S. cities, Ellis and Beattie (1983) found that locations with the greatest disparity between gender in political and economic status tended to have lower rape rates than cities with a more equitable power distribution—a finding repeated using a state-by-state analysis one year later (Baron & Strauss, 1984). Herman (1990) has argued that residence in a patriarchal society that worships a male deity and glorifies male strength increases a woman's potential to be sexually assaulted. Indeed, differential geographic data appear to support this notion (Abramson & Hayashi, 1984).

Feminists have also directed attention to pornography as a contributing factor, feeding rape acceptance by depicting women as promiscuous and craving sexual submission (Fraser Commission, 1985; MacKinnon, 1986). However, we do not yet know about pornography's influence on sexual assault. Baron and Strauss (1984) reported a significant correlation between pornography use and rape rates in 50 states. More recently, Boeringer (1994), showed, in 477 college males, a relationship between use of pornography and sexual coercion. Other studies, however, have questioned pornography's contribution (Attorney General's Commission, 1986; Scott, 1985). Liberalization of publication laws in the 1960s and 1970s increased availability of pornography and altered its content, with an increase in sexually violent and degrading themes (Donnerstein, Linz, & Penrod, 1987; Palys, 1986). However, there is no evidence that rape is increasing. Moreover, a number of analogue studies (Hall & Hirschman, 1993) exposing men to various aggressive and dehumanizing scenes failed to demonstrate that this exposure increased callousness toward women and acceptance of rape myths.

Given the state of research in this area, even an ardent feminist would admit that sociopolitical theories of sexual aggression cannot answer all questions of etiology, both ultimate and proximate. Feminist theories fail to account for male victims and female sexual aggression (Anderson, 1998; Anderson & Newton, 1997). In addition, the popular characterization of rape as a nonsexual act cannot answer the question of why it ends with the attacker's orgasm. In most cases, even stranger rape, the offender uses only enough force to require sexual compliance (Prentky & Knight, 1991). The sole objective finding in men who have raped is not arousal to aggression as much as failure to inhibit arousal with cues of victim refusal or suffering (Howes, 1998). The feminist position that male-generated pornography maintains sexual assault has not been convincingly demonstrated; indeed, most pornography depicts willing females enjoying sexual experiences.

It appears that most men, even those who rape, do not attack women for the purpose of inflicting physical harm, absent a sexual goal. Thus, the feminists' hope that improving conditions for women worldwide will result in the reduction of sexual assault has yet to be realized. More evident is the contribution to women's rights that the feminist movement has inspired, and the advances it has already created for *both* genders in present-day civilization.

The Addiction Model

The current popularity of addiction as an explanation for sexual crimes compels examination (Carnes, 1983). Recently, Laws (1996b) has pointed to similarities between compulsive drug and alcohol use and sexual behavior. Some offenders, particularly pedophiles and serial rapists, develop a preoccupation with deviant sexual activity and repeatedly entertain fantasies about it, often abandoning many other potentially rewarding activities and "casting their lives adrift in perilous seas." Often, the offender feels "driven" to aggressive sexual activity and, after completing it, is contrite, only to begin the chain again after a variable delay. To bolster the connection, a significant proportion of sexual offenders have been reported to abuse alcohol (Seto & Barbaree, 1995).

If a sexually aggressive man is addicted to sex, he would be more likely to coerce a woman to obtain sexual gratification and would lack adequate internal controls to maintain his behavior within societal norms. External motivations, such as peer and family pressure and legal sanctions, will be required to effect a change. An analogy to alcohol continues: Abstinence and peer pressure via twelve-step support groups will be necessary for treatment; there is no hope for a cure, but risk reduction is a realistic goal.

However, there are profound differences between alcoholism and sexual aggression. Almost everyone enjoys sexual activity and experiences increasing sexual urgency as abstinence progresses. The alcoholic begins in a nonaddicted state, drinks increasingly, then suffers withdrawal with abstinence; continued sobriety often leads to a *reduction* in urges to drink. In one case, universal urges exit, in the other, urges must be created. Perhaps most significantly, the victims of alcoholism are distal and largely unintentional; the victims of sexual assault are proximal and, in many cases, are affected lifelong. While the addiction model has become fashionable with a segment of the lay and clinical populations, it remains an analogy without a presently realized attachment to ongoing research in this area.

Behavioral Theories

The demonstration that some men who rape demonstrate deviant sexual arousal on the plethysmograph (Abel, Barlow, Blanchard, & Guild, 1977; Freund & Blanchard, 1981) lent confirmation to clinical histories of offenders who often reported aggressive sexual fantasies. In contrast to feminist theories, behaviorists maintain that sexual gratification is the primary motivation for sexual crimes. Indeed, the most complex models subdefining types of rapists were initially based on sexual preferences (Rosenberg et al., 1988).

If behavioral principles apply to all organisms, then in humans, when sexual release (with its inherently reinforcing properties) is associated with previously neutral stimuli, they come to signal reward as well: New pairings with any stimulus are possible. In situations in which a previously unassociated stimulus is similar to an unconditioned stimulus, it too, will begin to contain reinforcing properties, a fact only insignificantly noted thus far in research on child sexual abuse. For example, a man living with his girlfriend and her 12-year-old daughter, a female he did not raise from infancy, may, outside of his awareness, take account of similarities in their manner and appearance. In having associated sexual release with a similar woman (her mother), he may become increasingly attracted to her, especially living in proximity. In a similar fashion, chance pairings in youth, as sexual senses are developing, have been thought to be responsible for some sexual aggression. A young boy may associate early arousal with a movie he surreptitiously has seen containing sexual aggression, or with a story, eagerly received, of coercion against a woman. He may pair these images in his mind's eye with masturbation and climax, thereby repeatedly strengthening them. Eventually, under certain conditions, he may act in a coercive fashion. If not immediately punished, and especially if reinforced by sexual compliance on the part of a female confederate, this behavior is likely to continue or escalate. Because sexual release is the result of a chain of behaviors (each stimulus and response paving the way for the next), triggering stimuli can initiate the cycle again under the right circumstances. In this manner, a sexually aggressive individual can be seen as responding to environmental stimuli, greatly dependent upon his peers and surroundings, and compelled to make "sea changes" based upon the "winds of circumstance and chance."

Even the most strict behaviorist, however, would not adhere to such a "black box" model. For if all sexually aggressive males are aroused to the aggressive elements of sex, one would have expected plethysmograph data to be far more definitive than reported. Moreover, human sexual behavior may be learned not only by the standard processes of operant and respondent conditioning, but by vicarious social learning as well (Freeman-Longo, 1986). Genetic variance, combined with the idiosyncracies of upbringing and circumstance, may be responsible for the heterogeneity seen in sexually aggressive males. Nonetheless, there has been too quick and reflexive a disavowal of behaviorism to feel entirely comfortable about abandoning it altogether. Behavioral principles apply to all organisms of which we are aware. Ignoring stimulus generalization, contingency, and the power of sexual reinforcement, is like fleeing your home because you learned that houses can burn. In future models of sexual assault, behavioral explanations will probably continue to play a supporting role.

Sociocultural Theories

The role of social and cognitive processes in sexual assault has long been recognized. Societies characterized by patriarchal organization have been reported to be higher in levels of both sexual and nonsexual aggression (Clark & Lewis, 1977; Sanday, 1981), a finding true to communities both undeveloped and industrialized. Some of these communities may also have higher levels of rape tolerance (Hall, Howard, & Boezio, 1986), the extent to which people minimize the seriousness of sexual assault, discount its traumatic effects, blame the victim for the attack, or question her credibility (O'Donohue et al., 1996). It appears that sexual aggression against women may be influenced by a male's perception of his social environment, of a woman's role in society, and of himself.

In contrast to behavioral theories, social learning theory (Bandura, 1977) posits three overlapping processes: (1) *participant modeling*, in which the learner observes, then copies, another's behavior; (2) *vicarious learning*, in which the individual learns by observation only; and (3) *symbolic modeling*, in which the individual anticipates consequences through forethought and mental imagery. Also, humans observe their behavior and devise a set of self-statements through which they define what sort of person they are.

Early champions of social influence, Groth and Birnbaum (1979) characterized three types of rapists: (1) the *anger rapist*, for whom sex is a hostile act; (2) the *power rapist*, for whom sex represents conquest; and (3) the *sadistic rapist*, for whom sex and aggression have fused. Attempts, however, to validate these types have not fared well. The instruments designed to measure hostility to women and acceptance of myths are woefully transparent, while the plethysmograph cannot adequately distinguish men with a propensity to aggress (Quinsey & Earls, 1990). Moreover, reports from offenders are suspect. Confidential research has helped matters just a little. Heterogeneity conspires against accuracy in this regard, not just in type of offender, but in type of offense as well.

One area, however, that has received some recent attention is the issue of social skills. Anecdotal reports (and popular notions) describe sexual offenders as being raised in emotional isolation (Marshall & Mazzucco, 1995), and unable to bond to others (Ward, Hudson, Marshall, & Siegert, 1995). For example, Lipton, McDonel, and McFall (1987) examined social information processing in rapists. They reported that these men experienced problems in accurately identifying cues in first-date scenarios, particularly negative mood states. Subsequent studies also implied deficits in intimacy and greater loneliness in some sexual offenders (Bumby & Marshall, 1994; Seidman, Marshall, Hudson, & Robertson, 1994), but the evidence is inconclusive. A larger, well-controlled study in New Zealand reported that a simple division between sexual offenders and other groups in intimacy was less than clear-cut (Ward, McCormack, & Hudson, 1997).

There has been some evidence that men who rape view their victims' behavior as being provocative before a sexual assault and as enjoying rape, whereas nonaggressive men interpreted these signals quite differently (Hanson & Scott, 1995). Pryor and Stoller (1994) showed that males likely to sexually harass perceived a stronger link between sexuality and dominance, while O'Donohue and colleagues (1996) detected a hypermasculinity profile in men with self-reported past and future coercive behavior. This has led to the supposition that such men lack empathy (Marshall, Hudson, Jones, & Fernandez, 1995), a notion that presupposes that deficiency as a prerequisite for rape. However, empirical data do not support this contention; deficits in this area were more apparent in offenders *not* using force (Hanson & Scott, 1995). Clinically, it is not uncommon to learn that a young man arrested for acquaintance or partner rape is a church-going, job-holding, family-supporting member of his community. At the moment of the act, it is unlikely that he underwent a total personality change. Rather, the circumstances of that moment, combined with his internal drive state and disregard for consequences, may have propelled him to an unfortunate action. Some aggressive acts are planned, but most are not (Marshall, 1996a). The rapist therefore, might not lack the capacity for empathy in general, but, simply disregards it at the time of the deed. Thus, empirical support for sociocultural theories of sexual aggression is modest, and, where it exists, appears overly dependent on university student and survey research. Nonetheless, it has provided an enduring image of the sexually aggressive male as an unattached loner which, if not taken as an icon, could well contribute to developing more comprehensive theories in the future.

Cognitive and Affective Theories

As conscious creatures, humans are endowed with the capacity to plan, ponder, and interpret their actions. On that basis, it has been proposed that sexually aggressive behavior can be initiated, facilitated, and justified by distorted thinking. This notion has been supported by the clinical observation that offenders frequently fail to recognize the harm that aggressive behavior has caused. In people who do not aggress, this lapse causes considerable discomfort and prompts explanations in cognitive terms: Men who aggress sexually unconsciously distort what they are doing to preserve a favorable self-image (Ward, Hudson, & Marshall, 1995). In order to bear the conflict of what they are doing, they must suspend regulatory mechanisms presumed to be operative in all individuals at all times (Ward, Hudson, & Keenan, 1998).

There is evidence for such deconstruction (Marshall, Jones, Hudson, & McDonald, 1993), but it is anecdotal. Indeed, recent findings indicate no general lack of empathy in such men (Hanson & Scott, 1995). Thus, the deficits displayed may be situation-specific. Such men often deny or minimize their actions in several ways: They may deny that the act occurred, deny it was nonconsensual, or deny that it created any ill effects upon the victim, even when confronted by incontrovertible evidence. In cognitive theory, attention is paid to four sequential processes by which a sexually aggressive act might occur:

1. *Covert planning.* The aggressor might not be aware of preparing the victim and/or situation in which an aggressive act may occur (Pithers & Gray, 1996).
2. *Affect and immediate gratification.* The aggressor does not have a problem with delaying gratification, but possesses a cognitive style that focuses on the immediate present and ignores issues of victim harm and long-term consequence (Ward et al., 1995).
3. *Cognitive deconstruction.* The aggressor suspends cognitive processes to accomplish the act without experiencing affective distress (Hartley, 1998).
4. *Cognitive distortion.* The aggressor minimizes, denies, and distorts his memory of the act(s) to better preserve self-esteem (Bumby, 1996; Schlank & Shaw, 1996).

In a cognitively-based study of this sequence, Malamuth and Brown (1994) found that faulty information-processing fueled higher levels of mistrust and hostility toward women and paved the way to sexual aggression. Partly based on these results, Johnson and Ward (1996) proposed the use of a sociocognitive framework in considering the factors contributing to offending. They noted that research, to date, has focused on cognitive distortions *after* the aggressive acts and hence, has not controlled for responses emitted as a consequence of offending. They cogently point out the need for improved research in this area using adequate nonoffender control groups, and systematically investigating information-processing in known aggressors.

One concern for current cognitive theorists is the lack of accounting for affective, motivational, and biological factors, a problem not insurmountable (Fiske & Taylor, 1991). Cognitive theorists also need to better explain blitz attacks, and acquaintance and partner aggression. Research in this area needs to better control for postoffense variables, because what a man will say after a crime might have been determined by the circumstances of the crime itself. Because some theorists propose that affective states, such as anger and disappointment at the time of the offense, are significant contributors to attacks (Pithers, 1990), cognitive theory must begin to measure emotional states among aggressors retrospectively, and then devise ways to assess affective predispositions that might help us understand aggressive sexual acts. Offenders can see others' distortions sharply; their vision is apparently dimmed by the proximity of their own minimization and justification. It is hoped that cognitive theory can further help them, and us, see the light.

Sociobiological Theories

There is no domain in psychology over the past two decades that has not been informed by an understanding of the significance of evolutionary mechanisms in affecting human behavior. Broad differences in gender-related behavior have been supposed to underlie males' hunting and mating abilities—particularly orientation, physical strength, and aggression, tempered by a need to function in a hierarchal team of male confederates. Females remain closer to home, rearing young, and gathering food. They may have developed a greater capacity to interpret social cues and, hence, a more finely-tuned sensitivity to interpersonal conflict (Maccoby, 1987). Undoubtedly, flexibility in evolutionary mechanisms would be desirable to help individuals prosper in increasingly complex human societies. Therefore, broad overlap in masculine and feminine traits would be seen in real-life interactions, with each individual possessing a predisposition on which life's experiences would act in shaping gender-related behavior.

Evolutionary theory advances our understanding of sexual aggression by linking these gender differences with *ultimate* (rather than *proximate*) motivation for the sexual nature of assault: reproduction. Ultimate cause (the reason for sex) differs from proximate cause (the pleasure of sex) and is not linguistically mediated; consequently, it can be studied in animals. Differences have evolved in all species to the benefit of each gender. Females, who bear the total initial burden of parental investment, and much of it after birth, have been favored to compete for males who would offer them the best chance of nurturing their offspring to maturity. To pass on their DNA, males must impress females with their resources (physical strength, health, appearance, and possessions) to gain sexual access. From a female perspective, displaying hesitancy and coyness could gain more attention and time to discriminate a better choice among men. However, males who are sexually aggressive might be favored because they may be more successful in mating than their subassertive compatriots. While genetic variables may contribute to aggression (McLaren, 1990), experiential factors must also be taken into account. The process of a rape, for example, may relate to evolutionary mechanisms perhaps gone awry in the service of sexual interest, but the content (attraction to the victim, circumstances of the crime) is idiosyncratically determined.

Evolutionary theory leads to the following testable hypotheses (followed by some confirmatory references):

1. Males employ aggression and dominance to perpetuate their genes to a greater degree than do females (Ellis, 1993).
2. If reproduction is an ultimate goal, males will prefer the females most likely to conceive, and deliver a viable infant after intercourse, such as those who are young and healthy (Quinsey & Lalumière, 1995).
3. Females will prefer males with the greatest resources to guarantee that their own genes survive.
4. The period of increased sexual aggression in males should coincide with the years in which males are most likely to produce viable offspring (Henn, Herjanic, & Vanderpearl, 1976).
5. Rape should be more common in lower than upper socioeconomic strata (Peterson & Bailey, 1988).
6. Male and female brains should differ structurally, either at the macroscopic (Allen & Gorski, 1992) or microscopic (LeVay, 1991), levels.
7. Male reproductive interests are best served by compromising between the strategies of impregnating as many females as possible and devoting maximum attention to raising a single female's young (Ellis, 1993).

Much more is needed, of course, to constitute a theory of why men rape. Individual differences in risk-taking, absence of impulse control, and disinhibition of arousal in the face of female distress cannot be directly accounted for by evolutionary theory. Moreover, situational factors remain to be specified. In addition, the present theory attributes little significance to the potential influences of pornography and social modeling (e.g., gang rapes). Nonetheless, it has formed a significant addition to our understanding of human sexual behavior that has the potential to prevent sexual assault in the future.

Integrated Theories

No current theorist, regardless of bias, adopts a unilateral position uninformed by the work of others. All workers in this field recognize the significant contributions of feminist, behavioral, social learning, cognitive-affective, and sociobiological perspectives, and all attempt to integrate significant components from each. The first of these was developed by Malamuth in the mid 1980s (Malamuth, 1986), although more recently enhanced (Malamuth, Heavey, & Linz, 1993). These workers proposed two pathways that must interact to cause sexual aggression: *hostile masculinity* and *sexual promiscuity*. The first path stems from a hostile early home environment, antisocial personality characteristics, and acceptance of male strength as a desirable trait. Evidence indicates that such men show greater levels of plethysmographic arousal to aggressive elements of sexuality, accept rape myths more readily, show antisocial traits, and see sex as an opportunity for aggression (Huesmann, 1988; Marshall, 1996b). The second path, *sexual promiscuity,* is characterized by a high sexual drive, use of sex as a means of boosting self-esteem, and an increased tendency to employ coercive tactics in the pursuit of sex (Marshall & Barbaree, 1990a).

This reasoning led Malamuth to propose six predictor variables for the occurrence of sexual aggression:

1. Hostility to women
2. A dominance motive
3. Acceptance of rape myths
4. Arousal to depictions of rape
5. Antisocial personality traits
6. Sexual experience (as a measure of opportunity to aggress)

Based on these ultimate causes, they proposed three proximate conditions necessary for sexual aggression:

1. Motivation to commit an aggressive sexual act
2. Reduction in inhibition preventing sexual arousal in the face of victim distress
3. Opportunity

To bolster the model, Malamuth and colleagues present empirical evidence demonstrating the synergistic interactions of the six variables with the three proximate causes, and demonstrated a six-fold increase in frequency of sexually aggressive acts when all six factors were present.

Unfortunately, this theory relies mainly on data obtained from retrospective surveys of college students. As yet, the role of genetic contributions, affective state at the time of the offense, motivational drive state, and influence of peers, are not taken into account. Moreover, if hostility to women really plays a role in aggressive sexual behavior, one must explain why these males spend a great deal of time with, and around, women companions, why they are heterosexual instead of homosexual, and why they aggress against males as well as females.

Components of Malamuth's theory appear in a more recent, comprehensive approach by Marshall and Barbaree (1990a). These authors emphasize adverse developmental experiences, such as distant, unavailable parents and the presence of harsh discipline, leading to poor social skills (Ward et al., 1997); negative attitudes toward relationships (Ward, Hudson, & Marshall, 1995); lack of adequate behavioral controls (Monto, Zgourides, & Harris, 1988); intimacy deficits (Marshall & Mazzucco, 1995); impaired ability to distinguish between aggression and sexuality (Ward et al., 1997); a fluctuating, ambivalent attachment style (Ward, Hudson, Marshall, & Siegert, 1995); poor parental bonding (Kobayashi, Sales, Becker, Figueredo, & Kaplan, 1995); low self-esteem (Marshall et al., 1997); more gender-biased attitudes (Wegner, 1994); less sensitivity to victim issues (Marshall, Barbaree, & Fernandez, 1995); endorsement of aggression as a more appropriate intervention in conflict (Marshall, Barbaree, & Fernandez, 1995); and the expectation of fewer negative consequences following aggression (O'Donohue et al., 1996).

Marshall and Barbaree did not ignore evolutionary and biological factors. They noted that physiological substrates evolved to perpetuate an individual's DNA and, therefore, establish a predisposition, but one that can only be activated by a poor upbringing and a lack of capacity to form satisfying relationships.

While this model is broad and flexible, it will need to expand in a number of directions to satisfy current critics (Hudson & Ward, 1997). It has presented data mainly on stranger rapists, ignoring what may be a larger issue of acquaintance and partner rape. Moreover, it fails to explain how rapists, supposedly lacking self-esteem, are actually more confident than other groups of offenders (Marshall, Barbaree, & Fernandez, 1995). Also, it does not yet take into account proximate factors, such as affective state and the use of alcohol. Nonetheless, it leaves great opportunity for expansion to include these variables in future formulations.

A third overarching theory, proposed by Hall and Hirschman (1991), stems from their initial observations that empirical evidence for deviant sexual arousal in cases of rape is largely lacking (Howes, 1998). In rape (as opposed to pedophilia), sexual arousal may not be deviant (Barbaree & Serin, 1993). These authors, therefore, propose a quadripartite model of rape, in which a high level of general sexual arousal, combined with cognitive processes (benefits of sexual aggression at the time versus potential negative consequences), affective components (depression due to loneliness, anger at rejection), and trait characteristics (antisocial attitude, inadequate socialization) all combine to lead to an increased likelihood of sexual aggression. This theory combines situational variables (such as state at the time of the crime) with predispositional factors, but is weak in defining the latter. It takes into account feminists' notions on anger toward women and social learning theories with their emphasis on environmental antecedents to rape. However, it focuses on rape, not the majority of sexual aggression, which may be carried out by otherwise normal-appearing males, and deals mainly with proximate rather than ultimate causation.

More recently, Hudson and Ward (1997) have proposed an integrated theory based on their work with relapse prevention and their own attempts at theory-knitting (Ward & Hudson, 1998). They propose a model of sexual aggression as a result of nine steps in an offense chain:

1. Abnormalities in self-regulation, including underregulation or misregulation of sexual drive

2. Developmentally adverse events, such as being the victim of sexual abuse
3. Distal planning, such as unconscious planning and circumstance (victim vulnerability and the use of alcohol)
4. Nonsexual contact with the victim with the ultimate purpose of offending
5. Cognitive planning, such as a conscious evaluation of benefits and risks of aggressing
6. Proximate planning, such as an immediate decision to initiate sexual contact with the victim
7. The sexual offense itself
8. The evaluation process thereafter, which usually involves cognitive distortions
9. Resolutions about future behavior and conclusions that it is wrong and not to be repeated, or that it is too enjoyable to stop the chain from being reinitiated

These authors consider intimacy deficits and deficits in attachment style as important, but at a middle level, providing a conceptual basis for more comprehensive theories. Microtheories, as in their nine-point conceptualization outlined above, specify cognitive, behavioral, motivational, and contextual factors related to the offense chain. They concluded that overarching theories are not yet at hand, but that more attention to coordinated hypotheses at lower levels will eventually produce a global working model of the offending process.

However, their model relies on cognitive processes not easily amenable to scientific scrutiny, and fails to take into account that most rapists—70 to 80 percent (Maletzky, 1994)—are not usually abused as children; that genetic factors may account as well for the chaos in the childhood homes of future rapists; and that there is no convincing evidence that men who aggress sexually (as opposed to rapists) have deficits in female attachments (Marshall, Hudson, Jones, & Fernandez, 1995). Nonetheless, the work of Hudson and Ward in this area has helped to combine a number of ultimate and proximate factors into testable hypotheses, and to explain how hypothetical constructs can be subdivided into different levels of theory.

Ellis (1993) and Maletzky (1996) have proposed a biosocial theory of rape designed to incorporate the strengths of feminist, behavioral, social learning, and evolutionary models. It advances four propositions necessary to understand sexual assault:

1. Humans have two inherent drives that motivate sexual aggression: sexual drive and the drive to possess.
2. These drives are stronger in males than females.
3. The motivation for, and process of, assault is unlearned; however, the behavioral surroundings and content of the assault are dependent on environmental factors, such as upbringing, modeling, stimulus generalization, availability of a victim, level of intoxication, and immediate affective state.
4. The strength of immediate sexual drive increases propensity to sexually aggress. This theory pays attention to biological and gender differences and

speaks to ultimate as well as proximate factors. It fails, however, to take into account the role conditions might play in the sexual assault and, at present, provides satisfying conceptions in preference to promising solutions to the problem of sexual aggression.

In fact, all of the integrated theories advanced thus far have failed to account for the fact that perhaps 20 to 30 percent of victims of sexual aggression are male (McConaghy, 1993b) and that some of these were victims of *female* sexual aggression (Anderson, 1998). In addition, these theories are based mostly on surveys of college students and analogue research. Most centrally, no theory explains why, given the advantages of sexual aggression for a male, most men do not rape and, instead, chose to live amicably both with female and male rivals.

Moreover, comprehensive theorists often appear to strain to include every conceivable factor influencing assault—a probable reflection of the fact that rape in particular, and sexual assault in general, is heterogeneous, and may not represent a single phenomenon. Sexual assault may be situation specific and individual specific—so idiosyncratic as to thwart comprehensive theory-building.

Assessment

There are commonly two goals in the assessment of males with sexual aggression: forensic and therapeutic. The first asks questions of safety, disposition, and treatability; the second focuses on elements of a treatment plan. Both share much, however, and are often combined. In assessing a sexual offender, it is important for the clinician to recognize inherent differences from other patient populations. Offenders are often seen, not at their own request, but on referral from a criminal justice agency, such as a corrections division, children's services agency, or the courts. Absent judicial influence, most such men would not enter treatment voluntarily, as most (and, most often, sincerely) hold fast to one of two beliefs: "I didn't do it" or "Even if I did do it, it could never happen again."

To further hinder a therapeutic relationship, many offenders minimize or deny sexual aggression. Some minimize by denying coercion ("it was consenting"), sexual intent ("I was pushed into her"), victim harm ("she enjoyed it" or "she didn't even fight me off"), or seriousness ("she wasn't a virgin"; "we were friends afterward"). Some blame the victim ("she provoked me"), while others deny outright that the event ever occurred. For many, it is certainly advantageous to maintain relative innocence, as a number of offenders are first evaluated following arrest, but before trial or sentencing. However, even aggressors not involved in the legal system have ample reason to deny, for the admission of loss of sexual control is not an easily confessable sin, and pardon comes only after arduous public humiliation. Indeed, it is a wonder that a slim majority of men *do* admit to some culpability (Maletzky & Steinhauser, 1996).

Under such circumstances, proper assessment cannot rely on an offender's initial self-report. Trust-building over a number of sessions is necessary to obtain meaningful information. As in any clinical assessment, attention must be directed to an offender's history, that is, development and upbringing, education, military history, vocational history, social and marital patterns, medical history, patterns of drug and alcohol use, criminal record, and genetic history. The clinician should focus particularly on the sexual developmental history, including sexual abuse history, childhood sexual games, age of first masturbation and intercourse, sexual fantasies, dating experiences, erectile difficulties, premature ejaculation, and unusual attractions (e.g., to children or aggressive sex). While most individuals are embarrassed when describing sexual intimacies with a relative stranger, most clinicians develop their own empathic style, which can ease the transition from adamant denial to begrudging minimization to outright admission and, occasionally, to additional confessions.

Although trained by profession, clinicians are not clairvoyant. They cannot automatically gauge truth or deceit. Moreover, individual offender style betrays attempts at easy classification. Nonetheless, a thorough mental status examination can inform conclusions about risk and treatment options. Does the patient avoid eye contact and speak hesitantly? While this is no guarantee of deception, these observations lessen credibility. Are there limitations in orientation, vocabulary, memory, abstracting, and mathematical abilities? Special programs may be necessary for the developmentally disabled offender. Is affective range restricted? Lack of spontaneous displays of normal emotion *may* betray an attempt to conceal information. Is there any evidence of a thought disorder or affective disorder that may require psychiatric treatment? Often these observations are useful, not only in building a treatment program, but in learning how to best interact with each offender.

This information must be supplemented with additional input from official agencies, such as police reports, presentence investigations, and reports from children's services agencies. Firsthand accounts by victims are the most salient. A comparison of offender and victim reports is crucial to understanding the nature and level of an offender's cognitive distortions and denial, if any. Indeed, a review of collateral materials should be accomplished *before* the initial visit to better evaluate the manner in which the offender regards his offense. Even in the face of denial, one can adopt a nonjudgmental approach (Schlank & Shaw, 1996), such that an offender, first regarding the examiner as an extension of the judicial system prosecuting him, can gradually come to think of her or him as an ally in therapy, helping rid him of an unwanted part of himself.

Psychological Testing

Psychological assessment of an offender can be undertaken with a variety of purposes. Is this offender suffering from a psychiatric illness? Does he harbor intellectual deficits? Will antisocial tendencies render adherence to a treatment program difficult? What other treatment issues must be addressed? Alternatively, we may wish to measure progress in treatment by comparing responses on the same assessment device over time. It might be especially important to assess risk in this population and to explore whether any instrument can distinguish men likely to aggress.

Although a heroic effort has been devoted to attempts to delineate a sexual offender profile or a rapist typology based on standard psychological tests, such as the MMPI (Marshall & Hall, 1995) or MCMI (Carpenter, Peed, & Eastman, 1995), no sexual offender profile has been distinguished—a probable reflection of the heterogeneity seen within these populations. Thus, more narrowly focused instruments have been developed to measure predispositions to sexually aggress. However, most of these are surveys (Attraction to Sexual Aggression Scale [Malamuth, 1989]; Multidimensional Assessment of Sex and Aggression [Knight, Prentky, & Cerce, 1994]) or are, at best, indirect analogues (Hostility Toward Women Scale [Check, 1985]; Rape Empathy Scale [Dietz, Blackwell, Daley, & Bentley, 1982]; Fear of Intimacy Scale [Descutner & Thelen, 1991]).

Over the past decade, much attention has been devoted to the cognitive style of rapists. Burt's Rape Myth Acceptance Scale (RMA) (1980) has been accepted as an indicator of potential for aggressive sexual behavior, but no study has (nor perhaps can) truly test whether deviant scores *predict* such behavior. It also appears to be a transparent instrument, especially for men accused of rape. Given the present state of knowledge, it would seem reasonable to suppose that men who endorse such myths are at greater risk to aggress. Of concern, however, is the impact of social desirability and the scale's focus on issues of age, race, and familiarity, as much as on sexual aggression.

The Hare Psychopathy Checklist (PCL) (Hare, 1980) has been suggested as relevant for the investigation of rapists (Ward, McCormack, Hudson, & Polaschek, 1997). This scale, revised in 1990 (Hare et al.) uses an interviewer-administered guide to assess 20 items divisible into two factors: selfish use of others and socially deviant behavior. Although men who rape have scored higher on this scale than have child molesters (Barbaree, 1990), they do not differ from other, nonsexual offenders. It is possible, however, that greater scores on this instrument can portend greater risk of future offending (Quinsey, Harris, Rice, & Lalumière, 1993).

Assessment instruments have been devised to measure sexual behavior in aggressors (Langevin, Paitich, Russon, Handy, & Langevin, 1990), sexual experiences (Koss & Oros, 1982), fantasies (Daleiden, Kaufman, Hilliker, & O'Neil, 1998), the extent of denial (Baldwin & Roys, 1998), empathy (Dietz et al., 1982), and intimacy (Ward, McCormack, & Hudson, 1997). Many of these tests are contaminated, however, by questions of transparency and clinical relevance. A recent attempt to disguise an assessment instrument for sexual aggressors (Schewe & O'Donohue, 1998) awaits independent verification using larger numbers of subjects.

In summary, there is inconclusive evidence that any single psychometric test, or cluster of tests, can provide meaningful information for detection or prediction of sexually aggressive acts. This failure, despite attempts spanning decades, may argue strongly for wide variability, not only in sexually coercive acts, but in those who perpetrate them.

Physiological Assessment

While sexual arousal may be characterized by a number of physiologic reactions, the most distinctive marker in males is penile erection. The penile plethysmograph, first used to measure nocturnal erections for the evaluation of impotence, has been widely adopted to assess sexual offenders. In a typical paradigm (Maletzky & Steinhauser, 1996), an offender watches a video screen after placing a thin, nonconstricting rubber gauge around his penis at midshaft. Penile circumference can then be obtained as he watches slides or videos and/or listens to sexually arousing stories. Techniques have been developed to maintain attention and prevent faking (Barbaree & Serin, 1993). Figures 10.1a and 10.1b demonstrate typical tracings for an aggressive offender before and following a course of treatment.

While standardized stimuli are being developed for the detection of child molesters and pedophiles (Card & Dibble, 1995; Laws, Gulayets, & Frenzel, 1995), none have proven effective in reliably distinguishing men who aggress from those

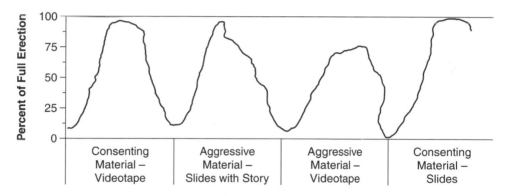

FIGURE 10.1a   Baseline Plethysmograph Recording for a Sexual Aggressor

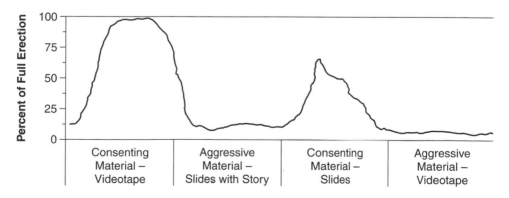

FIGURE 10.1b   End-of-Treatment Plethysmograph Recording for a Sexual Aggressor

who do not. Although early evidence indicated the rape index (arousal to nonconsenting sex divided by arousal to consenting sex) could discriminate among types of sexual offenders (Abel, Barlow, Planchard, & Guild, 1977), most studies suggest extreme caution. For example, Baxter, Barbaree, and Marshall (1986) reported that both rapist and nonrapist offenders showed equal arousal to rape and mutually consenting cues. Similarly, Murphy, Krisak, Stalgaitis, and Anderson (1984) and Langevin, Paitich, and Russon (1985) could not distinguish between men with or without aggressive sexuality, based on plethysmograph findings alone. Marshall and Barbaree (1994) evaluated 60 rapists and found that only 30 percent were equally or more aroused to depictions of coercive sex than by consenting relations. In this study, almost 27 percent of nondeviant males displayed equal or greater arousal to rape than to mutually consenting sex, underscoring the difficulty in differentiating aggressive males from those not likely to rape. Eccles, Marshall, and Barbaree (1994) reported on 38 men who listened to audiotapes describing aggression and degrading sexual scenes. They found that neither aggression nor degrading rape indices discriminated between offenders and nonoffenders, suggesting that many men in random samples are aroused to scenes of coercive sexual activity. When differential patterns are demonstrated, they have always been in a highly selected population, such as sadistic and serial rapists (Langevin, Paitich, & Russon, 1985; Quinsey & Earls, 1990).

Multiple problems have occurred in the use of the plethysmograph. Standardization of stimuli is progressing (ATSA, 1997), but wide acceptance will not be easily gained. Each laboratory has developed its own collection of stimulus materials that may be powerful for some offenders and not others. Comparing one site's data to another's may be scientifically impossible under such conditions. Moreover, the mere possession of child pornography has been interpreted by some as immoral (as reviewed in Laws, 1996a) and illegal by others (Civil Action Suit, 1993, p. 22) because it may promote child pornography. In addition, while the plethysmograph has been demonstrated to be valid and reliable in distinguishing pedophiles from other offenders and nonoffender populations (Howes, 1995), trust is limited in its capacity to detect sexual aggression lurking in the background. It cannot prove guilt or claim predictive accuracy. In addition, faking is not uncommon, and it can sometimes be successful (Howes, 1998; Quinsey & Earls, 1990; Wilson, 1997). Indeed, while false positives are rare, false negatives are not (Looman, Abracen, Maillet, & DiFazio, 1998; Ward, McCormack, Hudson, & Polaschek, 1997). The test is conducted under cold laboratory conditions (although time for habituation is allowed) and administered by strangers, often under adversarial conditions. It is embarrassing and expensive for the subjects, some of whom may be innocent.

Despite its abundant limitations, the plethysmograph carries several distinct advantages:

1. It is, at present, the only objective way to measure male sexual arousal (Card & Olsen, 1996).
2. It can be individualized by choosing offender-specific visual stimuli and recording actual scenes (Maletzky, 1995).

3. Safeguards against the misuse of pornographic stimulus materials can be taken (Maletzky, 1995).
4. It has been demonstrated to predict success in treatment programs (Abel & Rouleau, 1990; Maletzky, 1993).
5. It has delineated a particularly severe class of sexually aggressive men: sadistic rapists (Rice, Chaplin, Harris, & Coutts, 1994).
6. It may prove useful in measuring inhibition of arousal, as most men will gradually lose their erections when shown increasingly aggressive scenes; those who do not may represent aggressors at greater risk (Earls, 1988).
7. It may be much more useful as a treatment device than as a tool for assessment.

Because serious concerns about the reliability, validity, and ethics of the procedure have been raised, attention has recently been directed toward other assessment devices. Abel, Huffman, Warberg, and Holland (1998) have described a computerized procedure measuring duration of time an offender chooses to look at selected slides, called *reaction time*. The authors showed that this duration was longer in selected offenders when viewing scenes linked with their past history of offending. They believed the data were sufficient to discriminate offending from nonoffending populations, although others (Fischer & Smith, in press) disagree and cite this test's transparency as a drawback.

Polygraph testing (the "lie detector"), and even the knowledge of an impending polygraph, can have a profound effect on disclosure by a sexual aggressor (Emerick & Dutton, 1993). Blasingame (1998) has proposed guidelines for the use of this instrument with sexual offenders in the community. As with the plethysmograph, the polygraph is often more useful for treatment than assessment purposes.

It must be left to the twenty-first century to ponder the ethics of using neuroimaging devices, such as PET scans, to measure sexual arousal in humans. The technology is being developed (Raine, 1993; Stoléru et al., 1999), but its deployment is far from clear.

Assessment of Risk

Most men who aggress sexually continue to live in their communities, either undetected, unincarcerated, or under supervision. It is incumbent on treatment providers to accurately assess how safe each offender is to be at large. While many researchers have examined risk in general offending populations (sexual and nonsexual), just a handful have addressed the more specific issue in sexual aggressors.

Quinsey and colleagues (1993) have suggested an actuarial scheme for mathematically predicting risk based on a number of offense and historical variables previously shown (Hanson & Bussiere, 1996; Maletzky, 1993) to predict risk to be at large in sizable samples of child molesters, pedophiles, and rapists. Factors indicating risk include history of prior sexual and nonsexual offenses, predatory manner of offending, younger age, history of interpersonal and vocational instability, minimization, denial, force used in the crime(s), and greater plethysmographic arousal to aggressive sexuality. Findings have consistently demonstrated that men who chose victims who are strangers and who have multiple victims are at greatest risk.

More recently, Hudson and Ward (1997) have argued that these static factors should be augmented with variables that are more amenable to change, and assessable throughout a course of treatment. Plethysmographic measurement of deviant arousal is one such factor. Proulx and colleagues (1997) examined 113 rapists, 21 percent of whom reoffended after treatment. Reconvicted rapists did not differ from nonrecidivists at initial or final assessment. However, Rice, Quinsey, and Harris (1991) reported the opposite. Maletzky and Prueitt (1999) found that the initial plethysmographic assessment of deviant arousal was inversely correlated with success in a cognitive/behavioral treatment program. Methods and large subject numbers were common to all three studies, thus these differences remain unexplained and are, as yet, further unexplored.

Proulx and colleagues (1997) also attempted to investigate another potentially changeable or dynamic factor: performance on psychometric testing. Results of this study were not statistically significant, because the number of recidivists was too small; other work has suggested that higher scores on the PCL predicted treatment failure (Rice et al., 1991).

Other researchers are also examining factors that may change with treatment, such as attitudes about therapy (Beech & Fordham, 1997), sexual fantasies (O'Donohue, Letourneau, & Dowling, 1997), cognitive distortions (Bumby, 1996), and victim empathy and offense disclosure (Anderson, Gibeau, & D'Amora, 1995). One drawback to work done thus far concerns specificity. It is difficult to know how to apply predictive variables studied only in adjudicated rapists and apply these to the wider category of men who are sexually aggressive. It is likely that work in the future will take a broader approach and incorporate both static and dynamic factors as variables in making predictions about amenability to treatment and safety to be at large, given the potential for ill consequence and human suffering with an error in either direction.

Treatment

The most important task for clinicians is influencing the lives of their clients and of those in their community in a positive direction. Treatment is the act that must transform this vision into deed. Yet, treatment for sexual aggressors, and rapists in particular, has often been questioned in two directions: *Should* such men be treated or punished? Even if treated, does any form of treatment work for sexual aggressors?

Indeed, treatment for all sexual aggressors has often been seen as coddling offenders who, in this view, should be treated like other criminals (as reviewed in Brake & Shannon, 1997). An alternative view, not surprisingly held by most workers in this field, does not diminish the criminal responsibility of the offender, but attempts to combine this with the provision for opportunity of treatment to prevent future abuse (Maletzky, 1998; Marshall, 1996b). Indeed, treatment, particularly that employing what have become known as the cognitive-behavioral approaches, has been shown to be effective in general populations of incarcerated sexual offenders (Marques, 1997), exhibitionists (Maletzky, 1997a), outpatient child molesters (Dwyer, 1997), and men who rape (Maletzky, 1993).

A detailed explication of these techniques is beyond the scope of this chapter, but brief descriptions will be outlined, followed by several case examples. While *techniques* will be highlighted, it must be noted that one of the most important approaches, not amenable to technical description, is *trust-building*. Meeting with an offender to obtain a history and beginning to explore levels of resistance and issues of denial are unlike the start of therapy for most psychiatric clients. Most offenders are under treatment by mandate; many deny or distort what they have done. Establishing trust under these circumstances is no easy task, but still a vitally necessary one and attainable using a variety of communication and paradoxical techniques (Maletzky & Steinhauser, 1998; Winn, 1996).

While most institutions and clinics utilize group therapy almost exclusively, one-to-one therapy remains a valuable part of treatment as well. Ideally, combinations offer both advantages. Building of social skills and confrontation of denial are best facilitated in groups, but because each offender is unique, individual therapy can utilize cognitive and behavioral techniques to pinpoint the idiosyncracies of deviant sexual attractions. It still surprises veteran clinicians that, even though we treat under court order, and must develop close liaisons with corrections officers, sufficient trust *is* developed in most offenders. Disclosure following initial denial often occurs and many once hostile, sexually aggressive men become our staunchest allies through the therapy process.

Case Illustrations

Case A.   Client A had separated physically, but not emotionally, from his wife, who had been seeing the same lover for the past year. However, under pressure from A, Mrs. A had allowed him to visit twice and, on one occasion, had sexual relations after he verbally coerced her. Saturday nights were particularly difficult for A because he and Mrs. A often had gone dancing on the weekends. One Saturday night he broke in and fought with Mrs. A's lover, who fled. He forced sex on his wife, despite her physical struggles. He tied her to the bed and forced a banana into her vagina, then made her eat it. Mandated into anger management training and sexual offender treatment, he steadfastly denied that the sex was anything but consensual. In the beginning of treatment, the therapist reviewed police reports with A and discussed the acts in a theoretical fashion: "I wonder how a woman would feel having this done?" and "How would you feel if you had done this?" This progressed to "I wonder if a part of you could have done this?" and "Part of you may not be able to admit this ... if it were me, it would also be difficult." Gradually after a number of months in group and individual therapy, A admitted to the use of force.

Any clinic can cite successes ad nauseam. In the following case examples, readers should be aware that failures occur, although less frequently than previously imagined. To facilitate the discussion, the following techniques are presented singly, although, in practice, one merges into another in a variable sequence, dependent on individual client needs.

Cognitive Techniques

Therapists have identified a number of *cognitive distortions* common in sexual offenders (McGrath, Cann, & Konopasky, 1998). Here, group therapy is often helpful, because offenders can see themselves and others' behavior more objectively, and senior group members can challenge distortions at times more effectively than therapists. Steps include identifying cognitive distortions particular to each offender, the relationship they may have to his offending, then providing contradictory evidence and negative consequences, and role-playing prosocial alternatives (Ward, Hudson, McCormack, & Polaschek, 1997).

A second facet of cognitive therapy is *relapse prevention*. If sexual assault is the end result of a chain of behaviors, what starts the chain? Identifying triggering stimuli, including emotions and events, is a first step in devising options to block it or divert it to positive ends. In many offenders, this internal management needs to be supplemented by external management techniques as well (Pithers & Gray, 1996).

Case B.   Following his conviction for sexual abuse, B was mandated into an outpatient treatment program. This was his third such charge (with many more actual crimes committed) stemming from attempts to fondle women's breasts surreptitiously, pretending to accidently brush against them in elevators, crowded stores and the like. In examining sexual logs that he was asked to keep, B recognized that these episodes usually occurred when his wife was out of town on business. It did not appear that sexual deprivation was involved, however, because they had been abstinent for a number of years. A plan was devised in which Mrs. B would notify B's family and probation officer of her upcoming trips and B would stay with his sister and brother-in-law during those time periods. This plan included ways to help B use his free time while his wife was away by volunteering at a local health agency.

A third element of cognitive therapy utilized in almost all treatment programs is *empathy training*, helping offenders gain an appreciation for the process of victimization. Part of such training includes sensitization to others' affective states, while part includes a general education about the harm sexual aggression can cause.

Case C.   C dismissed his five (reported) rapes as exaggerations by victims who were not physically harmed and thus, in his view, not emotionally damaged by the experience. C was asked to read aloud in group therapy several letters written by women who had been raped by others. He viewed on several occasions a series of videotapes interviewing victims describing the manner in which they suffered. C seemed, however, to show little response. On one occasion, however, a rape victim attended the group therapy (at her request) to talk to the men about her life since the assault. C appeared visibly shaken, not so much by her tragic story, but by the fact that as they made eye contact, she said, "And I can forgive you."

Cognitive therapy has been one of the main forms of treatment for sexual offenders in the past decade. While all programs surveyed recently used some form of cognitive therapy (Knopp, Freeman-Longo, & Stevenson, 1992), techniques are not ideally standardized, and variations exist about timing and duration of such interventions. Further work will undoubtedly be forthcoming to justify the present inclusion of cognitive therapy techniques in the therapeutic armamentarium.

Behavioral Techniques

Although mired in historical controversy, *aversive conditioning techniques* remain a fixture in the treatment of the sexual offender. *Electric shock aversion* was the first aversive stimulus used (Evans, 1970; Maletzky, 1980). It is now considered unnecessarily painful and perhaps not a direct deconditioner of sexual arousal (Maletzky, 1990). Instead, covert techniques are preferred. These carry twin advantages of simplicity and minimal cost. In a typical paradigm, called *covert sensitization,* an offender is taught relaxation techniques and asked to imagine, under relaxation, scenes combining inappropriate arousal with adverse consequences.

Case D.   D, a college student, had been convicted of a second rape at the age of 22. He was asked to imagine under relaxation that he was stalking, then attacking, an attractive woman he had seen on campus. Sexual pleasure was built early in the scene followed by instructions to imagine the woman actually being a police officer. The scene became a trap, and he was taken to jail.

Case E.   After continually harassing female employees at his office, E, a local business manager, was referred by his employee assistance program. He was asked to imagine a series of scenes in which he approached women aggressively, each ending with negative consequences. In one scene, the woman screamed and coworkers came to her aid; in another, he was caught by his wife and daughter making sexual advances to women at work. These scenes were recorded for him, with the assignment of listening to the tape four nights each week.

It has sometimes proven advisable, in cases of very high deviant arousal, to build a hierarchy of scenes in a technique called *minimal arousal conditioning* (Gray, 1995; Jensen & Gray, 1997). In such scenes, the earliest steps in a chain leading to abuse are deconditioned first because they may be more susceptible to such techniques. Later, steps closer to sexual release are deconditioned successively.

Although widely used, covert sensitization at times proves too mild and must be boosted with the use of real-world aversive stimuli. These are usually noxious odors such as ammonia or rotting tissue. These odors can be introduced at crucial points in the scene to decondition arousal.

Case F.   F had a history of aggressively raping girls 11 to 13 years old. He was asked to imagine approaching such a girl, but as he lifted her dress (in the scene), he found her hygiene was poor and she had sores in her genital area dripping pus, with lice crawling in her pubic hair. Such nauseating images were paired with the odor of rotting meat and cat feces, and were tape recorded for F to listen to in the office and at home daily while using a bottle of the foul odor. Escape from the scene, such as running away from the girl, was associated with removal of the odor.

Ammonia has been employed as the odor most frequently administered. However, this substance, while chemically noxious, produces a burning, painful sensation which can, over many sessions, damage the olfactory mucosa. Nauseating odors, such as rotting meat, appear to directly decondition sexual arousal, perhaps due to the direct link between the olfactory nerve and limbic system (Maletzky, 1990).

Aversive behavior rehearsal is a different technique that may work by similar mechanisms. In this approach, originally crafted for exhibitionists (Wickramaserka, 1980), the offender is asked to demonstrate the crime using anatomically correct, life-size human dolls. At times, the procedure is videotaped. Having to demonstrate what he did, and view it again on tape, creates a painful and embarrassing experience for the aggressive offender, makes a private, shameful act public, and usually results in diminished arousal to deviant stimuli (Maletzky & Steinhauser, 1998). As with all such techniques, offenders, as patients, must give consent to undergo such rigors; most do. (Often, scenes taken from police and victim reports must be used at first with such patients.) Aversive behavior rehearsal has been remarkably effective in certain cases, although, the technique often causes extreme anxiety in some patients and in some witnessing staff as well.

Therapists have worked hard to take the "aversive" out of aversive conditioning due to its unpopularity and expense. *Plethysmographic biofeedback* offers an aversion-free method of deconditioning deviant arousal while promoting a sense of control for the offender. In a typical session, the patient views or listens to stimulus material, such as videotapes and audiotapes of scenes of aggressive sexuality, while wearing a plethysmograph gauge attached to a series of biofeedback lights positioned to the side of the viewing screen, often in a vertical array, as depicted in Figure 10.2. Each 5 percent of increasing arousal triggers a light above the last one to flash on. Thus, the offender can see his arousal increasing or decreasing and, combined with instructions from the therapist, can engage in attempts at self-control.

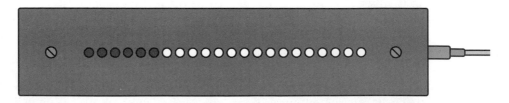

FIGURE 10.2   **Plethysmograph Biofeedback Lights**

Case G. G, a sexual sadist, was asked to keep his arousal under 20 percent of previously measured full erection while viewing slides of sexual torture of women. He had previously shown a high arousal to such scenes. His therapist gradually presented more arousing slides in successive sessions as G, seeing the erections made manifest, eventually demonstrated increasing control.

Such control in a laboratory setting cannot automatically be assumed to transfer to the real-world situation; again, a variety of techniques is necessary to be reasonably assured some will take hold. Usually contained within this blend is some variety of *satiation*. It appears that the central element in this technique is repetition leading to boredom (Laws, 1995), although some (Maletzky & Steinhauser, 1998) maintain it is the aversive elements in such methods that render them successful.

Case H. Following the failure of purely cognitive techniques, H, a 43-year-old serial rapist aroused by the aggressive elements of sex, was asked to masturbate (in private) to scenes of mutually consenting relations until ejaculation occurred. He was then asked to continue to masturbate for 30 minutes thereafter using images of aggressive sexuality. Compliance was checked by asking H to tape record his fantasies while masturbating. The procedure proved painful and boring because H was then pairing deviant sexual images (of aggressive sexuality) with the point of lowest possible arousal (immediately after orgasm). He was asked to repeat this procedure three times each week.

Case I. I, an adolescent offender who attacked two adult women on the running track at his school, was asked to repeat again and again his aggressive sexual fantasies for two 30-minute periods separated by one hour five days each week for two months and to tape record the procedure (to check for compliance). By focusing on this imagery repeatedly and monotonously, the images became less arousing to him by the second month.

Such *verbal satiation*, absent the masturbatory element, has also been demonstrated to reduce the chance of reoffending (Gray, 1995). A related technique, *masturbatory fantasy change* (Maletzky, 1990) asks the offender to masturbate to aggressive fantasies until the point of ejaculatory inevitability, at which time he is asked to switch to mutually consenting fantasies. He is then asked to make that switch earlier and earlier in the masturbation process, until he is masturbating fully to nonaggressive scenes. These methods, again, are useful only with selected offenders and must be combined with cognitive techniques for maximal efficacy.

A technique related to plethysmographic biofeedback, *sexual impulse control training*, is particularly appropriate for the sexual aggressor. In this technique, the offender is asked to engage in a variety of homework assignments with the consent of a partner.

Case J. Following trust building with J and his wife, both were asked to alter their sexual behavior for limited amounts of time. J had been arrested for attempting to rape his 17-year-old stepdaughter who was subsequently placed outside the home.

The therapist asked J to become purposely aroused by exposing himself to mutually consenting pornography, then to practice restraining himself from sexual release for at least 24 hours. In similar fashion, J and his wife were asked to first begin fore- play but not proceed to intercourse for 24 hours. Later they were asked to begin intercourse and voluntarily interrupt it and not complete it for at least 24 hours.

The purpose for such difficult tasks is practice of control. In the case of the sexual aggressor, the arousal itself may not be terribly deviant (as in J's case), but the behavior following it may produce irreparable harm.

A more recent aversive technique, *vicarious sensitization* (Weinrott, Riggan, & Frothingham, 1997) asks the offender to view videotaped vignettes, typically with negative content. In a typical scene, an offender gets attacked by the neighbors of a victim; in another, a man incarcerated for rape describes his own anal rape by inmates; in a third, a female victim off-screen relates what she would like to do to her rapist as a surgical castration is depicted on-screen. This technique combines elements of cognitive therapy with classical conditioning: The scenes are so aver- sive that they induce in most offenders a visceral feeling of disgust. Indeed, such combinations of elements may best explain many therapeutic effects. The genera- tion of such novel techniques is limited only by human ingenuity. Their effective- ness will take considerably longer, however, to evaluate.

Adjunctive Techniques

Most often, in treating the sexual aggressor, a variety of nontechniques will offer important contributions, based on individual need. *Assertive training, social skills training, family and partner therapy,* and *anger management training* form integral parts of the treatment process. There are no strict rules about when to interpose such techniques. Treatment must be customized to the individual offender, although at times beginning with such traditional techniques proves less threaten- ing to some offenders.

Biological Approaches

Because the testes are responsible for producing most of the testosterone in human males, castration was proposed early in the twentieth century as a solution to the problem of sexually aggressive behavior, particularly in European countries (as reviewed in Heim & Hursch, 1979). It is unlikely that castration would be adopted in this country, due to ethical and medical concerns (Maletzky, 1997b). Instead, hormonal therapy to reduce circulating testosterone levels has been advocated for treating the most recalcitrant of cases. While estrogen was employed originally (Whittaker, 1959), progesterone, the hormone produced by women in the late luteal phase, has proven more effective at reducing testosterone level (Whalen, 1984) and sexual drive in males (Money & Bennett, 1981). Progesterone is available in the United States as *Provera* and in its long-acting intramuscular preparation, *depo-Provera.* Cyproterone acetate, an unrelated antiandrogen, is available in Europe and Canada.

A number of studies (as reviewed in Prentky, 1997) have testified to *depo-Provera*'s efficacy in reducing the risk of reoffending in sexual aggressors. In most studies, 80 to 95 percent of offenders did not reoffend while on the drug (Maletzky, 1991), impressive results when realizing that only the most incorrigible of offenders are usually given the opportunity to receive it.

Case K.   K, now 31, had been diagnosed as suffering from moderate mental retardation (IQ estimated at 60) his entire life. Lack of impulse control was manifested not only by easy frustration and anger outbursts, but by repeatedly touching breasts and buttocks of males and females. A variety of behavioral approaches had failed and, prior to total institutionalization, his guardian agreed to a trial of *depo-Provera* for K, who has been receiving 200 mg intramuscularly every two weeks for the past three years without a recurrence of the sexually obtrusive behavior he previously could not control.

Legal and ethical problems in providing a drug which reduces sexual drive have often been addressed (Kafka, 1996; Prentky, 1997), but not yet solved. This is especially salient in clients, such as K, where legitimate questions about informed consent can be raised. Indeed, several jurisdictions have attempted to legislate compulsory antiandrogen treatment. At present, the courts have generally ruled that in the interest of public safety, some offenders can be mandated (usually by a corrections officer) to receive *depo-Provera* throughout their term of probation or parole (as reviewed in Pallone, 1990). While a case can be made requiring all dangerous offenders to receive such drugs, several disadvantages have been noted:

1. The uncertainties noted above about informed consent: Is an offender on parole able to exert free choice?
2. The possible destruction of trust with an offender.
3. The lack of any consistent evidence that once *depo-Provera* is discontinued (such as the end of supervision) its effects remain.
4. The possible complications secondary to side effects, including reduced competitiveness, and risks, although slight, of venous thrombosis and breast cancer.
5. The negative effects that lowering overall sexual drive can have on a partner.

It does not appear now that antiandrogens will offer anything but temporary relief from sexual aggression, although long-term studies are still in progress (Maletzky, 1991). While receiving the drug, offenders may be safer to be at large, but Prentky's (1997) quote is still accurate: "antiandrogen drugs should never be used as exclusive treatments . . . for aggressive sexual behaviors " (p. 344). Such treatment is best regarded now as a temporary safety net, making particularly aggressive offenders *safer* to be at large, while engaged in a cognitive-behavioral treatment program.

The same may be said of selective serotonin reuptake inhibitors (SSRIs) such as *Prozac, Paxil,* and *Zoloft.* Some authors have proposed that these antiobsessional antidepressants can reduce deviant sexual drive to a greater degree than nondeviant drive (Greenberg & Bradford, 1997; Kafka, 1995), although results are marginal in this direction thus far. SSRIs reduce overall sexual drive in the majority of males and can cause unpleasant side effects, including nausea and agitation. Nonetheless, the data are promising enough in this area to warrant further investigation, particularly if a differential effect on deviant arousal can be demonstrated.

Treatment Efficacy

With the widespread implementation of sexual offender treatment programs in North America, it has become increasingly important to evaluate their efficacy. A number of recidivism studies have been reported, but their interpretation remains controversial. Furby, Weinrott, and Blackshaw (1989), after reviewing the existing literature on treated versus untreated samples of sexual offenders, concluded that there was no effect of treatment on reoffending. However, Marshall and Barbaree (1990b), reviewing essentially the same studies, believed there *were* positive treatment effects. More recently, Barbaree (1997) has argued that scientific rigor has been insufficient to reach any conclusions thus far about cognitive-behavioral treatment programs, especially given the low base rate of offending for many types of offenders, such as situational or incest offenders.

A more optimistic view has been expressed by Hall (1995), who conducted a meta-analysis of all studies published between 1989 and 1995. Cognitive-behavioral and hormonal treatments appeared to be more effective than behavioral methods alone, as was community-based treatment compared with institutional treatment; a more robust treatment effect was shown with longer follow-ups. Indeed, the two longest-term follow-up studies published so far (Dwyer, 1997; Maletzky, 1993) show positive results of intensive cognitive-behavioral programs in reducing recidivism. However, these studies did not include matched controls, due to ethical concerns in withholding treatment in this population, most of which remained at large. Recently, Barbaree (1997) has proposed that treatment results are still sufficiently ambiguous to question public expenditure on such programs, particularly those which are institutionally based.

One problem in the analysis of outcome data thus far is the failure to separate offender subgroups. Only Maletzky (1993, 1998) has presented data on long-term follow-ups (up to 20 years) for rapists as opposed to pedophiles, child molesters, and exhibitionists. Unfortunately, outcome was *worse* for the sexually aggressive group than any other category. While over 90 percent of heterosexual pedophiles (both situational and predatory) did not reoffend, more than 25 percent of men who raped did, a figure which would not please a public concerned with risk of physical and emotional injury. Moreover, the characteristics of dangerous offenders also defined the most aggressive sexual predators: those who chose victims they did not know well, those who preyed on victims in their communities rather than their homes, those who had multiple victims, and those who used force in the commission of their crimes.

Criticism of existing studies, many clinically based, includes failure to use equivalent randomly assigned comparison groups, inadequate follow-up periods, and small sample sizes. However, an ongoing project in California aims to correct these deficiencies (Marques, 1997). The Sexual Offender Treatment and Evaluation Project is utilizing random assignment, extensive evaluations of offenders pre- and posttreatment, and the collection of 5-year follow-up data. Preliminary results (Day & Marques, 1998) indicate a positive, but very small, treatment effect for rapists. Unfortunately, two deficiencies remain: (1) The offenders are being drawn from the state's highest security facility and thus represent the most dangerous offenders; and (2) the treatment program omits most of the behavioral techniques that uncontrolled studies have suggested are effective, relying almost exclusively on the methods of relapse prevention. Nonetheless, the results of this project will be closely watched and may have already contributed to a trend away from relapse prevention as the *sole* mode of therapy (Marshall & Anderson, 1996).

Unfortunately, a widening gap exists between public outrage over sexual assault and willingness to fund research in this area. Given the small likelihood that this will change in the near future, researchers and clinicians need to coordinate efforts on larger studies, perhaps nationwide. While random assignment and strict controls are always desirable, they may not be as feasible as solidly-based clinical studies involving larger numbers of subjects, a broader array of geographic treatment sites, and a wider spectrum of treatment techniques. Double-blind studies do not have a monopoly on truth, nor is it only through them that we can focus our efforts to reduce sexual assault.

Summary

The multidimensional nature of sexual aggression is reflected in the broad array of aggressive behaviors described in this chapter and on the faces of its victims, which range from infants to older women and even younger men. Although empowerment of women kindled by the feminist movement has awakened a growing awareness of different forms of sexual aggression, there is still no other aggressive act in which the victim is so often blamed. Only recently have we become more informed about nonrape sexual aggression, partner and acquaintance rape, and sexual aggression toward those too young or disabled to consent. National awareness grows slowly, but it grows nonetheless, and will continue to inform and impact public decision making and, hopefully, lead to better ways of organizing and funding needed research in this critical area.

One glaring defect in present research programs is the inattention paid to rape *prevention*, an area that should attract a greater proportion of research funds in the future. Prevention programs might include self-defense and rape prevention classes for young women and rape sensitivity training for teenage males (Foshee et al., 1998; Lonsway et al., 1998) presently at highest risk for sexual aggression. Research and treatment efforts also need to be channeled toward the juvenile offender as all data point to the origin of sexual offending in early adolescent years. Treatment providers and researchers should look toward combining efforts to yield multisite studies with larger numbers of subjects as well as smaller, more closely controlled trials of individual treatment techniques. Special populations, such as female aggressors and the disabled, are only now being recognized.

While there is no firm evidence that sexual aggression is increasing, it need not increase to merit our continuing attention. The high prevalence of such assault and the documented trauma to its victims cause legitimate concerns for public safety, especially because most sexual aggressors will eventually return to their communities. Community-based notification laws, unevenly applied and of doubtful preventative efficacy (Freeman-Longo, 1996), are insufficient to protect most potential victims. Further, it is unlikely that stricter sentencing guidelines, tougher laws, and even mandated *depo-Provera* will accomplish the goal of reduced recidivism. Therefore, it is imperative to improve our treatment programs. Certainly, treatment is warranted in a cost-benefit analysis. Victim- and offender-related treatment and incarceration costs for each reoffense totaled approximately $180,000 in a 1991 study (Prentky & Burgess), a figure likely to be half that at the turn of the millennium (Cohen & Miller, 1998). The costs, in terms of victim harm, are incalculable.

Because sexual aggression is so diverse, a single etiological factor cannot be identified. Aggressors are heterogeneous, and their acts at any one point in time are unpredictable. Nonetheless, we can identify some males at greater risk for offending the first time, and on subsequent occasions as well. Why they do so may reside in a combination of currently fashionable bioevolutionary mechanisms; psychological and genetic predispositions toward poor impulse control; and situational variables, including access to a potential victim, level of drug and alcohol use, if any, and cognitive assessment of benefits (sexual gratification) and risks (detection, apprehension, and incarceration). For offenders, the sources of their aggression may remain a mystery, but for victims, the sources of their suffering assuredly are not. There is no shortage of work for the future.

REFERENCES

Abel, G. G., Barlow, D. H., Blanchard, E. B., & Guild, D. (1977). The components of rapists' sexual arousal. *Archives of General Psychiatry, 34,* 895–903.

Abel, G. G., Huffman, J., Warberg, B., & Holland, C. L. (1998). Visual reaction time and plethysmography as measures of sexual interest in child molesters. *Sexual Abuse: A Journal of Research and Treatment, 10,* 81–95.

Abel, G. G. & Rouleau, J. L. (1990). The nature and extent of sexual assault. In W. L. Marshall, D. R. Laws, & H. E. Barbaree (Eds.), *Handbook of Sexual Assault: Issues, Theories and Treatment of the Offender* (pp. 9–21). New York: Plenum.

Abramson, P. R. & Hayashi, H. (1984). Pornography in Japan: Cross-cultural and theoretical considerations. In N. M. Malamuth & E. Donnerstein (Eds.), *Pornography and Sexual Aggression* (pp. 173–183). New York: Academic.

Ageton, S. S. (1983). *Sexual Assault among Adolescents.* Lexington, MA: Lexington Books.

Alder, C. (1984). The convicted rapist: A sexual or a violent offender? *Criminal Justice and Behavior, 11,* 157–177.

Allen, L. S. & Gorski, R. A. (1992). Sexual orientation and the size of the anterior commissure in the human brain. *Proceedings of the National Academy of Sciences, 89,* 7199–7202.

Anderson, P. B. (1998). Variations in college women's self-reported heterosexual aggression. *Sexual Abuse: A Journal of Research and Treatment, 10,* 294–301.

Anderson, P. B. & Newton, M. (1997). The Initiating Heterosexual Contact Scale: A factor analysis. *Sexual Abuse: A Journal of Research and Treatment, 9,* 179–196.

Anderson, R. D., Gibeau, D., & D'Amora, D. A. (1995). The Sex Offender Treatment Rating Scale: Initial reliability data. *Sexual Abuse: A Journal of Research and Treatment, 7,* 221–227.

ATSA. (1997). *Standards in the Use of the Penile Plethysmograph.* Beaverton, OR: The Association for the Treatment of Sexual Abusers.

Attorney General's Commission on Pornography. (1986). *Final Report.* Washington, DC: United States Department of Justice.

Bain, J., Langevin, R., Dickey, R., Hucker, S. J., & Wright, P. (1988). Hormones in sexually aggressive men. I. Baseline values for eight hormones. II. The ACTH test. *Annals of Sex Research, 1,* 63–78.

Baldwin, K. & Roys, D. T. (1998). Factors associated with denial in a sample of alleged adult sexual offenders. *Sexual Abuse: A Journal of Research and Treatment, 10,* 264–279.

Bandura, A. (1977). *Social Learning Theory.* Englewood Cliffs, NJ: Prentice Hall.

Barbaree, H. E. (1990). Stimulus control of sexual arousal: Its role in sexual assault. In W. L. Marshall, D. R. Laws, & H. E. Barbaree (Eds.), *Handbook of Sexual Assault: Issues, Theories and Treatment of the Offender* (pp. 115–142). New York: Plenum.

Barbaree, H. E. (1997). Evaluating treatment efficacy with sexual offenders: The insensitivity of recidivism studies to treatment effect. *Sexual Abuse: A Journal of Research and Treatment, 9,* 111–128.

Barbaree, H. E., Bogaert, A. F., & Seto, M. C. (1995). Sexual reorientation therapy: Practices and controversies. In L. Diamant & R. D. McAnulty (Eds.), *The Psychology of Sexual Orientation, Behavior and Identity: A Handbook* (pp. 357–383). Westport, CT: Greenwood.

Barbaree, H. E. & Serin, R. C. (1993). Role of male sexual arousal during rape in various rapist subtypes. In G. C. Nagayama-Hall, R. Hirschman, J. R. Graham, & M. S. Zaragoza (Eds.), *Sexual Aggression: Issues in Etiology, Assessment and Treatment* (pp. 99–114). Washington, DC: Taylor & Francis.

Bard, L. A., Carter, D. L., Cerce, D. D., Knight, R. A., Rosenberg, R., & Schneider, B. (1997). A descriptive study of rapists and child molesters: Developmental, clinical and criminal characteristics. *Behavioral Sciences and the Law, 5,* 203–220.

Baron, R. A. & Strauss, M. (1984). Sexual satisfaction, pornography and rape in the United States. In N. Malamuth & E. Donnerstein (Eds.), *Pornography and Sexual Aggression* (pp. 185–209). New York: Academic.

Bart, P. B. & O'Brien, P. H. (1984). Stopping rape: Effective avoidance strategies. *Signs: Journal of Women in Culture and Society, 10,* 83–101.

Baxter, D. J., Barbaree, H. E., & Marshall, W. L. (1986). Sexual responses to consenting and forced sex in a large sample of rapists and nonrapists. *Behaviour Research and Therapy, 24,* 513–520.

Becker, J. V., Harris, C. D., & Sales, B. D. (1993). Juveniles who commit sexual offenses: A critical review of research. In G. C. Nagayama-Hall, R. Hirschman, J. R. Graham, & M. S. Zaraoza (Eds.), *Sexual Aggression: Issues in Etiology, Assessment and Treatment* (pp. 215–228). Washington, DC: Taylor & Francis.

Beech, A. & Fordham, A. S. (1997). Therapeutic climate of sexual offender treatment programs. *Sexual Abuse: A Journal of Research and Treatment, 9,* 219–237.

Berlin, F. S. & Meinecke, C. F. (1981). Treatment of sex offenders with antiandrogenic medication: Conceptualization, review of treatment modalities and preliminary findings. *American Journal of Psychiatry, 138,* 601–607.

Blader, J. C., Marshall, W. L., & Barbaree, H. E. (1988, June). *The Inhibitory Effect of Coercion on Sexual Arousal in Men and Disinhibition by Provocation.* Paper presented at the annual meeting of the Canadian Psychological Association, Montreal.

Blasingame, G. D. (1998). Suggested clinical uses of polygraphy in community-based sexual offender treatment programs. *Sexual Abuse: A Journal of Research and Treatment, 10,* 37–45.

Boeringer, S. B. (1994). Pornography and sexual aggression: Associations of violent and nonviolent depictions with rape and rape proclivity. *Deviant Behavior, 15,* 289–304.

Bowie, S. I., Silverman, D. C., Kalick, S. M., & Edbril, S. D. (1990). Blitz rape and confidence rape: Implications for clinical intervention. *American Journal of Psychotherapy, 44,* 180–188.

Bradford, J. & Maclean, D. (1984). Sexual offenders, violence and testosterone: A chemical study. *Canadian Journal of Psychiatry, 29,* 335–343.

Brake, S. C. & Shannon, D. (1997). Using pretreatment to increase admission in sex offenders. In B. K. Schwartz & H. R. Cellini (Eds.), *The Sex Offender: New Insights, Treatment Innovations and Legal Developments* (Vol. II, pp. 5-1–5-16). Kingston, NJ: Civic Research Institute.

Bumby, K. M. (1996). Assessing the cognitive distortions of child molesters and rapists: Development and validation of the MOLEST and RAPE scales. *Sexual Abuse: A Journal of Research and Treatment, 8*, 37–54.

Bumby, K. M. & Marshall, W. L. (1994, October). *Loneliness and Intimacy Deficits among Incarcerated Rapists and Child Molesters.* Paper presented at the annual Research and Treatment Conference of the Association for the Treatment of Sexual Abusers, San Francisco.

Byers, E. S. & Heinlein, L. (1989). Predicting initiations and refusals of sexual activity in married and cohabitating heterosexual couples. *Journal of Sex Research, 26*, 210–231.

Burgess, A. W. (1985). Sexual victimization of adolescents. In A. W. Burgess (Ed.), *Rape and Sexual Assault* (pp. 199–208). New York: Garland.

Burgess, A. W. & Holmstrom, L. L. (1985). Rape trauma syndrome and posttraumatic stress response. In A. W. Burgess (Ed.), *Rape and Sexual Assault* (pp. 46–60). New York: Garland.

Burt, M. R. (1980). Cultural myths and support for rape. *Journal of Personality and Social Psychology, 38*, 217–230.

Burt, M. R. & Katz, B. L. (1988). Coping strategies and recovery from rape. *Annals of the New York Academy of Sciences, 528*, 345–358.

Calhoun, K. S., Bernat, J. A., Clum, G. A., & Frame, C. L. (1997). Sexual coercion and attraction to sexual aggression in a community sample of young men. *Journal of Interpersonal Violence, 12*, 392–406.

Card, R. D. & Dibble, A. (1995). Predictive value of the Card/Farrell stimuli in discriminating between gynephilic and pedophilic sex offenders. *Sexual Abuse: A Journal of Research and Treatment, 7*, 129–141.

Card, R. D. & Olsen, S. E. (1996). Visual plethysmograph stimuli involving children: Rethinking some quasi-logical issues. *Sexual Abuse: A Journal of Research and Treatment, 8*, 267–271.

Carnes, P. (1983). *The Sexual Addiction.* Minneapolis, MN: CompCare.

Carpenter, D. R., Peed, S. F., & Eastman, B. (1995). Personality characteristics of adolescent sexual offenders: A pilot study. *Sexual Abuse: A Journal of Research and Treatment, 7*, 195–203.

Check, J. V. P. (1985). *The Hostility Toward Women Scale.* Unpublished doctoral dissertation, University of Manitoba, Winnipeg, Canada.

Christie, M. M., Marshall, W. L., & Lanthier, R. D. (1979). *A Descriptive Study of Incarcerated Rapists and Child Molesters.* (Report to the Solicitor General of Canada). Ottawa: Office of the Solicitor General.

Civil Action Suit. (1993, December 13). *Class Action Complaint for Injunctive and Declaratory Relief.* U.S. District Court, District of Vermont.

Clark, L. & Lewis, D. J. (1977). *Rape: The Price of Coercive Sexuality.* Toronto: Canadian Women's Educational Press.

Cohen, M. A. & Miller, T. R. (1998). The cost of mental health care for victims of crime. *Journal of Interpersonal Violence, 13*, 93–110.

Collins, S. J. (1994). Sexual aggression: A discriminant analysis of predictors in nonforensic sample. *South African Journal of Psychology, 24*, 35–38.

Daleiden, E. L., Kaufman, K. L., Hilliker, D. R., & O'Neil, J. N. (1998). The sexual histories and fantasies of youthful males: A comparison of sexual offending, nonsexual offending and nonoffending groups. *Sexual Abuse: A Journal of Research and Treatment, 10*, 251–263.

Darke, J. L. (1990). Sexual aggression: Achieving power through humiliation. In W. L. Marshall, D. R. Laws, & H. E. Barbaree (Eds.), *Handbook of Sexual Assault: Issues, Theories and Treatment of the Offender* (pp. 55–72). New York: Plenum.

Day, D. M. & Marques, J. K. (1998). Reply to Nathaniel McConaghy. *Sexual Abuse: A Journal of Research and Treatment, 10*, 162–166.

Delgado, J. M. R. (1969). Offensive-defensive behavior in free monkeys and chimpanzees induced by radio stimulation of the brain. In S. Garatini & E. B. Sigg (Eds.), *Aggressive Behavior: Proceedings of the International Symposium on the Biology of Aggressive Behavior.* Amsterdam: Exerpta Medica.

Dermen, V. H. (1990). *Against Her Will: The Effect of Alcohol Expectancy Set on Male "Sexual Aggression" Toward a Female Target.* Unpublished doctoral dissertation, State University of New York, Buffalo.

Descutner, C. & Thelen, M. H. (1991). Development and validation of the Fear of Intimacy Scale. *Psychological Assessment, 3*, 218–225.

Dietz, S. R., Blackwell, K. T., Daley, P. C., & Bentley, B. J. (1982). Measurement of empathy toward rape victims and rapists. *Journal of Personality and Social Psychology, 43*, 372–384.

Donnerstein, E., Linz, D., & Penrod, S. (1987). *The Question of Pornography: Research Findings and Policy Implications*. New York: Free Press.

Dwyer, S. M. (1997). Treatment outcome study: Seventeen years after sexual offender treatment. *Sexual Abuse: A Journal of Research and Treatment, 9*, 149–160.

Earls, C. M. (1988). Aberrant sexual arousal in sexual offenders. In R. A. Prentky & V. L. Quinsey (Eds.), *Human Sexual Aggression: Current Perspectives* (pp. 41–48). New York: The New York Academy of Sciences.

Eccles, A., Marshall, W. L., & Barbaree, H. E. (1994). Differentiating rapists and nonoffenders using the rape index. *Behaviour Research and Therapy, 32*, 539–546.

Ehrenkranz, J., Bliss, E., & Sheard, M. H. (1974). Plasma testosterone: Correlation with aggressive behavior and social dominance in man. *Psychosomatic Medicine, 36*, 469–475.

Ellis, L. (1993). Rape as a biosocial phenomenon. In G. C. Nagayama-Hall, R. Hirschman, J. R. Graham, & M. S. Zaragoza (Eds.), *Sexual Aggression: Issues in Etiology, Assessment and Treatment* (pp. 17–41). Washington, DC: Taylor & Francis.

Ellis, L. & Beattie, C. (1983). The feminist explanation for rape: An empirical test. *Journal of Sex Research, 19*, 74–93.

Emerick, R. & Dutton, W. (1993). The effect of polygraphy on the self-report of adolescent sex offenders: Implications for risk assessment. *Annals of Sex Research, 6*, 83–103.

Evans, D. R. (1970). Subjective variables and treatment effects in aversive therapy. *Behaviour Research and Therapy, 8*, 141–152.

Fischer, L. & Smith, G. (in press). Assessment of juvenile offenders: Technical adequacy of the Abel Assessment of Interest in Paraphilias. *Sexual Abuse: A Journal of Research and Treatment*.

Fiske, S. T. & Taylor, S. E. (1991). *Social Cognition* (2nd ed.). New York: McGraw Hill.

Foshee, V. A., Bauman, K. G., Arriaga, X. B., Helms, R. W., Koch, G. G., & Linder, G. F. (1998). An evaluation of safe dates, an adolescent dating violence prevention program. *American Journal of Public Health, 88*, 45–50.

Fraser Commission. (1985). *Report of the Special Committee on Pornography and Prostitution*. Ottawa: Canadian Government Publishing Centre.

Freeman-Longo, R. E. (1986). The impact of sexual victimization on males. *Child Abuse and Neglect, 10*, 411–414.

Freeman-Longo, R. E. (1996). Prevention or problem. *Sexual Abuse: A Journal of Research and Treatment, 8*, 91–100.

Freund, K. & Blanchard, R. (1981). Assessment of sexual dysfunction and deviance. In M. Hersen & A. S. Bellack (Eds.), *Behavioral Assessment: A Practical Handbook* (pp. 427–455). New York: Pergamon.

Furby, L., Weinrott, M. R., & Blackshaw, L. (1989). Sex offender recidivism: A review. *Psychological Bulletin, 105*, 3–30.

Galski, T., Thornton, K. E., & Shumsky, D. (1990). Brain dysfunction in sex offenders. *Journal of Offender Rehabilitation, 16*, 65–80.

Garvey, N. (1991). Sexual victimization prevalence among New Zealand University students. *Journal of Consulting and Clinical Psychology, 59*, 464–466.

Gray, S. R. (1995). A comparison of verbal satiation and minimal arousal conditioning to reduce deviant arousal in the laboratory. *Sexual Abuse: A Journal of Research and Treatment, 7*, 143–153.

Greenberg, D. M. & Bradford, J. M. W. (1997). Treatment of the paraphilic disorders: A review of the role of the selective serotonin reuptake inhibitors. *Sexual Abuse: A Journal of Research and Treatment, 9*, 349–360.

Groth, A. N. & Birnbaum, A. H. (1979). *Men Who Rape: The Psychology of the Offender*. New York: Plenum.

Grubin, D. & Mason, D. (1997). Medical models of sexual deviance. In D. R. Laws & W. O'Donohue (Eds.), *Sexual Deviance: Theory, Assessment and Treatment* (pp. 434–448). New York: Guilford.

Hall, E. R., Howard, J. A., & Boezio, S. L. (1986). Tolerance of rape: A sexist or antisocial attitude? *Psychology of Women Quarterly, 10*, 101–108.

Hall, G. C. N. (1995). Sexual offender recidivism revisited: A meta-analysis of recent treatment studies. *Journal of Consulting and Clinical Psychology, 63*, 802–809.

Hall, G. C. N. & Hirschman, R. (1991). Toward a theory of sexual aggression: A quadripartite model. *Journal of Consulting and Clinical Psychology, 59*, 662–669.

Hall, G. C. N. & Hirschman, R. (1993). Use of a new laboratory methodology to conceptualize sexual aggression. In G. C. Nagayama-Hall, R. Hirschman, J. R. Graham, & M. S. Zaragoza (Eds.), *Sexual Aggression: Issues in Etiology, Assessment and Treatment* (pp. 115–132). Washington, DC: Taylor & Francis.

Hall, G. C. N. & Hirschman, R. (1994). The relationship between men's sexual aggression inside and outside the laboratory. *Journal of Consulting and Clinical Psychology, 62,* 375–380.

Hanson, R. K. & Bussiere, M. T. (1996). *Predictors of Sexual Offender Recidivism: A Meta-Analysis.* (Report No. 1996–04.) Ottawa: Solicitor General of Canada.

Hanson, R. K. & Scott, H. (1995). Assessing perspective-taking among offenders, nonsexual criminals and nonoffenders. *Sexual Abuse: A Journal of Research and Treatment, 7,* 259–277.

Hare, R. D. (1980). A research scale for the assessment of psychopathy in criminal populations. *Personality and Individual Differences, 1,* 111–119.

Hare, R. D., Harpur, T. J., Hakstian, A. R., Forth, A. G., Hart, S. D., & Newman, J. P. (1990). The Revised Psychotherapy Checklist: Reliability and factor structure. *Psychological Assessment: A Journal of Consulting and Clinical Psychology, 2,* 338–341.

Hartley, C. C. (1998). How incest offenders overcome internal inhibitions through the use of cognitions and cognitive distortions. *Journal of Interpersonal Violence, 13,* 25–39.

Heim, N. & Hursch, C. J. (1979). Castration of sex offenders: Treatment or punishment? A review and critique of recent European literature. *Archives of Sexual Behavior, 8,* 281–304.

Henn, F. A., Herjanic, M., & Vanderpearl, R. H. (1976). Forensic psychiatry: Profiles of two types of sex offenders. *American Journal of Sex Offenders, 133,* 694–696.

Herman, J. L. (1990). Sex offenders: A feminist perspective. In W. L. Marshall, D. R. Laws, & H. E. Barbaree (Eds.), *Handbook of Sexual Assault: Issues, Theories and Treatment of the Offender* (pp. 177–193). New York: Plenum.

Howes, R. J. (1995). A survey of plethysmograph assessment in North America. *Sexual Abuse: A Journal of Research and Treatment, 7,* 9–24.

Howes, R. J. (1998). Plethysmographic assessment of incarcerated nonsexual offenders: A comparison with rapists. *Sexual Abuse: A Journal of Research and Treatment, 10,* 250–259.

Hucker, S. J. (1990). Necrophilia and other unusual philias. In R. Bluglass & P. Bowden (Eds.), *Principles and Practice of Forensic Psychiatry* (pp. 723–728). London: Churchill Livingstone.

Hucker, S. J. (1997). Sexual sadism: Psychopathology and theory. In D. R. Laws & W. O'Donohue (Eds.), *Sexual Deviance: Theory, Assessment and Treatment* (pp. 194–209). New York: Guilford.

Hudson, S. M. & Ward, T. (1997). Rape: Psychopathology and theory. In D. R. Laws & W. O'Donohue (Eds.), *Sexual Deviance: Theory, Assessment and Treatment* (pp. 332–355). New York: Guilford.

Huesmann, L. R. (1988). An information processing model for the development of aggression. *Aggressive Behavior, 14,* 13–24.

Jensen, S. & Gray, S. R. (1997, October). *Assessment and Management of Sexual Arousal.* Workshop presented at 16th Annual Research and Treatment Conference. The Association for the Treatment of Sexual Abusers, Washington, DC.

Johnson, L. & Ward, T. (1996). Social cognition and sexual offending: A theoretical framework. *Sexual Abuse: A Journal of Research and Treatment, 8,* 55–80.

Kafka, M. P. (1995). Current concepts in the drug treatment of paraphilias and paraphilia-related disorders. *CNS Drugs, 3,* 9–21.

Kafka, M. P. (1996). Hypersexual desire: Clinical implications for men with paraphilias and paraphilia-related disorders. *The Forum, Association for the Treatment of Sexual Abusers, 8,* 4–5.

Kilpatrick, D. G. (1993). Introduction to the special section on rape. *Journal of Interpersonal Violence, 8,* 193–197.

Kilpatrick, D. G., Veronen, L. J., & Resnick, J. P. A. (1979). Assessment of the aftermath of rape. *Journal of Behavioral Assessment, 2,* 133–149.

Knight, R. A. & Prentky, R. A. (1990). Classifying sexual offenders: The development and corroboration of taxonomic models. In W. L. Marshall, D. R. Laws, & H. E. Barbaree (Eds.), *Handbook of Sexual Assault: Issues, Theories and Treatment of the Sexual Offender.* New York: Plenum.

Knight, R. A. & Prentky, R. A. (1997, October). *A Unified Model of Sexual Aggression: Consistencies Across Noncriminal and Criminal Samples.* Paper presented at the annual Research and Treatment Conference of the Association for the Treatment of Sexual Abusers, Washington, DC.

Knight, R. A., Prentky, R. A., & Cerce, D. D. (1994). The development, reliability and validity of an inventory for the multidimensional assessment of sex and aggression. *Criminal Justice and Behavior, 21,* 72–94.

Knopp, F. H., Freeman-Longo, R. E., & Stevenson, W. F. (1992). *Nationwide Survey of Juvenile and Adult Sex Offender Treatment Programs and Models.* Orwell, VT: Safer Society Press.

Kobayashi, J., Sales, B. D., Becker, J. V., Figueredo, A. J., & Kaplan, M. S. (1995). Perceived parental deviance, parent-child bonding, child abuse, and child sexual aggression. *Sexual Abuse: A Journal of Research and Treatment, 7,* 25–44.

Koss, M. P. (1985). The hidden rape victim: Personality, attitudinal and situational characteristics. *Psychology of Women Quarterly, 9,* 193–212.

Koss, M. P. (1993). Detecting the scope of rape: A review of prevalence research methods. *Journal of Interpersonal Violence, 8,* 198–222.

Koss, M. P. & Deniro, T. E. (1989). Discriminant analysis of risk factors for sexual victimization among a national sample of college women. *Journal of Consulting and Clinical Psychology, 57,* 242–250.

Koss, M. P. & Gaines, J. A. (1993). The prediction of sexual aggression by alcohol use, athletic participation, and fraternity affiliation. *Journal of Interpersonal Violence, 8,* 94–108.

Koss, M. P. & Oros, C. J. (1982). Sexual experiences survey: A research instrument investigating sexual aggression and victimization. *Journal of Consulting and Clinical Psychology, 50,* 455–457.

Kutchinsky, B. (1991). Pornography and rape: Theory and practice? Evidence from crime data in four countries where pornography is easily available. *International Journal of Law and Psychiatry, 14,* 47–64.

Langevin, R. (1990). Sexual anomalies and the brain. In W. L. Marshall, D. R. Laws, & H. E. Barbaree (Eds.), *Handbook of Sexual Assault: Issues, Theories and Treatment of the Offender* (pp. 103–113). New York: Plenum.

Langevin, R., Bain, J., Ben-Aron, M. H., Couthard, R., Day, D., Handey, L. C., Heasman, R., Hucker, S. J., Purins, J. E., Roper, V., Ausson, A. R., Webster, C. D., & Wortzman, G. (1985). Sexual aggression: Constructing a predictive equation: A controlled pilot study. In R. Langevin (Ed.), *Erotic Preference, Gender Identity and Aggression in Men: New Research Studies* (pp. 39–76). Hillsdale, NJ: Lawrence Erlbaum.

Langevin, R., Paitich, D., & Russon, A. (1985). Are rapists sexually anomalous, aggressive, or both? In R. Langevin (Ed.), *Erotic Preference, Gender Identity and Aggression in Men: New Research Studies* (pp. 13–38). Hillsdale, NJ: Lawrence Erlbaum.

Langevin, R., Paitich, D., Russon, A., Handy, L., & Langevin, A. (1990). *Clarke Sex History Questionnaire for Males Manual.* Etobicoke, Ontario: Juniper.

Langley, T., Beatty, G., Yost, E. A., & O'Neal, E. C. (1991). How behavioral cues in a date rape scenario influence judgments regarding victim and perpetrator. *Forensic Reports, 4,* 355–358.

Laws, D. R. (1995). Verbal satiation: Notes on procedure with speculations on its mechanism of effect. *Sexual Abuse: A Journal of Research and Treatment, 7,* 155–166.

Laws, D. R. (1996a). Marching into the past: A critique of Card and Olsen. *Sexual Abuse: A Journal of Research and Treatment, 8,* 273–278.

Laws, D. R. (1996b). Relapse prevention or harm reduction? *Sexual Abuse: A Journal of Research and Treatment, 8,* 243–247.

Laws, D. R., Gulayets, M. J., & Frenzel, R. R. (1995). Assessment of sex offenders using standardized slide stimuli and procedures: A multisite study. *Sexual Abuse: A Journal of Research and Treatment, 7,* 45–66.

LeVay, S. (1991). A difference in hypothalamic structure between heterosexual and homosexual men. *Science, 253,* 1034–1037.

Lipton, D. N., McDonel, E. C., & McFall, R. M. (1987). Heterosocial perception in rapists. *Journal of Consulting and Clinical Psychology, 55,* 17–21.

Lonsway, K. A., Klaw, E. L., Berg, D. R., Walds, C. R., Kothari, C., Mazurek, C. J., & Hegeman, K. E. (1998). Beyond "No Means No": Outcomes of an intensive program to train peer facilitators for campus acquaintance rape education. *Journal of Interpersonal Violence, 13,* 73–92.

Looman, J., Abracen, J., Maillet, G., & DiFazio, R. (1998). Phallometric nonresponding in sexual offenders. *Sexual Abuse: A Journal of Research and Treatment, 10,* 325–336.

Lopez, P. A. & George, W. H. (1992, August). *Effects of Female Presence and Erotophilia on Male Pornography-Viewing Behavior.* Paper presented at the annual meeting of the American Psychological Association, Washington, DC.

Maccoby, E. E. (1987). The varied meanings of "masculine" and "feminine." In J. M. Reinish, L. A. Rosenblum, & S. A. Sanders (Eds.), *Masculinity/Femininity: Basic Perspectives* (pp. 227–239). New York: Oxford University Press.

MacKinnon, C. (1986). *Feminism Unmodified.* Cambridge, MA: Harvard University Press.

Malamuth, N. W. (1981). Rape proclivity among males. *Journal of Social Issues, 37,* 138–157.

Malamuth, N. W. (1986). Predictors of naturalistic sexual aggression. *Journal of Personality and Social Psychology, 50,* 953–962.

Malamuth, N. W. (1988). A multidimensional approach to sexual aggression: Combining measures of past behavior and present likelihood. In R. A. Prentky & V. L. Quinsey (Eds.), *Human Sexual Aggression: Current Perspectives* (pp. 124–132). New York: New York Academy of Sciences.

Malamuth, N. W. (1989). The attraction to sexual aggression: Part one. *Journal of Sex Research, 26,* 26–49.

Malamuth, N. W. & Brown, L. M. (1994). Sexually aggressive men's perceptions of women's communications: Testing three explanations. *Journal of Personality and Social Psychology, 67,* 69–72.

Malamuth, N. W., Heavey, C. L., & Linz, D. (1993). Predicting men's antisocial behavior against women: The interaction model of sexual aggression. In G. C. Nagayama-Hall, R. Hirschman, J. R. Graham, & M. S. Zaragoza (Eds.), *Sexual Aggression: Issues in Etiology, Assessment and Treatment* (pp. 63–97). Washington, DC: Taylor & Francis.

Maletzky, B. M. (1980). Assisted covert sensitization. In D. J. Cox & R. J. Daitzman (Eds.), *Exhibitionism: Description, Assessment and Treatment* (pp. 189–251). New York: Garland.

Maletzky, B. M. (1990). *Treating the Sexual Offender.* Newburg Park, CA: Sage.

Maletzky, B. M. (1991). The use of medroxyprogesterone acetate to assist in the treatment of sexual offenders. *Annals of Sex Research, 4,* 117–129.

Maletzky, B. M. (1993). Factors associated with success and failure in the behavioral and cognitive treatment of sexual offenders. *Annals of Sex Research, 6,* 241–258.

Maletzky, B. M. (1994, November). *Advanced Techniques in Behavioral Conditioning for the Sexual Offender.* Paper presented at the annual Research and Treatment Conference of the Association for the Treatment of Sexual Abusers, San Francisco.

Maletzky, B. M. (1995). Standardization and the penile plethysmograph. *Sexual Abuse: A Journal of Research and Treatment, 7,* 5–7.

Maletzky, B. M. (1996). Evolution, psychopathology and sexual offending: Aping our ancestors. *Aggression and Violent Behavior: A Review, 1,* 369–373.

Maletzky, B. M. (1997a). Exhibitionism: Assessment and treatment. In D. R. Laws & W. O'Donohue (Eds.), *Sexual deviance: Theory, Assessment and Treatment* (pp. 40–74). New York: Guilford.

Maletzky, B. M. (1997b). Castration: A personal foul. *Sexual Abuse: A Journal of Research and Treatment, 9,* 1–5.

Maletzky, B. M. (1998). The paraphilias: Research and treatment. In P. E. Nathan & J. M. Gorman (Eds.), *A Guide to Treatments that Work* (pp. 472–500). New York: Oxford University Press.

Maletzky, B. M. & Prueitt, M. (1999). *A Sexual Offender Orientation Group.* Manuscript in preparation.

Maletzky, B. M. & Steinhauser, C. (1996, November). *Advanced Behavioral Techniques in Treating the Sexual Offender.* Workshop conducted at the annual Research and Treatment Conference of the Association for the Treatment of the Sexual Abuser, Chicago.

Maletzky, B. M. & Steinhauser, C. (1998). The Portland Sexual Abuse Clinic. In W. L. Marshall, S. M. Hudson, T. Ward, & Y. M. Fernandez (Eds.), *Sourcebook of Treatment Programs for Sexual Offenders* (pp. 105–116). New York: Plenum.

Marques, J. K. (1997, October). *Collaborative Database of Sex Offender Treatment Outcome.* Presented at the annual Research and Treatment Conference of the Association for the Treatment of Sexual Abusers, Washington, DC.

Marshall, W. L. (1996a). Assessment, treatment and theorizing about sex offenders: Developments over the past 20 years and future directions. *Criminal Justice and Behavior, 23,* 162–199.

Marshall, W. L. (1996b). The sexual offender: Monster, victim or everyone? *Sexual Abuse: A Journal of Research and Treatment, 8,* 317–335.

Marshall, W. L. & Anderson, D. (1996). An evaluation of the benefits of relapse prevention programs with sexual offenders. *Sexual Abuse: A Journal of Research and Treatment, 8,* 209–221.

Marshall, W. L. & Barbaree, H. E. (1990a). An integrated theory of the etiology of sexual offending. In W. L. Marshall, D. W. Laws, & H. E. Barbaree (Eds.), *Handbook of Sexual Assault: Issues, Theories and Treatment of the Offender* (pp. 257–275). New York: Plenum.

Marshall, W. L. & Barbaree, H. E. (1990b). Outcome of comprehensive cognitive-behavioral treatment programs. In W. L. Marshall, D. R. Laws, & H. E. Barbaree (Eds.), *Handbook of Sexual Assault: Issues, Theories and Treatment of the Offender* (pp. 363–385). New York: Plenum.

Marshall, W. L. & Barbaree, H. E. (1994). *Erectile Preference Profiles Among Rapists and Nonrapists.* Unpublished manuscript.

Marshall, W. L., Barbaree, H. E., & Fernandez, Y. M. (1995). Some aspects of social competence in sexual offenders. *Sexual Abuse: A Journal of Research and Treatment, 7,* 113–127.

Marshall, W. L., Champagne, F., Surgeon, C., & Bryce, P. (1997). Increasing the self-esteem of child molesters. *Sexual Abuse: A Journal of Research and Treatment, 9,* 321–333.

Marshall, W. L. & Hall, G. C. N. (1995). The value of the MMPI in deciding forensic issues in accused sexual offenders. *Sexual Abuse: A Journal of Research and Treatment, 7,* 205–219.

Marshall, W. L., Hudson, S. M., Jones, R., & Fernandez, Y. M. (1995). Empathy in sexual offenders. *Clinical Psychology Review, 15,* 99–113.

Marshall, W. L., Jones, R. L., Hudson, S. M., & McDonald, E. (1993). Generalized empathy in child molesters. *Journal of Child Sexual Abuse, 2,* 61–68.

Marshall, W. L. & Mazzucco, A. (1995). Self-esteem and parental attachments in child molesters. *Sexual Abuse: A Journal of Research and Treatment, 7,* 279–284.

Marshall, W. L. & Nagayama-Hall, G. C. (1995). The value of the MMPI in deciding forensic issues in accused sexual offenders. *Sexual Abuse: A Journal of Research and Treatment, 7,* 205–219.

McConaghy, N. (1993a). *Sexual Behavior: Problems and Management.* New York: Plenum.

McConaghy, N. (1993b). Sexual coercion and assault. In N. McConaghy (Ed.), *Sexual Behavior: Problems and Management* (pp. 269–301). New York: Plenum.

McConaghy, N. & Zamir, R. (1997). *Heterosexual and Homosexual Coercion, Sexual Orientation and Sexual Roles.* Manuscript submitted for publication.

McGrath, M., Cann, S., & Konopasky, R. (1998). New measures of defensiveness, empathy and cognitive distortions for sexual offenders against children. *Sexual Abuse: A Journal of Research and Treatment, 10,* 25–36.

McLaren, A. (1990). What makes a man a man? *Nature, 346,* 216–217.

Miner, M. H., West, M. A., & Day, D. M. (1995). Sexual preference for child and aggressive stimuli: Comparison of rapists and child molesters using auditory and visual stimuli. *Behaviour Research and Therapy, 33,* 545–551.

Money, J. & Bennett, R. G. (1981). Postadolescent paraphilic sex offenders: Antiandrogenic and counseling therapy follow-up. *International Journal of Mental Health, 10,* 122–133.

Monto, M., Zgourides, G., & Harris, R. (1998). Empa-thy, self-esteem and the adolescent sexual offender. *Sexual Abuse: A Journal of Research and Treatment, 10,* 127–140.

Muehlenhard, C. L. & Cook, S. W. (1988). Men's self-reports of unwanted sexual activity. *Journal of Sex Research, 24,* 48–72.

Muehlenhard, C. L. & Linton, M. A. (1987). Date rape and sexual aggression in dating situations: Incidence and risk factors. *Journal of Counseling Psychology, 34,* 186–196.

Murphy, W. D., Krisak, J., Stalgaitis, S., & Anderson, K. (1984). The use of penile tumescence measures with incarcerated rapists: Further validity issues. *Archives of Sexual Behavior, 13,* 545–554.

O'Donohue, W., Letourneau, E. J., & Dowling, H. (1997). Development and preliminary validation of a paraphilic sexual fantasy questionnaire. *Sexual Abuse: A Journal of Research and Treatment, 9,* 167–178.

O'Donohue, W., McKay, J. S., & Schewe, P. A. (1996). Rape: The roles of outcome expectancies and hypermasculinity. *Sexual Abuse: A Journal of Research and Treatment, 8,* 133–141.

Pallone, N. J. (1990). *Rehabilitating Criminal Sexual Psychopaths.* New Brunswick, NJ: Transaction.

Palys, T. S. (1986). Testing of the common wisdom: The social content of video pornography. *Canadian Psychology, 27,* 22–35.

Peterson, R. D. & Bailey, W. C. (1988). Forcible rape, poverty and economic inequality in U.S. metropolitan communities. *Journal of Quantitative Criminology, 4,* 99–119.

Pithers, W. D. (1990). Relapse prevention with sexual aggressors: A method for maintaining therapeutic gain and enhancing external supervision. In W. L. Marshall, D. R. Laws, & H. E. Barbaree (Eds.), *Handbook of Sexual Assault: Issues, Theories and Treatment of the Offender* (pp. 343–631). New York: Plenum.

Pithers, W. D. & Gray, A. S. (1996). Utility of relapse prevention in treatment of sexual abusers. *Sexual Abuse: A Journal of Research and Treatment, 8,* 223–230.

Prentky, R. A. (1997). Arousal reduction in sexual offenders: A review of antiandrogen interventions. *Sexual Abuse: A Journal of Research and Treatment, 9,* 335–347.

Prentky, R. A. & Burgess, A. W. (1991). Hypothetical biological substrates of a fantasy-based drive mechanism for repetitive sexual aggression. In A. W. Burgess (Ed.), *Rape and Sexual Assault III* (pp. 235–256). New York: Garland.

Prentky, R. A. & Knight, R. A. (1991). Identifying critical dimensions for discriminating among rapists. *Journal of Consulting and Clinical Psychology, 59,* 643–661.

Proulx, J., Pellerin, B., Paradise, Y., McKibben, A., Aubut, J., & Oimet, M. (1997). Static and dynamic predictors of recidivism in sexual aggressors. *Sexual Abuse: A Journal of Research and Treatment, 9,* 7–27.

Pryor, J. B. (1987). Sexual harassment proclivities in men. *Sex Roles, 17,* 269–290.

Pryor, J. B. & Stoller, L. M. (1994). Sexual cognition processes in men high in likelihood to sexually harass. *Personality and Social Psychology Bulletin, 20,* 163–169.

Quinsey, V. L. & Earls, C. M. (1990). The modification of sexual preferences. In W. L. Marshall, D. R. Laws, & H. E. Barbaree (Eds.), *Handbook of Sexual Assault: Issues, Theories and Treatment of the Offender* (pp. 279–295). New York: Plenum.

Quinsey, V. L., Harris, G. T., Rice, M. E., & Lalumière, M. L. (1993). Assessing treatment efficacy in outcome studies of sex offenders. *Journal of Interpersonal Violence, 8,* 512–523.

Quinsey, V. L. & Lalumière, M. L. (1995). Evolutionary perspectives on sexual offending. *Sexual Abuse: A Journal of Research and Treatment, 7,* 301–315.

Rada, R., Laws, D. R., & Kellner, R. (1976). Plasma testosterone levels in rapists. *Psychosomatic Medicine, 38,* 257–268.

Raine, A. (1993). *The Psychopathology of Crime.* San Diego, CA: Academic.

Resnick, P. A. (1993). The psychological impact of rape. *Journal of Interpersonal Violence, 8,* 223–255.

Revitch, E. & Schlesinger, L. B. (1988). Clinical reflections on sexual aggression. In R. A. Prentky & V. L. Quinsey (Eds.), *Human Sexual Aggression: Current Perspectives.* New York: New York Academy of Sciences.

Rice, M. E., Chaplin, T. C., Harris, G. T., & Coutts, J. (1994). Empathy for the victim and sexual arousal among rapists and nonrapists. *Journal of Interpersonal Violence, 9,* 435–449.

Rice, M. E., Quinsey, V. L., & Harris, G. T. (1991). Sexual recidivism among child molesters released from a maximum security psychiatric institution. *Journal of Consulting and Clinical Psychology, 59,* 381–386.

Riggs, D. S., Murphy, C. M., & O'Leary, K. D. (1989). Intentional falsification in reports of interpartner aggression. *Journal of Interpersonal Violence, 4,* 220–232.

Riggs, D. S. & O'Leary, K. D. (1996). Aggression between heterosexual dating partners: An examination of a casual model of courtship aggression. *Journal of Interpersonal Violence, 11,* 519–540.

Rosenberg, R., Knight, R. A., Prentky, R. A., & Lee, A. (1988). Validating the components of a taxonomic system for rapists: A multipath analysis approach. *Bulletin of the American Academy of Psychiatry and the Law, 16,* 169–185.

Russell, D. E. H. (1988). The incidence and prevalence of intrafamilial and extrafamilial sexual abuse of female children. In L. E. A. Walker (Ed.), *Handbook on Sexual Abuse of Children* (pp. 19–36). New York: Springer.

Sanday, P. R. (1981). The socio-cultural context of rape: A cross-cultural study. *Journal of Social Issues, 37,* 5–27.

Schewe, P. A. & O'Donohue, W. (1998). Psychometrics of the rape conformity assessment and other measures: Implications for rape prevention. *Sexual Abuse: A Journal of Research and Treatment, 10,* 97–112.

Schlank, A. M. & Shaw, T. (1996). Treating sexual offenders who deny their guilt: A pilot study. *Sexual Abuse: A Journal of Research and Treatment, 8,* 17–23.

Scott, J. E. (1985, May). *Violence and Erotic Material: The Relationship Between Adult Entertainment and Rape.* Paper presented at the annual meeting of the American Association for the Advancement of Science, Los Angeles.

Seghorn, T. K. & Cohen, M. (1980). The psychology of the rape assailant. In W. J. Curran, A. L. McGary, & C. Petty (Eds.), *Modern Legal Medicine, Psychiatry and Forensic Science* (pp. 533–551). Philadelphia: F. A. Davis.

Seidman, B., Marshall, W. L., Hudson, S. M., & Robertson, P. J. (1994). An examination of intimacy and loneliness in sex offenders. *Journal of Interpersonal Violence, 9,* 518–534.

Seto, M. C. & Barbaree, H. E. (1995). The role of alcohol in sexual aggression. *Clinical Psychology Review, 15,* 545–566.

Sorenson, S. B., Stein, J. A., Siegel, J. M., Golding, J. M., & Burnam, M. A. (1987). The prevalence of adult sexual assault. *American Journal of Epidemiology, 126,* 1154–1164.

Stermac, L., Sheridan, P. M., Davidson, A., & Dunn, S. (1996). Sexual assault of adult males. *Journal of Interpersonal Violence, 11,* 52–64.

Stoléru, S., Grégoire, M. C., Gérard, D., Decety, J., Lafarge, E., Cinotti, L., Lavenne, F., Le Bars, D., Verney-Mavry, E., Rada, H., Collet, C., Mazoyer, B., Forest, M. G., Magnin, F., Spira, A., & Comar, D. (1999). Neuroanatomical correlates of visually evoked sexual arousal in human males. *Archives of Sexual Behavior, 28,* 1–21.

Stuckman-Johnson, C. (1988). Forced sex on dates. *Journal of Sex Research, 24,* 234–241.

Thornhill, N. W. & Thornhill, R. (1990). An evolutionary analysis of psychological pain following rape: 1. The effects of victim's age and marital status. *Ethology and Sociobiology, 11,* 155–176.

Truman, D. M., Tokar, D. M., & Fischer, A. R. (1996). Dimensions of masculinity: Relations to date rape supportive attitudes and sexual aggression in dating situations. *Journal of Counseling and Development, 74,* 555–562.

Ullman, S. E. & Knight, R. A. (1991). A multivariate model for predicting rape and physical injury outcomes during sexual assaults. *Journal of Consulting and Clinical Psychology, 59,* 724–731.

Waldner-Haugrud, L. K. & Magruder, B. (1995). Male and female sexual victimization in dating relationships: Gender differences in coercion techniques and outcomes. *Violence and Victims, 10,* 203–215.

Ward, T. & Hudson, S. M. (1998). The construction and development of theory in the sexual offending area: A metatheoretical framework. *Sexual Abuse: A Journal of Research and Treatment, 10,* 47–63.

Ward, T., Hudson, S. M., & Keenan, T. (1998). A self-regulation model of the sexual offense process. *Sexual Abuse: A Journal of Research and Treatment, 10,* 141–157.

Ward, T., Hudson, S. M., & Marshall, W. L. (1995). Cognitive distortions and affective deficits in sex offenders: A cognitive deconstructionist interpretation. *Sexual Abuse: A Journal of Research and Treatment, 7,* 67–83.

Ward, T., Hudson, S. M., Marshall, W. L., & Siegert, R. (1995). Attachment style and intimacy deficits in sexual offenders: A theoretical framework. *Sexual Abuse: A Journal of Research and Treatment, 7,* 317–335.

Ward, T., McCormack, J., & Hudson, S. M. (1997). Sexual offenders' perceptions of their intimate relationships. *Sexual Abuse: A Journal of Research and Treatment, 9,* 57–74.

Ward, T., McCormack, J., Hudson, S. M., & Polaschek, D. (1997). Rape: Assessment and treatment. In D. R. Laws & W. O'Donohue (Eds.), *Sexual Deviance: Theory, Assessment and Treatment* (pp. 356–393). New York: Guilford.

Wegner, D. M. (1994). Ironic process of mental control. *Psychological Bulletin, 101,* 34–52.

Weinrott, M. R., Riggan, M., & Frothingham, S. (1997). Reducing deviant arousal in juvenile sex offenders using vicarious sensitization. *Journal of Interpersonal Violence, 12,* 704–728.

Whalen, R. E. (1984). Multiple actions of steroids and their antagonists. *Archives of Sexual Behavior, 13,* 497.

Whittaker, L. H. (1959). Oestrogens and psychosexual disorders. *Medical Journal of Australia, 2,* 542–549.

Wickramaserka, I. (1980). Aversive behavior rehearsal: A cognitive-behavioral procedure. In D. J. Cox & R. J. Daitzman (Eds.), *Exhibitionism: Description, Assessment and Treatment* (pp. 123–149). New York: Garland.

Wilson, R. J. (1997). Psychophysiological signs of faking in the phallometric test. *Sexual Abuse: A Journal of Research and Treatment, 10,* 113–126.

Winn, M. E. (1996). The strategic and systemic management of denial in the cognitive/behavioral treatment of sexual offenders. *Sexual Abuse: A Journal of Research and Treatment, 8,* 25–36.

Yllo, K. & Finkelhor, D. (1985). Marital rape. In A. W. Burgess (Ed.), *Rape and Sexual Assault* (pp. 146–158). New York: Garland.

Zweig, J. M., Barber, B. L., & Eccles, J. S. (1997). Sexual coercion and well-being in adulthood: Comparisons by gender and college status. *Journal of Interpersonal Violence, 12,* 291–308.

11 Paraphilias

MICHAEL C. SETO

Centre for Addiction and Mental Health and University of Toronto

HOWARD E. BARBAREE

Centre for Addiction and Mental Health and University of Toronto

Description of the Problem

The paraphilias, from the Greek words for love (*philia*) beyond the usual (*para*), are usually defined as abnormal sexual preferences. They can be broadly divided into two categories: abnormal *target* preferences and abnormal *activity* preferences (see Freund, Seto, & Kuban, 1997). In the former, the preferred focus of sexual thoughts, fantasies, and urges are targets other than sexually mature people. In the latter, the preferred activities are highly atypical for individuals who prefer sexually mature people. A target or activity is considered to be preferred when it is consistently needed for sexual gratification. According to the latest edition of the *Diagnostic and Statistical Manual of Mental Disorders (DSM-IV)*, the primary classification guide used by mental health professionals in North America, the diagnostic criteria for paraphilias require (1) recurrent and intense sexually arousing fantasies, urges, or behavior directed towards body parts or nonhuman objects, suffering or humiliation of either partner in the sex act, or sexual activity with a nonconsenting person; and (2) these fantasies, urges, or behavior cause clinically significant distress or impairment in functioning (American Psychiatric Association, 1994). The *DSM-IV* specifically mentions more common types of paraphilias (the preferred target or activity is noted in brackets): fetishism (nonliving object), frotteurism (touching or rubbing against a nonconsenting person), pedophilia (prepubescent child), masochism (being humiliated, bound, or otherwise made to suffer), sadism (psychological or physical suffering of others), and transvestic fetishism (cross-dressing). For example, according to *DSM-IV*, voyeurism involves:

> the act of observing unsuspecting individuals (usually strangers) who are naked, in the process of disrobing, or engaging in sexual activity. The act of looking (peeping)

is for the purpose of achieving sexual excitement, and generally no sexual activity with the observed person is sought. Orgasm, usually produced by masturbation, may occur during the voyeuristic activity or later while the person remembers what he has witnessed. (p. 532)

Other abnormal sexual preferences fall under the diagnostic category of "Paraphilia Not Otherwise Specified." Many paraphilias have been described in the clinical literature, although some of these preferences are very rare (see Money, 1984). Table 11.1 lists examples of paraphilias. To date, nobody has developed a satisfactory theory to explain why some targets and activities are more likely than others to become paraphilic preferences, although the courtship disorder theory relates certain activity paraphilias—voyeurism, exhibitionism, frotteurism, and preferential rape—to disturbances in the typical human courtship process (see Freund, 1990). For example, fetishism for leather, rubber, or vinyl is much more likely than fetishism for wool or cardboard. Mason (1997) observed that fetish categories may be stable over time, but the objects in those categories may change (e.g., a fetishistic interest in clothing material has been stable over time, but interests in velvet or silk in the nineteenth century have been displaced by interests in polyvinyl chloride, rubber, or other synthetic materials in the latter twentieth century).

The distinction between normal and abnormal can be made in a number of ways, including statistical frequency, sociocultural norms, clinical judgment, and

TABLE 1.11 Examples of Clinically Identified Paraphilias.

Paraphilia	Preferred Stimulus
Acrotomophilia	Stump of an amputee and/or the desire to amputate someone's limb
Asphyxiophilia	Self-induced asphyxiation almost to the point of unconsciousness. Also known as autoerotic asphyxiation
Autagonistophilia	Being observed or being on stage while having sex with someone
Coprophilia	Handling and/or eating feces
Klismaphilia	Receiving or giving enemas
Morphophilia	A particular body shape and size
Necrophilia	A corpse or someone pretending to be dead
Partialism	Particular body part such as the foot or neck
Scoptophilia	Watching others engage in masturbation or sexual intercourse
Stigmatophilia	A partner who has been tattooed, scarified, or pierced in the genital area
Troilism	Observing one's partner engaging in sex with another person
Urophilia	Being urinated on and/or drinking urine ("golden showers")
Zoophilia	Engaging in sex with nonhuman animals

biological pathology (defined as a disturbance in a biological process or mechanism). These approaches do not necessarily agree. A good example is the argument over the normality or abnormality of homosexuality. Statistically, individuals who are attracted to and choose same-sex partners are uncommon, with population prevalence estimates consistently under 10 percent, depending on the survey methodology (e.g., Sell, Wells, & Wypij, 1995). In contrast, attitudes about homosexuality appear to have shifted toward greater tolerance over the past 30 years, at least in terms of legal treatment. Similarly, homosexuality was previously classified as a mental disorder in *DSM*, but is no longer recognized as such by most clinicians. The research regarding biological pathology is contentious. Recent evidence supporting a maternal immunosensitivity explanation (Blanchard & Bogaert, 1996) may speak to the biological disturbance underlying homosexuality. Of course, these ways of defining normality and abnormality are not independent (e.g., Ernulf, Innala, & Whitam, 1989).

Variations in the expression of sexual preferences need to be considered when making a diagnosis of paraphilia. For example, a distinction has been made between bondage and discipline, dominance and submission, and sadomasochism in what is often referred to as the BDSM subculture (see Ernulf & Innala, 1995). These authors note that bondage and discipline typically refers to sexual behavior involving physical restraint and/or commands requiring obedience. Dominance and submission is a broad term encompassing the other two terms, and focuses on the role of power in sex, sometimes in the context of fantasized roles such as teacher-student or guard-inmate. Sadomasochism refers to sexual behavior involving physical or psychological suffering. Freund and colleagues (1997) also described several variants that result from the combination of paraphilias. One patient who was voyeuristic and exhibitionistic did not practice frotteurism himself, but was sexually excited by watching other men engaging in frotteurism in buses or subway cars. McNally and Lukach (1991) described a case of zoophilic exhibitionism, in which a man repeatedly exposed his genitals and masturbated in front of large dogs, but did not expose himself to humans or have sexual contact with the dogs.

There are potential problems with the *DSM-IV* definition of paraphilia. First, the designation of a sexual preference for a particular target or activity as abnormal could be construed as socially or culturally arbitrary, reflecting the prevailing social values, attitudes, and biases (see Simon, 1994; Suppe, 1984). As mentioned earlier, homosexuality, a sexual preference for same-sex partners, was previously considered pathological by many psychiatrists and was not dropped from the *DSM* until 1973 (American Psychiatric Association, 1973). Similarly, some authors have suggested that pedophilia, a sexual preference for prepubescent children as partners, is considered pathological in Western society and is not legally and socially accepted at this time, but that it has been deemed more acceptable in other cultures or times. An established advocacy organization, the North American Man Boy Love Association, has argued that children are capable of giving consent to sex and are more likely to be harmed by the negative reactions of their families and society than the sexual activity itself (see Seto, 1999, for a philosophical counter-argument).

Another difficulty with the *DSM* definition of paraphilia is determining the threshold of frequency, intensity, or psychological importance to make a diagnosis. A substantial number of people have fantasized or engaged in sexual behavior that could be consistent with a paraphilic diagnosis, such as cross-dressing or spanking, but do not qualify because the frequency, intensity, or importance of the target or activity for sexual gratification is not sufficient. For example, *Playboy* magazine commissioned a survey of 3,700 college students in 1976. The survey found that 2 percent of the sample had tried and liked inflicting or receiving pain during sex, while another 3 percent had tried and liked bondage or master-slave role-playing. This does not mean these individuals regularly engaged in those activities, or required them in order to be sexually satisfied. In contrast, Moser and Levitt (1987) surveyed 178 men who either subscribed to a sadomasochism magazine or were members of a sadomasochism organization, and found that 95 percent of them found sadomasochistic activities were as satisfying or more satisfying than typical sexual intercourse. Thirty percent reported that sadomasochistic activity was essential for their sexual gratification.

Freund and colleagues (1997) examined the responses of two volunteer groups, one consisting of 69 university students and the other of 35 less educated men from the community, who completed a sexological questionnaire. This questionnaire contains the following item: "Since age 16, have you ever masturbated while watching or trying to observe a girl or woman who was unaware of your presence?" Twelve percent of the university student volunteers answered yes, compared to 23 percent of the less educated community volunteers. In comparison, 85 percent of a sample of 60 voyeurs admitted to masturbating while surreptitiously observing a female. The volunteers also answered the following question pertaining to exhibitionism: "Since age 16 have you ever shown your penis (from a distance) to a female who was almost or totally a stranger to you?" None of the volunteers answered yes, while 81 percent of 150 exhibitionists admitted they had exposed their penis to a female stranger. Freund and colleagues also examined the responses of 63 university students and 186 less educated volunteers to the following two questions: (1) "Since age 16, have you ever attempted to fondle the breasts or crotch of an unsuspecting female who was almost or totally a stranger?" and (2) "Since age 16, have you ever stood behind an unsuspecting female who was almost or totally a stranger to you and pressed (intentionally) your penis against her buttocks?" Thirty two percent of the university students and 30 percent of the less educated men answered yes to one or both questions. In contrast, 79 percent of 77 frotteuristic men admitted to this behavior. These data indicate that behaviors consistent with voyeuristic or frotteuristic interests are not rare in ostensibly normal men; however, exposing one's penis in a manner consistent with exhibitionism is very rare.

Finally, there can be inconsistencies in applying thresholds of frequency or intensity. For example, an individual who prefers partners with red hair, but who is also attracted to blondes or brunettes would not be diagnosed, while another individual who prefers prepubescent children, but who is also sexually aroused by adults might still be diagnosed as a nonexclusive pedophile by many clinicians using *DSM-IV* criteria.

Epidemiology

We do not know how common paraphilias are in the general population. Large, representative surveys of sexual behavior have not usually included items about sexual interests, fantasies, and behavior that would be diagnostically relevant. Clinical or forensic samples are not representative because certain paraphilias, such as exhibitionism or pedophilia, are more likely to be identified because they are illegal. Also, only some paraphilic individuals will be detected in this way. On the other hand, data gathered from social organizations or related forums may be vulnerable to socially desirable responding, because the members may be interested in presenting themselves in the best possible light (e.g., to counter negative public opinions about their sexual interests). Consequently, we know relatively little about paraphilias, such as transvestic fetishism, which usually take place in private and do not come to official attention unless the person is distressed or gets into legal trouble because of it (e.g., if they steal women's clothes to wear). We also know relatively little about paraphilias, such as scoptophilia, or urophilia, because these activities are not illegal between consenting adult partners. Some paraphilic interests can be met by prostitutes who specialize in serving these interests. For example, Chivers and Blanchard (1996) analyzed 329 escort advertisements from 10 consecutive issues of two free weekly newspapers in Toronto and found that 17 percent of the prostitutes mentioned domination, describing themselves as dominatrices, mistresses, or as involved in sexual activities such as spanking or bondage.

Surveys reporting the proportions of respondents who have fantasized about a particular target or activity or who have engaged in relevant sexual behavior are useful but they do not usually provide information about the frequency, intensity, or consequences of these fantasies or behavior. Briere and Runtz (1989) surveyed 193 male undergraduates and found that 9 percent had fantasized about having sex with a young child, 5 percent masturbated to fantasies of sex with children, and 7 percent indicated some likelihood of having sex with a child if they were guaranteed they would not be punished or identified. The proportion who had sexual fantasies about children, masturbated to these fantasies, and who had acted on their interest is unknown. Crepault and Couture (1980) surveyed 94 males about specific sexual fantasies during masturbation or intercourse, and found that 61.7 percent fantasized about having sex with a young girl, 11.7 percent fantasized about being humiliated, 5.3 percent fantasized about sexual activity with an animal, and 3.2 percent fantasized about having sex with a young boy. Templeman and Stinnett (1991) surveyed 60 college males and found that 7 percent expressed an interest in exposing themselves, 54 percent expressed an interest in peeping through windows at an unsuspecting female, and 5 percent expressed an interest in having sex with a girl under the age of 12. In a recent *Details* magazine sex survey of college students, there were approximately 2,000 male and female respondents (Elliott & Brantley, 1997). Thirty percent of men and 24 percent of women had tried spanking; 27 percent of men and 26 percent of women had tried bondage, and 6 percent of each sex had incorporated sadomasochistic elements into their sexual activities.

Social norms have changed over time. The recent proliferation of body piercing, tattoos, and scarification in popular culture suggests these forms of fetish- or BDSM-related adornment are more acceptable than they were even 20 years ago. Similarly, the greater availability of fetish- or BDSM-related items in stores selling sexual merchandise or mail order catalogues, and the appearance of advertisements for "dungeons" and "dominatrices" in mainstream newspapers suggests these interests are becoming less secretive.

Paraphilias appear to be much more common in males than females, with a typical onset in adolescence (American Psychiatric Association, 1994). The sex ratio may vary depending on the paraphilia in question. Frotteurism and transvestic fetishism seem to be present in males almost exclusively, while exhibitionism and pedophilia are more common in men than women (see Hunter & Mathews, 1997). In contrast, there seems to be a smaller sex difference in masochistic and fetishistic interests. There is limited information from cross-cultural studies, but victimization surveys indicate that exhibitionism and pedophilia are not limited to North American society (Cox, Tsang, & Lee, 1982; Finkelhor, 1994; Rhoads & Borjes, 1981). There are similarities in the BDSM subcultures in Germany and the United States (cf. Moser & Levitt, 1987; Spengler, 1977). There is no theoretical reason to expect differences in the variety and forms of paraphilias across cultures or times. However, there may be differences in the frequency that paraphilic interests are expressed, depending on the degree of legal or social sanction for sexually anomalous behavior.

We need large, anonymous, and representative surveys, in order to get a better idea of how common paraphilias are in the general population. Also, researchers need to develop alternative ways to gather information. One interesting approach is to use an unobtrusive measure of sexual interest. Dietz and Evans (1982) looked at pornographic imagery on magazine covers, and found that 17.6 percent depicted BDSM themes. This method is useful to the extent that the pornography marketplace is efficient (i.e., that the material being produced and distributed corresponds to the interests of consumers) within the limits of legal restrictions on pornography. Another method is to look at the media that facilitate anonymity. Ernulf and Innala (1995) studied 514 messages about sexual bondage (out of 3,560 messages) sent to an Internet discussion group, *alt.sex.bondage*, in 1990. Seventy-two percent of the messages were purportedly written by males, with the majority describing themselves as heterosexual. Among those senders who stated their orientation, 18 percent of the men and 11 percent of the women described themselves as homosexual. These prevalence rates are higher than found in surveys of the general population, suggesting homosexual individuals are more likely than heterosexual individuals to be involved in bondage-related activities (or, at least, more likely to participate in an Internet discussion group about bondage-related activities). Among those senders expressing a preference, 71 percent of the heterosexual males preferred the dominant-initiator role, compared to 89 percent of the heterosexual females. Only eight homosexual males and none of the homosexual females indicated a role preference. The most common theme regarding bondage was the "sense of play." Age or physical attractiveness of one's partner was rarely mentioned as important. Of course, this method is dependent on the truthfulness of anonymous postings; people can easily lie about their sex, age, or other information, and there is no way to verify it.

Characteristics

Not much information is available on individual characteristics, but paraphilic individuals clearly comprise a heterogeneous group. Much of the clinical literature is psychoanalytic in orientation, focusing on speculations about the underlying dynamics of the sexual preference. Some clinicians and researchers have suggested that paraphilic individuals, such as exhibitionists and pedophiles, have personality disturbances and social skill deficits (e.g., McCreary, 1975; Wise, Fagan, Schmidt, Ponticas, & Costa, 1991). Clinically, paraphilic individuals were described as unassertive, poor in heterosocial skills, and poor in handling feelings of anger or hostility. Although many of these individuals are married or involved in a common-law relationship, their marital adjustment was considered to be poorer than average. It has also been suggested that paraphilic men have a lower than average level of normative sexual activity and masturbation is a bigger part of their sexual lives (see Blair & Lanyon, 1981). However, others have not found supporting evidence (Smukler & Schiebel, 1975; Forgac & Michaels, 1982), and many of these studies have not included an appropriate comparison group.

Authors have usually reported no differences in terms of intelligence, education level, or socioeconomic status. Not surprisingly, respondents to surveys or Internet discussion groups may be higher in education and socioeconomic status than the general population. Some paraphilics have considerable contact with the law, suggesting the expression of some paraphilias that may involve violating the rights of others, such as exhibitionism or sadism, may reflect a more general problem of antisocial conduct (see Seto & Barbaree, 1997). Having a paraphilia does not seem to be associated with severe psychopathology. For example, Rosman and Resnick (1989) found that only 11 percent of the "true necrophiles" they identified showed evidence of psychosis. However, substance abuse was common and may have served as a disinhibiting factor in their behavior (see Seto & Barbaree, 1995, regarding the role of alcohol in sexual aggression). Some researchers have looked at neuropsychological differences between men with paraphilias and controls, with mixed results (see review by Langevin, 1990).

There is substantial evidence for the co-occurrence of paraphilias, in the sense that having one increases the likelihood of having others. In contrast to the notion that paraphilic individuals are very specific (e.g., exhibitionists prefer to expose their penises and engage almost exclusively in this kind of criminal sexual behavior), there are data showing nonspecificity in terms of age of victim, gender, and type of paraphilic acts (see Abel & Osborn, 1992). A number of authors have commented on the association of paraphilias. Taylor (1947) noted a co-occurrence of exhibitionism and frotteurism. Yalom (1960) described cases of co-occurrence of voyeurism, exhibitionism, and rape, while Grassberger (1964) found that 12 percent of subjects arrested for indecent exposure had committed other sexual offenses, especially rape. According to Gebhard, Gagnon, Pomeroy, and Christenson (1965), 1 in 10 incarcerated exhibitionists had also committed rape; these authors also reported an association between exhibitionism and frotteurism. Abel, Becker, Cunningham-Rathner, Mittelman, and Rouleau (1988) found a high degree of co-occurrence in paraphilic behaviors for a group of 561 male outpatients. For example, 28 percent of the 142 men reporting exhibitionistic activity also reported voyeuristic activity, while 63 percent of the 62 men reporting voyeuristic activity also reported exhibitionistic activity. Finally, Bradford, Boulet, and Pawlak (1992) reported on the co-occurrence of paraphilias in a sample of 443 men undergoing a psychiatric assessment. Of the 115 men reporting voyeuristic activity (the largest single paraphilic category in their study), 66 percent had engaged in frotteuristic activity, 52 percent had engaged in exhibitionistic activity, and 47 percent had committed rape.

Moser and Levitt (1987) described a wide variety of acts associated with BDSM activity, the most common being flagellation and bondage. Behaviors that caused pain with little physical risk (ice, hot wax, biting, and face-slapping) were relatively common, while behaviors that were more risky (burns, branding, piercing, tattoos, and pins) were much less common. A majority of their respondents had engaged in master-slave role-playing. Women were well-represented, unlike studies of other paraphilias. Nine percent of the respondents said they required sadomasochistic activity for sexual gratification. Some respondents also indicated interests in other paraphilic areas, including urophilia (33%), coprophilia (8.5%), klismaphilia (30%), fetishism (51%), and bestiality (4.5%). Some respondents had also been involved in group sex (39%), mate sharing (18%), and incestuous behavior (5.1%).

Assessment

Much of our information about the assessment and treatment of paraphilias comes from the sex offender literature. Paraphilias can be diagnosed using information from a number of sources: (1) the individual's self-report about his sexual fantasies, urges, and behavior; (2) questionnaires using scales that measure sexual interests; and (3) phallometric testing, which provides a physiological measure of sexual arousal to different stimulus categories (e.g., depictions of nude children, adolescents, and adults). Sexual histories are usually gathered through clinical interviews. Variables of interest include the number and duration of consensual, age-appropriate sexual relationships, number of sexual partners, exposure to pornography, the age of onset of sexual interests, including other paraphilic acts, and a detailed description of sexual offenses, if any. Questionnaires that have been used include the Clarke Sex History Questionnaire and the Multiphasic Sex Inventory. Although self-report measures can be clinically useful, they are vulnerable to faking because of the obvious nature of the questions and the legal or social sanctions that some individuals may face if they answer honestly. As a consequence, more emphasis is usually given to phallometric testing in forensic settings.

The behavioral assessment and treatment of male sex offenders has depended a great deal on the phallometric measurement of sexual arousal. A number of detailed reviews on this methodology are available (see Murphy & Barbaree, 1994; O'Donohue & Letourneau, 1992). In phallometric testing, male sexual arousal is monitored by measuring changes in penile circumference or volume while the man is presented with stimuli that vary in their sexual and nonsexual content. A measure of blood engorgement in the vaginal wall based on the reflectance of light is available for measuring physiological sexual arousal in females (see Palace & Gorzalka, 1992, for a description of the typical apparatus).

There is good evidence for the validity of phallometric testing for gender or age preferences. Homosexual individuals can be clearly distinguished from heterosexual individuals in terms of their responding to depictions of same-sex and opposite-sex stimuli (e.g., Freund, 1967). Child molesters, on average, respond relatively more to stimuli depicting children than nonoffenders (e.g., Freund & Watson, 1991; Seto, Lalumière, & Kuban, 1999). Stronger responding to children is associated with having a male victim, having more victims, and having younger victims, and follow-up studies suggest stronger responding is associated with a greater probability of sexually reoffending (Barbaree & Marshall, 1988; Rice, Quinsey, & Harris, 1991). Other target preferences have been less studied, although the existing evidence suggests that phallometric testing can distinguish fetishists and transvestic fetishists from controls (Blanchard, Racansky, & Steiner, 1986; Freund, Seto, & Kuban, 1996). In terms of activity preferences, most of the published research has focused on sadism and paraphilic rape, because of the great concern about these activities (e.g., Seto & Kuban, 1996). A recent review of published and unpublished studies argued convincingly that rapists could be discriminated from nonrapists using phallometric testing, although the sensitivity (proportion who are rapists who are accurately identified as such) is lower than for gender or age preferences (Lalumière & Quinsey, 1993; 1994).

As we mentioned, there have been relatively few phallometric investigations of activity preferences other than paraphilic rape. Marshall, Payne, Barbaree, and Eccles (1991) found a significant difference between exhibitionists and controls in their relative responses to depictions of exposing. In contrast, Freund, Scher, and Hucker (1984) found no difference between exhibitionists and controls in their responses to consenting sex, while Fedora and his colleagues found that exhibitionists responded to slides depicting fully clothed women, while controls did not (Fedora, Reddon, & Yeudall, 1986).

One possible difficulty in developing tests for paraphilic preferences is the deliberate suppression of responses to the preferred stimuli (i.e., faking). We are interested in developing a phallometric test for masochism using subjects solicited from the community in order to evaluate this possibility. These volunteers would be willing to admit having a paraphilic preference for masochistic activities given that they were self-identified, and would subsequently be unlikely to fake their responses because there are no legal sanctions for such activities (see Freund, Seto, & Kuban, 1995). Failure to discriminate between masochists and controls would suggest that faking is not a sufficient explanation, at least on its own, for the difficulty in achieving high sensitivities (correctly identifying individuals who have the preference) and specificities (correctly identifying individuals who do not have the preference) in tests for activity preferences. Other possible contributing factors to the difficulty in developing tests for activity preferences are the characteristics of the stimuli used. For example, Lalumière and Quinsey (1994) found that studies using stimulus sets with more exemplars per category and more brutal descriptions of rape were better able to discriminate between rapists and controls.

Intervention

A variety of approaches have been used in the treatment of paraphilias. We focus on pharmacological and behavioral approaches because there is currently no evidence supporting nonbehavioral psychotherapies (see Barbaree & Seto, 1997, for a review regarding the treatment of pedophilia). The aim of drug therapy is to suppress sexual urges and behavior. The most common agents interfere with the actions of androgens, such as cyproterone acetate or medroxyprogesterone acetate. There is some preliminary evidence for their efficacy in reducing the frequency or intensity of sexual urges and arousal, but larger, better-controlled evaluation studies are needed (see review by Gijs & Gooren, 1996). Problems with drug therapy include side-effects and patient dissatisfaction with the nonspecificity of action, because appropriate sexual arousal and behavior are also suppressed. Not surprisingly, clinical trials of these agents often show a high dropout rate. It has recently been suggested that serotinergic agents, such as fluoxetine (Prozac) or buspirone (Buspar), can specifically reduce deviant sexual arousal without affecting normal sexual arousal (see Fedoroff, 1993). Compliance with this form of pharmacotherapy may be higher. It should be noted that this suggestion is based on uncontrolled case studies and has been evaluated in only one experimental drug trial (Kruesi, Fine, Valladares, Phillips, & Rapaport, 1992).

In behavioral approaches, aversion techniques are typically used to suppress inappropriate sexual arousal, while masturbatory reconditioning techniques are used to increase appropriate sexual arousal. In aversion procedures, unpleasant stimuli, such as mild electric shock or ammonia odors, are paired with repeated presentations of the preferred sexual stimulus, such as a nude child. In a variation called covert sensitization, the aversive stimulus is imagined, for example, being discovered by family, friends, or coworkers while engaging in paraphilic behavior. Satiation is a behavioral technique for decreasing inappropriate sexual arousal that does not depend on the use of aversive procedures. In this procedure, the subject masturbates to ejaculation while verbalizing aloud variations of his deviant fantasy. After ejaculating, and throughout the refractory period, he is told to continue masturbating to the same fantasies over several long sessions. Masturbatory reconditioning involves associating sexual arousal with appropriate stimuli. Techniques include thematic shift, in which the subject masturbates to a paraphilic sexual fantasy until the point of orgasm, then switches to a nonparaphilic fantasy. The efficacy of behavioral approaches for changing sexual arousal patterns was reviewed by Barbaree, Bogaert, and Seto (1995). Overall, the existing research suggests that behavioral methods can have a temporary effect on sexual arousal patterns, but it is unclear how long these changes are maintained and whether they result in actual changes in interests, as opposed to greater voluntary control over sexual arousal.

The relapse prevention approach to treating sex offenders was adapted from the addictions area. Marlatt and Gordon (1980, 1985) outlined a strategy for assisting individuals who have completed treatment to prevent the recurrence of drug-taking behavior. The strategy involves (1) identifying situations in which the individual is at high risk for relapse; (2) teaching the individual to identify these high risk situations and to avoid them; (3) identifying lapses as behaviors which do not constitute full-fledged relapses, but which constitute approximations to the drug-taking behavior and which may be a precursor to a relapse (e.g., spending time in bars as a precursor to drinking alcohol); (4) teaching the individual to identify a lapse; and (5) teaching the individual various coping strategies which might be used in response to both high-risk situations and lapses to minimize the chances of a relapse.

Case Illustration

The following is an example of an individual with pedophilia. This case illustrates how many paraphilic acts can go undetected, as well as some of the treatment issues when working with sex offenders. Potentially identifying details have been changed.

Mr. Smith (not his real name) is a 27-year-old offender currently involved in correctional treatment for sex offenders. Mr. Smith recently admitted to a long history of sexual interactions with children, starting in his childhood after he was himself sexually abused by older boys. He estimated that he had sexually abused hundreds of boys over the years.

Mr. Smith described a typical incident in which he would walk up to an 11-year-old boy and distract him by showing him something. Mr. Smith would then put his hand down the boy's pants and fondle his penis. If the child did not struggle too much, he would lay him down on the ground and attempt to perform fellatio. He would try to go as far as he could, including anal sex. He would cease his attempts if the boy struggled too much. The boy would often escape. Mr. Smith said he committed offenses like this in malls and restrooms and any public place where he might find young boys. Mr. Smith committed these offenses over many years without ever being caught or detected.

At the age of 24, Mr. Smith was convicted of providing alcohol to a minor in an incident which clearly had sexual overtones. He had met a group of teenaged boys in a remote camping site, and provided them with as much beer as they could drink. One youngster became very intoxicated and Mr. Smith got him away from his friends. In his later statement to police, the boy could not recall much, but he did remember Mr. Smith touching his penis. Mr. Smith explained to the police that the boy was so intoxicated that he could not even stand to urinate, so he was forced to assist the boy in his attempts to urinate. Apparently, this story was believed and Mr. Smith was not charged with a sexual offense.

At the age of 26, Mr. Smith befriended a 14-year-old boy's mother expressly in order to gain access to the boy. Upon discovering the boy was interested in getting work in the fast-food delivery business, Mr. Smith volunteered to show the boy what he knew. He made arrangements to take the boy on his delivery rounds from 8 P.M. to 4 A.M., and sought and received permission from the boy's mother to have the boy sleep over at his place afterward, in order not to disturb the mother's sleep when they were finished making deliveries. Upon returning to his apartment, Mr. Smith gave a mixed alcoholic beverage to the boy, telling him it was only soda. When the boy passed out on the couch, Mr. Smith disrobed him and performed fellatio on the boy. During this act, the boy regained consciousness and ran out of the apartment after he realized what was happening. He notified a neighbor and police were called. Mr. Smith was convicted of sexual assault for the first time.

Upon entering a prison-based sex offender treatment program, Mr. Smith denied that he had ever committed a sexual assault, describing his index offense as a misunderstanding. He was assessed in the phallometric laboratory and was found to have particularly strong arousal to depictions of young boys, and negligible arousal to adults of either gender. The treatment targeting his deviant sexual arousal was part of an overall program that addressed his denial, his lack of empathy for his victims, and his lack of appreciation of the harm experienced by sexual abuse victims. Additionally, the treatment was designed to increase his awareness of the situations which put him at high risk for sexual assault, and in the context of the program, he was encouraged to develop a relapse prevention plan. His progress in the treatment program was judged to be only "fair," and after treatment, the program assessed his risk for reoffense to be very high. Mr. Smith was denied parole and remains in custody at this time.

Summary

Paraphilias can be defined as sexual preferences for unusual targets or activities, although identifying paraphilic individuals is not straightforward. A wide variety of paraphilic interests have been described in the clinical or research literature, but most are very rare. Relatively more common examples include fetishism (nonliving objects), pedophilia (prepubescent children), sadism (physical or psychological suffering of others), and masochism (being humiliated, bound, or otherwise made to suffer). We do not know how common paraphilias are in the general population, but we do know they are likely to co-occur in the same individual. We do not understand the etiology of paraphilias, just as we do not have a good understanding of the normative development of sexual preferences (see Quinsey & Lalumière, 1995; Quinsey, Rice, Harris, & Reid, 1993).

From the existing evidence, paraphilic individuals are a heterogeneous group and do not consistently differ from nonparaphilic individuals in terms of biographic or personality characteristics. The only obvious difference is their unusual sexual preference for particular targets or activities. Individuals with paraphilias, such as exhibitionism, pedophilia, and sadism, are more likely to be studied by researchers, because these individuals are more likely to be identified in clinical or forensic settings. Also, there is greater concern regarding the consequences of their behavior for others, compared to paraphilias that do not involve others (e.g., fetishism) or that tend to take place between consenting adults. Paraphilias are more common in males and tend to appear in adolescence or early adulthood.

Paraphilias can be identified from self-report information and physiological assessments of sexual arousal patterns. In particular, because of the potential biases in self-report regarding criminal behavior, the measurement of erectile response (phallometric testing) has been very important in the study of rape and child molestation. There is a great deal of evidence for the validity of this assessment procedure. A physiological measure of sexual arousal in females based on the reflectance of light from the vaginal wall (vaginal photoplethysmography) is less studied at this time.

Interventions are geared toward individuals who are distressed by their paraphilic interests or who have caused harm to others through their actions. Pharmacological or behavioral interventions seem to be more promising than nonbehavioral interventions. The drug treatment literature has been recently reviewed by Gijs and Gooren (1996). They concluded that there is some support for the use of antiandrogens (which mainly affect testosterone) and that serotonergic agents such as fluoxetine (Prozac) show promise; however, methodologically rigorous evaluations still need to be conducted. Behavioral techniques, such as aversive conditioning using ammonia or mild electric shock, appear to have short-term effects on sexual arousal patterns, but the long-term maintenance of these changes has not been demonstrated (see Barbaree et al., 1995).

More research is needed to better understand the onset and development of paraphilic interests, the incidence and prevalence of these interests in the general population, to identify the distinguishing characteristics of paraphilic individuals, and the efficacy of drug or behavioral interventions targeting paraphilic behavior that is personally distressing or causes harm to others.

REFERENCES

Abel, G. G., Becker, J. V., Cunningham-Rathner, J., Mittelman, M., & Rouleau, J. L. (1988). Multiple paraphilic diagnoses among sex offenders. *Bulletin of the American Academy of Psychiatry and the Law, 16,* 153–168.

Abel, G. G. & Osborn, C. (1992). The paraphilias: The extent and nature of sexually deviant and criminal behavior. *Psychiatric Clinics of North America, 15,* 675–687.

American Psychiatric Association. (1973). *Diagnostic and Statistical Manual of Mental Disorders* (2nd ed.). Washington, DC: Author.

American Psychiatric Association. (1994). *Diagnostic and Statistical Manual of Mental Disorders* (4th ed.). Washington, DC: Author.

Barbaree, H. E., Bogaert, A. F., & Seto, M. C. (1995). Sexual reorientation therapy for pedophiles: Practices and controversies. In L. Diamant &

R. McAnulty (Eds.), *The Psychology of Sexual Orientation, Behavior, and Identity: A Handbook* (pp. 357–383). Westport, CT: Greenwood.

Barbaree, H. E. & Marshall, W. L. (1988). Deviant sexual arousal, offense history, and demographic variables as predictors of reoffense among child molesters. *Behavioural Sciences and the Law, 6,* 267–280.

Barbaree, H. E. & Seto, M. C. (1997). Pedophilia: Assessment and treatment. In D. R. Laws & W. O'Donohue (Eds.), *Sexual Deviance: Theory, Assessment, and Treatment* (pp. 175–193). New York: Guilford.

Blair, C. & Lanyon, R. I. (1981). Exhibitionism: Etiology and treatment. *Psychological Bulletin, 89,* 439–463.

Blanchard, R. & Bogaert, A. F. (1996). Homosexuality in men and number of older brothers. *American Journal of Psychiatry, 153,* 27–31.

Blanchard, R., Racansky, I. G., & Steiner, B. W. (1986). Phallometric detection of fetishistic arousal in heterosexual male cross-dressers. *Journal of Sex Research, 22,* 452–462.

Bradford, J. M. W., Boulet, J., & Pawlak, A. (1992). The paraphilias: A multiplicity of deviant behaviors. *Canadian Journal of Psychiatry, 37,* 104–108.

Briere, J. & Runtz, M. (1989). University males' sexual interest in children: Predicting potential indices of "pedophilia" in a nonforensic sample. *Child Abuse and Neglect, 13,* 65–75.

Chivers, M. & Blanchard, R. (1996). Prostitution advertisement suggest association of transvestism and masochism. *Journal of Sex and Marital Therapy, 22,* 97–102.

Cox, D. J., Tsang, K., & Lee, A. (1982). A cross cultural comparison of the incidence and nature of male exhibitionism among female college students. *Victimology, 7,* 231–234.

Crepault, C. & Couture, M. (1980). Men's erotic fantasies. *Archives of Sexual Behavior, 9,* 565–581.

Dietz, P. E. & Evans, B. (1982). Pornographic imagery and prevalence of paraphilia. *American Journal of Psychiatry, 139,* 1493–1495.

Elliott, L. & Brantley, C. (1997). *Sex on Campus: The Naked Truth about the Real Sex Lives of College Students.* New York: Random House.

Ernulf, K. E. & Innala, S. M. (1995). Sexual bondage: A review and unobtrusive observation. *Archives of Sexual Behavior, 24,* 631–654.

Ernulf, K. E., Innala, S. M., & Whitam, F. L. (1989). Biological explanations, psychological explanations, and tolerance of homosexuality: A cross-national analysis of beliefs and attitudes. *Psychological Report, 65,* 1003–1010.

Fedora, O., Reddon, J. R., & Yeudall, L. T. (1986). Stimuli eliciting sexual arousal in genital exhibitionists: A possible clinical application. *Archives of Sexual Behavior, 15,* 417–427.

Fedoroff, J. P. (1993). Serotonergic drug treatment of deviant sexual interests. *Annals of Sex Research, 6,* 105–121.

Finkelhor, D. (1994). The international epidemiology of child sexual abuse. *Child Abuse and Neglect, 18,* 409–417.

Forgac, G. E. & Michaels, E. J. (1982). Personality characteristics of two types of male exhibitionists. *Journal of Abnormal Psychology, 91,* 287–293.

Freund, K. (1963). A laboratory method of diagnosing predominance of homo- and hetero-erotic interest in the male. *Behaviour Research and Therapy, 5,* 85–93.

Freund, K. (1967). Erotic preference in pedophilia. *Behaviour Research and Therapy, 5,* 339-348.

Freund, K. (1990). Courtship disorder. In W. L. Marshall, D. R. Laws, & H. E. Barbaree (Eds.), *Handbook of Sexual Assault: Issues, Theories, and Treatment of the Offender* (pp. 195–207). New York: Plenum.

Freund, K., Scher, H., & Hucker, S. J. (1984). The courtship disorders: A further investigation. *Archives of Sexual Behavior, 13,* 133–139.

Freund, K., Seto, M. C., & Kuban, M. (1995). Masochism: A multiple case study. *Sexuologie, 4,* 313–324.

Freund, K., Seto, M. C., & Kuban, M. (1996). Two types of fetishism. *Behavior Research and Therapy, 34,* 687–694.

Freund, K., Seto, M. C., & Kuban, M. (1997). Frotteurism and the theory of courtship disorder. In D. R. Laws & W. O'Donohue (Eds.), *Sexual Deviance: Theory, Assessment, and Treatment* (pp. 111–130). New York: Guilford.

Freund, K. & Watson, R. J. (1991). Assessment of the sensitivity and specificity of a phallometric test: An update of phallometric diagnosis of pedophilia. *Psychological Assessment, 3,* 254–260.

Gebhard, P., Gagnon, J., Pomeroy, W., & Christenson, C. (1965). *Sex Offenders.* New York: Harper & Row.

Gijs, L. & Gooren, L. (1996). Hormonal and psychopharmacological interventions in the treatment of paraphilias: An update. *Journal of Sex Research, 33,* 273–290.

Grassberger, R. (1964). Der Exhibitionismus [Exhibitionism]. *Kriminalistik in Osterreich, 18,* 557–562.

Hunter, J. A. & Mathews, R. (1997). Sexual deviance in females. In D. R. Laws & W. O'Donohue (Eds.), *Sexual Deviance: Theory, Assessment, and Treatment* (pp. 465–480). New York: Guilford.

Kruesi, M. P. J., Fine, S., Valladares, L., Phillips, R. A., & Rapaport, J. (1992). Paraphilias: A double-blind cross-over comparison of clomipramine versus desipramine. *Archives of Sexual Behavior, 21,* 587–593.

Lalumière, M. L. & Quinsey, V. L. (1993). The sensitivity of phallometric measures with rapists. *Annals of Sex Research, 6,* 123–138.

Lalumière, M. L. & Quinsey, V. L. (1994). The discriminability of rapists from non-sex offenders using phallometric measures: A meta-analysis. *Criminal Justice and Behavior, 21,* 150–175.

Langevin, R. (1990). Sexual anomalies and the brain. In W. L. Marshall, D. R. Laws, & H. E. Barbaree (Eds.), *Handbook of Sexual Assault: Issues, Theories, and Treatment of the Offender* (pp. 103–113). New York: Plenum.

Marlatt, G. A. & Gordon, J. R. (1980). Determinants of relapse: Implications for the maintenance of behavior change. In P. O. Davidson & S. M. Davidson (Eds.), *Behavioral Medicine: Changing Health Lifestyles.* New York: Brunner/Mazel.

Marlatt, G. A. & Gordon, J. R. (1985). *Relapse Prevention: Treatment Strategies in the Treatment of the Addictive Behaviours.* New York: Guilford.

Marshall, W. L., Payne, K., Barbaree, H. E., & Eccles, A. (1991). Exhibitionists: Sexual preferences for exposing. *Behavior Research and Therapy, 29,* 37–40.

Mason, F. L. (1997). Fetishism: Psychopathology and theory. In D. R. Laws & W. O'Donohue (Eds.), *Sexual Deviance: Theory, Assessment, and Treatment* (pp. 75–93). New York: Guilford.

McCreary, C. P. (1975). Personality profiles of persons convicted of indecent exposure. *Journal of Clinical Psychology, 31,* 260–262.

McNally, R. J. & Lukach, B. M. (1991). Behavioral treatment of zoophilic exhibitionism. *Journal of Behavioral Therapy and Experimental Psychiatry, 22,* 281–284.

Money, J. (1984). Paraphilias: Phenomenology and classification. *American Journal of Psychotherapy, 38,* 164–179.

Moser, C. & Levitt, E. E. (1987). An exploratory-descriptive study of a sadomasochistically oriented sample. *Journal of Sex Research, 23,* 322–337.

Murphy, W. D. & Barbaree, H. E. (1994). *Assessments of Sex Offenders by Measures of Erectile Response: Psychometric Properties and Decision Making.* Brandon, VT: Safer Society Press.

O'Donohue, W. T. & Letourneau, E. (1992). The psychometric properties of the penile tumescence assessment of child molesters. *Journal of Psychopathology and Behavioral Assessment, 14,* 123–174.

Palace, E. M. & Gorzalka, B. B. (1992). Differential patterns of arousal in sexually functional and dysfunctional women: Physiological and subjective components of sexual response. *Archives of Sexual Behavior, 21,* 135–159.

Quinsey, V. L. & Lalumière, M. L. (1995). Evolutionary perspectives on sexual offending. *Sexual Abuse: A Journal of Research and Treatment, 7,* 301–315.

Quinsey, V. L., Rice, M. E., Harris, G. T., & Reid, K. S. (1993). The phylogenetic and ontogenetic development of sexual age preferences in males: Conceptual and measurement issues. In H. E. Barbaree, W. L. Marshall, & S. M. Hudson (Eds.), *The Juvenile Sex Offender* (pp. 143–163). New York: Guilford.

Rhoads, J. M. & Borjes, E. P. (1981). The incidence of exhibitionism in Guatemala and the United States. *British Journal of Psychiatry, 139,* 242–244.

Rice, M. E., Quinsey, V. L., & Harris, G. T. (1991). Sexual recidivism among child molesters released from a maximum security psychiatric institution. *Journal of Consulting and Clinical Psychology, 59,* 381–386.

Rosman, J. P. & Resnick, P. J. (1989). Sexual attraction to corpses: A psychiatric review of necrophilia. *Bulletin of the American Academy of Psychiatry and the Law, 17,* 153–163.

Sell, R. L., Wells, J. A., & Wypij, W. D. (1995). The prevalence of homosexual behavior and attraction in the United States, the United Kingdom and France: Results of national population-based samples. *Archives of Sexual Behavior, 24,* 235–248.

Seto, M. C. (1999). [Review of the book *Paedophiles and sexual offenses against children*]. *Archives of Sexual Behavior.*

Seto, M. C. & Barbaree, H. E. (1995). The role of alcohol in sexual aggression. *Clinical Psychology Review, 15,* 545–566.

Seto, M. C. & Barbaree, H. E. (1997). Sexual aggression as antisocial behavior: A developmental model. In D. Stoff, J. Breiling, & J. D. Maser (Eds.), *Handbook of Antisocial Behavior* (pp. 524–533). New York: Wiley.

Seto, M. C. & Kuban, M. (1996). Criterion-related validity of a phallometric test for paraphilic rape and sadism. *Behaviour Research and Therapy, 34,* 175–183.

Seto, M. C., Lalumière, M. L., & Kuban, M. (in press). *The Sexual Preferences of Incest Offenders.*

Simon, W. (1994). Deviance as history: The future of perversion. *Archives of Sexual Behavior, 23,* 1–20.

Smukler, A. J. & Schiebel, D. (1975). Personality characteristics of exhibitionists. *Diseases of the Nervous System, 36,* 600–603.

Spengler, A. (1977). Manifest sadomasochism in males: Results of an empirical study. *Archives of Sexual Behavior, 6,* 441–456.

Suppe, F. (1984). Classifying sexual disorders: The Diagnostic and Statistical Manual of the American Psychiatric Association. *Journal of Homosexuality,* 9–28.

Taylor, F. H. (1947). Observations on some cases of exhibitionism. *Journal of Mental Science, 93,* 681–683.

Templeman, T. L. & Stinnett, R. D. (1991). Patterns of sexual arousal and history in a "normal" sample of young men. *Archives of Sexual Behavior, 20,* 137–150.

Wise, T. N., Fagan, P. J., Schmidt, C. W., Ponticas, Y., & Costa, P. T. (1991). Personality and sexual functioning of tranvestic fetishists and other paraphilics. *Journal of Nervous and Mental Disease, 179,* 694–698.

Yalom, I. D. (1960). Aggression and forbiddenness in voyeurism. *Archives of General Psychiatry, 3,* 305–319.

Zuckerman, M. (1971). Physiological measures of sexual arousal in the human. *Psychological Bulletin, 75,* 297–329.

12 Homicide

MARC RIEDEL
Southern Illinois University

Description of the Law

Homicide is the "killing of one human being by the act, procurement, or omission of another" (Black, 1979, p. 661). The term *homicide* is neutral; that is, the killing of another is behavior without judgement as to its moral or legal quality. Figure 12.1 gives the major distinctions in homicide law.

Once charged with some manner of homicide, defendants may raise defenses based on justification or excuse to avoid criminal liability. Justifiable homicides are done under circumstances of duty or necessity, such as, killing of felons by police officers, self-defense, or legal executions.

Excusable homicides are those where the defendant argues he or she should not be held accountable under the circumstances. These killings involve misadventure or accident where there is some liability, but not sufficient to be criminal. Excusable homicides also include offenders who suffer from a mental disease or defect that prevented them from understanding the nature of the offense; that is, the insanity defense (Gardner & Manian, 1975).

Criminal Homicide

The Model Penal Code (MPC) was drafted to help courts and legislatures revise their penal codes to avoid redundancies and inconsistencies. Since its approval in 1962, it has led to a revision of the penal code in more than thirty states and has had a significant impact on the reasoning of state courts and the U.S. Supreme Court (Kadish & Schulhofer, 1989; Low, 1984).

According to the MPC (American Law Institute, 1962) "A person is guilty of criminal homicide if he purposely, knowingly, recklessly, or negligently causes the death of another human being" (p. 125). Criminal homicide is divided into manslaughter, murder, and negligent homicide (see Figure 12.1).

Criminal homicide is considered manslaughter when "a homicide which would otherwise be murder is committed under the influence of extreme mental or emotional disturbance for which there is reasonable explanation or excuse" (American Law Institute, 1962, p. 125). For example, abused women who kill their spouses are sometimes given the opportunity to plead guilty to manslaughter (Gillespie, 1989). Negligent homicide refers to kinds of negligence found in current state statutes where criminal liability occurs by automobile.

Murder is divided into three types: intent-to-kill, extreme recklessness, and felony murder. Intent-to-kill is the most familiar type of murder and refers to behavior in which there is intent and conduct that result in the death of another. Jones intends to kill Smith, points a loaded gun at him, shoots Smith in the heart and kills him. While intent-to-kill generally refers to affirmative behavior such as shooting a gun, a person may be charged where he or she failed to act and there was a clear duty to do so. For example, a parent who does nothing to save his child from certain death by an approaching train is guilty of an omission to act.

Murders manifesting extreme recklessness are committed under circumstances that manifest extreme indifference to the value of human life. Examples include shooting into a room full of people, driving an automobile at very high speed down a crowded street, or playing Russian roulette with another person.

The felony murder rule in many jurisdictions is controversial because of the large disparity between culpability required for murder and an individual's actual behavior when a murder is committed in the course of a rape or robbery. For

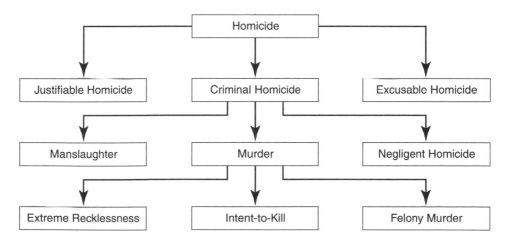

FIGURE 12.1   The Law of Homicide

instance, the driver of a getaway car may have no prior knowledge or role in the murder during a robbery, but he or she may be criminally liable under the felony murder rule.

The MPC abolishes the felony murder rule, but it does permit a *presumption* that the required degree of recklessness exists when a murder occurs during some specified felonies. Most states believe the felony murder rule has a deterrent value and those that have revised their penal code retain the felony murder rule in some form.

A Criminological Perspective

It is important to understand the legal character of criminal homicide because much of the social and psychological research draws on data gathered by law enforcement using legally based definitions. Homicide researchers also use data drawn from death certificates that rely on a medical definition of homicide. Fortunately, the definitions are similar, and data from the two sources agree well (Riedel, 1999).

Researchers attempt to understand and explain homicide using social science perspectives, which are different from legal definitions and procedures. But, if researchers are going to provide information useful to policy makers and practitioners, they have to use data rooted in legal classifications. On the other hand, homicide researchers need not be limited to legal classifications, if combining or modifying them in an explicit manner leads to new understandings.

For example, the legal distinction between aggravated assaults and murders is a dead victim. Thus, a person may be unconscious for several days as the result of a severe beating and the offender can be charged with aggravated assault, but if the victim dies, the charge is increased to murder.

While these two offenses carry very different penalties, behaviorally, the research shows few differences between the two events (Harries, 1989; Pittman & Handy, 1964). Rather than causally relevant characteristics of offenses, victims, and offenders, fortuitous factors play a role in distinguishing between the two offenses. These include such factors as faulty weapons or bad aim, type of weapons, and nearness to emergency medical facilities. The behavioral similarities, in other words, outweigh the differences. Given these circumstances, it makes more sense to study both offenses as a form of violence. While the resulting social science classification may have not legal standing, per se, it helps policy makers and practitioners because the original data are based in legal categories.

Second, researchers are interested in using data as close to the event as possible. This means using law enforcement sources or mortality statistics based on death certificates. The more homicides processed through various legal decisions and distinctions, the more selective the resulting set of cases may be. Hence, generalizations based on offenders convicted of murder may not be representative of all offenders—a problem that will be discussed in more detail later.

Finally, researchers are not consistent in their use of the terms, *murder* and *homicide,* as Wilbanks (1982) and Wolfgang (1958) have suggested. In this chapter we follow the practice of using terms favored by the cited source.

Trends in Criminal Homicide

The Uniform Crime Reporting Program of the FBI collects data on crime from police jurisdictions throughout the United States and publishes it in *Crime in the United States, Uniform Crime Reports (UCR)* (Federal Bureau of Investigation, 1996). In 1995, the *UCR* reported there were 21,597 murders and nonnegligent manslaughters in the United States. In order to make comparisons with other years, rates are used. Murder rates are constructed by dividing the annual number of murders by the annual population and multiplying the result by 100,000. Figure 12.2 gives murder rates in the United States from 1962 through 1994.

Murder rates peaked in 1980 at 10.2 per 100,000, with secondary peaks in 1974 and 1991 (9.8). The most recent (1995) available murder and nonnegligent manslaughter rate was 8.2. This represents a percent decline in rates of 16.3 from 1991 according to the FBI (1996).

The decline in murder rates nationally and in major urban areas has been proclaimed throughout the land and attributed to the policies of President Clinton's administration. Such claims should be viewed with caution. For example, during President Reagan's first term in office, there was a 19 percent decline in rates when 1984 is compared to 1981.

There are two substantive issues. First, murder rates fluctuate annually and for short periods for unknown reasons. Any of a variety of gratuitous claims can be supported by juxtaposing statistics. Second, attributing long-term shifts in murder rates to one or more causes is a difficult research endeavor. It requires, for example, controlling for the effect of competing causes and short-term fluctua-

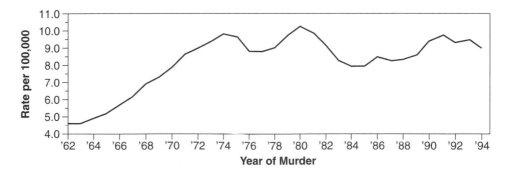

FIGURE 12.2   Murder Rates in the United States: 1962–1994

Source: Annual editions of the *Uniform Crime Reports*

tions, and a careful evaluation of data. Showing parallels between time series does not demonstrate causal relationships. Murder rates are determined by a host of demographic, cultural, and social factors of which the policies of a sitting President are a very small part.

Indeed, there is little room for optimism if homicide rates in the United States are compared with other advanced industrial countries. In a comparison of U.S. homicide rates to twelve other comparable countries from 1966 through 1988, homicide rates in the United States were two- to three-times higher than the next highest country, Finland (Riedel, 1995).

Transnationally, U.S. homicide rates are most comparable to rates found in developing countries (see Table 12.1). Table 12.1 shows that among 20 developing nations, the United States ranks ninth in homicide rates. Taking into account that many of these countries have unreliable statistical reporting systems and many

TABLE 12.1   Deaths by Homicide per 100,000 Population

Rank	Year	Country	Rate per 100,000
1	1984	El Salvador	40.4
2	1981	Columbia	37.4
3	1988	Switzerland	22.4
4	1986	Mexico	19.9
5	1988	Puerto Rico	17.5
6	1985	Bahamas	15.1
7	1986	Brazil	14.8
8	1983	Venezuela	12.9
9	1987	United States	8.5
10	1985	Barbados	7.5
11	1987	Panama	6.9
12	1986	Zimbabwe	6.9
13	1988	Northern Ireland	6.8
14	1987	U.S.S.R.	5.0
15	1985	Suriname	5.3
16	1983	Trinidad & Tobago	5.1
17	1985	Argentina	5.0
18	1985	Dominican Republic	4.8
19	1987	Ukraine	4.6
20	1987	Martinique	4.5

Source: Demographic Yearbook of the United Nations (1989)

homicides are not reported, it may be that the U.S. rate should be ranked lower. Nonetheless, the best available evidence suggests a homicide problem of substantial proportions.

Modernization theory is one explanation of transnational homicide rates. According to this theory, societies at different stages will show different patterns reflecting differences in criminal motivations, controls, and opportunities. A major prediction of modernization theory is that property crimes will be higher and violent crimes lower in modernized societies, while the reverse is true for developing countries (Shelley, 1981).

Gartner (1997) has suggested that sociocultural contexts are important in explaining crime. Societies conducive to low rates of violence have strong systems of informal social control and highly consensual normative systems, strong networks of communal obligation, and cultural orientations that discourage interpersonal aggression. These societies are characterized by collectivist rather than individualistic principles. While each of these theories receives some support, rigorous testing of the theories has been hampered by unreliable and inadequate statistics.

The Homicide Situation

It is useful to proceed by demolishing the myth that a homicide is the work of a scheming and diabolical killer who leaves the police with a dead body. This scenario usually includes a detective with an unprecedented amount of skill and intelligence who unravels the tangled threads that lead to an arrest. This does occur, but only in a very tiny proportion of homicides. On the contrary, it is ironic that the most serious of criminal offenses is frequently caused by the most trivial of events.

Many homicides originate in a dispute between two people who come to play the role of victim and offender. Such dispute-related homicides appear to be caused by any of a large number of small incidents. Arguments that begin over the ownership of a can of beer; flirting with a woman accompanying one of the participants; performance of a sports team; parking places; or whether one of the participants was deliberately jostled starts with insults and ends with a dead victim.

It is not the loss of a can of beer or parking place that is the cause, but what the behavior means to the involved parties. One of the actors takes exception to the behavior of another; he sees the other's behavior as an attempt to compel or prevent certain behavior or achieve a favorable self-image at the actor's expense. The actor counters with behavior to protect his or her own sense of self. This can take the form of refusing to do what is demanded, insisting that the person justify his or her demand, or retaliating with insults (Felson, 1993; Luckenbill, 1977).

This verbal exchange escalates in intensity with threats and counterthreats until physical violence occurs. Sometimes death results from the pushing, shoving, and hitting; more often one or the other produces a weapon to inflict a fatal wound. In many cases, it is the victim rather than the offender who first displays physical violence or uses a deadly weapon. In one study, 26 percent of the homicides were victim-precipitated (Wolfgang, 1958).

Situational components are also important in predatory violence (Felson, 1993), such as robbery murders. It is not clear to what extent murder is planned as part of the robbery and the extent to which it is the "outcome of events which somehow progressed beyond the degree of harm intended by the offender" (Block, 1977, p. 10). Generally, it is thought that robbery offenders are more interested in money or property than murder, but studies suggest that murder may be planned in some instances (Cook, 1980; Lorenz Dietz, 1983).

The circumstances of the following case suggest that robbery was intended, but homicide occurred because the offenders misinterpreted the victim's behavior.

> During the graveyard shift, two offenders drove up to the gas pumps to refuel their car. As they entered the gas station, one offender pointed a gun at the 19-year-old attendant and demanded money. As the attendant opened the cash drawer, the handle broke off. The action of putting the handle in his back pocket led the offender to believe the attendant was going for a gun. He shot and killed him. (Lundesgaarde, 1977, pp. 135–136)

But the preceding account does not leave us with a full understanding of homicide. For example, all of us have taken exception or been insulted by the careless remark of another. We may have hotly denied the content and implications of the remark and may have countered with another insult. But we do not kill. The interaction ends with nothing more serious than a slammed door or silence. What is the difference between the latter and those situations that end in homicide?

We lack a comprehensive explanation of homicide that will integrate the various factors that predispose offenders and victims to act in a lethal manner. Race/ethnicity, gender, age, weapons, drugs, and prior relationships are important, but an understanding of their role in relation to other factors is not complete. We can, however, examine these elements and how they, in some instances, interact to produce a lethal effect.

Race/Ethnicity, Gender, and Age

Membership in certain demographic categories put victims and offenders at greater risk of being both offenders and victims of homicide. In the United States, being a young African American male places the person in the highest risk category. Table 12.2 gives homicide rates for race, gender, and age groups. The table shows that in the age group 15–24 years, the homicide victimization rate for African American males (101.8) is more than eight-times higher than for white males (11.5). For African American females in the same age group, the homicide rate (17.4) is more than four-times higher than for white females (3.9) (Centers for Disease Control, 1992).

TABLE 12.2   Homicide Victimization Rates by Racial Groups, Gender, and Age, 1988

Age	African Americans			Whites		
	Male	*Female*	*Both*	*Male*	*Female*	*Both*
< 1	19.3	23.6	21.4	5.6	6.0	5.8
1–4	7.5	6.3	6.9	2.2	1.6	1.9
5–9	2.7	1.9	2.3	0.8	0.7	0.7
10–14	5.7	4.4	5.1	1.3	0.8	1.0
15–24	101.8	17.4	59.0	11.5	3.9	7.8
25–34	108.9	25.5	64.8	13.2	4.4	8.9
35–44	79.3	14.6	44.0	10.4	3.2	6.8
45–54	45.3	7.7	24.5	7.6	2.5	6.0
55–64	29.1	6.8	16.9	6.0	2.0	3.9
> 64	27.8	9.7	16.9	4.2	2.6	3.3
Total	58.1	13.2	34.4	7.9	2.9	5.3

Source: CDC, Homicide Surveillance (1992)

The results presented in Table 12.2 have been generally confirmed using FBI statistics on murder and nonnegligent manslaughter at least since the 1940s. The ranking of rates for race and gender groups begins with African American males being highest by a wide margin, followed by African American females, which are slightly higher than white males. The lowest murder rates are for white females (Wilbanks, 1982).

Homicides involving African American and white females predominantly involve family-related situations. Both groups are generally victimized by spouses and lovers.

Most homicides involve victims and offenders of the same race. According to FBI statistics, 86 percent of white victims and 93 percent of African American victims are slain by members of the same racial group (Reiss & Roth, 1993).

It is also important to note in Table 12.2 that homicide rates for African American males and females remain higher throughout their life span. The lifetime risk of being an African American male homicide victim in 1987 is 4.16 per 100. For African American females, it is 1.02 per 100. For white males, it is 0.46 per 100, and for white females, it is 0.26 per 100. Thus, while the risk of homicide victimization is extremely high for young African American males, it is very high for African American males of *all* ages (Reiss & Roth, 1993).

Numbers in general, and rates in particular, are sometimes difficult to put in an easily understood context. To say that the overall age-adjusted homicide rate in

1989 for African American males (61.5) is more than seven-times the rate (8.1) of white males does not convey much meaning to white students, primarily because they lack any personal knowledge or experience of homicide. Many African American students, on the other hand, are all too aware of the painful reality.

To put it in context, many white students have known someone who has been killed in a motor vehicle accident. The white male motor vehicle death rate is 26.8. If the white students were African American, it is likely that they would know of more than one homicide, because the rate (61.5) is more than twice the rate for motor vehicle accidents (Reiss & Roth, 1993).

Latino Homicides

What is ignored, until comparatively recently, is the epidemiology of Latino homicides. Latino homicides are not distinguished in racial classifications because they are an ethnic, not a racial category. Despite the sparse research, Latino homicides are important to understand for several reasons.

There has been a dramatic increase in the Latino population in recent decades. In the past 30 years, the largest number of immigrants have Hispanic backgrounds. The largest number have come from Mexico and are concentrated in California and Texas (Kennedy, 1996). Recent government reports indicate that by 2006, Latinos will be the largest minority population, surpassing the African American population (Martinez, 1997). Because of their increasing size and influence, it is important to understand Latino homicide patterns and how they differ from white and African American patterns.

Amounts of Latino homicide victimization tend to be intermediate between whites and African Americans. In five southwestern states (Arizona, California, Colorado, New Mexico, Texas) for 1977–1982, whites had a rate of 7.9 per 100,000; Hispanics followed with a rate of 21.6; while African Americans were highest with a rate of 46.0 (Centers for Disease Control, 1986). In Chicago for 1989, Block (1993) reports whites and other males had a rate of 10.3, followed by 43.9 for Latino males, and 74.2 per 100,000 for African American males. Finally, Martinez (1997) notes that whites comprised 10 percent of the population in Miami from 1990 through 1995 and committed 7 percent of the homicides. Latinos were almost 63 percent of the population, but committed 38 percent of the homicides. African Americans were 27 percent of the population and committed 56 percent of the homicides.

Drawing on the author's unpublished research, there were 15,186 murders reported in Los Angeles County from 1987 through 1995. During that period, there were 7,111 Latino; 5,358 African American; 1,995 white; and 678 murder victims of other race/ethnic groups. There were 44 cases where race/ethnic identification was missing. While this is a large number of Latino murders, when the risk of victimization is taken into account by looking at variations in the size of the group population, the picture changes dramatically as Figure 12.3 shows. Thus, when annual murder rates are used, it is apparent that African Americans continue to be at greatest risk, followed by Latinos, and white victims.

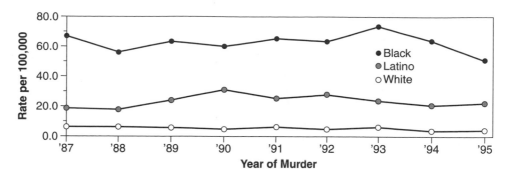

FIGURE 12.3   Race/Ethnic-Specific Murder Rates

There are two other characteristics of Latino homicides. First, as Martinez (1997) suggests, Latino female victimization is similar to that of whites. Using the Los Angeles County data, the mean race/ethnic gender-specific rates were 3.6 for white females, 5.0 for Latino females, and 19.6 for African American females.

Second, the rates of victimization among older age categories are similar for whites and Latinos. Race/ethnic age-specific rates (65 to 75 years) for whites was 4.1, for Latinos, it was 4.3, and for African Americans, it was 24.6.

Alcohol and Psychoactive Drugs

The use of alcohol is among the most important contributing factors to homicide situations. Goode (1993) puts it in unequivocal terms:

> Of all drugs, nationally, internationally, and cross-culturally, alcohol is *by far* the one most likely to be implicated in violent crimes. The empirical evidence linking alcohol and violence is overwhelming. More individuals who commit violent offenses are under the influence of alcohol than of any other single drug. The research supports a strong association between alcohol consumption and homicide. (p. 130)

Goodman and his colleagues (1986) found that 46 percent of murder victims surveyed in Los Angeles had a detectable alcohol level, and 30 percent had a blood-alcohol level of 0.10 or above. Block, Block, Wilson, and Daly (1990) found that the prevalence of alcohol use by victim or offender in Chicago homicides from 1988 through 1989 varied between 18 and 39 percent.

Chronic drinking is also associated with homicide and crimes of violence (Collins, 1986). Greenberg (1981) found that alcoholism had been diagnosed in 20 to 40 percent of convicted murderers.

Psychoactive Drugs

Illegal psychoactive drug use is implicated in a substantial share of urban homicides. National estimates of drug-related homicides range between 8 and 10 percent (Reiss & Roth, 1993).

The research seems most consistent about the effects of cocaine and marijuana. Inciardi (1989) compared homicide trends and cocaine arrests in six U.S. cities and found no simple aggregate relationships between the two. Chronic use of cocaine in powdered or smokable forms sometimes leads to mental states in which aggressive and violent behavior is expressed. One hospital study showed that 6 percent of all cocaine-related emergency admissions involved violent behavior; another showed no difference in the frequency of violence between institutionalized cocaine users and other inpatients (Reiss & Roth, 1993). Goldstein, Brownstein, Ryan, and Bellucci (1989) concluded that homicides arising from the pharmacological effects of cocaine are rare.

The effect of marijuana on violent crime is summarized by the following paragraph:

> During the past two decades, five major scientific reviews of the research literature have concluded that violent human behavior is either decreased or unaffected by cannabis use. Similarly, studies of many animal species demonstrate that acute doses of THC, the psychoactive ingredient in marijuana, promote submissive and flight responses and, at least in large doses, inhibit attack and threat behavior. These effects persist during chronic administration to animals. (Reiss & Roth, 1993, p. 195)

Studies of prevalence and dosage do not tell the whole story. Drug use and its violent effects are due to individual differences such as a long-term pattern of drug use, dosage levels, and even genetic mechanisms. Further, such differences interact with group, social, and cultural factors in ways that are not well understood with the most familiar drug—alcohol. We have barely begun to understand the intricate interrelationships that characterize other drugs and homicide.

Economic and Systemic Violence

The process of obtaining and distributing illegal drugs makes possible two kinds of violence. The first, economic violence, occurs when some drug users obtain money to buy drugs by robberies. The second, systemic violence, occurs in disputes over marketing practices. Since illegal markets are not subject to legal dispute resolution mechanisms, violence may result (Goldstein et al., 1989).

While violence is clearly part of obtaining money to buy drugs, the type of violence is primarily robbery. Burglaries are also frequent and can become violent if the burglar encounters an occupant of the property. Heroin users prefer nonviolent alternatives such as burglaries. However, robbery by heroin users is common (Blumstein, Cohen, Roth, & Visher, 1986).

Two important forms of systemic violence are related to organizations and transactions. Processing, importing, and distributing illegal drugs is a complicated organizational task. Violence and homicide is used to enforce organizational rules such as not using drugs while selling or trafficking; resolving territorial disputes; punishing informers; protecting sellers; and battling police.

Transaction-related violence is used in robberies of drugs and money from sellers; resolving disputes over the quantity or quality; and resolving disputes over how much money low-level sellers pay higher-level sellers (Reiss & Roth, 1993). Goldstein (1989) found that robberies of dealers and assaults to collect debts were the most common.

Firearms and Homicide

Firearms are the most common weapons used in homicide; about 60 percent involve firearms. No precise count of the number of firearms owned in the United States is available; the most recent estimate by the Bureau of Alcohol, Tobacco, and Firearms (1991) places the number of firearms at 200 million. The percent of all households owning a firearm has remained stable at about 50 percent for at least three decades. However, the fraction owning handguns has increased from 13 percent in 1959 to 24 percent in 1978, where it has remained stable (Bureau of Justice Statistics, 1989).

The risk of homicide victimization by gun is very high for adolescents, especially African American males. The gun homicide rate in 1988 was 8 per 100,000 for teenagers and 6 per 100,000 for the total population. For African American males ages 15 to 19 years, the firearms homicide death rate was 83.4, while for white males in the same age range, it was 7.5 per 100,000 (Reiss & Roth, 1993).

The pervasiveness of firearms and their disproportionate use by teenagers have been studied by Sheley and Wright (1995). They surveyed 758 male students in 10 inner-city high schools and 835 male inmates in 6 correctional institutions in 4 states. The more important findings from the survey of males in inner city schools are included in the text following.

First, the social environment of the students was such that 37 percent had males in their families who carried guns; 42 percent had friends who carried guns. Second, when the student sample was asked if it was okay to shoot someone, 10 percent agreed if it was to get something they wanted. The percentages were higher if the person was not from their neighborhood, injured, or insulted them.

Third, 12 percent of the student sample carried a gun all or most of the time. Automatic and semiautomatic sidearms and large-caliber revolvers were the weapons of preference. Students preferred weapons that were well-made, accurate, easy to shoot, and not easily traced; "Saturday Night Specials" play a very small role in teenage use of firearms.

Fourth, 41 percent of the students felt that they could obtain a gun with almost no trouble. Most felt they could buy one from family or friends; only 28 percent of the students would purchase one from a gunshop. Where gunshop purchases were made, teenagers typically have someone over 21 years old make the purchase for them.

What is most amazing was the cost of handguns. For the majority (53%) of instances reported by students, the cost of a handgun was between $50 and $100, which is generally cheaper than legally purchased weapons. From the perspective of supply and demand, the low price indicated an ample supply of handguns, many of which were stolen. Given this informal network of people who can provide firearms, legislation and regulation of legal firearms is likely to have little effect.

Finally, while there was an association between guns, drug dealing, and violent crime, the more important finding was that most of the students purchased guns to protect themselves (Sheley & Wright, 1995). Among students who were involved in drug dealing, guns are obtained because they are the tools of the trade. This results in an "arms race" in which other teenagers feel compelled to carry weapons for self-protection. The presence of lethal weapons leads to a major escalation of violence that frequently characterizes teenage males (Blumstein, 1995).

Relationships: Friends and Gangs

It is frequently said that the average person stands a greater chance of being killed by someone they know than a stranger. This is true—with a major qualification.

According to the *UCR* (Federal Bureau of Investigation, 1996), 11.6 percent of murders in 1995 involved family members and 33.9 percent involved friends, acquaintances, and such relationships as boyfriend, employee, neighbor, and so on; thus, 45.5 percent of murder victims had a prior relationship with their offenders. By comparison, 15.1 percent of the victims were strangers to their offenders.

However, information on victim/offender relationships was missing for 39.4 percent of murders. Most of these are offenses for which no offender has been arrested (Riedel & Rinehart, 1996). Because it is not known what types of relationships are contained in cases with missing data, the claim that we are more likely to be killed by someone known to us is limited to what is known about victim/offender relationships.

The presence in a situation of third parties whose good opinion is valued by the actors contributes to a lethal outcome. Such third parties as friends, spouses, and gang members more frequently encourage violence than mediate or reduce it. When the initiating insult represents an attack on male identities, the presence of other male third parties makes the violence more severe (Felson, 1978; Felson, Ribner, & Siegel, 1984; Felson & Steadman, 1983).

But the importance of peer influence extends beyond the immediate situation with respect to gangs and motivation for homicide. Determining the number of gang homicides presents a problem, because counting rules depend on the definition of a gang and gang involvement. Law-enforcement agencies take two approaches.

Los Angeles follows a broad gang-member definition: A gang homicide is one in which either victims or offenders are gang members. Chicago law enforcement, on the other hand, uses a narrower gang-motive definition in that the homicide is a direct link to gang function. There must be some positive evidence that gang activity or membership was the motive for the encounter. Examples include quarrels over territory, retaliation, recruitment, and "representing" (graffiti, shouting gang slogans, wearing gang colors). The difference is that a killing of a convenience store clerk by a gang member during a robbery would be a gang homicide in Los Angeles, but may not be in Chicago (Maxson & Klein, 1996).

The difference in definition makes a difference in the number of gangs. Maxson and Klein (1996) note that using the Los Angeles gang-member definition, 44 percent of all homicides occurring in the city in 1994 were gang homicides. In Chicago for the same year, using the gang-motive definition, 32 percent of all homicides were gang related.

Definitions make a difference in terms of *prevalence*, because the number of gang homicides plays a powerful role in motivating public opinion and resources; an equally important question is whether the two definitions make a difference in the *nature* of gang homicide. Comparisons of the two definitions to nongang homicide in Los Angeles using a large number of variables related to homicides indicate few differences, at least at the bivariate level. In other words, gang-member or gang-motive homicides are more similar to each other than to nongang homicides.

One characteristic that distinguishes gang from nongang homicide is the presence of guns. Among gang homicides in Los Angeles, 95 percent involved firearms; among nongang homicides, 75 percent involved firearms. In addition, male victims (90% versus 77%) and male offenders (9% versus 83%) are more prevalent in gang homicides than nongang homicides. The mean ages of victims (24.2 versus 34.4 years) and offenders (20.5 versus 31.3 years) are younger for gang homicides than for nongang homicides (Maxson, 1997).

While there are differences among gangs, the research does not support media reports of high levels of drug-motivated homicides among gangs. Meehan and O'Carroll (1995) found that 5 percent of gang-motivated homicides in Los Angeles involved narcotics, compared with 23 percent for other homicides. Just 2.2 percent of Chicago street gang-related homicides between 1965 and 1974 involved drug motives (Block, Christakos, Jacob, & Przybylski, 1995). At least with respect to what is found in law-enforcement records, drug-related homicides do not occur with a high frequency among gangs.

Relationships: Intimate Partners and Family

Most prior relationships between victims and offenders involve limited knowledge of another: *acquaintances* are the single largest category of victim/offender relationships tabulated by the FBI. Among gang homicides, victim and offender may know little more than the other is a member of an opposing gang.

Intimate partner and family homicides are different; they involve continuing relationships, and repeated violent victimization commonly occurs before the actual homicide. For example, Browne (1987), in her classic study of women who kill, documents frequent serious violent acts, many of which resulted in permanent injury to the woman, stretching over several years before the actual killing.

Intervention and research are hampered, because victims are relatively powerless and vulnerable in comparison to offenders. This means that offenders can threaten victims with additional violence if incidents are disclosed to others. Victims may also refrain from disclosure, anticipating stigmatization and denigration. Finally, many of these acts occur in private places where they are not visible to others and are less likely to be detected and reported to police.

There are relatively few homicide victims reported among young children. For 1995, the *UCR* reported that newborns, infants, and children ages 1 through 4 years are more frequently (3%) the victims of homicide than children ages 5 through 8 years (0.5%). Infants and small children are more likely to be killed by their mothers than their fathers and the risk of homicide for children less than 5 years is greater for male than female children (Federal Bureau of Investigation, 1996; Reiss & Roth, 1993).

Violence between family members and intimate partners is a serious problem, but family-related homicides, primarily homicides involving spouses, have been declining (Browne & Williams, 1993). According to the *UCR*, in 1977, family-related homicides made up 19.4 percent of all homicides; they have shown a decline over the years to 1995 where they make up 11.6 percent.

Rosenfeld (1997) examined the question further by studying intimate partner homicides. Marital intimate partners are those victims who have been married, separated, or divorced to their offenders, and those in a common-law relationship. Nonmarital intimate relationships includes boyfriends, ex-boyfriends, girlfriends, and ex-girlfriends.

Using homicide data from St. Louis, Rosenfeld found that total intimate partner homicide rates declined for African American females from 1970 to 1990. African American males, white males, and white females showed a decline from 1980.

Marital intimate homicide rates declined for African American males and females from 1970 to 1990 and for white males and females from 1980. Nonmarital intimate partner homicide rates decreased for all race and gender groups from 1980 to 1990.

Much of the decline in intimate partner homicide is a consequence of changes in marriage patterns among the young adult population that are at greatest risk for homicide victimization. In 1970, 55 percent of U.S. males between ages 20 and 24 years had never married; by 1992, this percentage had increased to 80 percent. Rosenfeld (1997) reports a decrease in percent married in St. Louis, especially among African Americans. Between 1970 and 1990, the percent of African American women never married dropped from 58 percent to 43 percent. With the increase in relationships that are not legally binding (marriage), intimate partners in conflict simply leave the relationship rather than remain and escalate it to the point of murder.

There are two additional factors that may contribute to a decline in intimate partner homicides. First, in the last few decades, there has been a shift away from the view that murders, particularly those between intimates, are crimes that cannot be prevented. Nothing can be done, it was said, when a man or woman suddenly kills their intimate partner "for no apparent reason." What is slowly sifting into public consciousness is the recognition that few spouses or intimate partners kill "for no apparent reason." The public is becoming increasingly aware that intimate partner homicides are frequently the culmination of a long history of extremely violent abuse. Murders are the result of battering or a last desperate attempt by abused women to free themselves of their tormentor (Gillespie, 1989). This awareness shifts the burden of social concern to the prevention of violence preceding the homicide. Doing something to prevent less serious forms of violence may also contribute to preventing more lethal forms.

Second, consensus about norms and values in a society are typically given formal shape and substance by law. For example, the immorality of murder is given expression by legislation, criminal justice processes, and penal sanctions. But legal formalization can also strengthens norms. With changes in legislation, wife battering is no longer a minor irritant for police and the source of gossip, but a crime with substantial penalties.

There has been a variety of legislative changes besides making abuse a criminal offense. These include making restraining orders more readily available; creating statutes permitting warrantless arrests based on probable cause in domestic violence cases; providing funds for family violence shelters; and developing abuse programs that offer counseling (Browne & Williams, 1989). While not eliminating the problem of domestic violence, the latter steps may contribute to preventing its most serious expression.

Preventing Homicides and Violence

Punishment and Deterrence

The obvious popular approach to reducing number of homicides is to arrest, convict, incarcerate, and/or impose the death penalty. While that approach is politically popular, by and large, it is ineffective.

No offender is arrested for more than one-third of murders and nonnegligent manslaughters in the United States. When police arrest someone for murder, it is called "clearing the offense by arrest." Jurisdictions routinely compute clearance rates or percentages by dividing the number of murders per year by the number cleared. Unfortunately, the clearance rate in the United States has been declining steadily since 1961, as Figure 12.4 shows. Except for an increase in 1983, arrest clearances for murder and nonnegligent manslaughter have declined from 93 percent in 1961, to 65 percent in 1995.

Deterrence is divided into general and specific deterrence. General deterrence occurs when a punishment applied to one offender has the effect of preventing others from committing the same act, because they fear the punishment they have seen applied. Specific deterrence refers to the effect the punishment has on the offender: It prevents him or her from committing crimes again.

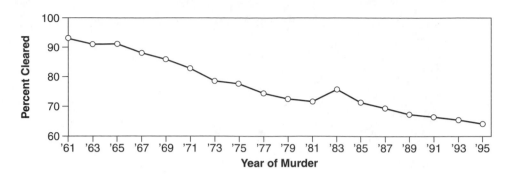

FIGURE 12.4 Percent Murders Cleared by Arrest

Source: Annual editions of *Uniform Crime Reports*

It is difficult to argue that arrests have either a specific or general deterrent effect when over one-third of murder offenders are not arrested. Research evaluating changes in policing practices and procedures have shown modest and short-term effects. Variations in police clearances have been related to number of police (Bottomley & Pease, 1986); workload, skills, training, and police-community relations (Greenwood & Petersilia, 1975); education level, age, and experience of the officers (Bozza, 1973); the extent of follow-up investigations (Bynum, Cordner, & Greene, 1982); information-processing technology (Skogan & Antunes, 1979); and the relative clearance effectiveness of patrol officers and detectives (Eck, 1992).

More research is needed to decide what elements of homicides are most important in clearing an offense (Cardarelli & Cavanagh, 1992). Because community participation is essential in arrest clearances, there is also a need to better understand the conditions under which citizens are willing to cooperate with police (Riedel, 1994).

Further winnowing of the number of offenders takes place after arrest. Persons arrested for a killing may or may not be charged with murder, those charged may plead guilty to a less serious charge (plea bargain) or acquitted, and those convicted may or may not be incarcerated in state institutions.

Greenwood (1982) tracked 1,813 homicide arrests in California through the system to final disposition. Of the 1,813 arrests for homicide, 848 (46%) were sentenced to state institutions. Of course, the latter does not include uncleared offenses. If we take 100 hypothetical murder cases, take into account that there will be only 65 arrests, and use Greenwood's conditional percentages at each stage, 30 of the offenders will be sent to state institutions. Other research indicates a much lower proportion of incarcerated offenders. Is it reasonable to believe that a punishment applied to less than one-third of the offenders has a general deterrent effect?

The Death Penalty.   A much smaller percent of those incarcerated is sentenced to death. But, the research on the death penalty consistently shows little deterrent effect. It appears that prison sentences are more effective with murder offenders than with other kinds of violent offenders. For 6,835 males released on parole, Sellin (1980) found only 21 (0.3%) were returned because they had committed another murder. These persons were less likely to commit murder while on parole than persons originally sentenced for armed robbery, forcible, or aggravated assault.

The most persistent argument advanced for the death penalty is that it is a specific deterrent: Once the offender is executed, it is certain that he or she will not commit any additional homicides. But would this offender have committed more if he or she had been sentenced to life and eventually released? One way to answer that question is to examine the behavior of offenders who were sentenced to death, but allowed to live.

In 1972, the U.S. Supreme Court concluded in *Furman v. Georgia* (408 U.S. 238) that the existing form of the death penalty was unconstitutional. As a result, over 600 offenders under sentence of death were resentenced. Some of these offenders were eventually released on parole.

In a study of 47 Texas offenders taken off death row by *Furman,* none was implicated in a prison homicide. Among those released into the community, only one offender committed another murder (Marquart & Sorenson, 1988). In another study of 272 *Furman* offenders, there were two additional murders of correctional workers and one of an inmate. Among the 185 offenders released on parole, there were three additional murders. Whether the six additional murders represent an acceptable level of risk requires comparison to the reincarceration records of comparable offenders not sentenced to death. From that perspective, the imposition of the death penalty appears *not* to prevent significantly more murders (Vito, Koester, & Wilson, 1991).

Preventing Violence

Another approach focuses on the broader problem of preventing violent behavior rather than homicides. There are two reasons that support that approach. First, from our early description of homicide situations, it is clear that it takes two or more people to perform the interaction sequence that leads to homicide. Homicides do not occur unless there are others who respond aggressively to the insult. When the potential victim is nonresponsive or leaves the setting, homicides do not occur. This suggests that we need to examine what are the social and cultural commonalities of victims and offenders that lead them to escalate conflicts to a violent end.

Second, many homicide offenders have a prior record of violent behavior. There are people who commit homicide with no previous record of violence. For example, Magargee (1973) noted that overcontrolled persons may suddenly erupt in a violent episode. But we have noted that many spousal killings involve a record of prior violence; this is true for other homicides as well. This suggests that we need to examine developmental patterns that contribute to violence.

Social and Cultural Factors.   Homicide victims and offenders are not randomly distributed through the population. Describing social and demographic variables that contribute to homicide shows what groups and strata in society are most at risk of homicide. In the United States, the highest risk is found among young African American males and females and Latino males. Knowing something about the social and economic conditions faced by young people in these categories leads to explanations and prevention programs.

The extent of poverty, racism, lack of opportunity in inner-city neighborhoods and prevention programs has been discussed elsewhere (Reiss & Roth, 1993). In their study of gun ownership and use in inner-city neighborhoods, Sheley and Wright (1995) paint a compelling picture of inner-city life, in which gun ownership seems a very reasonable response to the dangerous conditions of daily life.

There is much talk these days about family values and the importance of family in socializing children against the use of violence. What seems to be forgotten is that many families function in communities and neighborhoods that undermine their efforts to inculcate values opposing violence. The presence of gangs, availability of drugs and guns, and daily exposure to violence in the neighborhood mean that many families in inner-city neighborhoods face insuperable difficulties in raising children to avoid violent victimization.

For example, I became very good friends with a well-educated professional African American woman who came from a very close family in an inner-city neighborhood of Houston. Over the years, I met her family and many people with whom she had grown up. Very frequently, when I would ask her about the background of the people I met, she would relate stories of violence and crime: one or both parents became drug addicts, their mother killed their father, brothers were imprisoned for murders or robberies, sisters were prostitutes, and so on. I once ask her if she knew any conventional people; that is, people who grew up in families in which the most traumatic event was getting the mumps! She said she did not, which says a great deal about the impact of neighborhood and community. Unfortunately, this anecdote has a sadder ending: When she moved to Houston from Carbondale to take another job, she was stabbed to death by a 15-year-old African American male during the course of a burglary.

Criminologists have suggested that inner-city conditions generate a shared cluster of beliefs about the use of violence. These beliefs describe a subculture of violence that is most prevalent among young males, African Americans, and lower-income persons. Subcultural beliefs predispose actors to respond to certain behaviors, such as insults, with force. Because they believe that violence is a way of solving interpersonal problems, they are more likely to escalate a verbal conflict and use violence to resolve the dispute (Wolfgang & Ferracuti, 1967).

Developmental Factors.   There is a significant relationship between childhood aggression and violence: Aggressive children tend to become violent teenagers and violent adults. Farrington (1991) has shown that aggressive children at ages 8 to 10 years and 12 to 14 years tended to have later convictions for violence and tend to be violent at age 32. Predictors and correlates of violence include low IQ, low school attainment, high impulsivity, and poor concentration. Family factors include low income, large family size, parents with criminal convictions, harsh discipline, poor supervision, and parental separations (Farrington, 1989).

Cognitive-behavioral theories have resulted in prevention programs. Huesmann and Eron (1989) have developed a cognitive model of aggression development in which the expression of aggression is controlled by *scripts* learned during early development. These scripts suggest what events are about to occur, the expected reaction, and what the outcome will be. These scripts are retrieved with appropriate environmental cues and guide behavior. In this theory, a repeatedly aggressive child is one who consistently retrieves and uses aggressive scripts which are learned, in part, from the behavior of parents.

The prevention of violence focuses on changing these scripts to foster nonviolence. Social skills training can have positive effects in changing aggressive behavior in children. The Earlscourt Social Skills Group Program attempted to improve self-control and social skills of aggressive children. The program teaches such social skills as problem solving, knowing your feelings, using self-control, responding to teasing, and keeping out of fights. An evaluation of the program showed improvement in dealing with aggression, and these improvements were maintained over a three-month follow-up (Pepler, King, & Byrd, 1991).

Poor parental training techniques predict delinquency and may have an effect in reducing violence. Parental intervention programs, aimed at families with delinquent and predelinquent children, focus on noticing what the child is doing; monitoring his or her behavior over long periods; clearly stating and standing by house rules; making rewards and punishment consistently contingent on behavior; and negotiating disagreements so that conflicts and crises do not escalate (Reiss & Roth, 1993). Many parent training programs have been evaluated and have been shown to be effective in reducing aggression in children (Kazdin, 1985).

Summary

This chapter has examined homicide law and how criminologists use information gathered by the criminal justice process to better understand the phenomena. Based on this research and theories, the most important conclusions are described in the text following.

First, the United States has an extremely high homicide rate when compared with comparable industrialized countries. As has been shown, homicide rates are two- to three-times higher than Finland, the next highest, and are most comparable to third-world countries.

Second, homicide is a situational crime. Whether we consider killings between spouses, family members, or robbery murders, there is a conflict based on insults or some other form of miscommunication, which escalates to violence and, on occasion, a lethal outcome.

Third, there is a large number of characteristics of victims, offenders, and situations that increase the risk of a violent outcome. Demographically, homicide is clearly an offense of young males, particularly African American males. Women are involved in much smaller numbers and they tend to be involved in family-related conflicts. Alcohol is the most prevalent drug present in a homicide. Gang membership contributes to homicide, although drug transactions are not generally an important part of the picture. Easy access and the prevalence of firearms contributes to the lethality of the situation, especially in areas where adolescents perceive that carrying firearms is a necessary form of protection. Finally, a subculture of beliefs in which violence is seen as a way of resolving interpersonal conflicts interacts with other characteristics to make violence a prominent feature of U.S. society.

Can homicides be prevented? The view of this author is that they can. The decline in spousal killings over the past few decades suggests that what was once viewed as a private matter between intimate partners is susceptible to modification by a program of legislation, education, and providing resources to victims. What seems to offer the greatest promise for reducing other kinds of violence are social skills programs that focus on showing young people how conflicts can be reduced and resolved without violence.

Even assuming that social skills programs to reduce violence are successful beyond what can be demonstrated currently, harsher sanctions such as prison terms will still be necessary. Given the evolutionary and historical capacity for violence of all types expressed by humans, the best we may be able to do is make prisons the last alternative for violence. But that would be a significant improvement over the present where it is seen as the first.

REFERENCES

American Law Institute. (1962). *Model Penal Code: Proposed Official Draft*. Philadelphia: American Law Institute.

Black, H. C. (1979). *Black's Law Dictionary* (5th ed.). St. Paul, MN: West.

Block, C. R. (1993). Lethal violence in the Chicago Latino community. In A. V. Wilson (Ed.), *Homicide: The Victim/Offender Connection* (pp. 267–342). Cincinnati: Anderson.

Block, C. R., Block, R. L., Wilson, M., & Daly, M. (1990). *Chicago Homicide from the Sixties to the Nineties: Have Patterns of Lethal Violence Changed?* Paper presented at the American Society of Criminology, Baltimore, MD.

Block, C. R., Christakos, A., Jacob, A. P., & Przybylski, R. (1995). *Street Gangs and Crime: Patterns and Trends in Chicago (Research Bulletin)*. Chicago: Illinois Criminal Justice Information Authority.

Block, R. (1977). *Violent Crime: Environment, Interaction and Death*. Lexington, MA: Lexington.

Blumstein, A. (1995). Youth violence, guns, and the illicit drug industry. *Journal of Criminal Law and Criminology, 86*, 10–36.

Blumstein, A. J., Cohen, J., Roth, J., & Visher, C. (Eds.) (1986). *Criminal Careers and "Career Criminals."* Washington, DC: National Academy.

Bottomley, K. & Pease, K. (1986). *Crime and Punishment: Interpreting the Data*. Philadelphia: Open University Press.

Bozza, C. M. (1973). Motivations guiding policemen in the arrest process. *Journal of Police Science and Administration, 1*, 468–476.

Browne, A. (1987). *When Battered Women Kill*. New York: Free Press.

Browne, A. & Williams, K. R. (1989). Exploring the effect of resource availability and the likelihood of female-perpetrated homicides. *Law and Society Review, 23*, 75–94.

Browne, A. & Williams, K. R. (1993). Gender, intimacy, and lethal violence. *Gender and Society, 7*, 78–98.

Bureau of Alcohol, Tobacco, and Firearms. (1991, May 22). How many guns? *ATF News* (Press Release).

Bureau of Justice Statistics. (1989). *Criminal Victimization in the United States, 1987*. Washington, DC: Bureau of Justice Statistics.

Bynum, T. S., Cordner, G. W., & Greene, J. R. (1982). Victim and offense characteristics. *Criminology, 20,* 301–318.

Cardarelli, A. P. & Cavanagh, D. (1992). *Uncleared Homicides in the United States: An Exploratory Study of Trends and Patterns.* Paper presented at the American Society of Criminology, New Orleans, LA.

Centers for Disease Control. (1986). *Homicide Surveillance: High-Risk Racial and Ethnic Groups— Blacks and Hispanics, 1970–1983.* Atlanta: Center for Environmental Health and Injury Control.

Centers for Disease Control. (1992). Homicide surveillance. *Surveillance Summaries, Morbidity and Mortality Weekly Report, 41* (No. SS-3), pp. 1–33.

Collins, J. J. (1986). The relationship of problem drinking to individual offending sequences. In A. Blumstein, J. Cohen, J. A. Roth, & C. A. Visher (Eds.), *Criminal Careers and "Career Criminals"* (Vol. 2). Washington, DC: National Academy.

Cook, P. J. (1980). Reducing injury and death rates in robbery. *Policy Analysis, 6,* 21–45.

Eck, J. E. (1992). Criminal investigation. In G. W. Cordner & D. C. Hale (Eds.), *What Works in Policing?* (pp. 19–34). Cincinnati: Anderson.

Farrington, D. P. (1989). Early predictors of adolescent aggression and adult violence. *Violence and Victims, 4,* 79–100.

Farrington, D. P. (1991). Childhood aggression and adult violence: Early precursors and later-life outcomes. In D. J. Pepler & K. H. Rubin (Eds.), *The Development and Treatment of Childhood Aggression* (pp. 5–29). Hillsdale, NJ: Erlbaum.

Federal Bureau of Investigation. (1996). *Crime in the United States: 1995 Uniform Crime Reports.* Washington, DC: U.S. Government Printing Office.

Felson, R. (1978). Aggression as impression management. *Social Psychology, 41,* 205–213.

Felson, R. B. (1993). Predatory and dispute-related violence: A social interactionist approach. In R. V. Clarke & M. Felson (Eds.), *Routine Activity and Rational Choice* (Vol. 5, pp. 103–125). New Brunswick, NJ: Transaction.

Felson, R. B., Ribner, S. A., & Siegel, M. S. (1984). Age and the effect of third parties during criminal violence. *Sociology and Social Research, 68,* 452–462.

Felson, R. B. & Steadman, H. J. (1983). Situational factors in disputes leading to criminal violence. *Criminology: An Interdisciplinary Journal, 21,* 59–74.

Gardner, T. J. & Manian, V. (1975). *Criminal Law: Principles, Cases, and Readings.* St. Paul, MN: West.

Gartner, R. (1997). Crime: Variations across cultures and nations. In C. Ember & M. Ember (Eds.), *Cross-Cultural Research for Social Science.* Englewood Cliffs, NJ: Prentice Hall.

Gillespie, C. K. (1989). *Justifiable Homicide: Battered Women, Self-Defense, and the Law.* Columbus: Ohio State University Press.

Goldstein, P. J., Brownstein, H. H., Ryan, P. J., & Bellucci, P. A. (1989). Crack and homicide in New York City, 1988: A conceptually based event analysis. *Contemporary Drug Problems, 16,* 651–687.

Goode, E. (1993). *Drugs in American Society* (4th ed.). New York: McGraw Hill.

Goodman, R. A., Mercy, J. A., Loya, F., Rosenberg, M. L., Smith, J. C., Allen, N. H., Vargas, L., & Kolts, R. (1986). Alcohol use and interpersonal violence: Alcohol detected in homicide victims. *American Journal of Public Health, 76,* 144–149.

Greenberg, D. F. (1981). Methodological issues in survey research on the inhibition of crime. *Journal of Criminal Law and Criminology, 72,* 1094–1108.

Greenwood, P. W. (1982). The violent offender in the criminal justice system. In N. A. Weiner & M. E. Wolfgang (Eds.), *Criminal Violence.* Beverly Hills, CA: Sage.

Greenwood, P. W. & Petersilia, J. (1975). *The Criminal Investigation Process: Vol. 1, Summary and Policy Implications* (R-1776-DOJ). Santa Monica, CA: Rand Corporation.

Harries, K. D. (1989). Homicide and assault: A comparative analysis of attributes in Dallas neighborhoods, 1981–1985. *The Professional Geographer, 41,* 29–38.

Huesmann, L. R. & Eron, L. D. (1989). Individual differences and the trait of aggression. *European Journal of Personality, 3,* 95–106.

Inciardi, J. A. (1989). *The Crack/Violence Connection within a Population of Hard-Core Adolescent Offenders.* Paper presented at the National Institute on Drug Abuse Technical Review on Drugs and Violence, Rockville, MD.

Kadish, S. H. & Schulhofer, S. J. (1989). *Criminal Law and Its Processes: Cases and Materials* (5th ed.). Boston: Little Brown.

Kazdin, A. E. (1985). *Treatment of Antisocial Behavior in Children and Adolescents.* Homewood, IL: Dorsey.

Kennedy, D. M. (1996, November). Can we still afford to be a nation of immigrants? *The Atlantic Monthly, 278,* 52–54, 56, 58, 61, 64, 65–68.

Lorenz Dietz, M. (1983). *Killing for Profit.* Chicago: Nelson-Hall.

Low, P. W. (1984). *Criminal Law.* St. Paul, MN: West.

Luckenbill, D. F. (1977). Criminal homicide as a situated transaction. *Social Problems, 25,* 176–186.

Lundesgaarde, H. F. (1977). *Murder in Space City: A Cultural Analysis of Houston Homicides.* New York: Oxford University Press.

Magargee, E. I. (1973). Recent research on overcontrolled and undercontrolled personality patterns among violent offenders. *Social Symposium, 9,* 37–50.

Marquart, J. W. & Sorenson, J. R. (1988). Institutional and post-release behavior of *Furman*-commuted inmates in Texas. *Criminology, 26,* 677–693.

Martinez, R. (1997). Homicide among Miami's ethnic groups: Anglos, blacks, and latinos in the 1990s. *Homicide Studies, 1,* 17–34.

Maxson, C. L. (1999). Gang homicide. In M. D. Smith & M. Zahn (Eds.), *Homicide Studies: A Sourcebook of Social Research* (pp. 239–254). Newbury Park, CA: Sage.

Maxson, C. L. & Klein, M. W. (1996). Defining gang homicide: An updated look at member and motive approaches. In C. R. Huff (Ed.), *Gangs in America* (2nd ed., pp. 3–20). Thousand Oaks, CA: Sage.

Meehan, P. J. & O'Carroll, P. W. (1995). Gangs, drugs, and homicide in Los Angeles. In M. W. Klein, C. L. Maxson, & J. Miller (Eds.), *The Modern Gang Reader* (pp. 236–241). Los Angeles: Roxbury.

Pepler, D. J., King, G., & Byrd, W. (1991). A social-cognitively based social skills training program for aggressive children. In D. J. Pepler & K. H. Rubin (Eds.), *The Development and Treatment of Childhood Aggression* (pp. 361–379). Hillsdale, NJ: Erlbaum.

Pittman, D. & Handy, W. (1964). Patterns in criminal aggravated assault. *Journal of Criminal Law, Criminology, and Police Science, 55,* 462–470.

Reiss, A. J. & Roth, J. A. (Eds.). (1993). *Understanding and Preventing Violence.* Washington, DC: National Academy Press.

Riedel, M. (1994). *Getting Away with Murder: An Examination of Arrest Clearances.* Paper presented at the Workshop of the Homicide Research Working Group, Atlanta, GA.

Riedel, M. (1995). Questions and answers about murder. In C. Calhoun & G. Ritzer (Eds.), *Introduction to Social Problems* (pp. 1–21). New York: McGraw Hill.

Riedel, M. (1999). Sources of homicide data. In M. D. Smith & M. Zahn (Eds.), *Homicide Studies: A Sourcebook of Social Research* (pp. 75–95). Newbury Park, CA: Sage.

Riedel, M. & Rinehart, T. A. (1996). Murder clearances and missing data. *Journal of Crime and Justice, 19,* 83–102.

Rosenfeld, R. (1997). Changing relationships between men and women: A note on the decline in intimate partner homicide. *Homicide Studies, 1,* 72–83.

Sellin, T. (1980). *The Penalty of Death.* Beverly Hills, CA: Sage.

Sheley, J. F. & Wright, J. D. (1995). *In the Line of Fire: Youth, Guns, and Violence in Urban America.* New York: Aldine de Gruyter.

Shelley, L. I. (1981). *Crime and Modernization: The Impact of Industrialization and Modernization on Crime.* Carbondale: Southern Illinois University Press.

Skogan, W. G. & Antunes, G. E. (1979). Information, apprehension, and deterrence: Exploring the limits of police productivity. *Journal of Criminal Justice, 7,* 217–241.

Vito, G. F., Koester, P., & Wilson, D. G. (1991). Return of the dead: An update on the status of *Furman*-commuted death row inmates. In R. M. Bohm (Ed.), *The Death Penalty in American: Current Research* (pp. 89–99). Cincinnati: Anderson.

Wilbanks, W. (1982). Murdered women and women who murder: A critique of the literature. In N. H. Rafter & E. A. Stanko (Eds.), *Judge, Lawyer, Victim, Thief: Women, Gender Roles, and Criminal Justice.* Boston: Northeastern University Press.

Wolfgang, M. E. (1958). *Patterns in Criminal Homicide.* Philadelphia: University of Pennsylvania Press.

Wolfgang, M. E. & Ferracuti, F. (1967). *The Subculture of Violence: Towards an Integrated Theory in Criminology.* London: Tavistock.

13 Serial Murder and Sexual Homicide

WADE C. MYERS
University of Florida

ALLEN G. BURGESS
Data Integrity, Inc.

ANN W. BURGESS
University of Pennsylvania

JOHN E. DOUGLAS
Mind Hunters, Inc.

Description of the Problem

The crimes of serial and sexual murderers regularly attract the attention of the lay press, and the response of the public on learning of these acts is typically outrage and disgust. Paradoxically, a number of box office hits have been based on serial killers (*Copycat, Seven,* and, to a lesser extent, *Heat*), suggesting at the same time a certain fascination by many people with this form of violence. Adding to the macabre and mysterious quality of these violent crimes is the limited scientific literature available to explain them. This void is slowly being filled by the combined effort of workers in the fields of law enforcement, mental health, and sociology.

Definitions

To proceed in describing the phenomena of serial murder and sexual homicide, it is first necessary to define these separate, yet related, terms. From a historical perspective, a variety of terms, including lust murderer, sadistic murderer, compulsive murderer, sexually sadistic murderer, and erotophonophilia have been applied to this type of criminal.

Sexual homicide refers to murders with evidence demonstrating a sexual component to the crime (Burgess, Hartman, Ressler, Douglas, & McCormack, 1986; Ressler, Burgess, & Douglas, 1988). Observations at the crime scene to suggest sexual interest or sadistic fantasy may include removal of the victim's clothing, exposure of the victim's sexual organs, sexual positioning of the body, evidence of oral, vaginal, or anal intercourse, or other signs of sexual exploitation. This sexual component may involve penile penetration of the victim, or a sexually symbolic act, such as the insertion of a foreign object into one of the victim's orifices (Douglas,

Burgess, Burgess, & Ressler, 1992). The elements of power, brutality, and callousness in the offender's personality are often revealed through psychological clues available at the crime scene.

There are varying definitions of serial murder. Douglas and colleagues (1986) succinctly define serial murder as three or more separate homicidal events in three or more separate locations with a *cooling-off* period in between. This cooling-off period can last for days, weeks, or months, and is the key feature that distinguishes the serial killer from other multiple killers. Egger (1990) provides a more restrictive definition, stating that serial murder occurs when one or more individuals, typically male, commit a second, unrelated murder of an unknown victim at a different time and geographical location. The motive is not for material gain, but instead for the murderer to exert power over his hapless, vulnerable victim.

This latter definition designates that two murders are sufficient. Other sources believe there should be a minimum of three or more victims to definitively establish the occurrence of serial murder (Douglas et al., 1986; Hickey, 1991; Jenkins, 1988). A minimum of three victims is certainly a more convincing demonstration of a *serial* pattern. Furthermore, some disagree that serial murderers only kill strangers, or that nearly all offenders are male (Hickey, 1991). In a review of serial murders over almost 200 years, Hickey (1991) found that 17 percent were female.

A confounding factor in the literature, particularly in earlier works, was the use of nonspecific classification schemes, and thus a failure to make a distinction between the terms *serial murder* and *sexual homicide*. Yet, as the above definitions show, there can be significant overlap between sexual homicide and serial murder. For example, someone who commits a series of sexual murders becomes a serial murderer. On the other hand, not all serial murderers commit murders that are sexual in nature, although the majority do (Ressler et al., 1988).

It is also important to make a distinction between serial murder, spree serial murder, and mass murder. The National Center for the Analysis of Violent Crime (1992a) divides serial murder into *spree* and *classic* types. Spree serial killings involve two or more murders at separate locations with no cooling-off period between acts. The time period between spree murders can be minutes or days, and the offender tends to have a high excitation level and may be a fugitive.

In contrast, mass murder involves the killing of multiple victims by one offender during a single episode at one location. The time period for the mass killings may cover minutes, hours, or even days. The prototype of a classic mass murderer is a mentally disordered individual whose problems have increased to the point that he acts out against groups of people who are unrelated to him or his problems, unleashing his hostility through shootings and stabbings. Other mass murderers direct their deadly hostility at their own family members.

There are other differences that distinguish the mass, spree, and serial murderer. In addition to the number of events and locations, and the presence or absence of a cooling-off period, the classic mass murderer and the spree murderer are not concerned with who their victims are. They will indiscriminately kill anyone who crosses their path. In contrast, the serial murderer usually selects a preferred type of victim, and commonly stalks his victims in a predatory fashion. He believes he will not be caught, and carefully monitors his behaviors to avoid detection.

Classification Efforts

The few studies that specifically address homicidal aggression suggest the existence of two types of sex murderers: the vindictive or displaced anger murderer (Cohen et al., 1971; Groth, Burgess, & Holmstrom, 1977; Knight & Prentky, 1990; Prentky, Burgess, & Carter, 1986; Rada, 1978) and the sadistic, or lust murderer (Becker & Abel, 1978; Bromberg & Coyle, 1974; Cohen et al., 1971; Guttmacher & Weihofen, 1952; Groth, Burgess, & Holmstrom, 1977; Knight & Prentky 1990; Podolsky, 1966; Prentky, Burgess, & Carter, 1986; Rada, 1978; Ressler, 1985; Scully & Marolla, 1985). Podolsky (1966) notes that the former, the rape murderers, kill after raping their victims, primarily to escape detection. These murderers, according to Rada (1978), rarely report sexual satisfaction from their murders or perform postmortem sexual acts with their victims. In contrast, the sadistic murderer kills as part of a ritualized, sadistic fantasy (Groth et al., 1977). For this murderer, aggression and sexuality become fused into a single psychological experience—sadism—in which aggression is eroticized. According to Brittain (1970), subjugation of the victim is of importance to this type of sexual killer, cruelty and infliction of pain are merely the means to effect subjugation.

The most notable classification system to date for serial murder and sexual homicide was developed by Ressler and colleagues (1988). They defined four categories of sexual homicide: organized, disorganized, mixed, and sadistic. Organized crimes are planned, conscious, methodical acts in which the victim is typically not known. Disorganized crimes are spontaneous, unplanned acts often against a known victim. Mixed crimes contain elements of these two categories. Sadistic crimes are marked by the offender's satisfaction gained from causing suffering and pain through torture. This classification system has been expanded in the FBI's *Crime Classification Manual* (Douglas et al., 1992), a pioneering work that seeks to classify all types of homicide (as well as arson and sexual assault) by motive.

Historical Background

Historical Case Examples

Serial homicide is not a new phenomenon. Gilles de Rais, a fifteenth-century French nobleman, is believed to have tortured, raped, and killed hundreds of children (Hickey, 1991). He practiced necrophilia on his victims, and also reportedly decapitated victims in order to later use their heads for sexual activities. Another serial killer from the fifteenth century, was Countess Elizabeth Bathory, who tortured and killed young girls, her preferred victim. She also washed herself with their blood to keep her complexion fair (Hickey, 1991). In sixteenth-century Germany, a "werewolf" named Peter Stubb murdered numerous men and women. He also raped, sexually tortured, and murdered a number of girls and women before cannibalizing them (Hill & Williams, 1967). Fritz Haarman, "The Ogre of Hanover," sodomized, murdered, and cannibalized scores of young boys in nineteenth-century Germany. Part of his sexual gratification may have been obtained from ripping out the throats of his victims (Holmes & DeBurger, 1985). Perhaps the most infamous of all serial murderers throughout history is Jack the Ripper. He terrorized England in 1888 by killing and mutilating five or six prostitutes. Similar cases have occurred in twentieth-century England.

Evolution of FBI Research on Serial and Sexual Killers

Recognizing the need for national crime statistics in the 1920s, the International Association of Police formed a committee to develop a system of uniform violent crime statistics. The *Uniform Crime Report (UCR)* was the first official system developed for the classification of homicide in the United States. The *UCR*, prepared annually by the FBI in conjunction with the U.S. Department of Justice, presents statistics for crimes committed in the United States within a given year. Originally, seven offenses were chosen: murder, nonnegligent manslaughter, forcible rape, robbery, aggravated assault, and the property crimes of burglary, larceny, theft, and motor vehicle theft. Arson was added in 1979. The *Uniform Crime Report* provides information about age, race, sex of victims and offenders, types of weapons used, and situations in which the killings took place. There are no specific categories for serial or sexual murder in these statistics. Such crimes are placed under the rubric "Other Motives or Circumstances" or "Unknown Motives" categories.

The FBI Academy's Behavioral Science Unit at Quantico, Virginia first published a system for typing lust murder approximately 15 years ago (Hazelwood & Douglas, 1980). The typology delineated two categories, the organized nonsocial category and the disorganized asocial category. This early work on lust murder evolved into a programmatic effort to devise a classification system for serial sexual murder (Ressler et al., 1988).

In the late 1980s, FBI Academy agents from the Investigative Support Unit teamed up with the Behavioral Science Unit to begin working on a crime classification manual. An advisory committee representing federal and private associations was formed. This endeavor was modeled on the format of the American Psychiatric Association's *Diagnostic and Statistical Manual of Mental Disorders (DSM)*, and covers the major crime categories of murder, arson, and sexual assault. Sexual homicide has its own section in the results of this collaboration, the *Crime Classification Manual (CCM)* (Douglas et al., 1992). The other three major categories are criminal enterprise, personal cause, and group cause homicides.

The purpose of the *CCM* is fourfold: (1) to standardize terminology within the criminal justice field; (2) to facilitate communication with the criminal justice field and between criminal justice and mental health; (3) to educate the criminal justice system and the public at large to the types of crimes being committed; and

(4) to develop a data base for investigative research (Douglas et al., 1992). Efforts are underway to expand the classification of additional crimes. For example, a typology of interpersonal stalking has been proposed by Wright and colleagues (1996).

Epidemiology

The number of serial and sexual murderers currently operating in American society is unknown, and estimates vary (Egger, 1990). Many variables make it difficult to arrive at confident prevalence figures. For example, a percentage of serial murder victims are never identified as such. Serial murderers sometimes kill in different geographic regions, which prevents the establishment of a connection between victims. Law enforcement may not detect the linkage between homicides; at other times, it is difficult to determine the sexual element to a homicide (Ressler et al., 1988). Some offenders may escape apprehension altogether. As an illustration, the "Green River Killer" has killed as many as 30 victims in Washington state over the last decade, yet remains at large despite an intensive investigation that has cost millions of dollars. Thus, no interview can take place to help determine the crimes for which he is actually responsible. The linkage of deaths to one killer can be especially difficult to establish when the offender's modus operandi changes along with the geographic locations of his crimes. More readily identified is the killer who follows a consistent modus operandi in the same locale. For example, a serial killer was identified in Miami in the mid-1990s (Staff, 1996). He was targeting homeless female crack cocaine addicts in a poverty stricken area of the city called "Mean Streets." The victims were beaten and set ablaze.

The FBI has calculated that there are about 35 to 70 of these killers active in the United States (Egger, 1990). Others place the number as high as 100 or more (Egger, 1990; Hickey, 1991; Holmes & Holmes, 1994; Wilson, 1988). As many as 3,500 to 5,000 Americans each year may be victims of serial killers (Holmes & DeBurger, 1988; Norris, 1988). Egger (1990) criticized this estimate as being too high, explaining that it is a gross misrepresentation of the available data on homicide.

Hickey (1991) estimates that there has been an almost ten-fold increase in the number of U.S. serial murder cases in the last two decades in comparison to the eighteenth and nineteenth centuries. Most serial killings are stranger-to-stranger crimes. It is hypothesized that the steady increase since the 1960s of unknown motive murders, into which most stranger-to-stranger killings fall, reflects an increase in serial killings (Egger, 1990). Percentages for other categories of murders (e.g., intimate family and acquaintance killings) have remained relatively stable or dropped over the past few decades (Block, 1987). Critics of these figures reason that the prevalence of serial murder is stable, and the supposed increase is simply the result of enhanced reporting procedures by the media.

As of 1990, 47 U.S. states have had one or more serial killers active in their territory (Hickey, 1991). Only Hawaii, Iowa, and Maine are believed to have been spared. Serial murderers have been active in other countries as well (Holmes &

Holmes, 1994; Jenkins, 1988; Myers, Recoppa, Burton, & McElroy, 1993; Smith, 1987).

Characteristics of the Offender

General Offender and Victim Findings

Different from other violent crimes, the great majority of serial murderers, as well as their victims, are white (Ressler et al., 1988). The offenders are generally male, less than 35 years old, and first begin killing in their 20s (National Center for the Analysis of Violent Crime, 1992a; Ressler et al., 1988). They typically commit their offenses while alone, although up to one-third may have one or more partners. Although there have been a number of documented cases of female serial killers (Hickey, 1991), only equivocal evidence exists for there having been a female lust murderer (Holmes & Holmes, 1994; Myers et al., 1993). One possibility was Carol Wuornos. While working as a prostitute in Florida, she fatally shot five men in Florida during the course of having sex for hire with them.

Data on 222 classic serial murderers collected by the National Center for the Analysis of Violent Crime (1992a) revealed that the mean age of their first murder was 27.5 years, and their last murder 30.1 years. For the period of approximately 1960 though 1990, the center identified 357 serial killers. Their careers spanned years on average, and they are responsible for or suspected of killing 3,100 victims—an average of nine victims each. Sexual murderers sometimes commit their first sex killings as juveniles (Myers, 1994). Indeed, Burgess and colleagues (1986) found that 10 out of 36 (28%) sexual homicide offenders first committed murder as juveniles.

Some serial killers are far more prolific in numbers of victims than this average of nine. Henry Lee Lucas, arguably the most prolific serial murderer in U.S. history, is reputed to have murdered over 140 victims in the United States between 1976 and 1982, although this figure ranges from 40 to 600 victims (Hickey, 1991). Others give this distinction to Theodore Bundy, who by his own questionable report may have killed hundreds of young women.

Usually, serial killer victims share the characteristics of being vulnerable and easy to control (Egger, 1984; Levin & Fox, 1985). Young women, children, prostitutes, hitchhikers, and vagrants are frequently targeted (Egger, 1984). Favorite hunting grounds of serial killers include red light districts, places where men engage in casual homosexual contacts, skid row areas, and college campuses (Jenkins & Donovan, 1987).

Most serial killers engage in some sort of sexual activity with their victims. This activity may include sexual intercourse, masturbation, necrophilia, or other acts. Unlike the average murder victim, serial homicide victims are often mutilated. Bite marks, even signs of cannibalism, may be discovered. Body areas commonly disfigured include the breasts, genitals, rectum, and stomach (Geberth, 1993). While firearms are the most common weapon in most murders, serial killers more often kill by such "hands-on" methods as mutilation, asphyxiation, strangulation, beating, or bludgeoning (Holmes & DeBurger, 1985; Ressler et al., 1988). It is hypothesized that firearms are too impersonal, and do not allow the murderer to experience the psychosexual gratification he could otherwise obtain during a close range, personal contact killing. As in adult sexual murderers (Douglas et al., 1992), Myers, Scott, Burgess, and Burgess (1995) found that use of a knife, being armed beforehand, and overkill (excessive trauma or injury beyond that necessary to cause death) was significantly more common in juvenile sexual murderers than nonsexual murderers.

Another common characteristic found at the crime scene is evidence of bondage. Dietz, Hazelwood, and Warren (1990) noted that three-quarters of a series of sexually sadistic offenders had used bondage with their victims. Also present in this sample were the use of stage, props, costumes, and sometimes a script to be followed for the sadistic activities.

Some offenders will arrange the victim's body apparently in an effort to shock discoverers of the crime (Douglas & Olshaker, 1995). Danny Rollings, the serial murder who slayed five college students in Gainesville in 1991, decapitated one of his victims, and then placed the head on a shelf so anyone coming into the residence would be startled upon seeing it.

Eckert, Katchis, and Donovan (1991), writing from the perspective of forensic pathology, provided a classification of sexually related injuries and deaths, one of which covers serial murderers. This work brings to attention the need to be careful of labeling a death a sexual homicide in the face of bondage, asphyxiation, anorectal injuries, or other signs of sexual aberrance. Some cases prove to be accidental deaths during consensual sexual activity, despite appearances to the contrary, such as the rare participant who dies during anal or vaginal fisting, or the victim of erotic asphyxiation.

In Hickeys (1991) review of serial murderers since 1795, 34 female offenders were identified, or 17 percent of his total sample. These women, generally in their early 30s, murdered an average of 11 victims each. Their killing careers lasted just over nine years. Many tended to fall into the "black widow" or nurse category. Unlike male serial killers, sexual gratification was rarely found to be an aspect of these women's crimes. Poisoning was the most common method of death for their victims, with money and "enjoyment" being the two most often cited motives. One example of a female serial killer was Nanny Doss, the "Giggling Grandma," who apparently took pleasure in killing people. Over a two-decade killing career, she used rat poison and arsenic to kill four husbands, her mother, two sisters, two children, and two other relatives.

Organized versus Disorganized Crimes

The organized versus disorganized crime scene and life history characterization of sexual homicide offenders is a useful concept in understanding these crimes (Ressler, Burgess, Douglas, Hartman, & D'Agostino, 1986). The organized crime scene reveals a well-planned and executed act, as distinguished from the spontaneous, chaotic behavior evident at the disorganized murder site. When the time is right for the organized serial killer, and he has cooled off from his last homicide, he selects his next victim and proceeds with his plan. Conversely, the disorganized killer acts impulsively; a blitz attack may be used to overwhelm the victim. Organized murders appear to be nearly twice as common as disorganized murders. In a study by Prentky, Burgess, Rokous, Lee, Hartman, Ressler, and Douglas (1989), crime scene organization was significantly more likely to be organized for serial murderers than for single murderers (68% versus 24%).

The organized offender appears to take pride in his planning and staging of the murderous act, and is typically driven by fantasy. In addition to premeditating the act, the organized offender is more likely to commit sexual acts with live victims, show or display control of the victim, use restraints, and drive to the crime scene. Disorganized offenders are more likely to perform sexual acts with the corpse, leave weapons at the scene, position the dead body, and possibly even keep it. Disorganized crimes more often exhibit depersonalization of the body. This refers to actions taken to obscure the identity of the victim, as through mutilation or covering of the face.

With time, the career of organized killers will sometimes drift toward more disorganized crimes. This may reflect growing confidence in their ability to avoid detection, or an acceleration of their withdrawal into an idiosyncratic world further removed from reality.

Mobility Classification of Serial Murderers

Another feature of serial killers to consider is whether they are *geographically stable* or *transient* (Holmes & DeBurger, 1985), or in Hickey's (1991) terms, *local, place-specific,* or *traveling*. The geographically stable or local murderer lives and kills in one particular area, usually urban. An example of this type of offender is Wayne Williams, who murdered up to 30 young black males in the Atlanta area over the course of 2 years, before being arrested.

John Wayne Gacy serves as an example of a place-specific killer; someone who carries out their murders within one location, such as at home or a place of employment. He lured 33 young male victims back to his Chicago home where he then tortured and murdered them. Many of the bodies were hidden in a crawl space under his home. Another example of the place-specific killer was registered nurse Terri Rachals. She was charged in the deaths of six surgical intensive care unit hospital patients in the 1980s, and was implicated in many other mysterious hospital deaths. Her murder method was to inject potassium chloride into her victims intravenous line, causing cardiac arrest, supposedly to relieve their suffering (Hickey, 1991).

The geographically transient or traveling offender covers wide areas in committing his crimes. In the 1920s, serial killer Earle Nelson committed 21 murders in 9 states and 2 countries, ranging from California, to New York, to Canada. Ted Bundy murdered people in at least six states, spanning the width of the country from the state of Washington to Florida.

Social Background Characteristics

In their study of 36 men who had committed at least one sexual homicide (four-fifths had killed more than one victim for a total of 109 known murders, or an average of 3 victims per offender), Ressler and colleagues (1988) found that these men had the native intelligence to perform well in school, yet academic failure was the norm. The majority had to repeat elementary grades and did not finish high school. In addition, school failure was frequently mentioned by the men as an early fortifier of their sense of inadequacy. The men also had the ability to perform skilled jobs. In reality, however, most offenders had poor work histories in unskilled jobs, and only 20 percent had ever held steady jobs. Examination of performance behavior of these murderers reveals another paradox. Despite reasonably high intelligence and potential in many areas, performance in school, employment, social relationships, and military service was often poor. In all of these areas, performance fell far short of potential.

The sadistic offender often will gain employment at jobs that have the qualities of offering control over others or connections with suffering and death. Work as a security guard, or at hospitals, correctional facilities, mortuaries, and butcher shops can fill this niche (Holmes & DeBurger, 1985). Relatedly, a history of extreme cruelty to animals is common. A strong interest in horror movies, violent pornography, weapons, and police paraphernalia is also common.

In an interesting study with offenders in England, Grubin (1994) compared those who had committed sexual murders with rapists. One of the most robust findings he discovered was the social isolation and lack of sexual relationships in the sexual murderers. Even as children, many of them had experienced trouble fitting into peer groups.

Most sexual murderers are heterosexual, but sexual dysfunction, discomfort with ordinary sexual relations, and paraphilias of a nonsadistic nature (i.e., voyeurism, fetishism, exhibitionism, transvestism) are frequently present (Gratzer & Bradford, 1995; Prentky et al., 1989; Ressler et al., 1988). Prentky and colleagues (1989), in comparing serial sexual murderers with sexual murderers who only committed one offense, found that the former had significantly higher paraphilias, especially fetishism and cross-dressing. In another study of sexual homicide offenders, over three-quarters of the group rated pornography as their top sexual interest (Burgess et al., 1986). A high rate of paraphilias in sexually sadistic offenders appears to be common.

Etiology

There is as yet no clear answer to what causes a person to commit serial or sexual homicide. Theories addressing this question offer sociocultural, psychologic, psychodynamic, and biological explanations (Hickey, 1991).

From a sociocultural perspective, a number of investigators who have studied serial murder cases believe that violent pornography may be contributory in the vulnerable (Douglas & Olshaker, 1995). Others feel that the widespread societal bombardment by and acceptance of mass media violence plays a role in sexual violence. Inundation by violence and the devaluation of life, with the resultant message that violence is acceptable, seems to create a climate of apathy in society. This in turn may lower individuals' resistance to aggressive and sexual drives. Ted Bundy, shortly before his execution, pointed to media violence and pornography as spawning his career of murder.

The acts of the serial killer can be viewed as compulsive behavior. Revitch (1980) described the need to commit the sexually murderous act as compelling and likely to be repeated. Resisting this need purportedly brings on severe anxiety in the offender, akin to the feeling those with obsessive compulsive disorder experience when their compulsions are blocked. Other types of sexual offenses also have been described by some as a compulsive disorder.

Liebert (1985) offered a psychodynamic explanation for serial murder, noting that most killers of this type have a borderline or narcissistic personality structure. The destructive elements of the early mother-child relationship remain in the unconscious. These aggressive, dissociated elements are eventually split from the self and projected onto the female victim. In another psychodynamic view, Weinshel and Calet (1972) hypothesized that the mutilations associated with serial killing represent a wish to re-enter and explore the mother's womb.

There is a modicum of literature on the biological basis of sexual and serial killers. Money (1990) looks at this behavior as a disease. The diseased brain is postulated to send messages of attack along with messages of sexual arousal and mating behavior simultaneously, perhaps in a fashion similar the psychomotor seizures in temporal lobe epilepsy. No studies have examined the role of hormones and neurotransmitters in sexual killers. One study found that subjects who had killed a sexual partner had significantly lower cerebrospinal fluid levels of 5-HIAA, a metabolite of serotonin (Lidberg, Tuck, Asberg, Scalia-Tomba, & Bertilsson, 1985). There are scattered case reports in which sexual homicide perpetrators are found to have histories of serious head trauma and abnormalities on CT head scans, EEGs, and neuropsychological testing. However, such findings are nonspecific and common in other populations of nonsexual murderers.

Role of Fantasy

A relatively consistent psychological finding in many studies of serial and sexual murderers is the presence of violent fantasy. This is believed to play a critical role in these types of crimes (Brittain, 1970; MacCulloch, Snowden, Wood, & Mills, 1983; Ressler et al., 1988).

Prentky and colleagues (1989) compared serial sexual killers to subjects who had killed a single victim in examining the role of fantasy. Significantly more serial murderers had violent fantasies (86% versus 23%). Classical conditioning may help explain the power of fantasy in serial murders. Many sexual murderers are believed to masturbate to sexually sadistic themes (MacCulloch et al., 1983). As with other sexual offenders, it is hypothesized that the selective reinforcement of deviant fantasies through paired association with repeated masturbation contributes to sexual homicide, particularly the organized type.

MacCulloch and colleagues (1983) evaluated the presence of sadistic fantasy in 16 forensic hospital patients with psychopathic personality disorder who had committed violent sexual crimes. Most of these offenders' crimes were specifically linked to preceding fantasies. Progressively more sadistic behavioral "try-outs" linked to fantasy were conducted by these offenders, only stopping when they were apprehended.

Burgess and colleagues (1986) advanced a motivational model for sexual homicide based on the role of fantasy. Five factors in this model include the following: impaired early attachments; early psychologic trauma; patterned responses that generate fantasy; a violent fantasy life; and a "feedback filter" that nourishes repetitive thinking patterns. In this study, many of the murderers described the central role of fantasy in their early development, expressed in part through a variety of paraphilias. When asked to rank their sexual interests, the highest ranking activity was pornography (81%), followed by compulsive masturbation (79%), fetishism (72%), and voyeurism (71%). These fantasies were often violent and sadistic in nature. Twenty offenders had rape fantasies prior to the age of 18, and seven of these men acted out these fantasies within a year of being consciously aware of them. There was evidence of physical and sexual abuse in close to half of the killers and a higher percentage of emotional neglect. In general, it is interesting to note the isolated pattern of these deviant sexual expressions. The men seemed either to engage in paraphilias that were solitary in practice or in sexually violent activities; neither of which reflected any degree of interpersonal contact.

In addition, when questioned about the murders themselves and their preparations for the murders, the men identified the importance of fantasy to the crimes. After the first murder, the men found themselves deeply preoccupied and sometimes stimulated by the memories of the act, all of which contributed to and nurtured fantasies about subsequent murders.

One begins to see how an early pattern used to cope with a markedly deficient and abusive family life might turn a child away from that reality and into his own private world of violence where he cannot only exert control, but can exact retribution for the physical and emotional injuries inflicted on him. The control evidenced in these fantasies appears to be crucial not only to the child, but later to the adult. Importantly, these are not fantasies of escape to a better life, as one often sees in children recovering from sexual assaults and abusive treatment. These men did not compensate by retreating to a fantasy world in which love reigned and abuse was unheard of. Rather, their fantasies were fueled by feelings of aggression and mastery over those who were abusing them, suggesting a projected repetition of their own abuse and identification with the aggressor. As one murderer put it, "Nobody bothered to find out what my problem was and nobody knew about the fantasy world."

Family Patterns

It is often argued that the structure and quality of a family interaction is an important factor in the development of a child, especially in the way the child perceives family members and their interaction with him (and with each other). For children growing up, the quality of their attachments to parents and other members of the family is critical to how these children relate to and value other members of society. From developmental and social learning perspectives, these early life attachments evolve into detailed architectural plans for how the child will interact with his or her world.

In a study of 81 sexual offenders (54 rapists and 27 child molesters) incarcerated at the Massachusetts Treatment Center (Prentky, Knight, Sims-Knight, Straus, Rokous, & Cerce, 1989), three noteworthy findings were obtained. First, sexual and nonsexual aggression in adulthood each were related to distinct aspects of developmental history. Specifically, caregiver inconstancy and sexual deviation in the family were related to the amount of sexual aggression, whereas childhood and juvenile institutional history and physical abuse/neglect were associated with amount of nonsexual aggression. Second, contrary to previous studies of other criminal populations, the amount of aggression rather than frequency of crimes was predicted by developmental history. Third, the presence of caregiver inconsistency and family sexual deviation accounted for 87.5 percent of all cases of extreme sexual aggression in adulthood. The presence of an institutional history and physical abuse/neglect accounted for 81.2 percent of all cases of extreme nonsexual aggression in adulthood. Results of this study suggest that the quality of early interpersonal attachments and the experience of sexual abuse as a child may be important to understanding sexual aggression in adulthood. Given these rather compelling findings, we were especially interested in looking at factors that best addressed the level of interpersonal attachment in a sample of serial murderers.

By examining data from the most extensive study to date on sexual murderers, family histories of these 36 sexual murderers revealed multiple problems (Ressler et al., 1988). For example, one-half of the offenders' families had members with criminal histories and over one-half of the families had members with psychiatric problems, suggesting, at the very least, inconsistent contact between some family members and the offender as a child. In addition, however, there was evidence of irresponsible and maladaptive parenting in a large number of cases. Nearly 70 percent of the families had histories of alcohol abuse, and one-third of the families had histories of drug abuse. Sexual deviance among family members was present or suspected in almost one-half of the cases. Abuse of these subjects was also prevalent, as 74 percent had been emotionally abused, 42 percent physically abused, and 43 percent sexually abused. Thus, the likelihood that these offenders experienced a high quality of family life as children is remote.

When examining the childrearing patterns described by the murderers, one is most impressed by the high degree of family instability and by the poor quality of attachment among family members. Only one-third of the men reported growing up in one location. The majority said they experienced occasional instability, and six reported chronic instability or frequent moving. Over 40 percent lived out-side the family (e.g., in foster homes, state homes, detention centers, mental hospi-tals) before age 18 years. Twenty-five of the men for whom data were available had histories of early psychiatric difficulties. In general, these families were bereft not only of internal or nuclear attachments, but external or community attachments as well. Consequently, the children in these families had no opportunities to develop stable, healthy attachments within the community, thus reducing their opportuni-ties to develop positive, stable relationships outside the family—relationships that might otherwise have compensated for family instability.

These data suggest that most of the 36 murderers, as children, had little or no attachment to family members. Further, they felt a high degree of uninvolvement with their fathers, ambivalence toward their mothers, and little attachment to sib-lings. Their parents were preoccupied with their own problems of substance abuse, psychiatric disturbance, and criminality. They tended to engage in aberrant sexual behavior and often argued and fought with each other. Although the par-ents offered little constructive guidance, it appears that they did offer ample role-modeling of deviant behavior.

Retvitch (1980) also pointed out the presence of disturbed family functioning in sexually violent men, particularly centered around the mother. Such problems as maternal overprotection, infantilization, seductive behaviors toward the son, and even outright rejection of the son are noted. Maternal promiscuity, real or not, and a cold, distant, authoritarian, and punitive father are also cited as contributory factors (Brittain, 1970; Revitch, 1980).

Assessment and Diagnosis

In any criminal assessment, the interviewer must assess the intelligence of the offender in order to begin to make sense of who they are and what their unlawful actions represent. Certain studies have shown that the majority of serial killers have an average to superior level of intelligence (Burgess et al., 1986; Prentky et al., 1989). While organized serial murderers often have average to above average intelligence, disorganized sexual murderers tend to be below average in intelligence (National Center for the Analysis of Violent Crime, 1990). It has been suggested, however, that these offenders' ability to escape apprehension during their killing careers is more a sign of cunning and deceit rather than intellectual capacity (Hickey, 1991).

Only about one-fifth of serial murderers have had psychiatric treatment at some point in their lives (Hickey, 1991). Burgess and colleagues (1986), in their series of sexual murderers, found that 70 percent of them had undergone psychi-atric assessment or institutionalization as children.

Diagnostic Issues and Findings

It is generally believed that most serial murderers are not psychotic. The point has been raised that if they were truly psychotic, then they would not have the mental resources to escape apprehension (Dietz, 1986). In an early study, Retvitch (1965) diagnosed clinical schizophrenia in one-fifth of 43 male gynocidal offenders, some of whom had committed more than one murder. However, schizophrenia covered a broader spectrum of psychopathology at that time in history, and its unlikely that these nine offenders would meet current *DSM-IV* criteria for schizophrenia. Psychotic symptoms seen in this population after arrest may often represent malingering rather than true psychosis.

Generally, mental health professionals diagnose serial and sexual murderers as psychopaths, with corresponding qualities of inability to feel guilt, callousness, and irresponsibility, to name a few. Another common diagnostic finding in these offenders is sexual sadism, that is, the need to control others through domination, humiliation, or the infliction of pain to obtain sexual arousal (MacCulloch et al., 1983). Levin and Fox (1985) explain that these murderers are usually sociopathic personalities without guilt who have a powerful need to control and dominate others: "Though their crimes may be sickening, they are not sick in either a medical or a legal sense." Clifford Olson, Canada's most notorious serial murderer, was sentenced to life imprisonment for the torture and killing of at least 11 male and female children. A personality assessment following his arrest was consistent with that of a typical psychopath (Hare et al., 1990).

Occasionally the diagnosis of multiple personality disorder (MPD) will be raised in the serial murderer, and there may be an association between criminality and MPD (Coons, Bowman, & Milstein, 1988). Kenneth Bianchi, the "Hillside Strangler," strangled at least 10 women in the Los Angeles area two decades ago, and attributed his actions to MPD. His clinical presentation of MPD was contradictory, the corroborating evidence was equivocal, and experts were split over his diagnosis (Watkins, 1984). Ultimately, the court did not accept the diagnosis of MPD. To date, there are no well-documented cases of MPD in serial murder, and the possibility of malingering in such cases must be seriously considered (Hickey, 1991; Orne, Dinges, & Ornes, 1984).

Although several lust murderers equate their acts to overwhelming compulsions with repetitive, ritualistic features, and describe severe anxiety on attempts to resist these needs, these activities are not true compulsions (as in obsessive-compulsive disorder) because the person derives pleasure from the particular activity and may wish to resist it only because of its secondary deleterious consequences (American Psychiatric Association: *DSM IV*). Professionals with a more analytical approach have been prone to consider severe borderline or narcissistic personality disorders in these cases due to specific abnormalities in the ego functioning of these individuals.

Yarvis (1990) has brought attention to the point that research findings in the extant literature on the prevalence of psychopathology in murderers "are discordant and contradictory." For example, he noted that rates of psychosis range from 4 to 83 percent, substance abuse from 3 to 40 percent, antisocial personality disorder from 8 to 28 percent, dissociative reactions from less than 1 to almost 70 percent, and no psychiatric disorder from 0 to almost 90 percent. In his examination of 100 murderers, 10 were classified in the homicide/rape category. These sexual murderers were characterized by substance abuse (40%), all other diagnoses (40%), and no diagnosis (20%) on Axis I, and antisocial personality disorder (90%) on Axis II. This is consistent with the presumed high rate of antisocial personality and substance abuse in sexual murderers. Substance abuse may approach 50 percent in some samples of sexual murderers (Grubin, 1994; Ressler et al., 1988).

Diagnoses in Juvenile Sexual Homicide Offenders

Myers (1996) recently evaluated 12 incarcerated juvenile sexual murderers in an ongoing study using standardized psychological instruments, record review, and clinical interview. The sample's mean age at the time of the offenses was 15 years. All victims were female, and averaged 21 years of age. One-half of the sample had violent sexual fantasies.

The most common *DSM-III-R* diagnosis present at the time of the crimes was conduct disorder (82%), bringing to light their preceding pattern of serious antisocial behavior. Personality disorders at follow-up (mean age 19) were common (55%), with antisocial personality disorder the most frequent (36%). A measure quantifying psychopathy, the *Psychopathy Checklist—Revised* (Hare, 1990), found the sample to score in the general range of incarcerated young offenders. The group tended to came from chaotic, abusive backgrounds, and all were having serious school problems at arrest.

Course and Prognosis/Recidivism

Developmentally, sexual murderers often have a history of antisocial behaviors as youths. Conduct disorder symptoms in adolescence, such as assaultiveness toward adults (84%), stealing (81%), and lying (75%), were noted in the study by Ressler and colleagues (1988). These antisocial behaviors continued into adulthood for many of this group, as assaultiveness toward other adults (86%), stealing (56%), and lying (68%) continued to be commonplace. Most serial murderers will have a criminal history prior to their commission of sadistic acts, and nearly one-half will have committed other sex offenses (Hickey, 1991).

Once imprisoned, these offenders are not uncommonly easy to manage. However, they may not fit into the prison population, and other inmates may regard them with contempt or disgust, making their safety from other prisoners attacks an issue. Albert DeSalvo, the "Boston Strangler," was stabbed to death by another inmate (Levin & Fox, 1985). Jeffrey Dahmer, who killed 17 men and boys, met a similar fate in a Wisconsin prison by being bludgeoned to death.

The serial murderer has a strong psychological need to have absolute control, dominance, and power over his victims. The infliction of torture, pain, and ultimately death is carried out to meet this need (Levin & Fox, 1985). A psychological structure that supports this manner of thinking and feeling is believed to be deeply ingrained in their personalities. Personalities, especially in adults, are "enduring patterns of inner experience and behavior that deviates markedly from the expectations of the individual's culture, is pervasive and inflexible, has an onset in adolescence or early adulthood, is stable over time, and leads to distress or impairment" (American Psychiatric Association, 1994). In conceptualizing the occurrence of serial murder within the framework of an antisocial, sadistic personality, one would predict them to be highly recidivistic. That is what we find. More than one serial killer has warned authorities that he would reoffend if released back into society.

Clinical Management and Treatment

There are different ways to think about the management and treatment of an offender who has committed serial or sexual murder. Initially, there is the *management* and *treatment* of the societal problem created by the offenders' crimes through law enforcement and the judicial system. Energies of various agencies are vigorously focused on apprehending the murderer as rapidly as possible due to the high risk of repeat offenses. Next, the campaign of the opposing attorneys' offices begins in trying to establish guilt or innocence, and sometimes legal culpability—the insanity defense. On sentencing, the sexual murderer will usually receive a maximum sentence, often life imprisonment or the death penalty. There remains little room in this process for the application of classical psychological treatments. Perhaps guilty of hyperbole, Liebert (1985) has postulated that no lust murderer is psychologically capable of intensive psychotherapy because of their inability for intimacy.

However, the occasional sexual homicide offender will receive a limited sentence in prison, and thus will be released back into the community with a significant portion of his life remaining. In fact, the majority of juveniles who commit sexual homicide will eventually be released (Myers, 1996). Recidivism is a serious concern with regard to these offenders. Perhaps intensive community-based services, broader in scope and contact than parole measures, should be considered for the released sexual homicide offender to help lower the recidivism risk. Such *wraparound care* services that assist and monitor psychological, social, and occupational aspects of offenders' lives might be enlisted. Wraparound care has been used with limited early success with young sexual offenders released back to the community (Santarcangelo & Mandelkorn, 1995).

The Insanity Defense

A successful insanity defense for serial murders is a rarity. Even in cases where the defendant has a history of psychosis, and expert witnesses to testify to its existence, the court is rarely swayed (Jenkins, 1988; Jenkins, 1989). For example, Albert Fisk, who murdered many children in the 1920s and 1930s, was diagnosed with paranoid psychosis (Jenkins, 1989). He was subsequently found sane and executed. Two others who may well have had paranoid schizophrenia, John George

Haigh in 1949 and Peter Sutcliffe in 1980 (the "Yorkshire Ripper"), were found to be responsible for their actions (Jenkins, 1988). The difficulty for the defense team is in convincing the jury that the sadistic acts of murder are the product of psychotic thinking to the degree that the defendant did not know the nature and quality of his acts or their wrongfulness, or was unable to conform his conduct to the requirements of the law. It is especially difficult for the defense to prove an ongoing, consistent psychotic state in an offender who commits serial killings separated by long periods of time.

The National Center for the Analysis of Violent Crime

The National Center for the Analysis of Violent Crime (NCAVC), located at the FBI Academy in Quantico, Virginia, has been in existence now for over a decade. This organization seeks to assist law-enforcement agencies confronted with unusual, bizarre, or repetitive crimes by providing expertise in the areas of research, training, and investigative support (National Center for the Analysis of Violent Crime, 1992b).

One component of the NCAVC is the Violent Criminal Apprehension Program (VICAP). This program receives and distributes criminal reports from the United States and other countries in an attempt to link murders committed by serial violent offenders. VICAP requires all homicides to be reported to the NCAVC where the data are entered into a computer system and cross-checked to see if they match other reported homicides. To date, thousands of cases have been entered into the VICAP system.

Another component of NCAVC is the Criminal Investigative Analysis Program (CIAP). One of the functions of this subunit is criminal profiling, previously referred to by the term *psychological profile* (Douglas & Burgess, 1986). The profiling process seeks to identify major personality and behavioral characteristics of the offender based on crime analysis. These techniques require an in-depth knowledge of the criminal personality, an area, until recently, researched primarily by psychiatrists or psychologists (Yochelson & Samenow, 1977), who examined criminals from a psychological framework, or by sociologists and criminologists, who studied the demographics and social stratification of crime. Missing from these areas of inquiry were critical aspects of offender apprehension important to the law-enforcement community. Thus, researchers with a law-enforcement perspective began to shift the focus to the investigative process of crime scene inquiry and victimology.

Investigative Profiling

Investigative profiling is best viewed as a strategy enabling law enforcement to narrow the field of options and generate educated guesses about the perpetrator. It has been described as a collection of leads (Rossi, 1982), as an informed attempt to provide detailed information about a certain type of criminal (Geberth, 1981), and as a biographical sketch of behavioral patterns, trends, and tendencies (Vorpagel, 1982). Geberth (1981) has noted that the investigative profile is particularly useful when the criminal has demonstrated some clearly identifiable form of psychopathology. In such a case, the crime scene is presumed to reflect the murderer's behavior and personality in much the same way as furnishings reveal the homeowner's character. The process of profiling involves evaluating the criminal act, crime scene specifics, analysis of the victim, evaluation of police reports, and evaluation of the medical examiner's autopsy results. Then, a profile is developed with critical offender characteristics and investigative suggestions based on construction of the profile (Douglas & Burgess, 1986). At present, there have been no systematic efforts to validate these profile-derived classifications.

Community Issues

There is also a need to develop ways to treat society for the negative impact serial murderers exert. From a practical standpoint, serial murders are extremely expensive for local and state governments. The financial burden of investigations and the subsequent trial and appeals processes easily run into the millions of dollars. It is estimated that Ted Bundy's trial and appeals cost $9 million (Hickey, 1991). The costs of the legal defense alone for serial killer Danny Rollings was almost $1 million.

Then, there are the psychological effects of the serial murders on a community. It has been said that the community anxiety and excitement caused by the discovery of a serial murderer rival the risks of the murders themselves (Liebert, 1985). Herkov (1992), in an assessment of the psychological impact of a serial homicide on Gainesville, Florida, surveyed area resident adults and children (Herkov, Myers, & Burket, 1994) to determine the community's response to violent acts by a serial murderer. Over several days, the news was gradually released that the mutilated bodies of five college students had been discovered. Almost one-half of residents reported moderate to severe disruption of their daily lives. One-third felt panicked or frightened in the weeks following the murders. Many residents, adults and children alike, also experienced posttraumatic stress disorder symptoms, including an increased startle response, distressing thoughts, sleep difficulties, and trouble concentrating. Understandably, the most disturbed were female students living close to the murder sites. Of concern was the finding that a number of citizens purchased and began carrying firearms for protection; this certainly raised the probability of innocent people being maimed or killed by firearms in the hands of the inexperienced.

Case Illustration

Organized Sexual Homicide

Instead of going to school that morning, Skip got into his car and drove across town to the home of a female classmate. He was 17 years old and in his senior year.

He knew where this girl lived because they had carpooled with other students to several school functions in the past. Although they were only acquaintances, Skip knew that she would be home from school that day. She was recovering from an illness that had kept her out of school for two weeks already. He was also aware that her parents would be away at work that morning. In his coat pocket were several lengths of rope and a knife.

On arriving at her neighborhood, he parked his car around the block from her house so that his location would not be betrayed. He broke into her residence through the back door. Once inside, he cut the phone lines and checked to make sure that all the doors to the house were locked. He then began heading toward the rear of the home where her bedroom was located.

He found her still asleep as he entered her bedroom. As he approached her, she startled. She resisted him as came over to the bed, grabbed her breast, and tried to remove her nightgown. To gain her submission he began choking her with his hands from behind. He then informed her that she better comply "or else." At this point, he attempted to bind her wrists with the rope he had brought, but the length of the pieces were too short. However, she was lying there petrified with fear, so he abandoned his plan to tie her up. He then tore her clothing off and vaginally raped her. After the sexual assault he was feeling nervous, and forgot he had brought a knife with him. He left her temporarily in the room, and warned her not to move. Out in the garage he found a suitable garden instrument, and returned to her room. He then bludgeoned her to death.

Skip had been arrested twice before for sexual battery. These earlier crimes both occurred in his neighborhood. The first time, he grabbed a young girl's buttocks while she walked down a sidewalk in broad daylight. He did the same thing to an adult female a year later, although this time he grabbed the victim's breast. After the sexual homicide, Skip admitted to rape but not murder fantasies. Yet, he knew he would kill the victim, and felt a sense of "commitment" in his plans to go through with it while driving to the victim's home. When asked what drove him to decide to take her life, he responded, "Dead men tell no tales."

Summary

A review of the clinical and research literature on the crimes of serial and sexual murders suggests the importance of early detection and treatment of offenders, both juvenile and adult. Studies specific to sexual homicide suggest the importance of formative life events in the development of homicidal fantasies that are subsequently acted out. Further study is needed to determine clinical interventions that can assist in early detection and prevention.

REFERENCES

American Psychiatric Association. (1994). *Diagnostic and Statistical Manual of Mental Disorders.* Washington, DC: Author.

Becker, J. V. & Abel, G. G. (1978). Men and the victimization of women. In J. R. Chapman & M. R. Gates (Eds.), *Victimization of Women.* Beverly Hills, CA: Sage Publications.

Block, C. R. (1987). *Homicide in Chicago.* Chicago: Loyola University of Chicago.

Brittain, R. P. (1970). The sadistic murderer. *Med Sci Law, 10,* 148–207.

Bromberg, W. & Coyle, E. (1974, April 21–22). Rape: A compulsion to destroy. *Medical Insight,* 24–25.

Burgess, A. W., Hartman, C. R., Ressler, R. K., Douglas, J. E., & McCormack, A. (1986). Sexual homicide: A motivational model. *J Interpersonal Violence, 1,* 251–272.

Cohen, M. L., Garofalo, R. F., Boucher, R., & Seghorn, T. (1971). The psychology of rapists. *Seminars in Psychiatry, 3,* 307–327.

Coons, P. M., Bowman, E. S., & Milstein, V. (1988). Multiple personality disorder: A clinical investigation of 50 cases. *J Nerv Ment Dis, 176,* 519–527.

Dietz, P. E. (1986). Mass, serial and sensational homicides. *Bull NY Acad Med, 62,* 477–491.

Dietz, P. E., Hazelwood, R. R., & Warren, J. (1990). The sexually sadistic criminal and his offenses. *Bull Am Acad Psychiatry Law, 18,* 163–178.

Douglas, J. E. & Burgess, A. E. (1986, December). Criminal profiling: A viable investigative tool against violent crime. *FBI Law Enforcement Bulletin.*

Douglas, J. E., Burgess, A. W., Burgess, A. G., & Ressler, R. K. (1992). *Crime Classification Manual.* New York: Lexington Books of Macmillan.

Douglas, J. E. & Olshaker, M. (1995). *Mind Hunter.* New York: Scribner.

Douglas, J. E., Ressler, R. K., Burgess, A. W., & Hartman, C. R. (1986). Criminal profiling from crime scene analysis. *Behavioral Sciences and the Law, 4,* 401–421.

Eckert, W. G., Katchis, S., & Donovan, W. (1991). The pathology and medicolegal aspects of sexual activity. *Am J Forensic Med Pathology, 12,* 3–15.

Egger, S. A. (1984). A working definition of serial murder and the reduction of linkage blindness. *J Policy Sci Admin, 12,* 348–356.

Egger, S. A. (1990). *Serial Murder: An Elusive Phenomenon.* Westport, CT: Praeger.

Geberth, V. J. (1981). Psychological profiling. *Law and Order,* 46–49.

Geberth, V. J. (1993). *Practical Homicide Investigation: Tactics, Procedures, and Forensic Techniques.* Boca Raton, FL: CRC Press.

Gratzer, T. & Bradford, J. M. W. (1995). Offender and offense characteristics of sexual sadists: A comparative study. *J Forensic Sciences, 40,* 450–455.

Groth, A. N., Burgess, A. W., & Holstrom, L. L. (1977). Rape: Power, anger, and sexuality. *American Journal of Psychiatry, 134,* 1239–1243.

Grubin, D. (1994). Sexual murder. *British J Psychiatry, 165,* 624–629.

Guttmacher, M. S. & Weihofen, H. (1952). *Psychiatry and the Law.* New York: Norton.

Hare, R. D. (1990). *The Revised Psychopathy Checklist.* Vancouver, Canada: Department of Psychology, University of British Columbia.

Hare, R. D., Harpur, T. J., Hakstain, A. R., Forth, A. F., Hart, S. D., & Newman, J. P. (1990). The revised psychopathy checklist: Reliability and factor structure. *Psychological Assessment: A Journal of Consulting & Clinical Psychology, 2,* 338–341.

Hazelwood, R. R. & Douglas, J. E. (1980, April). The lust murderer. *FBI Law Enforcement Bulletin.*

Herkov, M. J. (1992). Community reactions to serial murder: A guide for law enforcement. *National Institute of Justice Contract,* Grant No. 90-IJ-RO35.

Herkov, M. J., Myers, W. C., & Burket, R. (1994). Children's reactions to serial murder in a community. *Behavioral Sciences and the Law, 12,* 251–259.

Hickey, E. W. (1991). *Serial Murderers and Their Victims.* Pacific Grove, CA: Brooks/Cole.

Hill, D. & Williams, P. (1967). *The Supernatural.* New York: Signet Books.

Holmes, R. M. & DeBurger, J. E. (1985). Profiles in terror: The serial murderer. *Federal Probation, 49,* 29–34.

Holmes, R. M. & DeBurger, J. E. (1988). *Serial Murder.* Newbury Park, CA: Sage.

Holmes, R. M. & Holmes, S. T. (1994). *Murder in America.* Thousand Oaks, CA: Sage.

Jenkins, P. (1988). Serial murder in England 1940–1985. *J Crim Just, 6,* 1–15.

Jenkins, P. (1989). Serial murder in the United States 1900–1940: A historical perspective. *J Crim Just, 17*, 377–391.

Jenkins, P. & Donovan, E. (1987, July–August). Serial murder on campus. *Campus Law Enforcement Journal*, 42–44.

Knight, R. R. A. & Prentky, R. A. (1990). Classifying sexual offenders: The development and corroboration of taxonomic models. In W. L. Marshall, D. R. Laws, & H. E. Barbaree (Eds.), *The Handbook of Sexual Assault: Issues, Theories, and Treatment of the Offender*. New York: Plenum.

Levin, J. & Fox, J. A. (1985). *Mass Murder: America's Growing Menace*. New York: Plenum.

Lidberg, L., Tuck, J. R., Asberg, M., Scalia-Tomba, B. P., & Bertilsson, L. (1985). Homicide, suicide and CSF 5-HIAA. *Acta Psychiatrica, 71*, 230–236.

Liebert, J. A. (1985). Contributions of psychiatric consultation in the investigation of serial murder. *Int J Offender Ther and Compar Criminology, 29*, 187–200.

MacCulloch, M. J., Snowden, P. R., Wood, P. J. W., & Mills, H. E. (1983). Sadistic fantasy, sadistic behavior and offending. *Br J Psychiatry, 143*, 20–29.

Money, J. (1990). Forensic sexology: Paraphiliac serial rape (biastophilia) and lust murder (erotophonophilia). *Am J Psychotherapy, 44*, 26–36.

Myers, W. C. (1994). Sexual homicide by adolescents. *J Am Acad Child Adolesc Psychiatry, 33*, 962–969.

Myers, W. C. (1996). An introductory study of juvenile sexual homicide (under editorial review).

Myers, W. C., Recoppa, L., Burton, K., & McElroy, R. (1993). Malignant sex and aggression: An overview of serial sexual homicide. *Bull Am Acad Psychiatry Law, 34*, 1483–1489.

Myers, W. C., Scott, K., Burgess, A. W., & Burgess, A. G. (1995). Psychopathology, biopsychosocial factors, crime characteristics, and classification of 25 homicidal youths. *J Am Acad Child Adolesc Psychiatry, 34*, 1483–1489.

National Center for the Analysis of Violent Crime. (1990). Criminal investigative analysis/sexual homicide. *U.S. Department of Justice, FBI Report*.

National Center for the Analysis of Violent Crime. (1992a, October). Serial, mass and spree murderers in the United States: Search of major wire services and publications on offenders operating from 1960 to the present. *U.S. Department of Justice, FBI Report*.

National Center for the Analysis of Violent Crime. (1992b). 1992 Annual report. *U.S. Department of Justice, FBI Report*.

Norris, J. (1988). *Serial Killers: The Growing Menace*. New York: Doubleday.

Orne, M. T., Dinges, D. F., & Orne, E. C. C. (1984). On the differential diagnosis of multiple personality in the forensic context. *Int J Clin Exp Hypnosis, 32*, 118–169.

Podolsky, E. (1966). Sexual violence. *Medical Digest, 34*, 60–63.

Prentky, R. A., Burgess, A. W., & Carter, D. L. (1986). Victim responses by rapist type: An empirical and clinical analysis. *Journal of Interpersonal Violence, 1*, 73–98.

Prentky, R. A., Burgess, A. W., Rokous, F., Lee, A., Hartman, C., Ressler, R., & Douglas, J. (1989). Presumptive role of fantasy in serial sexual homicide. *Am J Psychiatry, 146*, 887–891.

Prentky, R. A., Knight, R., Sims-Knight, J. E., Straus, B., Rokous, F., & Cerce, D. (1989). Developmental antecedents of sexual aggression. *Development and Psychopathology, 1*, 153–169.

Rada, R. T. (1978). *Clinical Aspects of the Rapist*. New York: Grune & Stratton.

Ressler, R. K. (Ed.) (1985). Violent Crimes. *FBI Law Enforcement Bulletin, 54*, 1–31.

Ressler, R., Burgess, A. W., & Douglas, J. E. (1988). *Sexual Homicide: Patterns and Motives*. Lexington, MA: Lexington Books.

Ressler, R. K., Burgess, A. W., Douglas, J. E., Hartman, C. R., & D'Agostino, R. B. (1986). Sexual killers and their victims: Identifying patterns through crime scene analysis. *J Interpersonal Violence, 1*, 288–308.

Revitch, E. (1965). Sex murderer and the potential sex murderer. *Diseases of the Nervous System, 26*, 640–648.

Revitch, E. (1980). Gynocide and unprovoked attacks on women. *Corrective and Social Psychiatry, 26*, 6–11.

Rossi, D. (1982). Crime scene behavioral analysis: Another tool for the law enforcement investigator. *Police Chief*, 152–155.

Santarcangelo, S. & Mandelkorn, D. (1995). Wraparound care approaches for youth with sexual offending behaviors and their families. In C. R. Ellis & N. N. Singh (Eds.), *Children and Adolescents with Emotional and Behavioral Dis-*

orders: Proceedings of the Fifth Annual Virginia Beach Conference (p. 141). Medical College of Virginia, Virginia Commonwealth University, Richmond, VA.

Scully, D. & Marolla, J. (1985). Riding the bull at Gilley's: Convicted rapists describe the rewards of rape. *Social Problems, 32,* 251–263.

Smith, H. E. (1987). Serial killers. *Criminal Justice International, 3,* 1–4.

Staff, T. (1996, January 27). Miami may have new serial killer. *The Gainesville Sun,* p. 4B.

Vorpagel, R. E. (1982). Painting psychological profiles: Charlantanism, charisma, or a new science? *Police Chief,* 156–159.

Watkin, J. G. (1984). The Bianchi (L.A. Hillside Strangler) Case: Sociopath or multiple personality? *Internation Journal of Clinical and Experimental Hypnosis, 2,* 67–101.

Weinshel, E. & Calet, V. (1972). On certain neurotic equivalents of necrophilia. *International Journal of Psychoanalysis, 53,* 67–75.

Wilson, P. R. (1988). "Stranger" child murder: Issues relating to causes and controls. *Forensic Science International, 36,* 267–277.

Yarvis, R. M. (1990). Axis I and Axis II diagnostic parameters of homicide. *Bull Am Acad Psychiatry Law, 18,* 249–269.

Yochelson, S. & Samenow, S. S. (1977). *The criminal Personality.* New York: Jason Aronson.

14 Alcohol, Drugs, and Violence

BRIAN M. QUIGLEY

Research Institute on Addictions

KENNETH E. LEONARD

Research Institute on Addictions

On Saturday, May 24, 1997 two Long Island men allegedly went on an all day drinking binge. At about 11 P.M., one man went to a bar while his friend waited in a nearby parking lot. After the bar refused to serve the man, he returned to find his friend asleep apparently passed out from drinking. The first man then proceeded to kick his drinking buddy and step on his throat. Acquiring a baseball bat, he then beat the other man until he believed him to be dead. He subsequently fled and held up a gas station with a knife. Police later arrested him, he confessed, and was charged with robbery and attempted murder ("Drinking Binge," 1997).

Stories such as this seem all too common. Alcohol and drugs are often associated with stories of violence and crime. Yet, the question remains: What impact do alcohol and drugs truly have on violence and crime? Studies examining the percentage of individuals using alcohol when committing a homicide range from 7 to 85 percent, but most estimates exceed 60 percent. Similarly, estimates of alcohol use by perpetrators of assaults range from 24 to 82 percent (Collins & Messerschmidt, 1993) and has been estimated to be 63 percent in violent crimes in general (Pihl & Peterson, 1995). In 64 percent of rapes, the victims report their attacker had been drinking (Koss, Deniro, Seibel, & Cox, 1988).

In the present chapter, we review the literature regarding the impact of alcohol and drug use on interpersonal violence. Although we will discuss numerous drugs when appropriate, the majority of the discussion will focus on the effects of alcohol. Alcohol is the substance most closely associated with aggression (Reiss & Roth, 1993), and due to the large amount of research, we are able to draw more conclusions about the effects of alcohol than about the effects of other drugs. However, one should not assume that the conclusions reached about the effects of alcohol can be generalized to other drugs. Other drugs (e.g., marijuana, cocaine, barbiturates) have different pharmacological effects than alcohol and, consequently, have different effects on behavior. Additionally, alcohol is often used by itself, while other substances are often used in combination with each other or in combination with alcohol (Chaiken & Chaiken, 1982). Consequently, it is often very difficult to disentangle the effects of other drugs from the effects of alcohol. Only in controlled laboratory settings in which drugs are used singularly can we draw clearer conclusions about the effects of drugs other than alcohol. Due to these problems, we will attempt to make clear when and what other drugs have the same effects as alcohol, and when and what other drugs have different effects.

In the present chapter, we will first describe several important distinctions that need to be drawn in order to understand why alcohol and drugs may facilitate violence. Then, we will outline the research methodologies which have been used to examine the relationship between alcohol, drugs, and aggression and present some illustrative studies addressing the link between alcohol, drugs, and violence. Following a description of the research methodologies, we will outline three hypothesized explanations for the alcohol/drug and aggression relationship and discuss evidence regarding these explanations.

Important Distinctions

Acute versus Chronic Effect

Alcohol and drugs may have an impact on violence through either acute or chronic effects. An acute effect occurs primarily when the substance is pharmacologically present and active in a user. For example, the intoxicating effects of several alcoholic drinks would be considered an acute effect. These effects occur both in naive users (i.e., inexperienced drinkers) as well as in experienced users (i.e., heavy drinkers), although the experienced users may require considerably more alcohol to experience the intoxication than naive users. Chronic effects refer to effects that occur only after the individual has used the substance for some time. Some chronic effects only arise after years of heavy substance use (e.g., alcoholic liver cirrhosis), while others may require considerably less exposure. More relevant to the issue of violence is the disrupted friendships and marriages that accompany more chronic use of a substance. For example, increased arguments and marital stress might occur as a result of chronic heavy alcohol use, and these might result in an increased likelihood of marital violence, even if the individual is sober at the time of the violence. Similarly, among individuals who are physically addicted, the agitation and irritation that accompany withdrawal might have an impact on aggressiveness.

Substance Use versus Substance Abuse

The second distinction that the reader should keep in mind is the distinction between substance use and substance abuse. Substance abuse may be thought of as a pattern of substance use that is harmful or potentially harmful to the user. This harm may involve physical harm (e.g., risk of injury due to intoxication, using substances in combination with medicines or in the presence of certain physical ailments), psychological harm (e.g., depression), or social harm (e.g., loss of family or friends, arrests). Although the conceptual distinction between use and abuse is fairly clear-cut, the practical distinction is sometimes difficult to draw. The use of any illegal drug is sometimes referred to as drug abuse, even if there is a minimal risk. In contrast, frequent use of alcohol, even daily use of moderate amounts, might not be labeled alcohol abuse.

A related distinction is often drawn between substance abuse and substance dependence. The crux of this distinction is whether the harmful pattern of consumption involves dependence on the substance, either physical dependence as evidenced by tolerance and withdrawal symptoms, or psychological, as evidenced by a variety of behavioral signs, such as giving up important social or recreational activities in order to use the substance.

In the research context, these distinctions are often made with the use of specific *diagnostic* criteria. The most commonly used set of criteria is the *Diagnostic and Statistical Manual* of the American Psychiatric Association, or *DSM-IV*. However, it is also the case that some research studies will utilize terms such as *alcoholic* (i.e., alcohol dependent), *problem drinker,* and *substance abuser* without using such criteria. As a result, an individual who simply admits to the use of an illicit substance may be described as a substance abuser, even though they may not have been classified as such with the use of *DSM-IV* criteria. Consequently, some studies may conclude that violent criminals are more likely to be substance abusers than nonviolent criminals, when what they should be concluding is that the violent criminals are more likely to report having used illegal drugs than nonviolent criminals.

Substance Use/Abuse versus Substance User/Abuser

The final distinction that is important to be aware of is the distinction between substance use or abuse and the substance user or abuser. The importance of this distinction is that an individual who is a substance user may differ from an individual who is not a substance user in a variety of important ways in addition to substance use. For example, a precondition of substance use is availability; if a person does not have access to a specific substance, he or she cannot use it. Consequently, a person who uses cocaine must be involved with others who can supply cocaine, a condition that occurs less often among nonusers. This connection with a drug supplying network may, by itself, have effects on the occurrence of criminal behavior (Goldstein, 1985). Similarly, one factor that seems to be causally implicated in the development of substance abuse is an impulsive, antisocial personality. This personality style is also associated with the occurrence of violence, even among individuals who are not substance abusers. Thus, differences in the occurrence of violence between substance abusers and nonabusers may come about because of the specific use of the substance of interest, or because of all of the other differences that characterize these two groups.

It is also important to remember that most individuals who are substance users, or even abusers, are not necessarily under the influence of substances at all times. Individuals with severe physical dependence may be experiencing the acute effects of the substance or the effects of withdrawal at most times. However, for most substance users, one cannot simply assume that they were using the substance at the time that violence occurred.

Research Methodologies

Descriptive Statistics

One very common research methodology that has been applied to issue of alcohol, drugs, and violence is the simple use of descriptive statistics. Although one would not typically consider this to be a formal research methodology, much of the information, particularly the earliest information reported on the relationship between substance and violence, is of this nature. This research, which spans 40 years, demonstrates that perpetrators of violent crime are often alcohol or drug abusers. Reviews of this literature, though somewhat dated, typically reported that nearly 50 percent of individuals who are incarcerated for homicide and other violent crimes are reported to be alcoholics (Greenberg, 1981; Pernanen, 1976). With the dramatic increase in the prevalence of drug use that has occurred over the past 40 years, more recent studies have been interested in extent to which violent criminals are substance abusers. For example, Wieczorek, Welte, and Abel (1990) found that 50 percent of homicide offenders were classified as "heavier" drinkers (2 to 5 drinks per day) or "much heavier" drinkers (more than 5 drinks per day). Johnson, Natarajan, Dunlap, and Elmoghazy (1994) examined the extent of assaults among individuals differing in their use of drugs. While 10 percent of individuals who had never used drugs had been assaultive in the past year, 20 to 30 percent of crack users had been assaultive. Rates of assault were also elevated for cocaine and, to a lesser extent, for heroin users. However, rates among individuals who only used marijuana were actually somewhat lower than the rates for nondrug users. Despite a variety of methodological problems with much of this research, it is clear that violent criminals are very likely to use alcohol excessively and to use illicit substances. The critical issue to recall is that data indicating that substance users and/ or abusers are likely to engage in violence does not necessarily suggest that the substance use or even substance abuse caused the violence.

There has also been a considerable body of research that has attempted to describe the extent of alcohol or drug use *immediately prior* to the occurrence of a violent event. For example, Wolfgang (1958) studied 588 criminal homicides and found that more than 60 percent involved drinking on the part of an offender, a victim, or both. Pittman and Handy (1964) studied aggravated assaults and reported that about 20 percent of the assaults involved drinking by either the offender or the victim. More recently, Wieczorek, Welte, and Abel (1990) examined the extent of alcohol and drug involvement among men incarcerated for homicide who participated in the National Survey of Jail and Prison Inmates. These authors reported that 36 percent of the offenders had consumed alcohol prior to the homicide, and an additional 13 percent had consumed alcohol in combination with some other drug. Only 7 percent of the offenders had consumed only drugs prior to the homicide. Thus, heavy alcohol use commonly precedes the occurrence of violent actions, but the use of other substances is less common.

In evaluating the meaning of such statistics, several issues need to be considered. First, while such studies report on the frequency of substance use in episodes of violence, they do not provide any information on the frequency of substance use in nonviolent interactions. For example, the finding that 50 percent of assaults were accompanied by alcohol consumption by either the victim or the offender would not be of interest if 50 percent of the time that two individuals got together, one or the other had been drinking. Even though we do not have information concerning the presence of drinking in nonviolent get-togethers, it seems unlikely that it would approach 50 percent. However, it is also clear that not everyone is equally likely to become involved in an assault. We know that violence is more common among young adults than older adults, and among men than among women. There are also individual difference factors that place some individuals at higher risk for assault than others, such as antisocial personality characteristics. Perhaps 50 percent of the time that antisocial young men get together, one or the other has been drinking. If this were the case, the fact that 50 percent of assaults occur under the influence of alcohol would not be impressive. The point of this discussion is that simple rates of involvement are interesting, but do not provide meaningful information concerning associations of substance use and violence.

Nonexperimental Research

Nonexperimental research differs from simple descriptive research in that there is an attempt to compare individuals who have experienced a given event with individuals who have not. One of the most critical issues confronting nonexperimental research on alcohol, drugs, and violence is identifying individuals who have been involved in violence. This can be accomplished in several different ways including the use of offender populations and general populations surveys.

The use of offender populations (i.e., individuals arrested and convicted for the commission of a violent crime) has the strength of ease and efficiency. Although violence seems very common, the overall prevalence of violent behavior is not particularly large. For example, statistics from the Uniform Crime Statistics indicated that 685 violent crimes occurred for every 100,000 inhabitants of the United States in 1995 (U.S. Department of Justice, 1996). This is an annual rate of under 1 percent of the population experiencing violent crime. Given this overall low prevalence rate, identifying violent individuals in the community for the purposes of research is quite difficult. Moreover, violent individuals who have not been arrested may be unwilling to participate in research or to admit to violent behavior for fear of possible incarceration. The use of an offender population is very convenient inasmuch as the individuals have already been identified and located. In addition, the violent behavior of interest has been documented by evidence and by the judicial process, and it is not reliant on the individual admitting responsibility.

Studies of incarcerated violent offenders have provided fairly clear results regarding the prevalence of alcohol and substance use/abuse among violent and nonviolent offenders. Myers (1982) compared 50 men incarcerated for assault, serious assault, and homicide with 50 men incarcerated for nonviolent offenses. In terms of usual drinking patterns (i.e., drinking in a typical week and drinking in the week that they committed the offense), violent and nonviolent offenders could not be distinguished. Similarly, Welte and Miller (1987) compared the alcohol and drug use for the year prior to incarceration for violent and property offenders. The usual drinking patterns of violent and property offenders were very similar. In contrast, the level of drug use was considerably higher among violent offenders than among property offenders. In a study of incarcerated murderers over 21 years of age, more than 50 percent reported regular alcohol use. Nearly one-third reported using alcohol at the time of the crime. Over 50 percent reported using any type of substance at the time of the crime and, with the exception of those over 36 years of age, over 35 percent reported using drugs (e.g., marijuana, cocaine, heroin) but not alcohol at the time of the murder (Fendrich, Mackesy-Amiti, Goldstein, Spunt, & Brownstein, 1995).

There are also drawbacks with respect to the use of offender populations. First, offender populations reflect a minority of individuals who have behaved violently. Many crimes of violence go unreported or unsolved. Pernanen (1991) compared police reports to victims' reports and found that only 4 percent of the violent incidents reported by victims come to the attention of the police. Consequently, the characteristics of violent offenders may reflect both the causes of violence as well as the factors that expedite arrest and conviction. For example, the common observation that about 50 percent of homicide offenders were drinking at the time of the homicide may reflect the inability of intoxicated offenders to avoid detection. Second, the selection of nonviolent individuals from incarcerated populations can be difficult. Although one can rely on the crime of conviction to identify the violent offenders (i.e., homicide offenders, assault offenders), conviction of a nonviolent crime does not ensure that the sample is not violent. The nonviolent conviction may be the result of a plea bargain for a violent offense, or it may reflect the most serious charge that the district attorney could substantiate. Also, many individuals engage in both violent and nonviolent crimes. Thus, many of the individuals convicted of a nonviolent crime will have committed violent crimes in the past.

Despite the difficulty and cost, studying the occurrence of alcohol and violence in the general population is an important approach to identifying a sample of violent individuals. For example, the Epidemiology Catchment Area (ECA) project studied the prevalence of psychiatric disorders in the general population as well as information regarding involvement in violent episodes (Robins & Regier, 1991). Evidence from analysis of this data demonstrated that 15.3 percent of individuals with alcohol problems had been involved in violent incidents. Only 2 percent of the individuals without alcohol abuse problems were involved in violent incidents (Swanson, 1993). Another general populations survey, the Household Survey of Drug and Alcohol Abuse found similar results. Among those with no alcohol use in the previous year, only 2.7 percent were involved in violence. When the respondents drank at least monthly, 14.6 percent had experienced violence in the previous year (Harrison & Gfroerer, 1992).

Drug use has also been found to be related to violent behavior in population surveys. Research by Goldstein, Bellucci, Spunt, and Miller (1991), in which a sample of street users of cocaine were followed over an eight-week time frame, found that 43 percent of male heavy users had perpetrated a violent event, whereas only 21 percent of male nonusers had been in violence. With regard to female cocaine users, only 19 percent of female heavy users were perpetrators of violence, and 27 percent of female nonusers were perpetrators of violence. However, cocaine use is not necessarily a protective factor for women, as 55 percent of heavy users were the victims of violence. Additionally, involvement in crack cocaine business makes involvement in violence more likely. In a survey of 254 crime-involved youths interviewed on the street, 4 percent of those involved as nondealers with cocaine were involved in assaults in the previous year. Eight percent of those involved only as users and/or dealers had been involved in assaults, and 17.4 percent of those who were deeply involved as dealers, manufacturers, and/or smugglers had been involved in violence in the previous 12 months (Inciardi & Pottieger, 1991).

The use of population-based surveys and interviews has been most effective in demonstrating a link between patterns of alcohol use and domestic violence. For example, Leonard, Bromet, Parkinson, Day, and Ryan (1985) assessed a sample of men employed in a factory with respect to current alcohol use, the presence of alcohol abuse or alcohol dependence, and physical aggression in the marriage. Although the average alcohol consumed was unrelated to the physical aggression in the marriage, men with a current diagnosis of either alcohol abuse or dependence were twice as likely to have engaged in physical aggression as men with no diagnosis or men who had a lifetime diagnosis, but were not currently having problems with alcohol. Kaufman, Kantor, and Straus (1990) assessed patterns of alcohol use and domestic violence in a nationally representative sample of households. Husband violence toward their partners was strongly related to the husband's drinking behavior, with the highest rates being observed among husbands who were binge drinkers (5 or more drinks per day, drinks from once a month to one to two times per week). In a national sample of 11,870 male U.S. army personnel from 38 bases, Pan, Neidig, and O'Leary (1994) found that having an alcohol problem significantly increased the likelihood of both mild and severe forms of husband-to-wife aggression. Importantly, this study was also able to assess the relationship between drug use and domestic violence, and found that drug use was significantly related to severe domestic violence. Two recent studies have suggested that heavy drinking is predictive of domestic violence later in the relationship (Heyman, O'Leary, & Jouriles, 1995; Leonard & Senchak, 1996). In both of these studies, men and women were assessed approximately at the time of marriage and reassessed later in marriage. Men who scored higher on standard scales of alcohol problems (i.e., Michigan Alcoholism Screening Test [Selzer, 1971]; the Alcohol Dependence Scale [Skinner & Allen, 1982]) engaged in higher levels of marital violence in the ensuing 12 months than those scoring low on these scales.

Although most nonexperimental research has been concerned with whether violent individuals are disproportionately *substance users or abusers*, recent research has attempted to use this approach to determine whether violent events are disproportionately accompanied by *acute substance use*. This approach has been utilized both within offender populations as well as with community samples. The basic premise behind such research is that if the acute use of a substance contributes to violence, then violent events should have a greater likelihood of involving a substance than some other control event. For example, some studies have compared a violent crime with a nonviolent crime, such as a property crime (e.g., Welte & Miller, 1987). Other studies have compared physical assaults with verbal altercations (e.g., Bard & Zacker, 1974), or severe physical assaults with less severe physical assaults (e.g., Martin & Bachman, 1997; Pernanen, 1991). Welte and Miller (1987) used data collected from jail and prison inmates by the Bureau of Justice Statistics to compare the use of alcohol and other drugs prior to violent versus property offenses. As noted above, the chronic use of alcohol did not differentiate violent offenders from property offenders. However, the use of alcohol prior to the crime of conviction was more common for violent offenses than property offenses. In contrast, these authors report that "those who were under the influence of drugs at the time of the crime were less likely to be in the violent group than those who were not" (p. 319). Although there has been relatively little research focusing on drug use at the time of violence, this latter finding is in general accordance with data from the Drug Use Forecasting program of the National Institute of Justice. Among individuals arrested for homicide and assault, the proportion who test positive for substance use is approximately 40 to 50 percent, while among those arrested for larceny, robbery, and burglary (acquisition crimes), the proportion testing positive exceeds 60 percent.

Several studies have taken a more fine-grained approach to the issue of alcohol in the violent event by more carefully specifying the nature of the violent event. In an early study, Bard and Zacker (1974) focused on family disturbances. These researchers trained police officers in observation and data recording. Officers reported on 962 families involved in 1388 disputes that required police intervention. Among those instances in which an assault was judged to have occurred, 21 percent were reported to involve alcohol use. Among the nonassaultive episodes, 40 percent were reported to involve alcohol. This difference was significant and suggested that alcohol use may have prevented violence. Pernanen (1991) interviewed a random community sample about their most recent victimization. Overall, alcohol was unrelated to the severity of the event, as indicated by whether an injury occurred. Focusing on a small subsample of domestic violence cases, he found that 13 percent of victims of sober violence were injured, while 26 percent of victims of intoxicated violence were injured. This difference was not significant, possibly due to a relatively small sample of subjects whose last victimization was from a spouse.

In evaluating these studies, it should be recalled that individuals who engage in the violent event may differ from individuals who engage in the nonviolent control event. Differences in the rate of substance use in violent versus control events might reflect the differential chronic use of substances by violent versus nonviolent individuals. It may also reflect different personality characteristics of violent and nonviolent individuals. Further, it is important to remember that other situational factors surrounding the violent event may differ from the situational factors surrounding the control event. For example, nonviolent crimes do not require the presence of another individual, while violent crimes do. Consequently, differences in substance use in violent versus nonviolent events could reflect differential presence of drinking in social versus nonsocial situations. Differences in substance use in violent versus nonviolent events would reflect the impact of the substance only if the other individual difference and situational factors are comparable or have been statistically controlled.

A few studies have examined the involvement of alcohol in violent events and have attempted to control for individual difference and situational factors. For example, Martin and Bachman (1997) utilized data from the National Crime Victimization Survey for 1992 and 1993 to determine whether the occurrence or severity of an assault was associated with drinking by the assailant. Severity was defined as a three-category variable of threat, assault without injury, and assault with injury. The survey found a significant association between assailant alcohol use on one hand and the occurrence of assault for male physical attacks on male strangers; 39 percent of the alcohol-involved episodes involved an actual assault, while only 26 percent of the sober episodes involved an assault. There was also a significant association between drinking by a male assailant and injury within intimate assaults; 54 percent of alcohol-involved assaults were severe (i.e., assault with injury), but only 43 percent of the sober assaults were severe. Moreover, these associations remained significant after controlling for several victim characteristics (e.g., marital status and age) and whether or not the incident took place in a public place. Finally, a recent study by Leonard and Quigley (in press) examined the relationship between alcohol use by husbands and wives in their most serious domestic dispute. One set of analyses compared the drinking of men whose most serious event was a verbal argument with men whose most serious dispute involved physical aggression. Because these two types of men might differ in terms of background variables, sociodemographic factors and stable dispositional variables that had been linked to marital aggression were controlled in the analyses. Also, because the circumstances surrounding verbal arguments might differ from the circumstances surrounding physical aggression, several contextual factors were also controlled in the analyses. After controlling for all of these factors, husbands' drinking was more common in domestic disputes that involved physical aggression than in disputes that involved simply arguments. This relationship did not hold for wives' drinking. In order to strengthen the argument, Leonard and Quigley then examined a subsample of individuals who reported on both a verbal argument and a physically aggressive episode. Alcohol was significantly more common in the physically aggressive episode than in the verbal argument.

Despite the promise of such nonexperimental event-based research, the inability to measure and control all of the potential confounding factors makes it difficult to determine causal links between acute alcohol or drug use and violence (Leonard & Jacob, 1988). Nonetheless, the findings to date are generally supportive of a relationship between acute alcohol use and violence in the event. In contrast, the few studies that have examined drug use in the event do not suggest that drug use is related to violence, but rather the reverse, that violence may be suppressed by acute drug use.

Experimental Studies

Laboratory studies are often used to examine the relationship between substance use and aggressive behavior. In such studies, subjects are placed in a laboratory context that allows for the expression of an aggressive response. For example, the subject may ostensibly be allowed to administer an aversive stimulus to an individual, often believed to be another subject, but in actuality, an experimental assistant or confederate. The aversive stimulus may be physical (such as noise or electric shock), verbal (such as an evaluation), or symbolic (as in a response that reduces the money that can be earned in a task). These approaches assume that behaviors, such as giving shocks or taking away points, are analogues to aggressive behavior outside of the laboratory. The usefulness of these laboratory methods depends on the validity of this assumption. Although there are questions about the validity of these experimental paradigms for studying aggression (see Anderson & Bushman, 1997; Giancola & Chermack, 1998; Tedeschi & Quigley, 1996), the procedures have generally been accepted as analogues to real-life aggressive situations.

The use of laboratory analogues is of considerable value in the study of the relationship between acute substance use and violence. The most important value of the experimental method is the control over extraneous variables. Experimental control allows the researcher to rule out alternative explanations for findings and to conclude that one variable has caused the changes observed in another variable. One set of variables that can be controlled in the context of laboratory studies concerns the actual administration of the substance of interest. For example, the pharmacological action of a substance is related to the amount of the substance in the bloodstream (as opposed to the amount in the stomach, intestine, etc.). In the natural environment, individuals differ with respect to the amount of alcohol they drink and the time periods for which they drink. As a result, alcohol consumption in the natural environment can lead to widely disparate blood alcohol levels. With respect to illegal drugs, the actual level of the substance depends on the strength and purity of the drug, which is often unknown. Moreover, illegal drugs, such as cocaine, sometimes contain varying amounts of other drugs. In the context of a laboratory study, precise amounts of a substance can be administered to subjects in such a manner as to ensure that fairly comparable levels are present in the body. In addition, the use of laboratory studies permits the assessment of any effects that occur simply on the basis of the individual's expectations concerning the drug. The administration of a placebo, a pharmacologically inactive substance, as though it were an active drug enables the investigator to assess behavior changes that occur on the basis of the belief that the drug causes certain behaviors.

Another element of control that is available in laboratory studies concerns the ability to separate the impact of substance *use* from any impact of the substance *user*. As described earlier, individuals who frequently use alcohol or illegal drugs differ in a number of ways from individuals who do not. The laboratory context enables the assessment of substance users with no substance use and with a specified dose. It also allows the investigator to determine whether other individual difference factors are important in understanding the acute effect of a substance. For example, one could examine the effects of a substance on light versus heavy users or on aggressive versus nonaggressive users. This control allows the investigator to specify more clearly who might become aggressive with the use of substances and who would be unlikely to become aggressive.

Another important control that the experimental method allows is the control over other situational features that are often a part of violent behaviors. The most critical aspect of this situational control is the ability of the investigator to control the behavior of the victim of aggression. In naturalistic settings, the occurrence of a violent event involves the interactional behavior of two, and sometime more, individuals. An individual can behave in a nonthreatening style, and perhaps, defuse a potentially violent situation. Alternatively, the individual can act provocatively and increase the stakes. Moreover, the potential "victim" might act differently with a clearly intoxicated individual than with a sober individual. In the laboratory situation, the behavior of the "victim" can be controlled such that both sober and intoxicated subjects are confronted with the same victim behavior. Alternatively, the behavior of the victim can be systematically varied to explore whether certain kinds of situations are more likely to result in substance-related violence than others.

In the study of aggression, a number of experimental procedures have been used with humans. The first of these procedures is referred to as the teacher-learner paradigm. In this paradigm, the subject administers shocks to another subject (really a confederate of the experimenter) for incorrect answers on a learning task. A second procedure is the essay evaluation procedure. In this task, a confederate of the experimenter evaluates the subject's essay through delivery of shock (a few shocks for a good essay, many shocks for a bad essay). The subject is then given the opportunity to evaluate an essay by the confederate through the delivery of shocks. Another procedure often used in the alcohol-aggression research is the point subtraction aggression procedure (PSAP), in which the subject plays a competitive game with a confederate. If the subject presses a key 10 times, it subtracts a point from the other person's score; if the subject presses another key 100 times, it adds a point to the participant's own score. These points translate into money. Since the behavior is causing a type of harm (monetary), it has been considered aggressive behavior. The most common procedure used in the laboratory when dealing with alcohol has been the Taylor reaction time paradigm (TAP; Taylor, 1967). In this procedure, subjects play a reaction time game with another subject (usually a confederate of the experimenter). On each trial, the subject sets a level of shock he or she wishes to deliver to the other person. The loser of the reaction time trial (i.e., the slower reactor) then g⟨ is shocked.

Overall in the laboratory paradigms, alcohol increases aggressive responding. Higher levels of alcohol intoxication (BAC = 0.10) have been found to lead to more aggressive responding in the TAP than low levels of intoxication (BAC = 0.03) (Taylor & Gammon, 1975). Bushman and Cooper (1990) conducted a quantitative review of 30 laboratory studies investigating the effects of alcohol on aggressive responding. Overall, they found a significant difference when comparing alcohol administration conditions to control conditions and to placebo conditions. There was no significant difference between control conditions and placebo conditions, indicating that alcohol does have a direct effect on aggressive behavior as measured in the lab. Recently, a second quantitative review of the laboratory literature was conducted (Ito, Miller, & Pollock, 1996), which also demonstrated a significant effect across 49 studies, indicating more aggression for intoxicated than for sober participants. Additionally, as provocation increased, the difference between the alcohol groups and the sober groups decreased, suggesting that even under low levels of provocation, in which sober participants do not become aggressive, alcohol seems to increase aggressive responding.

The effects of a few other drugs on laboratory measures of aggression have also been investigated, although not as extensively as alcohol. The category of drugs known as benzodiazepines are similar to alcohol in that, like alcohol, they act as depressants. The benzodiazepines diazepam (or Valium) and lorazepam have both been found to increase aggressive responding in laboratory studies of aggression (see Bond & Lader, 1988; Gantner & Taylor, 1988; Wilkinson, 1985). Gantner and Taylor administered 10 mg of diazepam to college students participating in the competitive reaction time game. Those who had consumed diazepam set higher shocks initially than did those who had consumed a placebo. The diazepam group also set higher shock in response to provocation than did the placebo group. Similar results were found by Wilkinson (1985), although the strongest effect of diazepam on aggression occurred in low-trait-anxious individuals. Cocaine has also been shown to increase aggressive responding in the Taylor reaction time game. Participants given a high dose of cocaine (2 mg/kg body weight) set higher shock levels than either those who received a low dose of cocaine (1 mg/kg) or those who received a placebo (Licata, Taylor, Berman, & Cranston, 1993).

However, not all drugs have been found to increase aggressive responding in the laboratory. Marijuana may act to suppress aggressive responding. Taylor and colleagues (1976) administered delta-9-tetrahydrocannabinol (THC), which is the active ingredient in marijuana, to participants in the reaction time game. Those who received a high dose of THC (0.3 mg/kg) set lower shock settings than those who received a low dose (0.1 mg/kg), although the effect was not statistically significant. Amphetamines also have not been found to increase aggressive responding. In the TAP, there is no effect of even a high dose of amphetamines (0.32 mg/kg) on aggressive behavior (Breezley, Gantner, Bailey, & Taylor, 1987).

Laboratory paradigms allow for control and the elimination of alternative explanations. However, these procedures also have limitations. Some have questioned the applicability of laboratory measures of aggression to real world situations of aggression (see Anderson & Bushman, 1997 and Berkowitz & Donnerstein, 1982 for discussions of the external validity of laboratory aggression paradigms). All of the studies in the analysis by Bushman and Cooper (1990) utilized only male participants; only rarely in this literature have females been used as subjects and in only one study have intoxicated males aggressed against female confederates (Richardson, 1981). Participants usually play against a confederate of the experimenter who is never shocked (for an exception to this see Leonard, 1984). Tedeschi and Quigley (1996) have questioned laboratory aggression paradigms because, although significant effects are found, the motivations of the subjects are rarely examined in laboratory studies on aggression. Thus, although we know alcohol and benzodiazepine lead to participants giving more shock in these paradigms, the explanation of why this happens is still unclear.

Explanations for the Relationship between Alcohol and Aggression

Noncausal Explanations

The first proposed explanation for the relationship of drugs and violence is not that the use of alcohol and drugs precipitates violence; rather, the use of alcohol and drugs and the commission of violent acts are precipitated by a common set of circumstances. According to this hypothesis, the relationship between drug use and violent behavior only exists because some third variable is the actual cause of both the behaviors.

The first of the noncausal explanations for the relationship of substance use to violence is the subculture of delinquency hypothesis. According to this hypothesis, certain subcultures emerge within society in which behavior that is condemned in the rest of society is encouraged. These subcultures are most likely to exist among lower socioeconomic classes, especially among men, and are distinguished by a concern for machismo and engaging in exciting or dangerous activities (Miller, 1958). When members of these subcultures attempt to integrate into the normative culture, conflict occurs. For example, lower-class school children who are asked to conform to the middle-class expectations of success in school often have problems fitting in. Those who cannot, tend to be attracted to others who also have trouble fitting in and form antinormative groups. In these groups, it is acceptable and even encouraged to engage in antinormative and delinquent behavior such as drug use, crime, and violence (Cohen, 1968).

What evidence exists for the subculture of delinquency hypotheses? Some exists in the data from the National Youth Survey (Elliott, Huizinga, & Ageton, 1985), which followed a representative sample of over 1,700 children ages 11 to 17 years over several years time. Analysis of these data, reported by Uihlein (1994), demonstrates that drug use and delinquency in these youth were correlated both within each year and across years. That is, drug use in each year was predictive of delinquency that year as well as delinquency in subsequent years. Conversely, delinquency was also predictive of drug use within a year and predictive of drug use in subsequent years. Also consistent with this subculture of delinquency hypothesis was the fact that both drug use and delinquency were negatively correlated with the adolescent's attachment to their parents, their school, and having goals in life, and was positively related to peer attachment.

However, it has been suggested that the antisocial feature may not necessarily be a subculture of delinquency, but rather a general deviance syndrome. According to this hypothesis, those individuals who are likely to engage in violent behavior also demonstrate predispositions to engage in other deviant behavior. It has been found that those with a history of substance dependence are more aggressive in laboratory measures of aggression than those who have no history of substance dependence (Allen, Moeller, Rhoades, & Cherek, 1997). Additionally, early onset of aggressive behavior in boys has been found to be predictive of later violence, criminal behavior, and alcohol use (Pulkkinen, 1983). Dembo and colleagues (1992) found, in a sample of juvenile offenders, that alcohol use and delinquency both related to a general factor of deviance, which was predictive of deviance 4 months later. It has also been suggested that the relationship of alcohol and drug use may be due to the relationship of the two variables to other personality disorders such as hyperactivity (Hechtman, Weiss, & Perlman, 1984). Consistent with this possibility is the finding of White (1991) that heavy marijuana users who are low on delinquency did not differ on measures of impulsivity, intensity of emotional outbursts, and disinhibition from those high in delinquent behavior but low on marijuana use. Although these personality measures did distinguish these two groups from a group consisting of individuals low on both delinquency and marijuana use, they could not be distinguished from each other on these measures. This is suggestive of a certain personality type which is likely to engage in both violence and substance use.

Alcohol and drugs can also be related to violence because violence can be involved in the acquisition of alcohol and drugs. For example, the mugger who engages in the act in order to obtain enough money to buy the drug to support his habit. This is referred to as economic-compulsive violence (Goldstein, 1985). A survey of prison inmates by the Bureau of Justice Statistics (U.S. Department of Justice, 1993) found that over a quarter of inmates committing property crimes such as robbery or burglary admitted committing the crime in order to get money for drugs. On the other hand, 12 percent of the inmates in prison for a violent crime also admitted committing the crime to obtain money for drugs. Drug dealing subcultures also may be more likely to use violence in connection with "business affairs." One type of Latino street gang identified by Feldman, Mandel, and Fields (1985) was basically concerned with active drug dealing, and when violence occurred in the gang, it was usually due to conflict over money or drugs. This is in contrast to other gangs that valued violence and used it mostly with regard to territorial disputes. Fagan and Chin (1990) examined individuals arrested for drug possession or sales in the upper Manhattan neighborhoods of Washington Heights and West Harlem. The authors suggested that with numerous crack-selling groups existing in neighborhoods, competition among drug dealers facilitates violence. In the sample, 38.5 percent of those dealing in crack cocaine and heroin reported being in fights with rival drug dealers, and 42.3 percent reported having fights with other dealers over the quality of drugs. Violence toward unpaying customers was also frequent, as 38.5 percent of dealers reported assaulting customers to collect debts.

Even in legal situations related to the acquisition of a substance, violence has been found to occur. Felson, Baccaglini, and Gmelch (1986), in a study of bars in Albany, New York, and Dublin, Ireland, found that the most commonly reported cause of violence was refusal to serve. However, although the desire to obtain alcohol definitely impacted the violence, it is likely that most of the individuals who became violent due to the refusal to serve also had been drinking previously. Because of this it is possible that some direct pharmacological effects may have also played a part in the violence.

Those committing crimes may use alcohol and drugs in order to help them prepare themselves for the act. Anxiety is said to be "soluble in alcohol and other drugs" (Pihl & Peterson, 1995, p. 143). Ritual behaviors engaged in by street gangs, such as the induction of a new member or the expulsion of old members, often involved the use of alcohol and drugs, as well as the commission of violent or criminal acts (Padilla, 1992). Vigil (1988) found that alcohol and drugs are used by Chicano gang members in Los Angeles to relax before engaging in acts of violence. To prepare themselves for conflict with other gangs, the members drank alcohol and smoked PCP-laced cigarettes. This ritualized type of drug use helped promote a solidarity among the gang members. The use of alcohol and drugs to prepare one's self for going into a dangerous situation is not restricted to street gangs. Burglars have been found to use drugs in order to reduce the stress associated with committing a crime as well as to "psych themselves up" before doing the crime (Cromwell, Olson, Avary, & Marks, 1991).

It is clear that alcohol and drugs have indirect effects on violence. There is evidence that a subculture exists in which heavy alcohol and drugs use, as well as violence are considered acceptable. Additionally, some individuals may be predisposed to engaging in deviant behavior, due to certain personality characteristics. Violence may also be instrumental in obtaining alcohol and drugs and conversely, alcohol and drug use may sometimes be used in order to prepare individuals to engage in criminal behavior. However, the relationship of drug use and violence cannot be totally explained by these types of mechanisms. They do not explain the laboratory research in which these variables are controlled, and yet alcohol and certain drugs still lead to higher levels of aggression. In order to more fully explain the relationship between drugs and violence, we must examine other mechanisms.

Expectancy Explanations

One of the primary social explanations for the alcohol-violence connection focuses on the symbolic value of alcohol consumption. Although this approach has been most clearly described with respect to alcohol and violence, it clearly could apply to drug use and violence as well. According to this perspective, periods of intoxication may be socially defined as a "time out" from usual social rules (Critchlow, 1986). Consequently, aggressive and other disruptive behaviors may occur with a lessened concern for possible social sanctions. The finding that alcohol has different effects in disparate cultures suggests that some of the effects of alcohol are socially determined rather than pharmacological (MacAndrew & Edgerton, 1969).

Within the field of psychology, this perspective has been represented by the concept of alcohol expectancies. According to this approach, individuals maintain certain learned (either socially or through direct experience) expectations concerning the effects alcohol has on behavior. These beliefs, in turn, serve both to motivate drinking behavior and to direct behavior of individuals who have consumed alcohol. In fact, there is strong empirical evidence that alcohol expectancies predict self-reported drinking (see Brown, Goldman, & Christiansen, 1987) and may have a significant impact on a variety of intoxicated behaviors.

Survey Studies.   Several nonexperimental studies have examined the relationship of expectancies to aggressive behavior. Leonard and Blane (1988) found, in males, that the belief that alcohol leads to aggression was positively correlated with the assault subscale of the Buss-Durkey Hostility Inventory. The men who reported believing alcohol lead to aggression were also more likely to report that they themselves were aggressive. However, since no measure of these men's aggression while intoxicated was taken, it is difficult to determine the meaning of this association. Dermen and George (1989) surveyed college students regarding their usual drinking behavior, alcohol-aggression expectancies, and their involvement in violence. For those with a low or moderate level of expectancy that alcohol led to aggression, the number of drinks per week was not related to aggressive behavior. However, for those with a high expectancy score, the number of drinks per week was positively and significantly associated with aggressive behavior. Leonard and Senchak (1993) examined the impact of alcohol expectancies on premarital husband violence. Frequent heavy drinking was associated with premarital aggression among husbands who believed that alcohol was a cause of aggression, but not among those who denied that alcohol caused aggression. Although these cross-sectional results tended to support the importance of alcohol expectancies in understanding marital aggression, the authors suggested the alternative explanation that heavy drinkers who have been aggressive may alter their alcohol expectancies accordingly. Thus, rather than alcohol use and alcohol-aggression expectancies influencing marital aggression, it could be that alcohol use and marital aggression influenced expectancies. In a longitudinal analysis of the same data set, Quigley and Leonard (1999) found no relationship between alcohol expectancies at the beginning of marriage and alcohol-related aggression one year later. Expectancies, however, were negatively related to the amount of severe violence in the first year of marriage. The less the husband believed alcohol led to aggression at the beginning of marriage, the more severe violence occurred later in the marriage.

Laboratory Studies.   Rather than relying on self-reports of aggression, laboratory studies have attempted to examine the role of alcohol expectancies both through measuring and manipulating expectancies. The placebo condition in lab studies, in which subjects are told that they have received alcohol when they have not, is meant to control for expectancy effects. Although some laboratory studies have shown that subjects in placebo conditions set higher levels of shock than do subjects in the control groups (e.g., Zeichner & Pihl, 1980), most investigations have not found significant differences between placebo groups and control groups. Bushman and Cooper's (1990) meta-analysis demonstrated an overall significant difference between the alcohol conditions and placebo conditions and an overall nonsignificant difference between placebo and control conditions. Taken together, these findings support a direct effect of alcohol on aggressive behavior that is not mediated by the belief that one has consumed alcohol.

Individual differences in expectancy have also been investigated in laboratory studies on alcohol and aggression. Rohsenow and Bachorowski (1984) measured alcohol expectancies in three laboratory studies investigating verbal aggression. All three studies produced different results regarding the impact of alcohol expectancies on aggressive behavior. In the first study, alcohol expectancies did not correlate with aggression among subjects who believed that they had consumed alcohol. In the second study, the expectancy that alcohol would increase verbal aggression was related to aggressive responding. The third study showed no correlation between expectancies of alcohol increasing aggression in general or verbal aggression in particular, and actual aggressive behavior. However, the expectancy that alcohol would increase social and physical pleasure was negatively correlated to aggressive behavior among those who believed that they had consumed alcohol. The relationship between alcohol consumption, alcohol-aggression expectancies, and aggression has also been assessed using the Taylor competitive reaction time task (Chermack & Taylor, 1995). Participants with low and high alcohol-aggression expectancies were randomly assigned to receive either a placebo or a high dose of alcohol. Although subjects who received alcohol were more aggressive than placebo subjects, neither the main effect of expectancy or interaction of alcohol and expectancy were significant.

The direct effects of expectancies regarding alcohol has received little support; however, it is possible that the effects of social expectancies may be complex and research has not yet been sophisticated enough to detect it. Alcohol use is more common among men (Cahalan, 1978), and is associated with a macho identity, hence those who use it may picture themselves as strong or powerful. When the situation allows for an aggressive response, these individuals may be more likely to engage in aggressive behavior. Additionally, alcohol expectancies may not proactively influence aggressive behavior. However, if someone believes alcohol makes one tougher or more aggressive and expects to enter a situation in which these qualities could be useful, they may be more likely to use alcohol before entering into a potentially violent situation.

Pharmacological Explanations

Current pharmacological explanations of alcohol's effects on aggression do not necessarily propose that alcohol itself automatically makes people more aggressive. Alcohol can have many effects including making one relaxed, happy, or sleepy, as well as aggressive. The pharmacological explanations of alcohol's relationship to aggression have to do with how alcohol influences cognitive processes. Early work suggested that alcohol works to reduce self-awareness. A study by Bailey, Leonard, Cranston, and Taylor (1983) compared intoxicated individuals to sober individuals on the Taylor reaction time game. Half of these individuals were seated in front of a mirror and a video camera, and the other half were not. The mirror and camera were meant to increase the subjects' self-awareness. Results showed that both intoxicated and sober subjects in the self-aware condition were less aggressive than those in the non-self-aware condition. The pharmacological explanations for alcohol's effects on aggression emphasizes the impact of alcohol's influence on what cues are attended to in the environment (Taylor & Leonard, 1983). For example, in the self-awareness study by Bailey and colleagues (1983), the mirror acted to make intoxicated individual's attend to self-relevant cues more than if the mirror had not been there. The question of why some cues are attended and others are not has been discussed by numerous theories, including alcohol myopia, anxiolytic effects of alcohol, and the social information processing theory.

One of the more intriguing hypotheses is that alcohol creates an attentional myopia which constrains the cues one attends to while under the influence (Steele & Josephs, 1990). This hypothesis, which arose from earlier theories of Pernanen (1976) and Taylor and Leonard (1983), posits that alcohol interferes with the processing of information and makes one attend to the most salient aspect of the situation. When two responses are likely (one an instigating and the other an inhibiting), intoxication will cause an individual to attend to instigating cues more so than to inhibitory cues. Alcohol is proposed to have its effect only under these situations of *inhibition conflict*, that is, when instigations and inhibitions are relatively equal. Myopia is proposed to effect the evaluation of information as well as the decision-making process regarding behavioral reactions to the situation. In a meta-analysis of several different types of social behaviors, including aggression, risk-taking, self-disclosure, and sexual interest, Steele and Southwick (1985) demonstrated that alcohol's effects on all of these social behaviors only occurred when situations of inhibition conflict existed. However, none of the studies examines explicitly manipulated inhibition conflict. Rather, the authors used a post hoc categorization of the studies to identify situations of inhibition conflict. Some primary research supportive of the myopia hypothesis has been reported by Steele, Critchlow, and Liu (1985). The authors demonstrated that helping behavior was more likely to occur under the influence of alcohol only when inhibition conflict exists (Steele et al., 1985). In this study, subjects who were given alcohol were most likely to volunteer for another study only when the study consisted of a boring task (i.e., a conflict situation, the person wanted to help, but the task was not enjoyable).

Actual effects of inhibition conflict on an intoxicated individual's decision making have only been demonstrated in a few studies. Banaji and Steele (1989) demonstrated that the difference between individual's estimates of real self and ideal self became smaller when under the influence of alcohol, due to alcohol's effect of making one attend to the more salient positive aspects of self-image and disregard the negative aspects. Alcohol has also been shown to make one attend to facilitory cues and disregard inhibitory cues in studies of driving while intoxicated and risky sexual behavior (MacDonald, Zanna, & Fong, 1995, 1996). When questions containing a facilitory cue (e.g., "If I only had a short distance to drive...") are asked of intoxicated individuals, these individuals indicate more intentions to drink and drive. Similarly, when facilitory cues are imbedded in questions asked of intoxicated males (e.g., "My partner is on the pill so there is little reason to worry if we have intercourse"), those males were less likely to report an intention to use a condom.

However, alcohol myopia is not the only theory as to why alcohol makes one attend to facilitory cues and disregard inhibitory cues. Another hypothesis has to do with the anxiety-reducing properties of alcohol. The anxiolysis-disinhibition model (Ito et al., 1996) proposes that in situations in which aggression has the potential to occur, anxiety is also present. This anxiety can be due to fear of retaliation for engaging in aggressive actions or fear of censure for aggressive actions. The anxiety arising from the situation may inhibit responses to the situation. Hence, in situations in which aggression is likely and alcohol is also present, those who have been drinking alcohol will feel less anxiety than those who have not been drinking, and will therefore be more likely to engage in aggressive behavior.

A recent meta-analysis (Ito et al., 1996) examined the myopia hypothesis in competition with the anxiolytic hypothesis, and found evidence supportive of both mechanisms. In terms of alcohol myopia, a significant effect of alcohol on aggressive behavior was found in situations of high inhibition conflict (as rated by the researchers). A small but significant effect was also found under situations of low inhibition conflict. However, the effect of alcohol was stronger for high versus low inhibition conflict suggesting a significantly stronger effect under situations of high inhibition conflict. Additionally, the influence of inhibition conflict depended on the dose of alcohol. When low dosages were used, a significant effect of alcohol on aggression was found in both low and high inhibition conditions. However, when high doses of alcohol were used, the effect of alcohol was present only under high conflict inhibition conditions. The low inhibition condition did not produce a significant effect. In support of the anxiolysis-disinhibition model, the difference between intoxicated and sober individuals in aggressive behavior increased as the amount of anxiety present in the studies increased.

Although these results suggest inhibition conflict and anxiolysis-disinhibition do play roles in the effect of alcohol on aggressive behavior, it is unclear if they are mutually exclusive hypotheses or really part of the same mechanism. Situations of high inhibition conflict may also be situations which produce high anxiety. At least one study (Zeichner, Pihl, Niaura, & Zacchia, 1982) has shown that the anxiolysis-disinhibition model may be preferred over the myopia model. In this study, participants delivered shocks to a confederate who administered noxious noise in return. The confederate was programmed to deliver levels of noxious noise that correlated perfectly with the shock levels that the subject set. In order to make the subjects attend to the inhibitory cues, they were asked to write down their shock level and the confederate's noise level. However, even though procedures forced subjects to attend to inhibitory cues (i.e., the lack of escalation by the confederate), those who were intoxicated still delivered higher levels of shock, suggesting that even though the inhibitory cues were attended to, they did not produce any anxiety and consequently no inhibition.

One other model has been used to explain the effects of alcohol on aggressive behavior. The social information processing perspective proposed that aggressive actions are a product of several separate cognitive skills, including the encoding and interpretation of cues existing in the interpersonal situation, response generation, outcome evaluation, response selection, and response enactment. Dodge (1986) has demonstrated deficits in these skills in aggressive children. Sayette, Wilson, and Elias (1993) attempted to determine if alcohol consumption causes deficits in intoxicated individuals similar to those observed in aggressive children. If intoxicated individuals did demonstrate the same deficits as aggressive children, it would provide a useful explanatory framework for alcohol's impact on aggression.

Sayette and colleagues (1993) examined the impact of alcohol on the different stages in the interpretation and decision process. Participants were presented with a videotape showing one individual rudely changing the channel on another person. Different versions of the tape varied whether the individual behaved aggressively or neutrally. Participants were then asked to rate the individuals on several dimensions and then decide what would happen next. Results showed that alcohol did not have an effect on participants' perceptions of the situation. Intoxicated individuals did not view the offending individuals action as any more intentional or aggressive than sober participants. However, there was a difference between intoxicated and sober subjects in terms of decision making. Those who had consumed alcohol made less adaptive (i.e., more aggressive) response options and were more likely to endorse the use of aggressive options then were subjects who received a placebo.

The evidence that alcohol does have pharmacological effects on aggressive behavior is substantial. It is clear that alcohol influences the cognitive decision-making ability of individuals; however, the mechanism for that effect is still not well understood. Alcohol myopia, anxiolysis-disinhibition, and social information models all have some support in the literature. At the moment, it is not yet clear which is the best explanation. It is possible all three may actually be aspects of a single mechanism. As mentioned earlier, alcohol myopia and anxiolysis-disinhibition are similar in the mechanisms they propose and in many hypotheses. Evidence seems to support both, although some (Ito et al., 1996; Zeichner et al., 1983) seems to support anxiolysis-disinhibition over myopia. Additionally, the anxiety-reducing properties of benzodiazepines, which have also been found to increase aggressive responding in the laboratory, would seem to support the anxiolysis-disinhibition model. The social information model is not necessarily at odds with either the myopia or the anxiolysis-disinhibition models. Consistent with the other two models, Sayette and colleagues (1993) demonstrated that alcohol has its effects on response generation, rather than the information encoding stages.

Summary

In this chapter, we have examined both the experimental and the nonexperimental research on the relationship between violence and alcohol or drugs. Both types of evidence converge to indicate that alcohol and some drugs do have an effect on aggressive behavior. Studies of offender populations, marital violence studies, and large-scale survey studies all indicate a relationship exists. Laboratory research has demonstrated that the relationship is not entirely a spurious one. Alcohol and some drugs increase aggression under the proper conditions. We have concentrated mostly on alcohol, because the majority of the research has been conducted on alcohol. However, we have attempted to also discuss other drugs, such as benzodiazepines, cocaine, and marijuana, where appropriate.

We should say more about the relationship of other drugs to violence. Anecdotal evidence links many drugs to crime and violence. For example, even though laboratory studies have clearly shown that marijuana does not increase aggressive responding, crime statistics show that the majority of arrestees test positive for drug use, mostly for use of marijuana and cocaine (U.S. Department of Justice, 1996). The noncausal explanations may be the best explanations for many of these findings. When subcultures and individuals are prone to engage in deviant behavior, violence and drugs often co-occur, even though there is no causal relationship between them. Additionally, involvement in illegal activities such as drug trafficking can also lead to the co-occurrence of drugs and violence, although the drugs are not technically causing the violence. However, controlled primary research on the effects of drugs other than alcohol on aggressive behavior is still lacking.

It is clear that alcohol use is related to violent behavior. However, even with alcohol, no single explanation satisfactorily explains the relationship. Violent criminals are often heavy drinkers, and may use alcohol as a form of relaxation or as a way to prepare themselves for engaging in criminal or violent actions. To the extent that these events occur, the relationship between alcohol and violence is spurious. Although spurious relationships explain a portion of the alcohol violence relationship, they cannot account for all of the evidence.

The explanation that alcohol does not cause aggressive behavior, rather it is the expectancy that alcohol leads to aggression that actually causes the aggression, has not found strong support in the literature. Studies rarely find differences between placebo and control conditions, and individual differences in expectancy are inconsistent in their prediction of alcohol-related violence. However, the social impact of drinking still needs to be more systematically examined. Some form of expectancy may help explain the relationship between alcohol and aggression, but the theory to this point has not had much explanatory power. It is clear that alcohol does have a direct effect on aggressive behavior; however, the mechanism of that effect is still unclear. Alcohol appears to interfere with cognitive decision making regarding behavior in potentially violent situations by influencing the cues that are attended to by the intoxicated individual. The intoxicated individual seems to attend to salient instigating cues more than potential inhibitory cues and to choose behavioral responses consistent with this cognitive bias. Consequently, alcohol instigation may increase the likelihood that violent behavior will occur among predisposed individuals in potentially provocative situations.

REFERENCES

Allen, T. J., Moeller, F. G., Rhoades, H. M., & Cherek, D. R. (1997). Subjects with a history of drug dependence are more aggressive than subjects with no drug use history. *Drug and Alcohol Dependence, 46,* 95–103.

Anderson, C. T. & Bushman, B. J. (1997). External validity of "trivial" experiments: The case of laboratory aggression. *Review of General Psychology, 1,* 19–41.

Bailey, D. S., Leonard, K. E., Cranston, J. W., & Taylor, S. P. (1983). Effects of alcohol and self awareness on human physical aggression. *Personality and Social Psychology Bulletin, 9,* 289–295.

Banaji, M. R. & Steele, C. M. (1989). Alcohol and self-evaluation: Is a social cognition approach beneficial. *Social Cognition, 7,* 137–151.

Bard, M. & Zacker, J. (1974). Assaultiveness and alcohol use in family disputes. *Criminology, 12,* 281–292.

Berkowitz, L. & Donnerstein, E. (1982). External validity is more than skin deep: Some answers to criticisms of laboratory experiments. *American Psychologist, 37,* 245–257.

Bond, A. & Lader, M. (1988). Differential effects of oxazepam and lorazepam on aggressive responding. *Psychopharmacology, 95,* 369–373.

Breezley, D. A., Gantner, A. B., Bailey, D. S., & Taylor, S. P. (1987). Amphetamines and human physical aggression. *Journal of Research and Personality, 21,* 52–60.

Brown, S. A., Goldman, M. S., & Christiansen, B. A. (1987). Do alcohol expectancies mediate drinking patterns of adults? *Journal of Consulting and Clinical Psychology, 53,* 512–519.

Bushman, B. J. & Cooper, H. M. (1990). Effects of alcohol on human aggression: An integrative research review. *Psychological Bulletin, 107,* 341–354.

Cahalan, D. (1978). Implications of American drinking practices and attitudes for prevention and treatment of alcoholism. In G. A. Marlatt & P. E. Nathan (Eds.), *Behavioral Approaches to Alcoholism* (pp. 6–26). New Brunswick, NJ: Rutgers Center for Alcohol Studies.

Chaiken, J. & Chaiken, M. (1982). *Varieties of Criminal Behavior.* Santa Monica, CA: Rand Corporation.

Chermack, S. T. & Taylor, S. P. (1995). Alcohol and human physical aggression: Pharmacological versus expectancy effects. *Journal of Studies on Alcohol, 56,* 449–456.

Cohen, A. K. (1968). The delinquent subculture. In E. Rubington and M. S. Weinberg (Eds.), *Deviance: The Interactionist Perspective* (pp. 211–212). New York: Macmillan.

Collins, J. J. & Messerschmidt, M. A. (1993). Epidemiology of alcohol-related violence. *Alcohol Health and Research World, 17,* 93–100.

Critchlow, B. (1986). The powers of John Barleycorn: Beliefs about the effects of alcohol on social behavior. *American Psychologist, 41,* 751–764.

Cromwell, P. F., Olson, J. N., Avary, D. W., & Marks, A. (1991). How drugs affect decisions by burglars. *International Journal of Offender Therapy and Comparative Criminology, 35,* 310–321.

Dembo, R., Williams, L., Wothke, W., Schmeidler, J., Getreu, A., Berry, E., & Wish, E. D. (1992). The generality of deviance: Replication of a structural model among high risk youths. *Journal of Research in Crime and Delinquency, 29*, 200–216.

Dermen, K. H. & George, W. H. (1989). Alcohol expectancy and the relationship between drinking and physical aggression. *The Journal of Psychology, 123*, 153–161.

Drinking binge on Long Island leads to charges of robbery, attempted murder. (1997, May 27). *The Buffalo News*, p. A7.

Dodge, K. A. (1986). A social information processing model of social competence in children. In M. Perlmutter (Ed.), *Cognitive Perspectives on Children's Psychology*, (Vol. 18, pp. 77–125). Hillsdale, NJ: Erlbaum.

Elliott, D. S., Huizinga, D., & Ageton, S. S. (1985). *Explaining Delinquency and Drug Use.* Beverly Hills, CA: Sage.

Fagan, J. & Chin, K. (1990). Violence as regulation and social control in the distribution of crack. In M. De La Rosa, E. Y. Lambert, & B. Gropper (Eds.), *Drugs and Violence: Causes, Correlates, and Consequences* (NIDA Research Monograph No.103, DHHS Pub. No. ADM 90-1721, pp. 8–43). Rockville, MD: Department of Health and Human Services.

Feldman, H. W., Mandel, J., & Fields, A. (1985). In the neighborhood: A strategy for delivering early intervention services to young drug users in their natural environments. In A. S. Friedman & G. M. Beschner (Eds.), *Treatment Services for Adolescent Substance Abusers.* Rockville, MD: National Institute on Drug Abuse.

Felson, R. B., Baccaglini, W., & Gmelch, G. (1986). Barroom brawls: Aggression and violence in Irish and American bars. In A. Campbell & J. J. Gibbs (Eds.), *Violent Transactions* (pp. 153–167). New York: Basil Blackwell.

Fendrich, M., Mackesy-Amiti, M. E., Goldstein, P., Spunt, B., & Brownstein, H. (1995). Substance involvement among juvenile murderers: Comparisons with older offenders based on interviews with prison inmates. *International Journal of the Addictions, 30*, 1363–1382.

Gantner, A. B. & Taylor, S. P. (1988). Human physical aggression as a function of diazepam. *Personality and Social Psychology Bulletin, 14*, 479–484.

Giancola, P. R. & Chermack, S. T. (1998). Construct validity of laboratory aggression paradigms: A response to Tedeschi and Quigley (1996). *Aggression and Violent Behavior: A Review Journal, 3*, 237–253.

Goldstein, P. J. (1985). The drugs-violence nexus: A tripartite conceptual framework. *Journal of Drug Issues, 15*, 493–506.

Goldstein, P. J., Bellucci, P. A., Spunt, B. J., & Miller, T. (1991). Volume of cocaine and violence: Comparison between men and women. *Journal of Drug Issues, 21*, 345–367.

Greenberg, S. W. (1981). Alcohol and crime: A methodological critique of the literature. In J. J. Collins (Ed.), *Drinking and Crime*, pp. 70–109. New York: Guilford.

Harrison, L. & Gfroerer, J. (1992). The intersection of drug use and criminal behavior: Results from the National Household Survey on Drug Abuse. *Crime and Delinquency, 38*, 422–443.

Hechtman, L., Weiss, G., & Perlman, T. (1984). Hyperactives as young adults: Past and current substance abuse and antisocial behavior. *American Journal of Orthopsychiatry, 54*, 415–425.

Heyman, R. E., O'Leary, K. D., & Jouriles, E. N. (1995). Alcohol and aggressive personality styles: Potentiators of serious physical aggression against wives? *Journal of Family Psychology, 9*, 44–57.

Inciardi, J. A. & Pottieger, A. E. (1991). Kids, crack, and crime. *Journal of Drug Issues, 21*, 257–270.

Ito, T. A., Miller, N., & Pollock, V. E. (1996). Alcohol and aggression: A meta-analysis on the moderating effects of inhibitory cues, triggering events, and self-focused attention. *Psychological Bulletin, 120*, 60–82.

Johnson, B. D., Natarajan, M., Dunlap, E., & Elmoghazy, E. (1994). Crack abusers and noncrack abusers: Profiles of drug use, drug sales, and nondrug criminality. *Journal of Drug Issues, 24*, 117–141.

Kaufman Kantor, G. & Straus, M. A. (1990). The "Drunken Bum" theory of wife beating. In M. A. Straus & R. J. Gelles (Eds.), *Physical Violence in American Families Risk Factors and Adaptions to Violence in 8,145 Families* (pp. 203–224). New Brunswick, NJ: Transaction.

Koss, M. P., Deniro, T. E., Seibel, C. A., & Cox, S. L. (1988). Stranger, acquaintance and date rape: Is there a difference in the victim's experience? *Psychology of Women Quarterly, 12*, 1–24.

Leonard, K. E. (1984). Alcohol consumption and escalatory aggression in intoxicated and sober dyads. *Journal of Studies on Alcohol, 45*, 75–80.

Leonard, K. E. & Blane, H. T. (1988). Alcohol expectancies and personality characteristics in young men. *Addictive Behaviors, 13*, 353–357.

Leonard, K. E., Bromet, E. J., Parkinson, D. K., Day, N. L., & Ryan, C. M. (1985). Patterns of alcohol use and physically aggressive behavior in men. *Journal of Studies on Alcohol, 46*, 279–282.

Leonard, K. E. & Jacob, T. (1988). Alcohol, alcoholism, and family violence. In V. B. Van Hasselt, R. L. Morrison, A. S. Bellack, & M. Hersen (Eds.), *Handbook of Family Violence*, pp. 383–406. New York: Plenum.

Leonard, K. E. & Quigley, B. M. (in press). Drinking and marital aggression in newlyweds: An event-based analysis of drinking and the occurrence of husband marital aggression. *Journal of Studies on Alcohol*.

Leonard, K. E. & Senchak, M. (1993). Alcohol and premarital aggression among newlywed couples. *Journal of Studies on Alcohol, 11*, 96–108.

Leonard, K. E. & Senchak, M. (1996). The prospective prediction of husband marital aggression among newlywed couples. *Journal of Abnormal Psychology, 105*, 369–380.

Licata, A., Taylor, S., Berman, M., & Cranston, J. (1993). Effects of cocaine on human aggression. *Pharmacology, Biochemistry, and Behavior, 45*, 549–552.

MacAndrew, C. & Edgerton, R. (1969). *Drunken Comportment: A Social Explanation*. Chicago: Aldine.

MacDonald, T. K., Zanna, M. P., & Fong, G. T. (1995). Decision making in altered states: Effects of alcohol on attitudes toward drinking and driving. *Journal of Personality and Social Psychology, 68*, 973–985.

MacDonald, T. K., Zanna, M. P., & Fong, G. T. (1996). Why common sense goes out the window: Effects of alcohol on intentions to use condoms. *Personality and Social Psychology Bulletin, 22*, 763–775.

Martin, S. E. & Bachman, R. (1997). The relationship of alcohol to injury in assault cases. *Recent Developments Alcoholism, 13*, 41–56.

Miller, W. B. (1958). Lower class culture as a generating milieu of gang delinquency. *Journal of Social Issues, 14*, 5–19.

Myers, T. (1982). Alcohol and violent crime re-examined: Self-reports from two sub-groups of Scottish male prisoners. *British Journal of Addiction, 77*, 399–413.

Padilla, F. (1992). *The Gang as an American Enterprise*. New Brunswick, NJ: Rutgers University Press.

Pan, H. D., Neidig P. H., & O'Leary, K. D. (1994). Predicting mild and severe husband-to-wife physical aggression. *Journal of Consulting and Clinical Psychology, 62*, 975–981.

Pernanen, K. (1976). Alcohol and crimes of violence. In B. Kissin & H. Begletier (Eds.), *The Biology of Alcoholism: Social Aspects of Alcoholism, 4* (pp. 351–444). New York: Plenum.

Pernanen, K. (1991). *Alcohol in Human Violence*. New York: Guilford.

Pihl, R. O. & Peterson, J. (1995). Drugs and aggression: Correlations, crime and human manipulative studies and some proposed mechanisms. *Journal of Psychiatry and Neuroscience, 20*, 141–149.

Pittman, D. & Handy, W. (1964). Patterns in criminal aggravated assault. *Journal of Criminal Law-Criminal Political Science, 55*, 462–470.

Pulkkinen, L. (1983). Youthful smoking and drinking in a longitudinal perspective. *Journal of Youth and Adolescence, 12*, 253–283.

Quigley, B. M. & Leonard, K. E. (1999). Husband alcohol expectancies, drinking, and marital conflict styles as predictors of severe marital violence among newlywed couples. *Psychology of Addictive Behaviors, 13*, 49–59.

Reiss, A. J. & Roth, J. A. (1993). *Understanding and Preventing Violence*. Washington, DC: National Academy.

Richardson, D. (1981). The effect of alcohol on male aggression toward female targets. *Motivation and Emotion, 5*, 333–344.

Robins, L. N. & Regier, D. A. (Eds.) (1991). *Psychiatric Disorders in America: The Epidemiologic Catchment Area Study*. New York: Free Press.

Rohsenow, D. J. & Bachorowski, J. (1984). Effects of alcohol and expectancies on verbal aggression in men and women. *Journal of Abnormal Psychology, 93*, 418–432.

Sayette, M., Wilson, G. T., & Elias, M. J. (1993). Alcohol and aggression: A social information processing analysis. *Journal of Studies on Alcohol, 54*, 399–407.

Selzer, M. L. (1971). The Michigan Alcoholism Screening Test: The quest for a new diagnostic instrument. *American Journal of Psychiatry, 127*, 1653–1658.

Skinner, H. A. & Allen, B. A. (1982). Alcohol dependence syndrome: Measurement and validation. *Journal of Abnormal Psychology, 91*, 199–209.

Steele, C. W., Critchlow, B., & Liu, T. J. (1985). Alcohol and social behavior: II. The helpful drunkard. *Journal of Personality and Social Psychology, 97*, 196–205.

Steele, C. M. & Josephs, R. A. (1990). Alcohol myopia: Its prized and dangerous effects. *American Psychologist, 45*, 921–933.

Steele, C. W. & Southwick, L. (1985). Alcohol and social behavior: I. The psychology of drunken excess. *Journal of Personality and Social Psychology, 48*, 18–34.

Swanson, J. W. (1993). Alcohol abuse, mental disorder, and violent behavior: An epidemiologic inquiry. *Alcohol Health and Research World, 17,* 123–132.

Taylor, S. P. (1967). Aggressive behavior and physiological arousal as a function of provocation and the tendency to inhibit aggression. *Journal of Personality, 35,* 297–310.

Taylor, S. P. & Gammon, C. B. (1975). Effects of type and dose of alcohol on human physical aggression. *Journal of Personality and Social Psychology, 34,* 938–941.

Taylor, S. P. & Leonard, K. E. (1983). Alcohol and human physical aggression. In R. G. Green & E. I. Donnerstein (Eds.), *Aggression: Theoretical and Empirical Reviews* (pp. 77–101). New York: Academic.

Taylor, S. P., Vardaris, R. M., Rawtich, A. B., Gammon, C. B., Cranston, J. W., & Lubetkin, A. I. (1976). The effects of alcohol and delta-9-tetrahydrocannabinol on human physical aggression. *Aggressive Behavior, 2,* 153–161.

Tedeschi, J. T. & Quigley, B. M. (1996). Limitations of laboratory paradigms for studying aggression. *Aggression and Violent Behavior: A Review Journal, 1,* 163–177.

Uihlein, C. (1994). Drugs and alcohol. In T. Hirschi & M. R. Gottfredson (Eds.), *The Generality of Deviance* (pp. 149–158). New Brunswick, NJ: Transaction.

U.S. Department of Justice. (1993). *Survey of State Prison Inmates, 1991.* Pub. No. NCJ-136949. Washington, DC: U.S. Government Printing Office, Bureau of Justice Statistics.

U.S. Department of Justice. (1996). *1995 Drug Use Forecasting Annual Report on Adult and Juvenile Arrestees.* Pub No. NCJ-161721. Washington DC: U.S. Government Printing Office, National Institute of Justice.

Vigil, J. D. (1988). *Barrio Gangs.* Austin: University of Texas Press.

Welte, J. W. & Miller, B. M. (1987). Alcohol use by violent and property offenders. *Drug and Alcohol Dependence, 19,* 313–324.

White, H. R. (1991). Marijuana use and delinquency: A test of the "independent clause" hypothesis. *The Journal of Drug Issues, 21,* 231–256.

Wieczorek, W. F., Welte, J. W., & Abel, E. L. (1990). Alcohol, drugs and murder: A study of convicted homicide offenders. *Journal of Criminal Justice, 18,* 217-227.

Wilkinson, C. J. (1985). Effects of diazepam (valium) and trait anxiety on human physical aggression and emotional state. *Journal of Behavioral Medicine, 8,* 101–114.

Wolfgang, M. E. (1958). *Patterns in Criminal Homicide.* Philadelphia: University of Pennsylvania Press.

Zeichner, A. & Pihl, R. O. (1980). Effects of alcohol and instigator intent on human aggression. *Journal of Studies on Alcohol, 41,* 265–276.

Zeichner, A., Pihl, R. O., Niaura, R., & Zacchia, C. (1982). Attentional processes in alcohol-mediated aggression. *Journal of Studies on Alcohol, 43,* 714–724.

15 The Prediction of Violence

CHARLES SCOTT
University of California

PHILLIP RESNICK
Case Western Reserve School of Medicine

The prediction of future violence is a challenging task. However, clinicians should be able to do a careful risk assessment for violence. Dangerousness is not a psychiatric diagnosis; the concept of dangerousness is a legal judgment based on social policy. In other words, dangerousness is a broader concept than either violence or dangerous behavior; it indicates an individual's propensity to commit dangerous acts (Mulvey & Lidz, 1984). With the increasing concern regarding violence in our communities, clinicians are frequently called on to evaluate an individual's risk for future aggression. Dangerousness assessments are required in a wide range of situations, such as involuntary hospitalization, notification of an individual about a threat, and release of a previously violent person into the community.

Unfortunately, no psychological test or interview can predict future violence with complete accuracy. Relatively infrequent events (e.g., homicide) are more difficult to predict than more common events (e.g., domestic violence), because they have a low base rate of occurrence. One of the best measures of violence prediction is a two-by-two table that assesses the relationship of a predicted event to the actual outcome. The prediction that a person will be violent or nonviolent can be compared to the actual behavior observed over time. The chart below outlines how this approach is presented.

	Predicted Behavior	
Actual Behavior	*Violent*	*Nonviolent*
Violent	True Positives	False Negative
Nonviolent	False Positive	True Negatives

In the chart, the term *true positive* refers to those individuals who are predicted to be violent and actually become violent. *False positive* refers to those who are predicted to be violent but do not become violent. *True negatives* include those who are predicted to be nonviolent and do refrain from violent behavior. Finally, those who commit a violent act, but were predicted to be nonviolent, are classified as *false negatives*. The term *predictive power positive (PPP)* is derived from dividing the true positives by the sum of the true positives and false positives and multiplying by 100. This number provides the percentage of those predicted to be violent who actually become violent.

An excellent opportunity to examine mental health professionals' ability to predict future violence occurred as a result of the 1966 legal case *Baxstrom v. Herald.* In this case, Mr. Baxstrom was transferred from prison to a hospital for the criminally insane. At the end of his prison sentence, he was committed to remain in the hospital without a full hearing regarding his future dangerousness. The U.S. Supreme Court ruled that this violated his constitutional right to due process. As a result, Mr. Baxstrom and other patients who had been involuntarily hospitalized were released. Those individuals who had been predicted to be violent were followed to determine if the predictions were accurate. This study indicated that psychiatrists had a very high rate of false positives (i.e., many more predictions of violence than actually occurred).

Following this study, a second generation of research examined specific clinical variables associated with violence over shorter periods of time. These investigations showed a modest improvement in clinicians' predictions of violence. In these studies, one in two predictions of short-term violence were accurate, compared to one in three for the earlier long-term predictions (Otto, 1992). It appears, therefore, that clinicians are more accurate when making predictions about violent behavior over shorter time intervals (e.g., weeks versus years).

Overview of Risk Assessment

When approaching assessment of dangerousness, it is helpful to divide the concept of dangerousness into four components. The first component is the magnitude of potential harm that is threatened. Behavior may involve physical harm to persons or property, as well as psychological harm to others. In addition to identifying the target of violence, the degree of expected harm should be clarified. For example, there is a difference between threatening to shoot someone in the head as opposed to punching someone in the nose.

The second component of dangerousness is the likelihood that a violent act will take place. Here, it is important to clarify the seriousness of the person's intent to cause harm. A person's past history of acting on violent thoughts is the best predictor that violent intentions will be carried out. The third component is the imminence of the threat. Is the person threatening harm in the next 10 hours or the next 10 days? The frequency of the proposed activity constitutes the fourth component of dangerousness.

Aggressive behavior can be divided into affective and predatory violence. Affective aggression involves hostile behavior as a reaction to some perceived threat, either from the environment or from an internal sense of fear or anxiety. An anxious emotional response is often characterized by a fast heart beat, sweating, shortness of breath, and feelings of panic and fear. In contrast, predatory aggression is planned, purposeful, and goal directed. Here, the individual seeks out a target to harm. Although there may be sense of heightened awareness, the individual is not reacting to a perceived threat. Predatory violence is more dangerous because it has no behaviors that foreshadow it (Meloy, 1987). The predator usually has no remorse and is comfortable using violence either to obtain a desired goal or to achieve a sense of pleasure and control.

The assessment of dangerousness requires the identification of risk factors associated with an increased likelihood of violence. Risk factors may be divided into static and dynamic categories. Although static risk factors are statistically associated with violent behavior, they cannot be changed. Examples of static factors include a person's age, gender, intelligence, and past history of violence. Dynamic risk factors are those in which change or intervention is possible. Dynamic risk factors include a person's employment, living situation, substance abuse, and probationary supervision. The following sections will examine risk factors associated with violence in adults, mentally ill people, children and adolescents, and people in the workplace.

Risk Factors Associated with Violence in Adults

The following demographic variables are associated with increased risk for violence:

1. *Age.* Violence peaks in the late teens and early twenties (Monahan, 1991).
2. *Gender.* Males perpetrate violent acts approximately 10-times more often than females (Tardiff & Sweillam, 1980).
3. *Socioeconomic status.* Violence is nearly three-times as common at the lowest socioeconomic status level than at the highest level.
4. *Intelligence.* The risk of violence increases for those with lower intelligence and mild mental retardation (Quinsey & Macguire, 1986).

One study found that intellectually handicapped men were 5-times more likely to commit violent offenses; and intellectually handicapped women were 25-times more likely to commit violent offenses (Hodgins, 1992). Those with less education also have a higher rate of violent acts (Link, Andrews, & Cullen, 1992).

A past history of violence is the single best predictor of future violent behavior (Klassen & O'Connor, 1988). Each prior episode of violence increases the risk of a future violent act. It is helpful to ask the individual about the most violent thing that he has ever done. Obtaining a detailed violence history involves determining the type of violent behavior; why violence occurred; who was involved; the presence of intoxication; and the degree of injury. Criminal and court records are particularly useful in evaluating the person's past history of violence and illegal behavior. The age of first arrest is highly correlated with persistence of criminal offending (Moffit, Mednick, & Gabrielli, 1989). Given four previous arrests, the probability of a fifth is 80 percent (Wolfgang, 1977).

A person who has used weapons against others in the past may pose a serious risk of future violence. The main difference between assault and homicide is the lethality of the weapon used. Loaded guns have the highest lethality of any weapon. An assault with a gun is five-times more likely to result in a fatality than an attack with a knife (Zimring, 1991). Approximately one in four U.S. households contain a gun, and 43 percent are kept loaded.

Subjects should be asked whether they own or have ever owned a weapon. The movement of a weapon, such as moving a gun from a closet to a nightstand, is particularly ominous in a paranoid person. The greater the psychotic fear, the more likely the paranoid person is to kill someone he misperceives as a persecutor.

Drugs and alcohol are strongly associated with violent behavior. Drug-related violence can be divided into three types: systemic, economically driven, and psychopharmacological (intoxication). Systemic drug violence results from activities associated with the illegal use of drugs, such as killing over drug "turf" or in retaliation for selling "bad drugs." Economically driven drug violence is committed to support the perpetrator's addiction. Psychopharmacological violence results directly from the drug's effects on the individual. The U.S. Department of Justice Statistics indicate that the vast majority of violent crimes are committed under the influence of either alcohol or drugs (Bureau of Justice Statistics [BJS], 1993).

The majority of persons involved in violent crimes, including murders, assaults, sexual assaults, and family violence are under the influence of alcohol (Murdoch, Pihl, & Ross, 1990). Up to 62 percent of violent offenders have been drinking when they commit crimes. Stimulants, such as cocaine, crack, amphetamines, and PCP, are of special concern. These drugs typically result in feelings of disinhibition, a sense of power, and paranoia. The violence associated with stimulants differs by gender. Men who abuse cocaine are more likely to perpetrate violent crimes, whereas women who regularly use cocaine are more likely to be the victims of violence (Goldstein, Bellucci, Spunt, & Miller, 1991). More than 60 percent of state prison inmates used drugs regularly prior to their incarceration; 30 percent were high at the time they committed their crimes (BJS, 1993).

Useful sources of information related to a person's potential for violence include military history and work history. The military history should include a history of fighting, being absent without leave (AWOL), disciplinary measures, and the type of discharge. An evaluation of the work history should review frequency of job changes and reasons for each termination. Frequent terminations increase the risk for violence. Persons who are laid off from work are six-times more likely to be violent than their employed peers (Catalano, Dooley, & Novaco, 1993).

Risk Assessment of Violence in the Mentally Ill

Overall, the presence of a major mental illness (mood disorder, anxiety disorder, or schizophrenia) increases a person's risk of violence. In a study that examined self-reported violence of over 10,000 persons in the community, individuals with a mental illness committed violent acts five-times more often than those without a mental illness. Individuals who abuse alcohol, however, are twice as likely to commit violent acts as those with mental illness alone. When illicit drugs are used, the rate is three-times as high. The worst combination for future violence is the presence of both mental illness and substance abuse (Swanson, Holzer, Ganju, & Jono, 1990).

The demographic risk factors of age and gender differ in individuals with mental illness. Whereas violence in the general population peaks at around age 18 years, the corresponding peak in psychiatric patients is in the mid-20s (Aquilina, 1991; Swanson et al., 1990). In contrast to the general population, where men show much higher rates of violent offenses than women, mentally ill men and women do not significantly differ in their rates of violent behavior (Borum, Swartz, & Swanson, 1996). In one study, women with major mental illnesses were nearly 28-times more likely than women in the general population to be convicted of violent crimes (Torrey, 1993).

Certain types of mental illness predispose individuals to violent behavior (e.g., psychosis). A psychotic disorder is characterized by the loss of touch with reality or disordered thinking. The experience of hearing voices when no one is present (auditory hallucinations) is a common symptom of psychosis. Other common symptoms include paranoia (extreme suspiciousness of others), disordered thinking, and delusions (fixed false beliefs). Delusions may range from a belief that one is being conspired against (paranoid delusion) to a belief that one has special powers (grandiose delusion). There is usually a substantial delay (about one month) between the onset of psychosis and the commission of serious violence (Humphreys, Johnstone, MacMillan, & Taylor, 1992).

One of the most serious psychotic symptoms associated with violence is paranoid delusions. Violence by paranoid psychotics is usually well planned and in line with their false beliefs. The violence is directed at a specific person who is perceived as a persecutor. Relatives or friends are often the targets of the paranoid individual. Paranoid persons in the community are more likely to be dangerous because they have greater access to weapons. Persecutory delusions are more likely to be acted on than any other type of delusion (Wessely et al., 1993).

Once one accepts the fact that psychotic symptoms are experienced as real, one can better understand the emergence of violent responses by individuals who either fear imminent harm or experience external forces as overriding their personal control. Certain types of delusions that are associated with an increased risk of aggression are called *threat- and control-override symptoms*. These delusions involve the following beliefs: that the mind is dominated by forces beyond the person's control; that thoughts are being put into the person's head; that people are wishing the person harm; and that the person is being followed (Link, Andrews, & Cullen, 1992).

Psychotic symptoms that are not associated with increased violence include the following: feeling dead, dissolved, or not existing; feeling that one's thoughts can be broadcast to others; and feeling that one's thoughts are being taken away by some external force. Individuals who experience threat/control-override symptoms are nearly twice as likely to engage in assaultive behavior as individuals experiencing other types of psychotic symptoms. If these individuals are abusing substances, their risk for violence increases to a rate of 8- to 10-times that of the general population (Borum et al., 1996). Delusional persons are more likely to be violent when they have feelings of fear or anger, and a history of acting on prior delusions.

Erotomania is a specific type of delusion in which a person falsely believes that another person is in love with him. The person about whom this belief is held is frequently of a higher status. Erotomania is more common in males. About 5 percent of erotomanics commit a violent act. Violence is most likely to be committed against the individual who stands in the way of the desired love object. For example, if the person has delusional beliefs regarding a relationship with a movie star, a bodyguard may be at risk if he is seen as a barrier to the desired person.

Some hallucinations are associated with an increased risk of violence. Hallucinations consist of sensory perceptions that have no basis in reality. Although hallucinations can involve all five senses (hearing, sight, taste, touch, and smell), auditory hallucinations are the most common type. Mental illnesses in which hallucinations are commonly experienced include schizophrenia, depression, mania, and substance abuse. Medical causes of hallucinations include organic diseases of the brain (particularly in the temporal lobe) and medication side effects. Hallucinations are associated with an increased risk of violent behavior, particularly if they occur with other psychotic symptoms, such as disorganization of thought and suspiciousness (Lowenstein, Binder, & McNiel, 1990).

Command hallucinations occur when a person hears voices directing him or her to perform a particular act. Commands to harm others are less frequently obeyed than harmless commands and commands to harm oneself (Kasper, Rogers, & Adams, 1996). Compliance with command hallucinations is associated with two factors. The first factor is the association of the command hallucination with delusions (Junginger, 1990). For example, if a person hears a voice telling him to kill his mother, he is more likely to do it if he has a concurrent delusion that she is an evil wizardess. Second, if a voice is familiar to the person, he is more likely to follow the command.

Depression is a common mental illness that affects more than 10 percent of the general population at any given time. Depression involves sustained feelings of either a depressed mood or irritability. Symptoms of depression include insomnia, difficulty with concentration, low energy, a change in appetite, social withdrawal, and suicidal thoughts. When people are depressed, they may strike out against others in despair. After committing a violent act, the depressed person may attempt suicide. Depression is the most common diagnosis in a murder-suicide (Marjuk, Tardiff, & Hirsch, 1992).

One pattern of murder-suicide involves depressed or psychotic parents (particularly mothers of very young children) who kill their children prior to attempting to take their own lives (Resnick, 1969). Murder-suicide in couples is associated with feelings of jealousy and possessiveness (Rosenbaum, 1990). In homicide-suicides, the homicide is often an extension of the suicidal act. The individual can no longer endure life without what is perceived to be a vital element (i.e., a spouse, a family, or a job). The perpetrator cannot bear the thought of other persons carrying on without him, so he forces others to join him in death.

Another mood disorder that increases the risk for aggressive behavior is mania. Mania (also called bipolar disorder) is a mental illness in which an individual has distinct periods of an elevated or irritable mood with increased energy, decreased need for sleep, pressured speech, and racing thoughts. Although persons with mania show a high percentage of assaultive or threatening behavior, serious violence is rare (Krakowski, Volavka, & Brizer, 1986). For example, manic patients show considerably less criminality than schizophrenic patients. Manic patients most commonly exhibit violent behavior when they are restrained or have limits set on their behavior.

Violence is associated with certain personality disorders. Personality disorders involve a long-standing maladaptive personality style that results in impairment in social or occupational functioning. While borderline (Tardiff & Sweillam, 1980) and sadistic (Meloy, 1992) personality disorders are associated with increased violence, the most common personality disorder associated with violence is antisocial personality disorder (ASPD).

Persons with ASPD have a disregard for others and frequently violate societal rules. ASPD is commonly found in the criminal population. Criminals with antisocial personalities are much more likely to use violent and aggressive behavior than are criminals in general (Hare & McPherson, 1984). The violence committed by those with antisocial personalities is often motivated by revenge or occurs during a period of heavy drinking. Violence among these persons is characteristically cold and calculated and lacks emotionality (Williamson, Hare, & Wong, 1987). Low IQ and antisocial personality disorder are a particularly ominous combination for increasing the risk of future violence (Heilbrun, 1990).

Individuals may have personality traits that increase their risk for violent behavior, but still not meet all the criteria for a diagnosis of personality disorder. Personality traits associated with violence include impulsivity, low frustration tolerance, inability to tolerate criticism, repetitive antisocial behavior, reckless driving, a sense of entitlement, and superficiality. The violence associated with these personality traits usually has a paroxysmal, episodic quality. When interviewed, these persons often have poor insight into their behavior and frequently blame others for their difficulties (Reid & Balis, 1987).

Risk Factors Associated with Juvenile Violence

Juveniles are generally defined as those individuals less than 18 years of age. The term *delinquency* refers to an illegal act or omission by a juvenile that would be considered a crime if committed by an adult. Nearly one out of every five persons arrested for a violent crime is less than 18 years old (U.S. Department of Justice, FBI, 1994).

In view of the increasing violent juvenile crime trends of the 1990s, the assessment of juvenile violence risk is extremely important. One measure of juvenile violence is the arrest rate for murder. Between 1984 and 1993, the rate at which juveniles were arrested for murder in the United States increased by nearly 170 percent. This trend reversed slightly between 1993 and 1995, with a 20 percent drop in the juvenile murder arrest rate and a 2.9 percent overall decrease in juvenile violent crime (Snyder, 1997). Nonetheless, the projected increase in the juvenile population during the next decade suggests that youth violence will continue to be a major problem.

Certain demographic factors are associated with increased rates of violence among juveniles. Juvenile males are arrested for violent offenses six-times more often than juvenile females. Boys are ten-times more likely to commit homicide than girls (Poe-Yamagata & Butts, 1996). Juvenile males most commonly kill male friends or acquaintances. Juvenile females kill family members nearly as often as they kill friends or acquaintances. Although girls most commonly murder with a gun, they are more likely than boys to kill with a knife (Snyder & Sickmund, 1995).

The age of juveniles is related to rates of violence. After age 13 years, the rate of homicide increases sharply during each year of adolescence until age 18 years (Federal Bureau of Investigation, 1993). On the surface, race also appears to be associated with increased juvenile violence. For example, the rate of violent crime arrests for black youth is approximately five-times the rate for whites (FBI, 1994). In addition, black juveniles commit murder at a rate six-times that of white juveniles (FBI, 1993). However, these racial differences have been linked to difficult living conditions and lower socioeconomic status, rather than race alone.

As with adults, one of the most important factors in determining juveniles' risk for future violence is their past history of violence. Juvenile offenders characteristically exhibit a variety of law-violating behaviors rather than repeating one particular illegal act. This pattern has been described as one of "diversification rather than specialization" (Snyder, 1995). The actual number of unlawful acts is more predictive of future criminal behavior than the specific act committed in the past (Robins & Ratcliff, 1980).

Chronic offenders (juveniles who have had more than five police contacts) represent less than 20 percent of all juvenile offenders, but they commit over 50 percent of all offenses (Wolfgang, Figlio, & Sellin, 1972). Even more disturbing is the fact that over 80 percent of the most frequent and serious juvenile offenders have no official police records (Elliott, 1994). In addition to asking about police contacts, therefore, juveniles should be asked, "What illegal acts have you committed for which you were never caught?" The greater the number of illegal acts, the greater the likelihood that the youth will eventually commit a violent act. Finally, the age of the first violent act helps determine the risk for violent crimes in adulthood. In the National Youth Survey, 45 percent of those juveniles who committed a serious violent offense prior to age 11 continued to perform violent acts into their twenties (Elliott, 1994).

The family history often provides useful information about risk for juvenile violence. Children with aggressive parents are more likely to be violent in adolescence and young adulthood (Farrington, 1991). Witnessing adults using knives or guns against each other doubles the risk that children will become serious violent offenders (Spaccarelli, Coatsworth, & Bowden, 1995). Children who experience abuse or neglect, and those whose fathers have been incarcerated, also have an increased risk for committing violent crime (Cellini, 1995; West & Farrington, 1977).

One of the greatest risk factors for juvenile homicide is the possession of a weapon. Knives and razors are the most common weapons carried by youths with the exception of black males, who more often carry firearms (Centers for Disease Control, 1991). Due to their lethality, firearms have played the most significant role in the increase in juvenile homicides. Other predictors of juvenile homicide are previous use of a weapon and a belief that it is acceptable to use violence to obtain a desired goal.

Juveniles belonging to gangs are involved in more violent behavior than those who are not. Approximately one-half of all crimes committed by gangs involve homicide or violence. The violence associated with gangs is most commonly related to disputes over territory or competition for status between gangs. The most common victims of gang violence are other gang members (Snyder & Sickmund, 1995).

While drug use has not been shown to cause the initiation of delinquent behavior, increase in substance abuse does worsen delinquent behavior once such behavior has developed. Because alcohol and drugs are disinhibiting, they increase the likelihood that juveniles will act on their violent impulses. Over 40 percent of juvenile murderers acknowledged that they were under the influence of alcohol or drugs at the time of their offenses (BJS, 1989). Juveniles who sell drugs are more likely than drug users to commit violent offenses. Juvenile drug dealers often carry concealed weapons that increase their potential for more serious aggression (Altschuler & Brounstein, 1991).

In addition to substance use, juvenile delinquents often meet the diagnostic criteria for emotional disorders outlined in the *Diagnostic and Statistical Manual of Mental Disorders (DSM)* published by the American Psychiatric Association. The most common disorder in juvenile delinquents is conduct disorder. Conduct disorder is a persistent pattern in which the youth violates the rights of others or frequently breaks the rules of society. Common symptoms of conduct disorder are aggression toward other people or animals, destruction of property, lying or stealing, and serious violation of rules (American Psychiatric Association, 1994). Over

80 percent of incarcerated male and female juvenile offenders meet the criteria for conduct disorder (Eppright, Kashani, Robison, & Reid, 1993). Those juveniles who have an earlier onset of conduct disorder and meet multiple criteria for this condition are involved in more serious and persistent juvenile delinquency.

Another diagnosis frequently present in juvenile delinquents is attention deficit hyperactivity disorder (ADHD). ADHD is characterized by persistent difficulties with concentration or hyperactivity/impulsivity that is in excess of that expected for the age group. These children frequently make careless mistakes, lose items, are easily distracted, fidget, and act impulsively (APA, 1994). Arrest rates of juveniles with ADHD range from 5- to 26-times higher than those without ADHD (Satterfield, Hoppe, & Schell, 1982). However, long-term follow up studies of these children indicate that it is the additional presence of conduct disorder, as opposed to ADHD alone, that predicts future criminality. Thus, children with ADHD who do not have conduct disorders are not at increased risk for later criminality (Satterfield & Schell, 1997).

Approximately 25 percent of delinquent children meet the criteria for a major depressive disorder (Chiles, Miller, & Cox, 1980). Depression in children often presents with irritability rather than depressed mood. There is high comorbidity of substance abuse and conduct disorder in depressed juveniles. As with ADHD, the presence of conduct disorder is a better predictor of future delinquency than the presence of depression alone.

Delinquent youth have often been exposed to repeated traumatic events. They have frequently witnessed the killing of friends or family members, seen violence in their neighborhoods, or personally experienced victimization. One study found that up to 30 percent of incarcerated juveniles met the criteria for Posttraumatic Stress Disorder (PTSD) (Steiner, Garcia, & Matthews, 1997). Individuals suffering from PTSD have been exposed to a traumatic event, such as witnessing a death or experiencing a threat of death. They react with horror, fear, or helplessness. Children exposed to repeated trauma sometimes develop an emotional numbing and have decreased reactions to subsequent traumatic events. The juveniles who have "seen it all" may present with an "I don't care" attitude. They often exhibit little empathy for their victims.

The vast majority of juveniles who commit violent offenses do not have psychotic disorders. In the small subset of juveniles who commit violent offenses due to psychosis, paranoia and delusional beliefs may contribute to their violence. Studies suggesting that mild neurologic abnormalities or seizure disorders are associated with violence have not been replicated by other researchers (McMannus, Alessi, & Grapefine, 1984).

Workplace Violence

In 1992, the Centers for Disease Control declared workplace violence to be a national epidemic. Workplace violence has been defined as "verbal and physical assault or any violence that occurs in the workplace even if its source is unrelated to the work environment" (Center for Mental Health Services, 1994). Each week, an average of 20 people are murdered and 18,000 people assaulted while working in the United States (National Institute for Occupational Safety and Health, 1996). Workplace homicide is the leading cause of death for women on the job, and the third leading cause of death for men at work (Centers for Disease Control and Prevention, 1993). The bombing of the Federal Building in Oklahoma City in 1995 brought international attention to the potential for massive violence at a work site. This one tragic event caused 12 percent of all job-related homicides in 1995 in the United States (Bureau of Labor Statistics, 1996).

Categories of violence in the workplace include the following: (1) employees who become emotionally enraged at supervisors or coworkers; (2) a spouse, relative, or significant other who attacks the employee and potential bystanders in the workplace, due to a domestic grievance; (3) violence associated with the commission of a crime, such as a robbery; (4) violence targeted against law enforcement; and (5) terrorism or hate crimes. The majority of workplace homicides are related to robberies.

The typical employee who becomes a workplace killer is a white man in his 30s or 40s. This individual may have lost his job or perceives that he will lose his job. The worker often feels he has been let go in an insensitive or dehumanizing manner. If the worker lacks a supportive family, and his job is his primary source of stability, the job loss may represent an even greater blow to his self-esteem. Other risk factors characteristic of the workplace killer include being a loner, having difficulty with authority figures, and having a tendency to hold grudges. A particularly ominous course of events is a demotion or firing after a divorce or home foreclosure. In these cases, the loss of the job may represent "the straw that broke the camel's back."

The FBI's Center for the Analysis of Violent Crime has developed the following profile of employees most at risk for violent flare-ups. The person has a tendency to blame others for problems and a history of cruelty to animals. He has a fascination with guns and mass crimes, a tendency to intimidate others, and a low frustration tolerance. Warning signs of an impending workplace mass murder by an employee include frequent references to shooting sprees and mass murder (real or fictional); a fascination with the military, survivalism, or police activities; a belief that he is being persecuted; and an exaggerated sense of self-importance or uniqueness.

Those employees most likely to use lethal violence in the workplace are those over 30 without a previous history of violence or substance abuse. Those individuals most likely to engage in nonlethal aggression in the workplace are those under 30 who have a previous history of violence and substance abuse.

Factors in the workplace that predispose to violence include a history of chronic labor management disputes, frequent grievances filed by employees, large numbers of injury claims, understaffing, excessive overtime, and an authoritarian management style.

The Prediction of Violence in Special Situations

Stalking

Stalking is the obsessional following or harrassment of another person. In the United States, 8 percent of adult women and 2 percent of adult men have been stalked at some time in their lives (Tjaden & Phoemmes, 1997). Stalking is recognized as a behavior that represents a serious risk of harm to the victim. The average stalker is a 35-year-old male whose love has been rejected. Stalking behavior often begins when a marriage or relationship ends. The risk of violence increases when the stalker devalues his previously overvalued love object. The most common motivation for stalking is control of the victim (Tjaden & Phoemmes, 1997).

Several characteristics of stalkers charged with criminal behavior have been delineated (Meloy, 1996). Stalkers are often chronic failures in social or sexual relationships and frequently have prior criminal and psychiatric histories. They are often unemployed or underemployed. Approximately 50 percent of stalkers threaten their victims. They are more likely to do so if there was a prior intimate relationship. However, the majority of stalkers do not actually carry out their threats. When violence occurs, it is usually limited to a physical assault without a weapon. Homicide occurs in about 2 percent of stalking cases.

A different set of risk factors has been identified for stalkers who kill strangers. They include the presence of a mental disorder and the stalker's belief that he is in some way special or unique. These individuals tend to identify with other stalkers. For example, they may save newspaper articles about stalking cases. Other risk factors include keeping a diary of their stalking and researching their target victim. They may purchase a weapon and show up uninvited at the victim's home or business. Stalkers who target strangers switch targets often. It is useful to learn why a stalker stopped following previous victims (Dietz, 1994).

Domestic Violence

Several risk factors have been identified for men who become physically abusive toward their domestic partners. Men who have less power in their relationship are more likely to be physically abusive toward their wives. Women who have more education or income may represent a higher position of authority to the abuser. If the wife is more verbally competent than her husband, his only way of winning an argument may be physical aggression. The most common justification husbands give for violent behavior is that they had "no other way" to handle the conflict (Babock, Waltz, Jacobson, & Gotman, 1993). The personality of male spouse abusers is often characterized by paranoid or antisocial traits (Meloy, 1992).

Fifty percent of abusive men have a problem with alcohol (Eichelman, 1994). Boys who witness their father's violence have a 1,000 percent greater likelihood of abusing their partners when compared with boys not exposed to such violence (Straus, 1980). Women are most at risk for homicide after leaving an abusive husband or announcing their intention to do so. Law-enforcement officers are at risk when they make domestic violence calls. In fact, 20 percent of police deaths occur while responding to domestic violence complaints (Eichelman, 1994).

Medical Illnesses

Brain diseases that increase violent behavior include infections, tumors, strokes, and head trauma. Up to 70 percent of patients with traumatic brain injuries have aggression and irritability that is of significant distress to the patients and their families (McKinlay, Brooks, & Bond, 1981). In particular, people with injuries to the frontal lobe of the brain demonstrate greater aggression than those with lesions in other brain areas (Grafman et al., 1996).

Violent behavior may occur during seizures. A seizure is defined as an abnormal electrical discharge in the brain that may be associated with changes in motor activity, consciousness, or sensation (Gumnit & Leppik, 1983). The vast majority of aggressive behavior associated with seizures occurs at the end of the seizure episode, when the individual is in a confused state and is resisting assistance. Epileptic aggression is not characterized by a targeted attack toward another person in the absence of other signs of seizure activity. The diagnosis of epilepsy by itself has not been demonstrated to increase the risk of violence between seizures (Treiman, 1994).

Assessment of Current Dangerousness

In addition to obtaining a thorough past history, the clinician should assess other risk factors for dangerousness. Individuals who are angry and lack empathy for others are at increased risk for violent behavior (Menzies, Webster, & Sepejak, 1985). In addition to anger, a paranoid person who feels afraid is at increased risk for commiting an assault. Behaviors associated with paranoid fear include changes of residence, long trips to evade persecutors, barricading rooms, carrying weapons for protection, and asking police for protection. In persons with paranoia, it is useful to inquire about what the person would do if confronted by his or her perceived persecutor.

Victims may be part of a specific delusional system or may be chosen randomly. Psychotic individuals are more likely to assault family members than strangers. Mothers of adult psychotic children are the most frequent targets of their violence (Estroff & Zimmer, 1994). There is a higher risk of violence if a person's prior violence has been directed toward a broad range of victims, or if there is a history of multiple assaults on a class of victims (e.g., wife, girlfriends) who are readily available (Monahan, 1981).

Evaluating the potential victim can provide insight as to how a potential confrontation may unfold. For example, if the intended victim is likely to be counter-provocative, an interaction is more likely to escalate into violence.

All threats should be taken seriously. When evaluating a threat, one should gather information about acts of preparation, possession of weapons, and the availability of the intended victim. It is also useful to ask about a grudge list. Finally, the individual who intends to kill himself after completing a homicide represents a particularly high risk. Since the perpetrator plans to die, he is unlikely to be deterred from committing a planned homicide.

Risk Assessment Instruments

Standardized assessment instruments for the prediction of violence have recently become available. Risk assessment instruments integrate risk factors for future violence. They vary as to the information gathered and how the information is scored. Assessment instruments may use clinical variables, actuarial variables, or both. Clinical risk factors have been theorized to be related to violent behavior. Actuarial risk factors have been statistically correlated to actual violence. Actuarial-risk-assessment approaches have been shown to predict violence better than those schemes that rely solely on clinical judgment (Borum, Otto, & Golding, 1993). Some overlap in risk factors exists between these two categories.

One of the best validated risk-assessment instruments is the Psychopathy Check List (PCL). Psychopathy in this context does not refer to a specific mental illness or personality disorder defined in *DSM-IV*. Rather, psychopathy refers to a personality style characterized by shallowness, superficial relationships, and concern only for oneself. These individuals are "coldhearted," lack feelings for their victims, and violate the laws of society without remorse (Hare, Hart, & Harpur, 1991).

Research with the Psychopathy Check List and its revision, Psychopathy Check List Revised (PCL-R), has examined the predictive validity of psychopathy to future violence and criminal behavior. The PCL-R consists of 20 items that evaluate a person's behavior and personality style. Psychopathy is determined to be present if the person achieves a certain score (Hare, Hart, & Harpur, 1991).

When the PCL was administered to 231 male inmates prior to their release from prison, those who scored in the top third were four-times more likely to commit a violent crime than those in the bottom third (Hart, Kropp, & Hare, 1988). The PCL-R has produced similar results for prison parolees (Serin, Peters, & Barbaree, 1990) and male juvenile offenders (Forth, Hart, & Hare, 1990). In one study of violent recidivism in men who had been released from a psychiatric hospital, 78 percent of those predicted to be violent on the basis of the PCL score actually committed violent acts (Harris, Rice, & Cormier, 1991). Assessment instruments based on the PCL include a screening version (PCL:SV) and a youth version (PCL:YV).

One risk-assessment scheme for dangerousness that combines both actuarial and clinical factors is entitled the Violence Prediction Scheme (Webster, Harris, Rice, Cormier, & Quinsey, 1994). The Violence Prediction Scheme was developed using individuals who had committed at least one violent offense. The actuarial component of this scheme is called the Violence Risk Appraisal Guide (VRAG). The VRAG uses the Psychopathy Check List as one of its 12 actuarial factors. The clinical component of the Violence Prediction Scheme is summarized by the mnemonic "ASSESS-LIST." This component scores 10 clinical variables, such as a person's antecedent history and sexual adjustment. The Violence Prediction Scheme has its primary emphasis on the 12 variables in the VRAG.

Risk assessment schemes have also been developed, which examine the risk for violence in particular situations. These include the risk of spousal assault (Spousal Assault Risk Assessment Guide), (Kropp, Hart, Webster, & Eaves, 1994), sexual reoffending (Recidivism Prediction Instrument), (Quinsey, Rice, & Harris, 1995), inpatient violence on a psychiatric unit (McNeil & Binder, 1994), and violence by mentally ill persons in the general population (Gardner, Lidz, Mulvey, & Shaw, 1996). The goals of these prediction schemes are to assist the clinician in gathering appropriate data and to anchor clinicians' predictions to established research.

Case Illustration

Dennis, a 24-year-old single male, was admitted to a psychiatric hospital after he threatened to kill his live-in girlfriend Sarah. He had a past history of hitting Sarah with his fists and threatening her with a gun. His earlier assaults toward Sarah occurred after he learned that she had been having affairs with different men in the neighborhood. Dennis' past legal history included four aggravated assaults, trespassing, and possession of cocaine with the intent to distribute.

Dennis was physically abused as a child. He was eventually removed from his home and placed in a juvenile detention facility, due to frequent fights with teachers and peers. He dropped out of high school in the ninth grade. Dennis was previously diagnosed with paranoid schizophrenia and cocaine dependence. He has an IQ of 72 (borderline intellectual functioning).

During the evaluation, Dennis told the examiner that he was hearing the voice of his mother commanding him to kill Sarah. He believed that she was the "anti-Christ" who was attempting to kill him with poison gas through the heater vents. He loaded his .357 magnum gun that morning with two bullets—one for Sarah and one for himself. Sarah called the police when Dennis began screaming at her that she was "the 'Great Liar'" and "should die so that others could be saved."

Analysis of the Case

Several important risk factors for violence are highlighted in this case. The magnitude of harm here is great—a possible murder-suicide. The likelihood of Dennis acting on his threat is high in view of his past history. In addition to being a young male (static risk factors), he has a childhood history of physical abuse, school failure, and low intelligence. He has a history of selling cocaine, and violent behavior since childhood. He also has a psychotic disorder (paranoid schizophrenia) with paranoid delusional beliefs. His command auditory hallucinations increase his risk of acting on his plan because he hears both a familiar voice (his mother's) and has a delusion associated with the commands. His current emotional state is characterized by fear and suspiciousness. His plan to kill himself after he murders Sarah indicates a high degree of commitment to his goal. The violence is also imminent. He recently loaded his weapon and began making statements that Sarah must die. Due to the numerous risk factors, the risk of lethal violence within the next few days is extremely high.

Summary

The prediction of violence remains an inexact science. Predicting violence has been compared to forecasting the weather. Like a good weather forecaster, the clinician does not state with absolute certainty that an event will occur. Instead, he estimates the likelihood that a future event will occur. Like weather forecasting, the correct prediction of future violence improves when only short time frames (next few days versus next few months) are considered (Monahan & Steadman, 1996). Finally, like weather forecasting, predictions of future violence will not always be correct. However, gathering a detailed past history and using appropriate risk assessment instruments can make the forecast as accurate as possible.

REFERENCES

Altschuler, D. & Brounstein, P. (1991). Patterns of drug use, drug trafficking, and other delinquency among inner-city adolescent males in Washington, DC. *Criminology, 29*, 589–622.

American Psychiatric Association. (1994). *Diagnostic and Statistical Manual of Mental Disorders* (4th ed.). Washington, DC: Author.

Aquilina, C (1991). Violence by psychiatric inpatients. *Medicine, Science and the Law, 31*, 306–312.

Babock, J. C., Waltz, J., Jacobson, N. S., & Gotman, J. M. (1993). Power and violence: The relation between communication patterns, power discrepancies, and domestic violence. *Journal of Consulting and Clinical Psychology, 61*, 40–50.

Borum, R., Otto, R., & Golding, S. (1993). Improving clinical judgment and decision making in forensic evaluation. *Journal of Psychiatry and Law, 21*, 35–36.

Borum, R., Swartz, M., & Swanson, J. (1996). Assessing and managing violence risk in clinical practice. *Journal of Practical Psychiatry and Behavioral Health,* 205–215.

Bureau of Justice Statistics. (1989). *Correctional Populations in the United States, 1987.* Washington, DC: U.S. Department of Justice.

Bureau of Justice Statistics. (1993). *Survey of State Prison Inmates, 1991.* Washington, DC: U.S. Department of Justice.

Bureau of Labor Statistics. (1996). *National Census of Fatal Occupation Injuries, 1995.* Washington, DC: U.S. Department of Labor.

Catalano, R., Dooley, D., & Novaco, R. (1993). Using ECA survey data to examine the effects of job layoffs on violent behavior. *Hospital and Community Psychiatry, 44*, 874–879.

Cellini, H. R. (1995, October). *Understanding Violent Juvenile Offenders,* (p. 8). Prepared for the National Violence Prevention Conference Program, Des Moines, IA.

Center for Mental Health Services. (1994, March). *Preventing Violence in the Workplace.* Washington, DC: U.S. Department of Health and Human Services, Substance Abuse and Mental Health Services Administration.

Centers for Disease Control and Prevention. (1991). Weapon-carrying among high school students—United States. *Morbidity and Mortality Weekly Report, 40,* 681–684.

Centers for Disease Control and Prevention. (1993, September). *National Institute of Occupational Safety and Health Alert: Request for Assistance in Prevention in the Workplace* (Publication No. 93–109). U.S. Department of Health and Human Services.

Chiles, J. A., Miller, M. L., & Cox, G. B. (1980). Depression in an adolescent population. *Archives of General Psychiatry, 137,* 1179–1184.

Dietz, P. (1994, October). *Stalking Syndrome of Pathological Attachments.* American Academy of Psychiatry and the Law Annual Meeting Presentation, Maui, HA.

Eichelman, B. S. (1994, August 22). Domestic violence. *Audio Digest Family Practice, 42.* (Audio-Digest Foundation).

Elliott, D. National Youth Survey [United States]: Wave V, 1980 [Computer File]. ICPSR version. Boulder, CO: University of Colorado, Behavioral Research Institute [producer], 1988. Ann Arbor, MI: Inter-university Consortium for Political and Social Research [distributor], 1994.

Eppright, T. D., Kashani, J. H., Robison, B. D., & Reid, J. C. (1993). Comorbidity of conduct disorder and personality disorders in an incarcerated juvenile population. *American Journal of Psychiatry, 150,* 1233–1236.

Estroff, S. E. & Zimmer, C. (1994). Social networks, social support, and violence. In J. Monahan & H. J. Steadman (Eds.), *Violence and Mental Disorder* (pp. 259–295). Chicago: The University of Chicago Press.

Farrington, D. (1991). Childhood aggression and adult violence. In D. Pepler & K. H. Rubin (Eds.), *The Development and Treatment of Childhood Aggression.* Hillsdale, NJ: Erlbaum.

Federal Bureau of Investigation. (1993). *Supplementary Homicide Reports 1976–1991* [machine-readable data files]. Washington, DC: U.S. Government Printing Office.

Federal Bureau of Investigation. (1994). *Age-Specific Arrest Rates and Race-Specific Arrest Rates for Selected Offenses 1965–1992.* Washington, DC: U.S. Government Printing Office.

Forth, A. E., Hart, S. D., & Hare, R. D. (1990). Assessment of psychopathy in male young offenders. *Psychological Assessment: A Journal of Consulting and Clinical Psychology, 2,* 342–344.

Gardner, W., Lidz, C. W., Mulvey, E. P., & Shaw, E. C. (1996). A comparison of actuarial methods for identifying repetitively-violent patients. *Law and Human Behavior, 20,* 35–48.

Goldstein, P. J., Bellucci, P. A., Spunt, B. J., & Miller, T. (1991). Frequency of cocaine use and violence: A comparison between men and women. In S. Scholber & C. Schade (Eds.), *The Epidemiology of Cocaine Use and Abuse* (Research Monograph 110, pp. 113–138). Rockville, MD: National Institute on Drug Abuse.

Grafman, J., Schwab, K., Warden, D., Pridgen, A., Brown, H. R., & Salazar, A. (1996). Frontal lobe injuries, violence and aggression: A report of the Vietnam head injury study. *Neurology, 46,* 1231–1238.

Gumnit, R. J. & Leppik, I. E. (1983). The epilepsies. *The Clinical Neurosciences* (pp. 409–440). New York: Churchill Livingstone.

Hare, R. D., Hart, S. D., & Harpur, T. J. (1991). Psychopathy and the proposed *DSM-IV* criteria for antisocial personality disorder. *Journal of Abnormal Psychology, 100,* 391–398.

Hare, R. D. & McPherson, L. M. (1984). Violent and aggressive behavior by criminal psychopaths. *International Journal of Law and Psychiatry, 7,* 35–50.

Harris, G. T., Rice, M. E., & Cormier, C. A. (1991). Psychopathy and violent recidivism. *Law and Human Behavior, 15,* 625–637.

Hart, S. D., Kropp, P. R., & Hare, R. D. (1988). Performance of male psychopaths following conditional release from prison. *Journal of Consulting and Clinical Psychology, 56,* 227–232.

Heilbrun, A. B. (1990). The measurement of criminal dangerousness as a personality construct: Further validation of a research index. *Journal of Personality Assessment, 54,* 141–148.

Hodgins, S. (1992). Mental disorder, intellectual deficiency, and crime: Evidence from a birth cohort. *Archives of General Psychiatry, 49,* 476–483.

Humphreys, M. S., Johnstone, E. C., MacMillan, J. F., & Taylor, P. J. (1992). Dangerous behavior preceding first admissions for schizophrenia. *British Journal of Psychiatry, 161,* 501–505.

Junginger, J. (1990). Predicting compliance with command hallucinations. *American Journal of Psychiatry, 147,* 245–247.

Kasper, M. E., Rogers, R., & Adams, P. A. (1996). Dangerousness and command hallucinations:

An investigation of psychotic inpatients. *Bulletin of the American Academy of Psychiatry and the Law, 24,* 219–224.

Klassen, D. & O'Connor, W. A. (1988). A prospective study of predictors of violence in adult male mental health admissions. *Law and Human Behavior, 12,* 143–158.

Krakowski, M., Volavka, J., & Brizer, D. (1986). Psychopathology and violence: A review of the literature. *Comprehensive Psychiatry, 27,* 131–148.

Kropp, P. R., Hart, S. D., Webster, C. D., & Eaves, D. (1994). *Manual for the Spousal Assault Risk Assessment Guide.* Vancouver, British Columbia, Canada: The British Columbia Institute on Family Violence.

Link, B. G., Andrews, H., & Cullen, F. T. (1992). The Violent Illegal Behavior of Mental Patiences Reconsidered. *American Phychological Review, 57,* 275–292.

Lowenstein, M., Binder, R. L., & McNiel, D. E. (1990). The relationship between admission symptoms and hospital assaults. *Hospital and Community Psychiatry, 41,* 311–313.

Marjuk, P. M., Tardiff, K., & Hirsch, C. S. (1992). The epidemiology of murder-suicide. *Journal of the American Medical Association, 267,* 3179–3183.

McKinlay, W. W., Brooks, D. N., & Bond, M. R. (1981). The short-term outcome of severe blunt head injury as reported by the relatives of the injured person. *Journal of Neurology, Neurosurgery, and Psychiatry, 44,* 527–533.

McMannus, M., Alessi, N., & Grapefine, W. (1984). Psychiatric disturbance in serious delinquents. *Journal of the American Academy of Child Psychiatry, 23,* 602–615.

McNeil, D. E. & Binder, R. L. (1994). Screening for risk of inpatient violence: Validation of an actuarial tool. *Law and Human Behavior, 18,* 579–586.

Meloy, J. R. (1987). The prediction of violence in outpatient psychotherapy. *American Journal of Psychotherapy, 41,* 38–45.

Meloy, J. R. (1992). *Violent Attachments.* Northvale, NJ: Jason Aronson.

Meloy, J. R. (1996). Stalking (obsessional following): A review of some preliminary studies. *Aggression and Violent Behavior, 1,* 147–162.

Menzies, E., Webster, C. O., & Sepejak, D. S. (1985). The dimensions of dangerousness: Evaluating the accuracy of psychometric predictions of violence among forensic patients. *Law and Human Behavior, 9,* 49–70.

Moffit, T. E., Mednick, S. A., & Gabrielli, W. F. (1989). Predicting careers of criminal violence: Descriptive data and predispositional factors. In D. A. Brizer & M. Crowner (Eds.), *Current Approaches to the Prediction of Violence.* Washington, DC: American Psychiatric Press.

Monahan, J. (1981). *The Clinical Prediction of Violent Behavior.* Baltimore, MD: National Institute of Mental Health.

Monahan, J. & Steadman, H. J. (1996). Violent storms and violent people: How meteorology can inform risk communication in mental health law. *American Psychologist, 51,* 931–938.

Moran, M. (1993, November 5). Seriously mentally ill do have higher rates of violence, Torrey Reports. *Psychiatric News, 28,* 5, 21.

Mulvey, E. P. & Lidz, C. W. (1984). Clinical considerations in the prediction of dangerousness in mental patients. *Clinical Psychology Review, 4,* 379–401.

Murdoch, D., Pihl, R. O., & Ross, D. (1990). Alcohol and crimes of violence: Present issues. *The International Journal of Addictions, 25,* 1065–1081.

National Institute for Occupational Safety and Health. (1996). *Violence in the Workplace: Risk Factors and Prevention Strategies.* Washington, DC: U.S. Government Printing Office.

Otto, R. (1992). The prediction of dangerous behavior: A review and analysis of "second generation" research. *Forensic Reports, 5,* 103–133.

Poe-Yamagata, E. P. & Butts, J. A. (1996, June). *Female Offenders in the Juvenile Justice System—Statistics Summary.* Washington, DC: Office of Juvenile Justice and Delinquency Prevention.

Quinsey, V. L. & Macguire, A. (1986). Maximum security psychiatric patients: Actuarial and clinical prediction of dangerousness. *Journal of Interpersonal Violence, 1,* 143–171.

Quinsey, V. L., Rice, M. F., & Harris, G. T. (1995). Actuarial prediction of sexual recidivism. *Journal of Interpersonal Violence, 10,* 85–105.

Reid, W. H. & Balis, G. U. (1987). Evaluation of the violent patient. In R. E. Hales & A. J. Frances (Eds.), *American Psychiatric Association Annual Review, 6,* 491–509.

Resnick, P. J. (1969). Child murder by parents: A psychiatric review of filicide. *American Journal of Psychiatry, 126,* 73–83.

Robins, L. N. & Ratcliff, K. S. (1980). Childhood conduct disorders and later arrest. In L. N. Robins, P. J. Clayton, & J. K. Wing (Eds.), *The Social Consequences of Psychiatric Illness* (pp. 248–263). New York: Brunner/Mazel.

Rosenbaum, M. (1990). The role of depression in couples involved in murder-suicide and homicide. *American Journal of Psychiatry, 147,* 1036–1039.

Satterfield, J., Hoppe, C., & Schell, A. (1982). A prospective study of delinquency in 110 adolescent boys with attention-deficit disorder and 88 normal adolescent boys. *American Journal of Psychiatry, 139,* 795–798.

Satterfield, J. H. & Schell, A. (1997, December). A prospective study of hyperactive boys with conduct problems and normal boys: Adolescent and adult criminality. *Journal of the American Academy of Child and Adolescent Psychiatry, 36,* 12.

Serin, R. C., Peters, R. D., & Barbaree, H. E. (1990). Predictors of psychopathy and release outcome in a criminal population. *Psychological Assessment: A Journal of Consulting and Clinical Psychology, 2,* 419–422.

Snyder, H. N. (1995). *Juvenile Arrests 1995.* Washington, DC: U.S. Department of Justice, Office of Justice Programs, Office of Juvenile Justice and Delinquency Prevention.

Snyder, H. N. & Sickmund, M. (1995). *Juvenile Offenders and Victims: A National Report* (pp. 49–55). Washington, DC: Office of Juvenile Justice and Delinquency Prevention.

Spaccarelli, S., Coatsworth, J. D., & Bowden, B. S. (1995). Exposure to serious family violence among incarcerated boys: Its association with violent offending and potential mediating variables. *Violence and Victims, 10,* 163–181.

Steiner, H., Garcia, I. G., & Matthews, Z. (1997, March). Posttraumatic stress disorder in incarcerated juvenile delinquents. *Journal of the American Academy of Child and Adolescent Psychiatry, 36,* 357.

Straus, M., Gelles, R., & Steinmetz, S. (1980). *Behind Closed Doors.* New York: Doubleday-Anchor.

Swanson, J. W., Holzer, C. E., Ganju, V. K., & Jono, R. T. (1990). Violence and psychiatric disorder in the community: Evidence from the epidemiologic catchment area surveys. *Hospital and Community Psychiatry, 41,* 761–770.

Tardiff, K. & Sweillam, A. (1980). Assault, suicide and mental illness. *Archives of General Psychiatry, 37,* 164–169.

Tjaden, P. & Phoemmes, N. (1997). *Stalking in America: Findings from the National Violence Against Women Survey.* Denver, CO: Center for Policy Research.

Treiman, D. M. (1994). Aggressive behavior and violence in epilepsy: Guidelines for expert testimony. In R. Rosner (Ed.), *Principles and Practice of Forensic Psychiatry,* 452–456. New York: Chapman & Hall.

U.S. Department of Justice, FBI. (1994). Crime in the United States. *Uniform Crime Reports.*

Webster, C. D., Harris, G. T., Rice, M. E., Cormier, C., & Quinsey, V. L. (1994). *The Violence Prediction Scheme: Assessing Dangerousness in High Risk Men.* Toronto, Ontario, Canada: Centre of Criminology, University of Toronto.

Wessely, S., Buchanan, A., Reed, A., Cutting, J., Everitt, B., Garety, P., & Taylor, P. J. (1993). Acting on delusions. 1: Prevalence. *British Journal of Psychiatry, 163,* 69–76.

West, D. J. & Farrington, D. P. (1977). *Who Becomes Delinquent?* London: Heinemann.

Williamson, S., Hare, R. D., & Wong, S. (1987). Violence: Criminal psychopaths and their victims. *Canadian Journal of Behavioral Science, 19,* 454–462.

Wolfgang, M. (1977). *From Boy to Man—From Delinquency to Crime.* Paper presented at the Serious Juvenile Offender National Symposium, Minneapolis, MN.

Wolfgang, M., Figlio, R., & Sellin, T. (1972). *Delinquency in a Birth Cohort.* Chicago: University of Chicago Press.

Zimring, F. E. (1991). Firearms, violence and public policy. *Scientific American, 257,* 48–54.

AUTHOR INDEX

SUBJECT INDEX